Time Out

Dubai

timeout.com/dubai

Time Out Guides Ltd
Universal House
251 Tottenham Court Road
London W1T 7AB
United Kingdom
Tel: +44 (0)20 7813 3000
Fax: +44 (0)20 7813 6001
Email: guides@timeout.com
www.timeout.com

Published by Time Out Guides Ltd, a wholly owned subsidiary of Time Out Group Ltd.
Time Out and the Time Out logo are trademarks of Time Out Group Ltd.

10 9 8 7 6 5 4 3 2 1

This edition first published in Great Britain in 2009 by Ebury Publishing.
A Random House Group Company
20 Vauxhall Bridge Road, London SW1V 2SA

Random House Australia Pty Ltd 20 Alfred Street, Milsons Point, Sydney, New South Wales 2061, Australia

Random House New Zealand Ltd 18 Poland Road, Glenfield, Auckland 10, New Zealand

Random House South Africa (Pty) Ltd Isle of Houghton, Corner Boundary Road & Carse O'Gowrie, Houghton 2198, South Africa

Random House UK Limited Reg. No. 954009

For further distribution details, see www.timeout.com.

ISBN: 978-1-84670-155-9

A CIP catalogue record for this book is available from the British Library.

Printed and bound by Firmengruppe APPL, aprinta druck, Wemding, Germany.

The Random House Group Limited supports The Forest Stewardship Council (FSC), the leading international forest
certification organisation. All our titles that are printed on Greenpeace approved FSC certified paper
carry the FSC logo. Our paper procurement policy can be found at http://www.rbooks.co.uk/environment.

Time Out carbon-offsets its flights with Trees for Cities (www.treesforcities.org).

Contents

jumeirah.com

SAVOUR THE BEST OF
ASIAN FLAVOURS AT JUNSUI

Chic and elegant, Junsui offers an array of Asian flavours. With 12 live
cooking stations, enjoy authentic cuisines from Japan, China, Thailand,
Indonesia and Korea. For a relaxing afternoon or evening drinks,
the uber-stylish cocktail lounge presents breathtaking views of the
Arabian Gulf.

Breakfast - International with Asian Twist:	AED 250
Lunch - Asian Live Cooking:	AED 325
Dinner - Asian Live Cooking:	AED 375
Asian Afternoon Tea:	AED 250
Junset Lounging All Day:	AED 125

To book your table call +971 4 3017600 or email BAArestaurants@jumeirah.com

Introduction

Amid all the hype, and there's been plenty of bad press alongside the good, it's easy to forget how far Dubai has come in recent decades. In 1970, this sprawling orgy of hotels, lifestyle developments and business hubs was little more than a sandy outpost. Even in the mid 1990s, the city boasted few landmarks and a negligible tourism industry. But through a mixture of ambition, audacity and a knack for self-promotion (man-made islands, towering skyscrapers, seven-star hotels), the city has transformed itself into a cultural and economic hub linking East and West in an ideological as well as geographical sense.

This metamorphosis from sleepy pearl-diving village to one of the most talked-about towns in the world has changed the locals' lives beyond recognition. Where their grandfathers eked out a hand-to-mouth existence in the desert, many of today's Emiratis live in a world of unbridled opportunity and financial plenty. They also find themselves a minority in their own city: thousands of people from around the globe have flocked here to help build Project Dubai, with millions more stopping by to enjoy the resort hotels, the shopping malls and the year-round sunshine.

That's not to say that the growth of Dubai has been one long success story. The emirate effectively transformed itself on foreign investment rather than oil receipts (which, surprisingly, make up just five per cent of GDP), which meant that Dubai suffered hugely when the credit crunch hit. But naysayers would do well to exercise caution before writing off its chances of a healthy recovery. Dig beneath the surface of 'Brand Dubai' and a whole new city opens up – one rarely documented in the international press, but a place nonetheless with all the colour and complexity of a modern metropolis.

As the city matures, its multiple communities will blend and interact to create a culture that is Dubai's own. Until then, the big, brash, headline-grabbing projects will continue to dominate the international image projected by the city, and visitors and residents will make of Dubai what they will. One thing is for sure, though. Anyone who pays more than a cursory visit to this city will find a place they did not wholly expect. *Chris Anderson, Editor*

Get the local experience

Over 50 of the world's top destinations available.

Dubai in Brief

IN CONTEXT

For a city with such a short history, Dubai certainly has a tale to tell. The opening section of the book traces the city's journey from its early days as a small, relatively isolated fishing village through the turbulent 20th century and on to the dazzling expansion of the present day. The Dubai Today chapter meets a parade of locals with different perspectives on this extraordinary place.

▶ *For more, see pp17-58.*

SIGHTS

Sightseeing in Dubai is unlike sightseeing in most other cities. For one thing, there are very few traditional sights here: you can count the number of notable museums on one hand, for instance, and historic monuments are conspicuous by their absence. The most notable sight in Dubai is its cityscape, extravagant and sprawling and still growing by the day.

▶ *For more, see pp59-83.*

CONSUME

Modern-day Dubai is all about conspicuous consumptionr. The city's array of luxury hotels is dazzling, overwhelming and almost certainly unmatched anywhere on earth; within them are high-end restaurants and, yes, a number of bars, especially popular with western expats. Add a shopping scene that blends traditional souks with glamorous malls, and you won't be short of ways to splash the cash.

▶ *For more, see pp85-182.*

ARTS & ENTERTAINMENT

The visual arts scene in Dubai has never been richer. Dealers are flooding here for parties, openings and festivals such as Art Dubai, but there's also a lot of home-grown talent on show. Elsewhere, this section of the book includes information on the city's major festivals, the strong nightclub scene and the many family-friendly activities around the city.

▶ *For more, see pp183-238.*

ESCAPES & EXCURSIONS

Beyond Dubai, the other emirates hold plenty of interest for the visitor. Chief among them, of course, is the capital Abu Dhabi, which is developing its own ambitions to become the country's cultural heart. The section also goes beyond the UAE to explore Muscat, which carries a fascinating Arabian authenticity and Musandam, nicknamed the Norway of Arabia on account of its amazing geography.

▶ *For more, see pp239-264.*

Dubai in 48 Hours

Day 1 History and Tradition

8AM Start your day with a taste of traditional Arabia in Dubai's **Bastakia** district (*see p69*), located by the Creek in Bur Dubai. Grab a quick bite and caffeine fix at the **Basta Art Café** (*see p113*), then wander through the maze of sand-coloured alleyways as the historic windtowers rise over you. There are several art galleries here, where you can peruse the works of local artists and even watch an Arabic calligrapher at work.

10AM To get to grips with modern living in Dubai, it's a short taxi ride to **Jumeirah Mosque** (*see p75*): the city's largest mosque, it's also the only one to which non-Muslims are allowed access for one of the regular tours (held every Tuesday, Thursday, Saturday and Sunday at 10am). Ask any question about life in Dubai, and the knowledgeable local guides will enlighten you.

2PM An exploration of Dubai's past isn't complete without a visit to the **Dubai Museum** (*see p70*), housed inside an old fort. The main displays are located underground, including a reproduction of a 1950s souk. From here wander to the **Creek** and take an abra ride across the water – it's Dhs1 from one side to the other, but you can also haggle to get the best price for a trip up and down (no more than Dhs50).

4PM The Creek houses a number of historical finds. You can visit the **Heritage & Diving Village** and the **Sheikh Saeed Al Maktoum House** (*see p70*), or head to the ancient souks. Haggle for material, and even ask for one of the tailors to make you something, at the textile souk in Bur Dubai, or jump over the Creek to Deira and visit the spice and gold souks. These areas tend to be a hive of activity from mid afternoon until the early evening.

8PM If you're in the mood for Arabic cuisine, the **Khan Murjan** restaurant at **Wafi** (*see p115*) is an excellent choice, located in the venue's recreated 14th century Baghdad souk.

NAVIGATING THE CITY

The city of Dubai is roughly divided in two halves by the Creek, a division that the defines the basic areas of **Deira**, to the north, and **Bur Dubai**, to the south. Beyond Bur Dubai lies **Jumeirah** and the **Marina**. The 'New Dubai' extends south through Jebel Ali and east into the desert, where recent developments such as Arabian Ranches and Sports City have added new districts away from Dubai's coastal strip.

One thing you'll quickly notice when travelling around Dubai is that there's an almost total lack of street names, and those that do exist are largely ignored. To get around, you'll need to know which landmark a place is near, or – more likely in a city where most of the activity occurs in malls and hotels – which landmark it's inside. Ask a resident for directions, and he or she will reel off a list of nearby malls, hotels, parks and banks. If you're heading off the beaten track, find out

Day 2 Modern Dubai

7AM If you're up early, see if you can book a tee time at one of Dubai's many state-of-the-art golf courses. The Ernie Els course in **Dubai Sports City** (*see p233*) is one of the city's newest; alternatively, follow in Tiger Woods' footsteps and play on the Majlis course at the **Emirates Golf Club** (see *p233*), home each year to the Dubai Desert Classic.

10AM Ride the city's first monorail across the Palm island, taking in the amazing views along the way, to the lavish **Atlantis** hotel (*see p105*). After marvelling at the huge **aquarium** (there's a separate Lost Chambers aquarium, a dolphinarium and Aquaventure waterpark, if you're fond of watery fun), pop to the **Atlantis Spa** (*see p217*) for some serious five-star pampering.

1PM Dubai is famous for its shopping, so a trip to **Mall of the Emirates** (*see p158*) and **Dubai Mall** (*see p157*) are a must. In addition to the many shops, these credit-card botherers feature a wealth of other attractions: Mall of the Emirates has its own theatre and indoor ski slope (**Ski Dubai**; *see p238*), while the Dubai Mall features an aquarium (in which you can go scuba diving), an ice rink, a gold souk and a pair of theme parks, **Sega Republic** and **Kidzania** (*see p201*).

4PM **Souk Madinat Jumeirah** (*see p159*) is a sprawling complex of hotels, bars and restaurants, complete with a souk, a theatre, waterways and abras. It's a modern twist on Dubai's past. Try a shisha pipe in the courtyard, sip a cocktail in a beanbag at **BarZar** (*see p147*), and get up close and personal with that Dubai icon, the **Burj Al Arab** (*see p101*).

8PM Dubai's booming restaurant scene means visitors are spoiled for choice. For all out decadence, try **Reflets Par Pierre Gagnaire** at the InterContinental Dubai Festival City (*see p125*). The **Exchange Grill** at the Fairmont (*see p141*) serves fantastic steaks, or try **Zuma** in DIFC (*see p121*) for excellent Japanese food.

---

beforehand what its nearest landmark is, and direct your taxi driver there.

GETTING AROUND
A city-wide metro system opened in September 2009, with dedicated buses ferrying passengers to and from the stations. The new metro system consists of two lines: the red line, running the length of Sheikh Zayed Road, and the smaller green line, serving Bur Dubai and Deira and due to open in 2010.

For destinations along the length of Sheikh Zayed Road, Deira and Garhoud, the metro is the cheapest form of transport. For anywhere further afield, taxis are the best way of getting around. You should have no problem getting a taxi at any major hotel, mall or attraction, but you might face problems tracking in more secluded locations or very late at night; if so, call Dubai Transport (208 0808). For more information on public transport in Dubai, visit http://wojhati.rta.ae.

Madinat Jumeirah
The Arabian resort of Dubai

Dubai in Profile

Dubai's rapid expansion has resulted in its fabric and geography changing radically over the last few years. New construction, both on land and (even more spectacularly) in the water, has resulted in the make-up of the city altering almost beyond recognition, while at the same time its population has soared from 674,000 in 1995 to nearly three times that figure some 15 years later. The global economic slowdown may yet have an effect on the city that proves just as profound as the one born during the boom years. But at any rate, stasis seems unlikely.

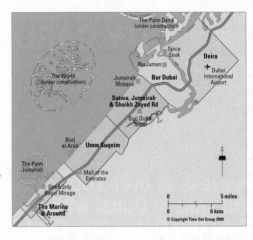

DEIRA

Glimpses of modern-day Dubai are certainly visible in Deira, a kind of umbrella neighbourhood that shelters a wide variety of smaller districts with their own particular characters. But for all the moneyed modernity of **Festival City**, the main attraction here is the area alongside the Creek, where newly built hotels and gleaming apartment complexes overlook the fascinating, chaotic bustle of Deira's old souk.

▶ *For more, see pp65-67.*

BUR DUBAI

Just as Deira is used as a catch-all term to denote the area to the north of the Creek, so Bur Dubai covers the south. There's history here, too: the enticing, handsome district of **Bastakia,** first settled in the 19th century by Iranian traders, has been preserved as a conservation area. But changes are also afoot here, as they are elsewhere in the city. The creekside remains unspoiled by modern development, but tower blocks dominate the landscape further inland.

▶ *For more, see pp68-71.*

SATWA, JUMEIRAH & SHEIKH ZAYED ROAD

A handful of old-timers remember when **Jumeirah** was a quiet little fishing village, distant from and different to Dubai itself. No longer. The city's extraordinary growth over the last few decades has seen this former outpost all but absorbed by the city itself, and in dramatic fashion; not for nothing have some Westerners dubbed it the 'Beverly Hills of Dubai'. Neighbouring **Satwa** is a different beast, an interesting and varied little community, but it's slated to be flattened to make way for another of the modern developments for which Dubai has become famous worldwide.

▶ For more, see pp72-76.

UMM SUQEIM

Running south from Jumeirah along the waterfront, Umm Suqeim isn't exactly a poor relation to its neighbour, but it's nonetheless in its shadow; some businesses in the district have even appended 'Jumeirah' to their names in the hope of picking up a little cachet from the illustrious area to the north. At the southern end of Umm Suqeim is the enormous Mall of the Emirates, complete with its own indoor ski slope.

▶ For more, see pp77-78.

THE MARINA

Directly south of Umm Suqeim, the Marina is at the heart of new Dubai. Entirely man-made, it's home to innumerable skyscrapers and luxury hotels, all clustered around or near the water. If you want to see how Dubai has changed in the last 25 years, this is the place to go.

▶ For more, see pp79-81.

PALM JUMEIRAH

For all the cloudbusting developments in and around the Marina, nothing says modern-day Dubai quite like Palm Jumeirah. A man-made island built from 21 billion gallons of sand and seven million tons of rock, it's an iconic addition to the city, home both to private residences and several predictably upscale hotels. It was originally planned as one of three similar 'Palm' islands; thus far, it's the one that's nearest completion.

▶ For more, see pp82-83.

Time Out Dubai

Editorial
Editor Chris Anderson
Deputy Editor Edoardo Albert
Proofreader Simon Cropper
Indexer Sally Davies

Managing Director Peter Fiennes
Editorial Director Ruth Jarvis
Series Editor Will Fulford-Jones
Business Manager Dan Allen
Editorial Manager Holly Pick
Assistant Management Accountant Ija Krasnikova

Design
Art Director Scott Moore
Art Editor Pinelope Kourmouzoglou
Senior Designer Henry Elphick
Graphic Designers Kei Ishimaru, Nicola Wilson
Advertising Designer Jodi Sher

Picture Desk
Picture Editor Jael Marschner
Deputy Picture Editor Lynn Chambers
Picture Researcher Gemma Walters
Picture Desk Assistant Ben Rowe
Picture Librarian Christina Theisen

Advertising
Commercial Director Mark Phillips
International Advertising Manager Kasimir Berger
International Sales Executive Charlie Sokol
Advertising Sales (Dubai) Gareth Lloyd-Jones,
  Michael Smith, Kamel Heikal, Charlotte Hurst

Marketing
Marketing Manager Yvonne Poon
**Sales & Marketing Director, North America
  & Latin America** Lisa Levinson
Senior Publishing Brand Manager Luthfa Begum
Art Director Anthony Huggins

Production
Group Production Director Mark Lamond
Production Manager Brendan McKeown
Production Controller Damian Bennett

Time Out Group
Chairman Tony Elliott
Chief Executive Officer David King
Group General Manager/Director Nichola Coulthard
Time Out Communications Ltd MD David Pepper
Time Out International Ltd MD Cathy Runciman
Time Out Magazine Ltd Publisher/MD Mark Elliott
Group IT Director Simon Chappell
Marketing & Circulation Director Catherine Demajo

Contributors

Introduction James Alexander, Chris Anderson, Jeremy Lawrence. **In Context** all chapters by James Alexander, Chris Anderson & Jeremy Lawrence. **Sights** all chapters by Jeremy Lawrence & Michelle Wranik. **Hotels** Becky Lucas. **Restaurants & Cafés** Daisy Carrington. **Pubs & Bars** James Wilkinson. **Shops & Services** Laura Chubb. **Calendar** Chris Anderson. **Art Galleries** Chris Lord. **Children** Ele Cooper. **Film & Theatre** Laura Chubb. **Health & Fitness** Daisy Carrington, Chris Lord. **Music & Clubs** James Wilkinson. **Sport** Daisy Carrington, Chris Lord. **Escapes & Excursions** Gareth Clark, Jonathan Wilks, Michelle Wranik. **Directory** Ele Cooper.

Maps john@jsgraphics.co.uk.

Photography ITP, except: pages 18, 20, 25 www.blinkimages.net; pages 22, 29 Getty Images. The following images were provided by the featured establishments/artists: pages 86, 87, 96, 97, 98 (bottom), 101, 102, 104, 107, 108, 155, 162, 163, 209, 210, 211, 212, 214, 216, 217, 218, 219, 220, 224.

The Editor would like to thank Celia Topping and all contributors to previous editions of *Time Out Dubai*, whose work forms the basis for parts of this book.

About the Guide

GETTING AROUND

The back of the book contains street maps of Dubai, as well as overview maps of the city and its surroundings. The maps start on page 289; on them are marked the locations of hotels (❶), restaurants (❶) and bars (❶). The majority of businesses listed in this guide are located in the areas we've mapped; the grid-square references in the listings refer to these maps.

THE ESSENTIALS

For practical information, including visas, disabled access, emergencies, lost property, useful websites and local transport, please see the Directory. It begins on page 265.

THE LISTINGS

Addresses, phone numbers, websites, transport information, hours and prices are all included in our listings, as are selected other facilities. All were checked and correct at press time. However, business owners can alter their arrangements at any time, and fluctuating economic conditions can cause prices to change rapidly.

The very best venues in the city, the must-sees and must-dos in every category,

have been marked with a red star (★). In the Sights chapters, we've also marked venues that offer free admission with a FREE symbol.

PHONE NUMBERS

The dialling code for Dubai is 04. All phone numbers in this book take this code unless otherwise stated. If you're calling from within Dubai, you need only dial the seven-digit numbers as listed in this book. From elsewhere in the UAE, preface the seven-digit numbers with the area code of 04.

To reach a Dubai number from outside the UAE, dial your country's international access code (00 from the UK, 011 from the US) or the '+' symbol (when using a mobile phone), followed by the UAE country code of 971, then 4 for Dubai (dropping the initial '0') and then the number as listed in this guide. So, to reach the Burj Al Arab hotel, dial +971 4 301 7777. For more on phones, *see p276*.

FEEDBACK

We welcome feedback on this guide, both on the venues we've included and on any other locations that you'd like to see featured in future editions. Please email us at guides@timeout.com.

Time Out Guides

Founded in 1968, Time Out has grown from humble beginnings into the leading resource for anyone wanting to know what's happening in the world's greatest cities. Alongside our influential weeklies in London, New York and Chicago, we publish more than 20 magazines in cities as varied as Beijing and Beirut; a range of travel books, with the City Guides now joined by the newer Shortlist series; and an information-packed website. The company remains proudly independent, still owned by Tony Elliott four decades after he launched *Time Out London*.

Written by local experts and illustrated with original photography, our books also

retain their independence. No business has been featured because it has advertised, and all restaurants and bars are visited and reviewed anonymously.

ABOUT THE EDITOR

Originally from the UK, **Chris Anderson** has lived in Dubai for five years, and has worked on many Time Out magazines and books about the city and the region. He contributes regularly to the weekly *Time Out Dubai* and the monthly *Time Out Abu Dhabi*, and has also launched magazines in Doha and Bahrain.

A full list of the book's contributors can be found opposite.

In Context

Burj Al Arab. *See p47 & p98*.

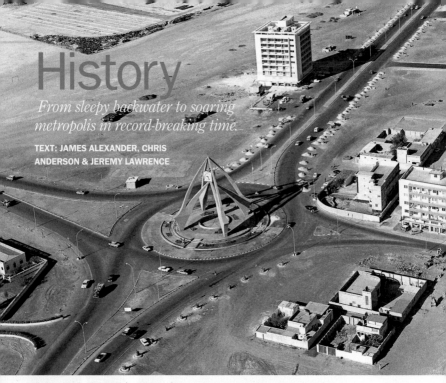

History

From sleepy backwater to soaring metropolis in record-breaking time.

TEXT: JAMES ALEXANDER, CHRIS ANDERSON & JEREMY LAWRENCE

With its gleaming skyscrapers, love of modernity and apparent lack of anything over ten years' old, you'd be forgiven for thinking that Dubai is a mere child of a city, albeit one undergoing an incredible growth-spurt. Although it's true that the city that headline writers know and love only really took shape over the last decade, settlements dating from the early fifth and sixth centuries AD have been found in what is now the modern suburb of Jumeirah. These relics indicate that with the advent of Islam, the Umayyad and the Abbasid Islamic dynasties, Dubai was already established as a stop-off point for the caravans serving Iraq.

Until recently, the emirate hasn't been very good at preserving its historic sites. The widespread and almost hysterical construction boom that began in the 1990s, and which went into overdrive in 2003, has morphed Dubai into a bustling metropolis, welding together Arab and Western cultures, sometimes successfully, other times awkwardly, but almost always at the cost of its traditional architecture and old buildings. Consequently, there are precious few mementoes of Dubai's more distant past.

It was the lure of pearl trading that put Dubai on the map; Venetian jeweller Gasparo Balbi made the first written reference to 'Dibei' in 1580, during a search of the East to uncover a lucrative source of the precious jewels.

TAMING THE GULF

Strategically located on a ten-kilometre (six-mile) creek, Dubai started its remarkable evolution from small, sleepy fishing village to dynamic city some time during the 18th century. The town was wedged between the two powerful clans that held sway over the lower Gulf, the Bani Yas of Liwa Oasis, who went on to settle in Abu Dhabi, the modern capital of the UAE, and the Qawasim, based in the northern emirates and parts of what would become Oman.

The Qawasim's powerful navy had already triggered the ire of the British Empire's ruling classes, which led to the area becoming known as the 'Pirate Coast' owing to the agile, armed Arab dhows that plundered ships from the East India Trading Company. The disruption to British commercial interests prompted a show of superior naval power that brought the ruling families of this part of the Arabian coastline to their knees. Britain, fearing attempts from Russia and France to challenge its dominance of the region, then signed exclusivity treaties with the leaders of the Trucial States, offering protection and non-interference in local politics on the condition that leaders didn't even correspond with other global powers. Dubai and the rest of the Trucial Coast were now firmly within the sphere of British influence.

MAKTOUM RULE

In 1833, the era of Maktoum family rule began, probably as a result of an internal quarrel among the Bani Yas of Abu Dhabi, when violent conduct on the part of its leader, Sheikh Khalifa, prompted the emigration of around 800 members of the Al Bu Falasah branch of the tribe. There was little resistance in Dubai to Obaid bin Said and Maktoum bin Butti, who took over the then village-sized settlement along the Creek. With Obaid's death a few years later, Maktoum took the reins of power, ushering in the bloodline that continues to rule Dubai today.

The Maktoums based themselves in Shindagah, which provided easy access to the sources of Dubai's wealth: the Gulf for pearling and fishing, and the Creek for trade. In 1820, Mohammed bin Hazza, then ruler of Dubai, signed the trading village's first preliminary truce with London, all too aware of the superior manpower of neighbouring Abu Dhabi and the Qawasim, who controlled much of the northern emirates and what is now Oman.

Under the protection of the British navy, which helped to stamp out the constant disruptions to trade caused by raids among the various tribes along the Trucial Coast, Dubai concentrated on making money. Like the other city ports that later formed the United Arab Emirates, Dubai evolved around its creek, an inlet from the sea. And like the other creeks along the northern coast, Dubai's suffered from sandbars formed at its entrance by strong tides but at least it was much longer than those of its neighbours, paving the way for the cargo ships that would make Dubai its fortune. Because the waves were pacified by sandbars, the pearling industry thrived, and its wares were exported to India and Europe. Trade with India and Persia encouraged more foreign traders to open up shop in the city port; the town was already developing its reputation as being not only open for business, but a place that warmly welcomed non-Arabs to take their share.

In the mid 19th century, Shindagah may have been the preserve of around 250 Arab homes, but the neighbouring Bur Dubai community was the base for almost 100 houses belonging to Indian traders. Across the Creek, Deira boasted 1,600 compounds, housing Arabs, Persians and Baluchis from what is now Pakistan. Deira souk was also thriving, with around 350 shops.

BUDDING DUBAI

It was the liberal, open-minded Maktoum bin Hashar, whose rule began in 1894, who capitalised on Dubai's emergence as a business and commercial centre. Foreshadowing a modern obsession with the tax-free environment, Dubai in the late

IN CONTEXT

19th century exempted from taxes almost half the men working in the pearling industry. Although more divers worked the pearl banks in Dubai than in any other Trucial State, the ruler ended up receiving only half the revenue of neighbouring Abu Dhabi.

No matter: Dubai's population exploded. As the pearl industry continued to bring more wealth to the town, Sheikh Maktoum implemented business-oriented policies that attracted traders from Lingah, the Persian port on the other side of the Gulf. Run by the Qawasim family, Lingah had, through the 1800s, acted as the main entry point for goods coming into the Gulf. The Persians, desperate for tax revenue, wrested control of the port from the Arabs at the turn of the century, replacing Arab officials with Persians and then Belgians, whose rigid bureaucracy and high tariffs persuaded merchants to head off in search of cheaper trade environments on the Arab side of the Gulf.

As the 20th century began, Sheikh Maktoum made Dubai a free zone by abolishing commercial taxes. He also courted the big players in the Persian warehousing trade, offering cheap land to important Indian and Persian traders. As he attracted these trade giants, others followed. In the first two decades of the 20th century, Dubai's population doubled to around 20,000, rapidly catching up with Sharjah, its larger neighbour and sometime trade rival.

Dubai Creek.

'Slaves came closer to freedom, not because the British decided to enforce their ban on slavery, but because owners could no longer afford them.'

Traders who had reckoned on a temporary sojourn in Dubai settled in the city once it became clear that taxes and regulations in Persia were there to stay. The pearling industry was now booming. Many people emigrated from the Persian district of Bastak, part of the Arab-dominated province of Lars, naming their newfound home on the Creek after their homeland; Bastakia soon became another thriving commercial area.

Sheikh Maktoum's power rose with the fortunes of his city state. He began the process of building bridges between the rival sheikhdoms of the coast, calling a meeting of the Trucial leaders in 1905 that foreshadowed the creation of the federation that was to be agreed just under 70 years later.

THE BUBBLE BURSTS

After years of growing prosperity, Dubai and the rest of the Gulf fell prey to the worldwide recession of the 1930s, a warning to leaders that the trade-based city's fortunes would ebb and flow with the tide of global economic prosperity. The pearling industry first became a victim of the weak international demand for luxury goods, and then the Japanese discovery of cultured pearls finished it off, throwing thousands of pearl fishermen out of work. In the final years of the trade, financiers were taking up to 36 per cent annual interest on the loans that captains needed to fit out boats and hire staff. As the pearling industry declined, traders redoubled their efforts in black market deals with Persia, where tariffs continued to soar far higher than in those ports on the Arabian Peninsula.

The pearling industry continued to decline. Dubaians with Persian connections built up their illicit cargo trade, making up for the city's lost revenue, but the increasing financial inequities between the traders and the recently unemployed Arab pearl divers amplified societal pressures. Further north in Kuwait, yearnings for political reform influenced the setting up of a parliament, giving the country the most developed political system in the Gulf.

Mirroring growing unease within Dubai society, splits within the royal family also emerged. The ruler's cousin, Mani bin Rashid, led the reform movement that challenged the ruling family's autocratic rule. Domestic slaves came closer to freedom, not because the British decided to enforce their ban on trading slaves, but because owners could no longer afford them. It wasn't until after World War II that the UK government started to enforce general manumission after having called a halt to the trading of slaves within the Gulf states a century earlier.

Against this background of social flux, events turned violent in October 1938. Sheikh Saeed and his followers set up their base in Bur Dubai, while his cousins lined up against the ruler across the Creek in Deira. After mediation from neighbouring sheikhs and the British political agent, or colonial ambassador, in Bahrain, Sheikh Saeed agreed to the setting up of a consultative council or *majlis* ('place of sitting'), heading up a cohort of 15 members, all of whom were proposed by leading members of the community who theoretically had the power to veto his decisions.

Sheikh Saeed was a reluctant leader, and only attended the first few sessions, smarting at a system in which his office was allocated an eighth of the national budget, the remainder earmarked for the *majlis*'s projects. He still controlled the treasury, and

IN CONTEXT

IN CONTEXT

was hesitant to open up the state coffers for the council's projects, such as building state-run schools for the general populace, regulating the customs service and its payroll, adjusting tariffs, and setting up a council of merchants to oversee the city-state's expanding commerce.

Six months after the council's foundation, Sheikh Saeed ordered loyal Bedouin to storm and dissolve it. A strong believer in benign autocratic rule, he suspected that some of his royal rivals were exploiting the *majlis* for their own benefit. Although short-lived, Dubai's six-month flirtation with democracy nonetheless had lasting implications at the highest levels. It sounded the political death knell for Sheikh Saeed; he devolved most of his authority to his son, Sheikh Rashid, who in time initiated many of the ideas of civic development proposed by the council's members.

POST WAR DEVELOPMENT

Although spared the horrors that Europe and Asia endured during World War II, Dubai still struggled during those six tough years. The flourishing business of trade was brought to a near standstill, and short supplies of rice and sugar caused hunger to grip parts of the city. The British government, which was landing seaplanes in the Creek throughout the conflict, imported food supplies that were to be rationed among the population. Never ones to miss a money-spinning trick, Dubai's traders began buying up some of these supplies and smuggling them to Iran's black market, where shortages were even more pressing.

Malnutrition was an even greater issue in the countryside, which was still ruled by autonomous nomadic tribes and where contacts with the coastal regions could be difficult. There was almost constant warfare as the tribes fought for rations, and the leaders of Abu Dhabi and Dubai argued over the boundary between their territories.

'The leaders of Dubai and the other Trucial States felt almost abandoned by the hasty nature of the British retreat.'

Open warfare between the two distant relatives, as well as among their allied and rival tribes of the hinterland, continued after World War II until the high level of casualties from Bedouin raids and counter-raids prompted the townsfolk and tribesmen to demand peace in 1948. The British authorities took it upon themselves to research the boundary dispute and draw the new frontier – London's first direct intervention in the internal politics of the Trucial States.

DUBAI STRIKES OIL

Although trade remained at the core of Dubai's development, a revolutionary new prospect came the Trucial States' way in the early 1950s: oil. For a couple of decades, most petroleum engineers had concluded that large deposits would be found somewhere along the Trucial Coast. After all, massive reserves had been found across the Middle East, and particularly in the Arabian Peninsula and the Gulf. Oil had first been discovered in Iran in 1908; Bahrain had started significant exports in 1936; and on the eve of World War II, neighbouring Saudi Arabia had found the first of its huge reservoirs. Companies began to explore across the region, frantically searching for more deposits of black gold. Petroleum Development (Trucial Coast), a British-owned company, won the concession to search for oil across the Trucial States and Oman.

But the war put a stop to the exploration, condemning the emirates to more years of poverty, and encouraging thousands of locals to emigrate to neighbouring Kuwait and Saudi Arabia to work on the massive post war oil development projects there. Although a consortium formed by British Petroleum and France's Total found commercially viable oil deposits off the coast of Abu Dhabi in 1958, progress was limited in Dubai's onshore and offshore exploration blocks.

COMMERCIAL WHEELS TURN

Nevertheless, Dubai sought to capitalise on the massive trade opportunities brought by oil companies. Mortgaging Dubai with a huge loan from oil-rich Saudi Arabia and Kuwait of around Dhs3.1 million, an amount that far outstripped the city's yearly income, Sheikh Rashid had the Creek dredged by an Australian firm. The ambitious project, which allowed vessels of up to 500 tonnes to anchor there, greatly increased shipping capacity. The emirate's trade levels jumped by 20 per cent, outpacing the growth in neighbouring Sharjah, which had been snapping at Dubai's heels. Gold smuggling, which peaked in 1970, contributed to the new surge in business. The 3.5 per cent import levies imposed on dhows and steamers docking along its wharfage became the emirate's biggest revenue earner after the war.

After seeing off Sharjah's maritime trade competition, Sheikh Rashid also took on his neighbour's airport. Sheikh Sultan of Sharjah had started levying taxes on gold arriving at Sharjah airport, which grew commercially on the back of the Royal Air Force base there. In 1960, Sheikh Rashid opened an airport, little more than an airstrip made from the hard sand found in Dubai's salt flats, which he expanded a few years later as demand for weekly flights to the UK grew. An open skies policy allowed any airline to use the airport at a cheaper cost than any other in the region, triggering its eventual rise as an international passenger and freight hub.

Before then, however, Dubai too struck black gold. In 1966, oil was discovered in an offshore field; exports began three years later. The prospect of imminent oil exports,

Architect of the UAE

How one man's legacy continues to shape the Emirates.

That the United Arab Emirates (UAE) stands as a model of success in a Middle East that is more generally known for being fraught with political tension, corruption and poverty owes much to the strength, courage and vision of a single man, **Sheikh Zayed bin Sultan Al Nahyan**. There was a genuine sadness among expatriates as well as Emiratis when the news of his death in November 2004 broke, so much so that even big business and the city's extraordinary tourist machine paused in their normally unceasing labours as a mark of respect at his passing.

Sheikh Zayed's greatest gift to the UAE was his ability to inspire unprecedented unity among peoples whose whole tradition emphasised fierce tribal independence. From these unlikely beginnings he went on to create an economic powerhouse from a desert land with little indigenous industry, bar a dying pearl trade, and people more familiar with the intricacies of raising camels than raising finance. Where once the country had only 200,000 inhabitants, and these thinly spread out across a desolate and inhospitable landscape, its population today numbers over three million, with residents coming from all walks of life and all parts of the planet. Upon assuming power in Abu Dhabi in 1966, Sheikh Zayed made it his personal goal to finance huge civic engineering projects through the Trucial States Development Office – recognising that only by using the financial might of Abu Dhabi as a fulcrum could the fledgling federal state be bound together.

Before the constitution that officially created the UAE was signed in 1971, Sheikh Zayed set off on a 'Unity Tour' through the lands that were to become the United Arab Emirates. In each sheikhdom he promised to make money available to improve the electricity supply. The tour, and subsequent flow of electrical power, took on an incredible significance for the people of the newly-fledged state, effectively symbolising a new national mindset. After all, this was a man who promised things – extraordinary things – and then got them done. This sense of unification would be carefully reinforced by many more national tours in the years of Sheikh Zayed's leadership.

The extraordinary bond with his people was a trait that British explorer Wilfred Thesiger would identify in his book *Arabian Sands*, having met with Sheikh Zayed during a much earlier tour of the Trucial Coast. Thesiger wrote of Zayed: 'He had a great reputation among the Bedu. They liked him for his easy, informal ways and his friendliness, and they respected his force of character, his shrewdness and his physical strength. They said admiringly, "Zayed is a Bedu. He knows about camels, can ride like one of us, can shoot, and knows how to fight."'

At the time of his death Sheikh Zayed had gained real stature as an international statesman, a reputation that resulted from something beyond the obvious mass of oil rigs and malls, or even the education system and abundant housing. Ever an ambassador for Arabic and Islamic values he drew praise from leaders the world over. In the words of another famous international statesman, former United States president Jimmy Carter: 'A man can only express his admiration for Sheikh Zayed and his leadership. Without his skilful policy, the infrastructure and civil progress of the United Arab Emirates could not have been accomplished in such a brief period.'

'The threat of international turmoil in the 1980s, as the Iran-Iraq War loomed large over the region, glued the emirates together.'

along with severe overcrowding of the Creek and the commercial centres around it, persuaded the government in 1967 to start building a Dhs367 million seaport, known as Port Rashid, which eventually opened in 1972 and was expanded again in 1978.

Trade and oil combined to give economic growth a massive injection. The petrodollar boom had finally arrived in Dubai, even though its oil reserves and revenues were minnow-like compared with its oil-rich neighbour Abu Dhabi. The population sky rocketed as migrant labour poured into the city to extract the oil and to build and maintain the public services that Sheikh Rashid, remembering the demands of the reform movement when he was being groomed for power, made a high priority for his government. In 1967, as the government planned Port Rashid, the population stood at 59,000. Five years later, in 1973, the city had doubled in size. By the end of the booming 1970s, 250,000 people lived in Dubai.

INDEPENDENCE

In 1967, Britain decided that its moment in the Middle East was over. London announced its intention to withdraw from its colonial outposts east of Suez, giving the Trucial States a departure date of 1971. Unlike in Aden, in southern Yemen, where years of insurgency showed a stark desire to see off the imperialists, the leaders of Dubai and the other Trucial States felt almost abandoned by the hasty nature of the British retreat. The Conservative opposition of the day also criticised the Labour government's decision to withdraw, arguing that British business exposure across the Gulf amounted to much more than the Dhs117.5 million annual cost of keeping British forces in the area, and that withdrawal would merely encourage new imperialists, such as the Soviet Union, to extend their influence over a region of vital strategic importance owing to its oil deposits.

Some Trucial leaders hoped the Conservative government, once it gained power, would reverse the decision to withdraw, but it wasn't to be. Sheikh Zayed of Abu Dhabi and Sheikh Rashid of Dubai met at the frontier between their two emirates, and agreed to form a federation that would jointly decide foreign, defence and social policy. At the encouragement of the British, the rulers of the Trucial States Abu Dhabi, Dubai, Sharjah, Ajman, Umm Al Quwain, Ras Al Khaimah and Fujairah met in Dubai with the leaders of Bahrain and Qatar in February 1968 to discuss a federation.

The nine leaders of these islands, city states and desert regions met on several occasions in the run-up to independence in 1971, discussing models of federation. Differences plagued the meetings, with Bahrain's larger, better-educated population suspicious of a federation in which political power would be spread evenly across the nine emirates, rather than being based on the population of each emirate. Bahrain, having ended border disputes with Iran, told the other prospective federation members that it would retain its independence. Qatar chose the same path. In July 1971, with the British withdrawal approaching, the seven Trucial leaders met and hammered out a federal document. Six of them, excluding Ras Al Khaimah, signed the provisional constitution, which was then used to proclaim a federation in November 1971.

Ras Al Khaimah had felt undervalued in the negotiations, and wanted to focus on three Gulf islands that Iran had occupied once the British forces left the area. But once the other emirates agreed to take on the issue of Abu Musa and the Greater and Lesser Tunb islands, it too acceded to the federation in February 1972.

The federation was born, led by Abu Dhabi, owing to its disproportionate financial contribution to the federal budget, but with significant autonomy for all emirates in local affairs. Sheikh Zayed Al Nahyan became the country's first president; Sheikh Rashid, who through the 1970s pressed for more autonomy for his free-wheeling emirate, acted as Zayed's Vice President and Prime Minister.

PETRODOLLAR BOOM

The 1970s were a decade of excess across the Gulf. Petrodollars flowed into the area as the world's seemingly unquenchable appetite for oil lapped up the region's exports. Oil revenues spiralled ever higher during the price shock of 1973 and 1974, triggered by the Arab producing states' boycott of nations supporting Israel in the third Arab-Israeli conflict. Dubai has never had the oil revenues that its rich neighbour Abu Dhabi enjoys (by 1980, Dubai's annual oil income stood at US$3 billion compared with Abu Dhabi's US$15 billion), but these revenues went a long way towards helping Dubai to develop the infrastructure it needed to realise fully the potential of its core economic activity trade and commerce.

FAMILY FEUD

Questioning the unity of purpose between the country's seven emirates is something of a taboo in the United Arab Emirates (UAE). However, historians privately recount stories of arguments between the leaders of all the emirates, especially the two powerhouses, oil-rich Abu Dhabi and commerce-friendly Dubai. Go back 50 years, and the two emirates were locked in all-out war, with the two leaders' Bedouin allies carrying out raids on the other's territory over three bloody years. Rivalries have cooled since the leaders of the seven Trucial States came together under one flag in the early 1970s. But even in those early days of unity, Dubai's Sheikh Rashid, although committed to the union, fought to give his emirate as much autonomy as possible.

Abu Dhabi's superior size and population has translated into greater political power. The discovery of huge oil reserves in Abu Dhabi gave Sheikh Zayed's emirate even more financial clout, as well as military muscle. When the UAE was formed, Abu Dhabi earned ten times more money from its oil revenues than Dubai and those earnings still vastly outstrip its neighbour. Factor in its huge investments in Western markets (one of the most recent and high profile being Manchester City football club) and the capital controls perhaps 90 per cent of the UAE's national wealth.

The federal government developed around Abu Dhabi's financial largesse. This helped the union's development, but sparked fears in Dubai and other poorer emirates, which were concerned that Abu Dhabi's bureaucrats, keen to control the disbursement of their funds, would whittle away at the emirates' close-knit tribal roots. In 1979, the UAE was in crisis, as Abu Dhabi pushed for more centralised authority than the other emirates would accept. The crisis abated as Sheikh Rashid accepted the post of UAE Prime Minister, while securing the rights of individual rulers to continue developing their emirates along their own lines.

The threat of international turmoil in the 1980s, as the Iran-Iraq War loomed large over the region, glued the emirates together. With the Islamic Revolution boiling in Iran and civil shipping under attack in their own backyard, the seven emirates' petty squabbles paled into insignificance. Abu Dhabi continued to fund generous welfare systems for the entire country, especially the resource-starved northern emirates.

Today, Abu Dhabi and Dubai still have different characters. Abu Dhabians are more restrained and conservative than go-getting Dubaians, and this was most evident when Dubai unilaterally allowed foreigners to own freehold property – triggering a massive building boom after 2003. Abu Dhabi sat silently on the sidelines for a while, but evidently took notes, as it has since embarked on an ambitious programme of its own, developing natural islands, building a Formula One race track and overhauling the city's infrastructure – although there are no plans for mile-high towers or flashy theme-parks.

IN CONTEXT

'It's Dubai's love affair with shopping that has sustained the emirate's tourist industry.'

There will no doubt have been a sense of *schadenfreude* at the level of pain the seemingly invincible Dubai suffered after the credit crunch. But nobody is denying that the city's dynamic economy has also brought international recognition and offers many lessons in how to move away from reliance on oil – along with a few hard-learned examples of what not to do.

DUBAI'S INDUSTRIAL REVOLUTION

Dubai, founded as a trade hub, quickly used growing oil revenues to diversify its economic base to include heavy industry. With abundant oil and gas resources, the emirates had a competitive advantage in large-scale industrial projects that require vast amounts of energy. Dubai's first great industrial project took the form of Dubai Dry Dock, constructed in 1973 as a ship repair yard, which Sheikh Rashid passed on to his third son and current ruler, Sheikh Mohammed. This venture also benefited from the outbreak of maritime war between Iran and Iraq, serving the steady stream of tanker war victims. Two years later, the Dubai Aluminium Co, or Dubal, was set up with an initial investment of Dhs5.1 billion, which took advantage of cheap oil to create one of the world's most profitable smelters.

As well as industrial projects, the oil wealth of the 1970s brought modern infrastructure. By the end of the decade, another bridge and a tunnel complemented the original Maktoum Bridge linking Bur Dubai with Deira. Dubai's population rose to 207,000 in 1977, compared with 20,000 in the 1940s.

As Dubai grew, so did the number of roads, hospitals and schools. The police force, set up in 1956 under the command of British officers, came under local control in 1975. Immigrants started their own schools, complementing the state-run schools that catered for locals and expatriate Arabs.

Whereas the 1970s spelt industrial development, the 1980s saw the arrival of big-time commerce. While strong global demand for oil underpinned the soaring revenues enjoyed by oil-producing countries, Dubai continued to diversify. The World Trade Centre, opened in 1979, attracted some of the world's biggest companies to set up local or regional headquarters in Dubai. Once again, cynics whispered that the centre, today dwarfed by the high-rises of Sheikh Zayed Road, was too far from the central commercial district in Deira. But little did it matter, as foreign companies set up shop in a land free of bureaucracy, boasting political stability and liberal social mores. The economy further diversified, and the city kept booming through the 1980s.

THE AGE OF TOURISM

In the 1970s, businessmen travelling to Dubai were hard pushed to find a single decent hotel. Sheikh Rashid even built a guesthouse for the businessmen and women who visited in the early days. By 1975, the InterContinental had opened on the Deira side of the Creek, but never satisfied the growing hordes of travellers touching down at the new airport; executives even used to share rooms.

How times change. By the 1990s, after the death of Sheikh Rashid, Dubai was busy reinventing itself as a tourist destination. There were 42 hotels in 1985, jumping to 272 by 2002 and 493 by 2008. The establishment in 1985 of Emirates, the Dubai-based international airline, helped the tourism sector flourish as the airline encouraged its passengers to stop over in the emirate en route to Asia, Africa or Europe. With start-up capital of Dhs36.7 million, the airline rapidly expanded, even staying profitable through the global travel slump after the terror attacks of 11 September 2001.

Father of Dubai

The Maktoum family continues to forge Dubai.

In an age in which the legacy of statesmen and politicians rarely escapes a cynical, retrospective makeover, Sheikh Maktoum bin Rashid Al Maktoum, who passed away in January 2006, is something of an exception. In his own land, he is remembered with honest affection and his achievements are highlighted with genuine admiration. The ruler of Dubai, who also held the position of UAE Vice President and Prime Minister, oversaw an economic and social miracle on the shores of the Arabian Gulf, turning a little-heard-of emirate into an economic powerhouse.

Sheikh Maktoum was educated at Cambridge University and then afterwards was groomed for power, being given the post of UAE Prime Minister until 1979. He helped to guide the fledgling country through some tough internal negotiations, but faced his biggest test in 1981 when his father fell ill. The burden of responsibility fell on Sheikh Maktoum, who took the opportunity to push through an ambitious economic plan to ween Dubai away from its dependence on oil while driving a social agenda to educate, house and empower the emirates' citizens. When his father eventually succumbed to a long illness in 1990, Sheikh Maktoum officially took control of Dubai's affairs and further quickened his business-friendly reforms, placing the emirate on its current path of ultra-fast growth.

Despite this business-friendly approach, or maybe because of it, he was keen to make sure all Emiratis shared in this newfound wealth, and he dramatically improved the living conditions of Dubai's population, an altruistic move rarely seen in the oil-rich countries of the Middle East. This move earned Sheikh Maktoum the respect and devotion of his people and of the wider Arab public, something which has been evident from the stream of international condolences and the genuine shock and sadness his death provoked on the street.

He was an avid race-goer and fan, and his hugely successful Godolphin stables helped raise the bar for standards across the racing world. Along with Sheikh Zayed, Sheikh Maktoum commanded universal respect and admiration across the UAE for being one of the country's founding fathers and for helping to create a peaceful, prosperous state in an extraordinarily short space of time.

IN CONTEXT

With its oil reserves running out, Dubai has turned increasingly to tourism. International events such as the Dubai World Cup horse race, desert rally and golf, tennis and rugby tournaments helped fuel the boom. But it's Dubai's love affair with shopping that has sustained the emirate's industry. The Dubai Shopping Festival, launched in 1996, attracts around 3.5 million people to the city every year. A second shopping festival, Dubai Summer Surprises, was introduced in 1998, attracting Gulf visitors who are used to the soaring summer temperatures that put off many Western tourists. Combined with sea, sun and liberal attitudes to entertainment, annual tourist numbers have now reached around 7.5 million, six times the city's resident population.

IN CONTEXT

A NEW ERA

In January 2006, following the death of Sheikh Maktoum bin Rashid Al Maktoum, his younger brother, Sheikh Mohammed, assumed power in Dubai. There was little doubt that he would be named leader. Accordingly, the transition between leaders was very smooth and any changes in government policy were barely noticeable.

BLACK GOLD TO WHITE COLLAR

Dubai's plan was, and continues to be, to attract professionals from across the globe. One of the emirate's most successful ventures to date is the formation of corporate free zones, where businesses in roughly the same industries are gathered in a corporate park, encouraging networking and new businesses. Dubai Internet City (DIC), announced in 1999, was the first such attempt to attract more professionals to the emirate. The venture was tailor-made to lure high-tech firms, offering tax-free 100 per cent ownership (outside free zones businesses need a local partner).

PROPERTY BOOM

Dubai's property boom, which exploded in 2003 with the introduction of freehold properties, is yet another reason why the emirate continues to make headlines across the globe. The repatriation of money from Western markets to the Middle East, especially the UAE, after 11 September 2001 gave Dubai's budding property industry a significant boost. Close to Dhs3.67 trillion poured into various sectors of the Middle Eastern market, a fair chunk of which went into Dubai's construction projects. Wealthy investors purchased dozens of apartments and villas, and small-time investors purchased an apartment or two at rock-bottom prices.

Developments such as Emaar's the Greens (the first rent-to-own scheme) and the Marina sparked buying crazes among expatriates and investors interested in making Dubai either their home or a destination for holidays. Nakheel's record-breaking Palm islands and the World attracted a number of heavyweight investors and celebrities as keen on owning a property in Dubai as they are about letting the world's media know about it. Local and international interest in Dubai's properties was substantial, with no one quite prepared for the unprecedeted influx of cash into the market.

Interestingly, for the first couple of years, there wasn't a single law to safeguard foreign homeowners and their properties. Instead, investors nervously relied on the clauses in their contracts with developers, and hoped that the imminent law they heard so much about would give them the comfort of government-sanctioned freehold status they desperately needed. In March 2006, after months of speculation, the law was implemented. Foreigners now have the legal right to buy properties in designated areas across the emirate, and they can register the properties in their own names with another new agency, the Real Estate Regulatory Authority (RERA).

Even before the law was announced, Dubai's property market was one of the fastest-growing in the world. In the first five years of freehold sales, the market broke through one financial ceiling after another in a dizzying rise into the financial stratosphere. People who bought properties off-plan in 2002 and 2003 saw their investments more than triple and sometimes quadruple in value.

If it seemed too good to last, that's because it was. As the world entered a new era of restricted credit in 2008, speculation on property in Dubai reached ludicrous proportions by that summer: anyone with enough money for a ten per cent deposit could make an initial payment on an off-plan property, then 'flip' it for a handsome profit. When the bubble burst at the end of that summer, those same investors were left high and dry. House prices fell by more than 40 per cent, many smaller developers went bust and thousands were stuck with properties that they couldn't afford. The bigger government-backed developers were not immune from the sudden exodus of cash from the market. Many multi-billion dollar projects were put on indefinite hold with little chance of them being finished – or even started – in the near future.

IN CONTEXT

Key Events

Dubai in brief.

1820 Dubai signs the 'General Maritime Peace Treaty' with Britain
1833 Dubai becomes an independent settlement of Abu Dhabi; rule of the Maktoum family begins
1841 Smallpox epidemic breaks out in Bur Dubai
1892 Trucial States are founded
1894 Fire devastates much of Deira
1947 Border dispute between Dubai and Abu Dhabi escalates
1954 Dubai Municipality established to help with city planning
1956 The Dubai police force is set up; first concrete house constructed in Dubai
1958 Sheikh Saeed dies; succeeded by Sheikh Rashid
1963 Maktoum Bridge opens, the first crossing over the Creek
1966 Oil is discovered in Dubai
1967 Building of Port Rashid begins; Britain announces its intention to withdraw
1971 Seven Trucial States meet, all but Ras Al Khaimah signing a federal document, forming the United Arab Emirates (UAE) with Sheikh Zayed Al Nahyan its first president
1972 Ras Al Khaimah joins the federation
1973 Port Rashid in downtown Dubai completed; the dirham adopted as the single UAE currency
1975 The Dubai police force comes under local control for the first time; Al Shindagha Tunnel opens, running beneath the Creek
1976 Building of Jebel Ali port begins; Garhoud Bridge opens across the Creek
1979 Dubai World Trade Centre opens; the Jebel Ali Free Zone is established; the border between Abu Dhabi and Dubai agreed
1980 Dubai's annual oil income stands at US$3 billion, Abu Dhabi's at US$15 billion

1983 Jebel Ali Port completed
1985 The Dubai-based international airline Emirates is established
1986 Sheikh Saeed's house is restored and opens for tourists
1990 Sheikh Rashid dies; he is succeeded as ruler by Sheikh Mohammed
1996 First Dubai World Cup, the world's richest horse race, takes place; first Dubai Shopping Festival
1998 First Dubai Summer Surprise takes place
1999 Burj Al Arab, the world's first seven-star hotel, even if it is self appointed to the mantle, opens on December 1; Dubai Internet City (DIC) opens
2001 Work begins on the first of the Palm islands, Palm Jumeirah
2003 Expatriates are granted permission to purchase freehold properties; Dubailand, the world's biggest collection of theme parks, announced
2004 Sheikh Zayed bin Sultan Al Nahyan dies; his son Sheikh Khalifa bin Zayed Al Nahyan becomes UAE president
2005 Ski Dubai, an indoor ski slope with real snow, opens at Mall of the Emirates; Dubai International Financial Centre (DIFC) opens
2006 Sheikh Maktoum bin Rashid Al Maktoum dies; his brother Sheikh Maktoum becomes ruler of Dubai; the official weekend changes from Thursday and Friday to Friday and Saturday
2007 Salik road toll system comes into effect; the Floating Bridge and Business Bay Bridge across Dubai Creek open
2008 New Garhoud Bridge opens; Atlantis hotel opens on The Palm
2009 Dubai Metro opens in September; construction finished on Burj Dubai, the world's tallest building

Dubai Today

The 21st-century city is a truly multi-cultural affair.

TEXT: JAMES ALEXANDER, CHRIS ANDERSON & JEREMY LAWRENCE

Among all the super-projects, luxury hotels and shopping malls, it's easy to forget that for over a million people, Dubai is simply home. The incredible influx of people from all over the world and the energy of Dubai's homegrown population has created a thriving, multicultural scene where new ideas and dreams can quickly become reality.

However, all too often expats remain hermetically sealed within their own communities, making little contact with the people in whose country they are living. Natives now constitute only a fifth of the population of Dubai.

Here, *Time Out* speaks to several Emiratis and expats to find out what Dubai means to them and how they are helping shape the future of the city.

THE ANIMATOR

Mohammed Harib is the creator of computer-animated TV show Freej.

Who are your UAE heroes?

HH Sheikh Mohammed, who helped cultivate a creative atmosphere in Dubai, and my father, who helped me become the person I am today. We have an Arabic phrase, 'When your son is grown you cease to be his father. You become his brother', and my father certainly heeded it. When I told him I wanted to be in animation, which is not a normal aspiration for people here, he told me to go for it despite everyone's opinions.

What does the future hold for the UAE?

The UAE has done in the past five years what many countries only aspire to: gone from being a third-world country to a developing monster. From sport to literature, we are the number one Arabic country. I'm a result of that, not part of it!

THE GALLERY DIRECTOR

Sunny Rahbar works at the Third Line, in the Al Quoz area.

What do you think has been the defining moment in the development of Dubai's art scene?

Events like Art Dubai have definitely created more public awareness and more support for the arts on a private and even a government level. But really, it felt like there was this combined energy and everyone just came together. It's still a small art scene, but the fact that it all happened at the same time and everyone depended on each other has been amazing.

What has been your favourite Dubai moment?

It has to be when we opened in 2005. We weren't even finished – we had a generator out the back running everything and it was really noisy, so we had to put the music up really loud [laughs]. It was great!

And what about the future of the art scene here?

The Dubai Cultural & Arts Authority has got some crazy plans – there are museums, theatres, opera houses… It's not that different from Abu Dhabi, but their strategy is more about inspiring the content from the ground rather than importing it. That's really exciting. Basically, I think it's just going to get bigger, better, faster, all those things – all very Dubai.

Sheikh Mohammed, Ruler of Dubai

The catalyst behind the growth.

Equestrian, fighter pilot, poet and, above all, businessman, **Sheikh Mohammed bin Rashid Al Maktoum** is the leading force behind the emirate's lightning modern-day development. Acting as chief executive of the huge holding company that is the Dubai government, the crown prince is behind the strategic and day-to-day running of the emirate. Following the death of his elder brother, Sheikh Maktoum, in January 2006, Sheikh Mohammed officially became ruler of Dubai, although he had been considered the de facto leader for several years.

With so much power vested in a single pair of hands, the cult of personality runs deep. The sheikh's daily schedule receives in-depth, adoring coverage from a fawning press; his presence at public gatherings commands reverential respect. But Sheikh Mohammed has a common touch too: he drives himself around in a white Mercedes 4x4 (licence plate #1, of course). The Noodle House in the Emirates Towers is one of the crown prince's frequent lunch spots

thanks in large part to its no-nonsense attitude and speedy service.

Equestrianism is both a hobby and a business for Sheikh Mohammed, who says his love of horses runs through his veins. His fascination with horseracing almost inevitably mutated into business. Set up in the mid 1990s, the royal family's stable, Godolphin, has quickly emerged as one of the world's top three equine operations, rivalled only by the Aga Khan and Ireland's Coolmore. The company's Dubai stables train their horses through the Gulf's winter, before dispersing the steeds across the world for the spring racing season.

The sycophancy surrounding Sheikh Mohammed may seem excessive to Western visitors, brought up to regard politicians with deep cynicism, but in a region of under-achieving leaders, the never-ending adulation of Dubai's 'Big Man' is for once well placed. Faced with a world economic crisis that has severely impacted the vision on which he staked his leadership, Sheikh Mohammed faces his biggest test yet.

THE FASHION DESIGNER

Buffi Jashanmal, is a fashion designer, stylist, costume designer and illustrator.

What's the biggest thing that has happened here in the fashion world?

I guess the last three Fashion Weeks have got people's attention, and they're just getting bigger and bigger and bigger.

What's your favourite part of Dubai?

I couldn't live without my 6.30am walks on the beach. The buzz of the city is amazing, but it's escaping from it all that means the most to me.

Describe your favourite moment in Dubai.

Probably seeing my dad cry as my models strutted down the catwalk at Dubai Fashion Week. He knew how much effort I put into it all, and there's nothing like having your family there to support you.

What does the future hold – for the UAE and for you?

I kind of get scared of my label growing because I want to keep things personal. The moment you get bigger, you have to play it safe and I don't want to be restricted. Dubai is a great place to try things out because people let you make mistakes. I do get worried that this place is too obsessed with money and growth. My apartment is half the size of my one in New York and more expensive. I just think it's all getting a little insane and could all suddenly come crashing down.

THE POET

Wael Al Sayegh is a poet and businessman.

Who are your UAE heroes?

HH Sheikh Zayed: he took his culture into the modern world and never forgot his Bedouin origins. He controlled billions of US dollars, but would sit on the floor with his fellow man. Without him, we would have no identity.

What's the biggest thing that has happened here in poetry?

The Zayed Book Award, which hands out big prize money to Arab writers every year. It's something every Arab writer aspires to winning.

What has been your favourite moment in the UAE?

Every time I see a UAE national succeeding on the world stage. As Emiratis, we've been given so much that excellence is not an option, it's a duty.

Dubai is...

... very entrepreneurial. We may have personal differences and contrasting beliefs, but we can come together to make a deal. That's the spirit of Dubai.

IN CONTEXT

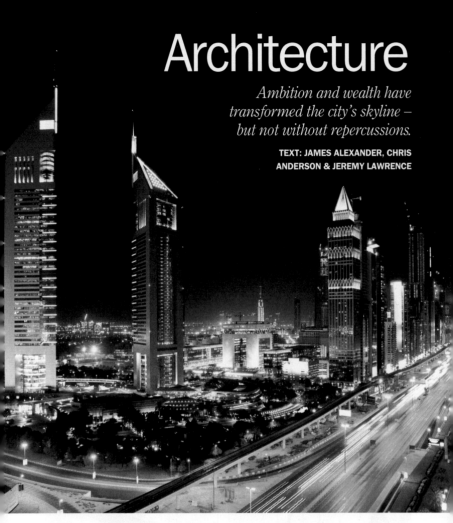

Architecture

Ambition and wealth have transformed the city's skyline – but not without repercussions.

TEXT: JAMES ALEXANDER, CHRIS ANDERSON & JEREMY LAWRENCE

With a hunger for innovative landmarks, and a peerless aptitude for publicising them, Dubai has produced multiple architectural feats to showcase its ambition and wealth around the world. When a *Vanity Fair* article hailed the city's 'skyline on crack', it wasn't far off the mark; Dubai, it can safely be said, is not the sleepy fishing town it was half a century ago.

But if you look behind the buzzwords and the bombast, you'll discover that something quite extraordinary has taken place. And although it's easy to scoff at the more outlandish projects, it's impossible not to be impressed by the outside-the-box thinking that has transformed this city.

IN CONTEXT

Bastakia

THE GROWTH SPURT

Unlike major cities such as London or New York, Dubai's architectural history is astonishingly compressed: wind tower houses replaced palm-frond shelters in the early 20th century; following the oil boom, these were torn down to make way for concrete apartment blocks; and those in turn were replaced by postmodernist skyscrapers. However, the city's design trend is turning full circle, with a penchant for Arabian chic seeing architects incorporating wind towers into their designs for five-star hotels.

With the first exports of oil from the area taking place in the early 1960s, Dubai set about dragging itself into the 20th century with an almost religious zeal. The mantra 'out with the old, in with the new' and the urgent need for mass housing resulted in the razing of most of its old town and the rapid rise of towers and cheap apartment blocks. It wasn't until the 1990s that the government turned its attention to preserving and restoring what was left of the old town. Critics maintain that only the UAE's neighbour, Oman, offers true examples of traditional Gulf architecture, but there are still pockets of authenticity left in early 21st-century Dubai, mainly in the Bastakia area.

In terms of contemporary architecture, the audacious Burj Al Arab hotel became an instant icon upon completion, and started Dubai's passion for breaking height records. Meanwhile, international architects have been busy creating cities-within-cities, the world's tallest tower and, of course, the Palm Islands. Unsurprisingly, the debate still rages among architects over ways to develop a local architectural language that looks to Dubai's past as well as its gleaming future.

BACK IN THE DAY

It was the Bani Yas tribe – ancestors of the Bedouin – who first set up camp in the deserts and mountains of Abu Dhabi and Dubai in the 18th century. They split their time between animal hide tents, ideal for winter wanderings, and *arish* or *barasti* (palm-frond shelters) for summer months spent on date plantations. *Barasti* were also popular among fishermen, pearlers and traders.

Coastal areas had blocky homes built from bricks of fossilised coral bonded with *sarooj* (a blend of Iranian red clay and manure, dried and baked in a kiln) or a lime mixture derived from seashells and plastered with chalk and water paste. Large courtyard houses built of *farush* (beach rock) and covered with lime plaster have been excavated in Jumeirah and dated to the second century of the Islamic era (ninth century AD). When a branch of the Bani Yas – the Maktoums – settled by the Creek in the early 19th century, more permanent homes were built using *guss* (mud blocks) and roofed with palm fronds, materials that kept the temperature down. Rooms usually opened on to an airy central courtyard restricted to family use, and male guests were entertained in a separate *majlis* (meeting room). In many newer villas the *majlis* is in the main house, a layout that is still familiar to Dubaians living in villas built in the 1970s and 1980s.

Public buildings in the 18th and 19th centuries were mostly stone forts, which doubled up as seats of government, and mosques. **Al Fahidi fort**, believed to be Dubai's oldest building, now home to Dubai Museum (*see p69*), was built around 1799 to guard landward approaches to the town. Parts of the old Dubai wall, built in the early 1800s, can be seen in Bastakia.

As Dubai's pearling industry boomed in the late 1800s, Bedouin and mountain communities began to gravitate towards the coastal trading villages. The simple, outwardly minimalist homes they built were decorated inside with intricate rugs and wooden latticework on windows, and outside by elaborately carved doors; this tradition has continued in the brightly painted metal doors and gates on old villas by the beach, and there are some great antique wooden examples in Bastakia. Historians disagree about whether these decorations were traditionally Arab, based on Islamic designs, or inspired by Indian decorative principles. Homes were built close to each other, with shady *sikkas* (narrow alleys) running down towards the water.

The Sky's the Limit

What should be, could be and probably never will be built.

Think you've heard it all? You haven't. Dubai's building boom led to the most outlandish projects ever conceived. We look at the ones that may, or may not, soon be gracing the city.

DEAD CERTS

Burj Dubai

Completed late in 2009, Burj Dubai stands 818m (2,684ft) tall – making it the world's tallest tower by some considerable distance. The centrepiece of a grandiose 'Downtown Burj' project, which includes residential and commercial towers and Dubai Mall, the city's biggest shopping centre, the gargantuan tower contains luxury apartments, business centres and an Armani Hotel.

Dubai Sports City

The initial stages of the world's first purpose-built sports city are already completed. International cricket is now played at the 25,000-capacity cricket stadium, the Ernie Els golf course is open and the keys to the first luxury villas are about to be handed over. Business towers and residential blocks

are being built, and the Manchester United Soccer School and International Cricket Council are set to relocate. However, at the time of going to press, the centrepiece of the project, a 60,000-seater stadium, is on hold.

Meydan

The huge horse racing city will include a luxury hotel and restaurants, a grand stand with a capacity of 60,000, a dirt and turf course and a presidential and commercial complex. Intersecting the creek is a four kilometre-long water canal linked to Dubai Creek. The brainchild of Sheikh Mohammed himself, it is still due to open in time for the World Cup in 2010.

Palm Jumeirah

With a total area larger than 800 football pitches, surrounded by an 11-kilometre (6.8-mile) breakwater, the Palm Jumeirah is a spectacular feat of engineering. It's also now a functioning home to thousands, thanks to its apartment blocks and shoreline villas. The brash, over-the-top but fun Atlantis Hotel is also open – complete with water slides, dolphin parks and celebrity restaurants. More hotels are set to follow, although the opening dates for many of these have been put back and the grandiose Trump Tower project is on hold.

REVISED
Arabian Canal

A 75-kilometre (47-mile) man-made waterway up to 150 metres (492 feet) wide and six metres (20 feet) deep, with public spaces for leisure and community events as well as a number of mixed-use projects, the US$50 billion waterfront development was supposed to be completed in phases over a 15-year period. Excavation has started, but has slowed drastically and there is little chance of it meeting the initial timetable, although the developers 'remain committed' to the project.

Dubailand

Announced back in 2003, Dubailand is supposed to be the largest collection of theme parks in the world. Plans were also on the table to build 'Bawadi' comprising 51 hotels with 60,000 rooms; and Falconcity of Wonders, which would have recreations of the Seven Wonders of the World. Projects such as the Autodrome and Sports City are up and running, but many of the more outlandish developments appear to be on hold.

Dubai Waterfront

A conglomeration of canals and artificial islands, the project is supposed to curve around Palm Jebel Ali, adding 70 kilometres (43 miles) to the coastline and housing 1.5 million people. Work has commenced on the first phase and homes have been sold, but whether it turns out to be as ambitious as first proposed is yet to be seen.

Palm Jebel Ali

Fifty per cent bigger than Palm Jumeirah, and expected to accommodate 1.7 million people by 2020, the project is set to include six marinas, a water theme park, a 'Sea Village' and housing. Completion dates have been repeatedly revised, but at some stage it should see the light of day.

The World

300 islands constructed in the shape of a world map four kilometres off the coast of Dubai, the development covers an area nine kilometres (six miles) in length and six kilometres (four miles) in width. The dredging cost billions of dollars, with islands up for sale for anything from US$15-US$250 million. Among the proposals for development was the recreation of Ireland, complete with rolling green hills and the Giant's Causeway. Several stars were also rumoured to have bought 'countries' for themselves – including Brad Pitt and Angelina Jolie. Dredging is more or less complete, but building work on the finished islands hasn't started.

ON HOLD
Nakheel Tower

Nakheel announced plans to build the gigantic 1,400-metre (4,593-foot) super-structure, but then almost immediately put the project on hold till 2010. No further news was forthcoming at the time of writing.

Palm Deira

The initial plan was to build an island ▶

The Sky's the Limit

▶ eight times larger than Palm Jumeirah, intended to house one million people. The drawings have been substantially revised since then, but developers Nakheel announced that more than a quarter of the total area of the Palm Deira had been reclaimed. However, work appears to have ground to a halt with no word of a revised deadline.

The Universe

How do you go one better than the World? Easy, you build the Universe. The proposed cluster of islands forming the shape of the solar system was dreamed up by Nakheel and is still in planning, filling the space between the shore and the World islands.

DON'T HOLD YOUR BREATH

Burj Al Arabi

This might be the most bizarre concept we've heard of. The proposed Burj Al Arabi project planned to represent an Arab man wearing national dress, with a special translucent fabric *kandura* suspended over what is planned to be the world's tallest concrete and steel realisation of the human form, at 140 metres (459 feet).

Dubai Sunny Mountain Ski Dome

If Willy Wonka were to be put in charge of designing a ski slope, it might end up looking something like Dubai Sunny Mountain. The plan was to feature real polar bears, the region's first Penguinarium, and – somewhat implausibly – a revolving mountain.

Hydropolis

The world's first underwater luxury resort was supposed to be a 'ten-star' the size of London's Hyde Park. There is no sign that construction ever started, though there was a nice billboard complete with artist's impression near the beach at one time.

International Chess City

A whole city dedicated to chess? Blame the Republic of Kalmykia, a self-governing entity in Russia, which built its own chess city in its capital Elista and wanted to repeat the trick in Dubai. Kalmykian leader Kirsan Ilyumzhinov unveiled plans to develop 32 buildings in the shape of chess pieces on a giant board. The pawns were normal homes, the rooks, knights and bishops five-star hotels, and the kings and queens were to be the last word in luxury.

Dubai Sports City. See p42.

'Soaring fortunes, built on increased trade, went stratospheric during the oil crisis of 1973, and the government began construction in earnest.'

By the late 19th century, spurred in part by a devastating fire in 1894, Deira's wealthy began to build their homes from coral stone and gypsum, although the poor still lived in *barasti* buildings. Today, *barasti* huts are constructed to shade farm workers in the desert, picnickers in villa gardens and cocktail drinkers at busy beach bars.

Sheikh Saeed Al Maktoum House (*see p70*) was built in 1896 on the southern bank of the Creek in Shindagha as a residence for the ruling family; it remained their home until Sheikh Saeed's death in 1958. Probably one of the first houses in the area to sport Iranian-inspired wind towers, it is a traditional coral-block structure built around a large central courtyard. The Emirati historian and architect Rashad Bukhash, formerly head of the Historical Buildings Section of Dubai Municipality, has described the Sheikh Saeed Al Maktoum House as 'the best example of traditional architecture, with all the wooden decorative elements – such as carved latticework and teak doors – that were typical of the times.' The restored house now acts as a museum, displaying old photographs and historical documents.

By the mid 20th century, a village of around 50 compounds, each with a wind tower or two, had built up in Bastakia along the Bur Dubai side of the Creek. It remained more or less intact until the 1980s. A collection of wind tower shops still exists by the *abra* (boat) station; other fine examples open to the public are the **Majlis Gallery** and **XVA**, a restored café, gallery and guesthouse. Former residents of Bastakia today look back with fondness to less hurried times, when families were self-sufficient – with livestock kept and slaughtered at home – and a shopping trip involved taking a rowed *abra* to the souks of Deira.

A CITY IS BORN

Dubai's pace of urbanisation – like every other facet of life in what was then the Trucial States – was dramatically accelerated by the discovery of oil in the early 1960s, first in Abu Dhabi and then in Dubai. The city's skyline was transformed following the formation of the UAE in 1971, largely due to the explosion in Dubai's population.

The first house built from concrete blocks was constructed in Dubai in 1956, but much of the population continued to live in *barastis* until well into the 1960s. Typically, extended families grouped together into compounds separated by thin alleyways; transport was by donkey, camel or *abra* until the 1960s, when the first roads opened.

Even before the oil days, Dubai's ambition was evident. Sheikh Rashid, who succeeded his father in 1958, spent his first few years in power setting up a Municipal Council, building and widening roads, constructing the first airport and bridging the Creek. The advent of the car created the need for the establishment of a system of land management and ownership – as people losing half their compound to a widened road required compensation – and the concept of town planning was introduced. Working out who owned what in the tribal quarters of the city proved tricky, but became essential as land value rose. Territory outside built-up areas and any reclaimed land belonged to the ruler – a decree that continues to this day.

International commentators were sceptical about Sheikh Rashid's grand plans, but there was no shortage of believers; Dubai's population doubled to 120,000 between the late 1960s and early '70s, and by 1981 had reached well over a quarter of a

IN CONTEXT

Burj Al Arab. *See p46.*

million. The few apartment blocks that sprung out of the desert around Deira's Clock Tower Roundabout (1963) in the 1960s weren't lonely for long, and by the mid '70s the Creek was lined with low- and high-rise structures. Already soaring fortunes, built on increased trade, went stratospheric during the oil crisis of 1973, and the government began construction in earnest. Developing infra-structure took precedence – the Shindagha tunnel and Al Maktoum Bridge, the dry docks at Port Rashid, mosques, hospitals, schools and power stations all date from around the late '60s and early '70s. Sadly, however, the need for urgent residential and office accommodation led to some entirely uncharismatic blocks being erected.

One exception is **Dubai Municipality** (1979), on the Deira side of the Creek, a building that's still widely admired for its abstract sensitivity – although the inner glass courtyard and water pools, which create a cool microclimate, weren't added until the 1980s. The **Dubai World Trade Centre** (DWTC), also built in 1979 and at the time the signature Dubai landmark, and its highest building at 39 storeys, hasn't enjoyed the same favour. Unmistakably of its time, the DWTC is now dwarfed in size and renown by Jumeirah Emirates Towers, and in function by the efficient Ibis and Novotel hotels, built to accommodate delegates to 2003's World Bank and IMF meetings.

Dubai's ritual building up and tearing down saw many of the smaller structures of the 1960s and '70s cleared to make way for a rising wave of brand-new skyscrapers. But tradition sat cheek by jowl with the shiny and the modern: timber for interiors and furniture was still imported to the Creek on wooden dhows and, even in the early 1980s, Bur Dubai was still a wind tower village compared to Deira's burgeoning metropolis across the water.

By the end of the decade, Dubai's passion for novelty began to soften slightly, perhaps owing in part to the emergence of the first wave of local architecture graduates. Rumour has it that Prince Charles, the UK's ambassador for architectural conservatism, expressed great enthusiasm for wind towers on a tour of Bastakia, encouraging Dubaians to start conservation projects. Meanwhile, the launch of Emirates airline in 1985 brought increasing numbers of tourists hungry for a taste of Arabia. The first restoration project, Sheikh Saeed's House, was completed in 1986, and through the 1990s another 70 buildings were saved. Architects began

Marina. *See p48.*

Green Thinking

The first initiatives to address Dubai's carbon footprint.

The UAE is the not-so-proud producer of one of the largest ecological footprints in the world, so 'the emirates' and 'environmentally friendly developments' aren't terms that often occur in the same sentence. In the 2008 Happy Planet Index, the UAE came 154th out of 178 countries in the ecological footprint category, meaning that the country consumes a huge amount of natural resources to sustain its lifestyle and culture, but hardly creates any of these resources itself. Environmentalists claim that offshore developments such as the World and the Palm islands are doing considerable damage to the region's marine life, as the digging up of the seabed suffocates it in a blanket of silt. Although the intelligent design of wind towers cooled down traditional Dubai buildings, today's malls, hotels, offices and indoor ski slopes are heavily reliant on air-conditioning units to beat the year-round heat, and this surplus of sun, so far, has not inspired many developers to consider solar power as a source of energy.

However, there are signs of a new awareness taking hold. The Dubai Desert Conservation Reserve, 45 minutes out of town, is a 225-square-kilometre refuge that will remain an untouched slice of the environment in the surrounding building frenzy.

And 27 October 2007 will always be remembered in Dubai's history. This was the start of Dubai's new 'green building' directive, enforcing all builders and developers across the emirate to comply with US standards from January 2008. In a city where a new skyscraper seemingly pops up every five minutes, this was big news. 'This decision will position Dubai as the first city in the Middle East – and among few cities in the world – to adopt the green building strategy', HE Mohammed Al Gergawi, Chairman of the Executive Office in Dubai, said. Of course, the change can't happen overnight. Developers are feeling the pressure to certify their buildings, but they're not sure how to do it, and existing buildings can't just become green overnight. But the change has at least started.

incorporating traditional or Islamic elements into their designs. The thoroughly 1980s **Deira Tower** (1980) in Baniyas Square, for example, has a distinctive circular white 'cap' like that worn by Emirati men under their *ghutra* (headdress).

INTO THE MILLENNIUM

Upon Sheikh Rashid's death in 1990, his sons set about furthering their father's plans to create the Hong Kong of the Middle East, with new buildings dedicated to commerce and tourism. Dubai's macho love affair with the tower became ever more fervent, and foreign architects' efforts to relate their buildings to the local environment ranged from the ultra-literal to the ultra-kitsch. Some managed to be both: visitors heading into the city from the airport can't miss the mock aircraft hull of **Emirates Aviation College**. **Jumeirah Beach Hotel** (1997) represents a surfer's dream wave, and the unusually low-rise **Dubai Creek Golf & Yacht Club** (1993), the billowing sails of a dhow. Other architects' favourites include Ott's **National Bank of Dubai** building (1998), known locally as the 'pregnant lady'. Supported by two giant columns, the gold, glass and granite sculptural tower nods to the curved hulls and taut sails of *abras* and dhows, but in a subtly contextual manner. Ott is also responsible for the nearby **Hilton Dubai Creek** (2001; *see p91*), a minimalist's dream.

   Jumeirah Emirates Towers (*see p106*) is equally sleek. The Australian design is the city's most spectacular corporate building. The hotel tower rises 355 metres (1,165 feet); if you can dodge security (it's officially for hotel guests only), take a ride in the exhilirating glass lifts. **Children's City** (*see p200*) in Creekside Park has a Duplo-style series of exhibition rooms, and is equally unashamedly modern and unusual in that it provides a spatial as well as a formal experience – as does the ultra-chic **One&Only Royal Mirage** hotel (*see p104*), which uses elements of traditional Islamic architecture. The impressive **Madinat Jumeirah** (*see p101*), a massive hotel and souk complex that opened in 2004, also harks back to the days of wind towers and coral block hues.

   Of course, it was with Madinat's neighbour, the **Burj Al Arab** hotel (*see p98* **Profile**), opened in late 1999, that Dubai really earned its reputation as an architect's playground. Tom Wright of Atkins aimed to build a 'state-of-the-art, almost futuristic building' that was 'Arabic, extravagant and super-luxurious'.

IN CONTEXT

Atlantis Hotel on Palm Jumeirah. *See p42.*

'Dubaians often wryly joke that they go to sleep alone at night only to wake up next to a skyscraper the next day.'

The Burj became an instant icon and the most recognised landmark in the city. Built some 300 metres (985 feet) off shore, it was the world's tallest hotel at 321 metres (1,053 feet) when it opened, and is supported by 250 columns descending 40 metres (130 feet) into the seabed. Rumour has it that sand from around the base has to be hoovered out every night to prevent subsidence, and that the tower sways by up to 30 centimetres (12 inches) at the top. Even if you can't afford a night's stay in the hotel, you can check out its 28 double-height floors of pure opulence by paying a Dhs250 entrance fee (redeemable in the bars and restaurants) and taking in the thrilling views from the Al Muntaha bar located in the oval pod at the top of the 'mast'.

By the late 1990s, local architects were beginning to mutter about an identity crisis among Dubai's buildings. For some, the attempts by the likes of the **Royal Mirage** and intimate eco-retreat **Al Maha Desert Resort & Spa** to allude to local or regional history were key to creating a contextual and distinctive Dubai 'look'. For people who question the notion of 'Islamic architecture', these attempts amounted to mere pastiche: they say that Dubai's age-old position on the trading crossroads and its new identity as a global city necessitate the sort of universal buildings that you'll see if you take a drive down **Sheikh Zayed Road** or walk by the **Marina**.

Dubaians often wryly joke that they go to sleep alone at night only to wake up next to a skyscraper the next day. Reflecting the transient and impatient nature of the new Dubai, many of the structures are impressive, but few of them are truly innovative, especially when it comes to environmental concerns (*see p47* **Green Thinking**). Old-timers asky why today's architects have yet to master the use of cool air, shade and natural light perfected in wind tower houses. While European, American and Asian capitals patronise the new breed of superstar architects, Dubai tends to rely on faceless foreign corporations for its construction needs, and the public's imagination has yet to be grabbed by many cultural or public buildings.

Dubai's new role as one massive real estate project has been facilitated by the launch of freehold property ownership for foreigners, enabling non-Emiratis to buy homes for the first time. Despite initial concerns about a lack of land and mortgage legislation, local and global investors proved to be more than willing to partake of the Dubai dream.

These moves created a fevered property boom that seemed unstoppable. New mega-projects were announced on what seemed like a daily basis, and each one was more audacious than the last. Dubai Waterfront would extend the coastline by 820 kilometres and house 750,000 people; the Arabian Canal would stretch 33 kilometres inland and cost over US$50 billion, to the east of a new international airport that would be easily the biggest ion the world. Bawadi, a leisure development in Dubai would house 51 hotels and 60,000 rooms. The list went on and on.

And then the global credit crunch hit Dubai in late 2008. With investors fleeing the market and credit all but impossible to find, many developments ground to a halt. Most are officially postponed rather than cancelled, but it is highly unlikely that they will see the light of day any time soon.

There is also increasing concern about the environmental cost and the apparent human rights abuses taking place on construction sites. These are problems the authorities will have to deal with, as the price of putting Dubai on the map has been increased scrutiny from the rest of the world.

IN CONTEXT

Sheikh Zayed Road.

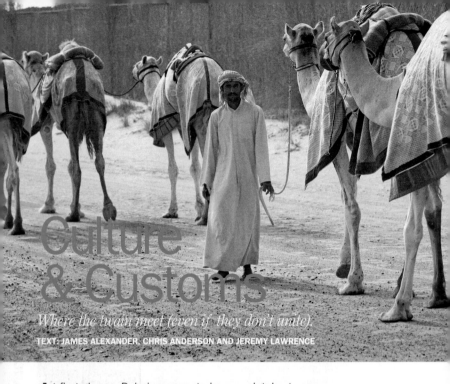

Culture & Customs

Where the twain meet (even if they don't unite).

TEXT: JAMES ALEXANDER, CHRIS ANDERSON AND JEREMY LAWRENCE

At first glance, Dubai appears to be completely at ease with its claim to be a tolerant, forward-thinking city. Walk through a shopping mall and you'll see traditional women covered from head to toe in traditional dress and Western girls in summer dresses; walk into a hotel nightclub and you could forgive yourself for thinking you were on a different continent altogether – and no one seems to mind. But scratch beneath the surface and things get a bit more complicated. The city has long walked a tightrope of trying to be all things to all men – accepting foreign customs while trying to maintain its own traditional, religious values. This leads to hideous inconsistencies: it's legal to drink in a hotel bar, for example, but it's illegal to have alcohol in your bloodstream once outside the door. And many people have fallen foul of the law because they simply didn't know what wasn't permissible.

The situation has become slightly clearer following the recent publication of what is and is not accepted behaviour. Nevertheless, many visitors will still be left in the dark by the lack of guidelines in public places and the lack of consistency in the application of these laws. But don't worry unduly: dress respectably, act courteously and remember that your Emirati hosts are known for their hospitality, good humour and tolerance.

'Even here today, gone tomorrow tourists can't fail to notice the busloads of workers who graft all year round.'

LAND OF CONTRADICTIONS

Most cities are full of inconsistencies, but you'll be hard-pushed to find a city with so many apparent contradictions as Dubai. It promotes itself as the entertainment capital of the Middle East, where clubbers can find enough venues to dance in for weeks, yet the local population is generally very conservative. As devout Muslims, many UAE nationals continue to uphold the numerous religious duties Islam enjoins, most of which have infiltrated local traditions and customs; yet, many of these practices also forbid them from indulging in the very entertainment services that the emirate is so keen to promote.

Dubai thrives on its image as an oasis in a mysterious and largely unapproachable region. In the midst of the political dramas happening around it, Dubai is a luxury destination for the wealthy and hordes of nouveau riche; people who aren't willing to give up their social freedoms, such as drinking alcohol, while on holiday. Celebrities flock to party in Dubai's massive hotels and trendy bars, whereas the city's locals are left on the sidelines, watching expatriates and visitors party away at clubs and bars that are deemed inappropriate by Emirati society. But as long as the cash keeps flowing, it's an oxymoronic reality that Dubai seems willing to live with.

IN CONTEXT

The Atlantis launch party.

Dubai Creek.

IN CONTEXT

'Dig beneath the surface and you'll find a complex, rapidly changing people.'

The result is an obvious dichotomy between foreigners and Emiratis – a rift so severe it physically separates most expatriates and visitors from locals; meeting and conversing with an Emirati is a special occasion rather than the norm. One of the drawbacks of this is the reinforcement of the expatriate bubble, in which foreigners forget or completely disregard the importance of adhering to and respecting local customs and traditions. No one's to blame; it's merely a consequence of Dubai's booming economy. The influx of foreigners, including an enormous number of Indian, Pakistani and Bangladeshi labourers brought in to build this city, has marginalised Emiratis and their way of life. Today, Emiratis constitute only around 20 per cent of the UAE's population, and the percentage of them living in the booming emirate of Dubai is much lower than that.

Scores of Emiratis have complained in the media that they feel like guests in their own nation, rather like cultural exiles within their palace walls. A natural consequence of this is a heightened sense of protectiveness over their culture and traditions. It is therefore advisable for visitors in Dubai to respect and adhere to the behavioural guidelines set by local custom, otherwise they risk offending Emiratis.

THE CITY OF IMMIGRANTS

Dubai's position at the crossroads of the Gulf, India and Africa has always made it home – or at least port-of-call – for expatriates from the region and beyond, but its transformation from a pearl-diving town to an economic powerhouse over the past 70 years has brought about a dramatic change in the city's ethnic make-up.

However, in spite of the emirate's attempts to eradicate racism, there are marked distinctions between 'workers' and 'expatriates', the former consisting of labourers from the subcontinent and the latter a combination of skilled men and women from the Middle East, Europe, Australasia and South Africa. Even here today, gone tomorrow tourists can't fail to notice the busloads of workers who graft all year round, even in the heat of the summer, building Dubai's new luxury hotels and homes. There are over half a million construction workers in the city at any time, living in what are openly called 'labour camps', and working long, round-the-clock shifts, for as little as US$180 a month. While some argue that the workers are better off earning money for themselves and their families in the Gulf rather than struggling to find jobs back home, stories abound of construction workers arriving in Dubai under false pretences, collapsing in high summer temperatures and slaving away in dangerous conditions.

The city's service sector – the lower rungs of the tourist and entertainment industries, and the maids and cleaners who look after local and expatriate families – tend to hail from the Philippines, Indonesia, East Africa and Sri Lanka. Dubai's labouring classes stay for years on end, sending money back via the informal *hawala* transfer system and visiting their families every two or three years. As every other taxi driver will tell you, many plan to come for a couple of years, but find themselves staying much longer; most can say the number of months and days until their next trip home.

Their exploitation contrasts strongly with the city's penchant for brash consumer luxury; for professionals, life in Dubai is a different story. Fewer companies offer the classic 'expat packages' (flights home, beach club membership, free housing) and the cost of living has risen dramatically in recent years, leading old-timers to complain that things aren't what they used to be. But Dubai can still provide a classic expat lifestyle.

However, change is afoot: today's IT, media, tourism and property industries have attracted young Arabs, Iranians and Indians, as well as Brits, other Europeans, South

IN CONTEXT

Africans and Australasians, some of whom have an interest in the Middle East beyond the lure of tax-free sunshine. The mantra is still 'work hard, play hard', but a new kind of sophistication is evident – and necessary, given Dubai's rapid pace of development.

DUBAI'S ARAB POPULATION

The Arab world's party people, the Lebanese, heavily influence Dubai's glamorous clubbing scene. The Lebanese tend to be Muslim or Christian, and have always immigrated to far-flung lands; there are substantial numbers in Dubai. Joining them are Palestinians, Syrians, other Levantine Arabs and Iranians, many of whom have been educated in Europe, the US or other Gulf states.

As for Emiratis, it's their passion for sport, business and shopping that brings them together, and the Thursday horse-racing nights attract huge crowds. As well as all things equine (racing, endurance riding, Arab horse racing and beauty contests), Emiratis are committed to their falconry – don't be surprised to see a row of hooded falcons coming through the airport's passport control, or in the gardens of the palaces in Jumeirah and Umm Suqeim. And finally, although shopping may be merely a pastime anywhere else in the world, here it's an obsession. Many families bond by hitting the mall every Friday afternoon, and with so many destinations to choose from, it's no wonder AA Gill observed that Dubai is the place where malls go on holiday.

THE ETHNIC FOOD CHAIN

Despite Dubai's generally harmonious and tolerant outlook, and its reputation as the most liberal of the emirates, some professionals do note a degree of racism – from the patronising attitude of some expatriates towards the service classes, to club bouncers refusing entry to groups of Indian men. At times, Dubai can seem to be made up of a collection of different ethnic groups that keep themselves to themselves, living parallel but separate lives. Certainly, the old order that places Emiratis at the top of the pile, followed by Europeans and then other Arabs, has shown staying power. But increasing numbers of professional Indians, the creation of democratically elected local councils, and laws allowing – even encouraging – foreigners to own property has created a class of 'stakeholders' in Dubai society that has blurred old boundaries. It will be fascinating to see how this plays out in future years.

LOCAL RULE

Although expatriates, particularly Westerners, might be highly visible, it's the local minority that defines and rules the city. Many foreigners mistakenly believe that Emirati society is as uniform as its choice of dress, but dig beneath the surface and you'll find a complex, rapidly changing people. Young professionals, whose grandparents may have lived on camel milk and dates in the desert, deftly straddle Dubai's twin towers of capitalism and tradition. They are likely to combine an arranged marriage, the wearing of the hijab and other traditions with business acumen and an international education, an absolute respect for the ruling Sheikhs with a deep love of Hollywood. An active programme of 'Emiratisation' aims to get more Emiratis into all areas of employment, but for now they tend to dominate only the public sector.

THE WEEKEND

In September 2006, the government changed the official weekend days from Thursday and Friday to Friday and Saturday and that modification has now been largely adopted by everyone. Around the same time, many companies also moved from one-day to two-day weekends – perhaps acknowledging the reality that Dubai is now a place to live rather than just work. Either way, Friday, the Islamic holy day, remains sacred. Many expatriates head for the beach or book large tables for an extensive Friday brunch – a long-established Dubai tradition. From noon onwards, they tuck into extraordinarily large buffets, and families gather at parks, beaches and homes.

Local Rules

What you really can and can't do in Dubai.

IN CONTEXT

DRINKING
There are plenty of restaurants and bars serving alcohol; the only restriction is that they must be inside a hotel or sporting stadium. The law states that everyone drinking in the bar should be a guest of that hotel but this is never enforced and people are free to drink where they choose. Residents are free to drink in their own home providing they hold an alcohol licence issued by the municipality. There are two main alcohol distributors, a+e and MMI, which distribute alcohol to bars and also sell it through their own shops to licence holders. Tourists are free to bring limited amounts of alcohol into the country (*see p271* **Customs**). It is illegal to drink in the streets or in public places.

EATING PORK
As with alcohol, pork is often freely served in hotel restaurants. Many larger supermarkets have a pork section for non-Muslims. You do not need a licence to purchase pork.

CLOTHING
Western women do not need to wear a headscarf, but should cover their shoulders and knees in public. This is especially important during Ramadan.

WOMEN DRIVERS
Women are subject to the same driving laws as men.

HOMOSEXUALITY
All sexual liaisons conducted outside of marriage are illegal in the UAE. As gay marriages are not recognised by Islamic law, all homosexual acts are illegal.

HIV
There is no test on entry to check if you are HIV positive. However, if you are found to be HIV positive during your stay, you will face deportation. If you're applying for residency, you have to pass a medical proving you aren't HIV positive.

HOTEL ROOMS
Strictly speaking, it is illegal for an unmarried couple to share a hotel room. However, very few establishments will actually ask to see a marriage certificate – particularly if you are a Western couple.

PUBLIC BEHAVIOUR
It is important to moderate your behaviour in public. Although kissing on the cheek is acceptable, even holding hands is technically illegal if you're unmarried, and more passionate displays of affection can result in fines and arrests.

Grand Mosque.

IN CONTEXT

THICKER THAN WATER

For Dubai's Emirati population – with only two generations of separation from tribal living – the extended family is of crucial importance, whether in business dealings and traditional gatherings or trips to the mall or the races. Names tend to define someone within their immediate family – as 'bin' ('son of') or 'bint' ('daughter of') – and within their tribe or extended family by the prefix 'al'. Protocol dictates that respect and thanks should always be given to the older generations in each family, especially when it comes to official matters. The existence of *wasta*, the 'old boys' network, favours those with family and friends in high places.

KNOW YOUR HOSTS

Emiratis are known for their warm hospitality and politeness. Traditionally, every guest who entered a Bedouin's tent or home had to be unconditionally fed and given shelter for three days. Nowadays, this kind of generosity is not essential for survival, but old habits die hard. If you're lucky enough to meet and be invited by locals (or other Gulf Arabs) for tea or coffee, do accept. The ritual of making and presenting coffee – strong, espresso-sized cups – is prized, and you'll be offered refill after refill. If your heart can't quite take it, just gently shake your cup from side to side; your host will know not to offer you any more. If you are doing the entertaining, make sure you press more refreshments on your guest – they may well refuse a few times out of politeness before caving in. If a meal presents itself, expect vast amounts of delicious food, much of which will end up being left – a sign of your host's generosity. Eat only with your right hand, since the left hand is traditionally used for wiping the backside in the toilet.

Most Emirati men favour the time-honoured – and extremely practical – *dishdasha* or *khandura* (a long, white shirt-dress), with *ghutra* (a white headdress) and *agal* (a black rope that holds the *ghutra* in place, traditionally used to hobble camels). In public, city women tend to wear an *abaya* (long black cloak) over a conservative dress, long skirt or tight designer jeans, with a *hijab* or *sheyla* (a scarf that either wraps around the face and hair, or covers the whole face). Older women sometimes wear a burka (a soft leather material covering a woman's nose and lips) that just leaves the eyes exposed, or a traditional hardened linen mask that sits on the nose. Although obviously influenced by the Islamic tenet for modesty, the clothes are also deeply practical, as anyone who has survived the biting sandy winds of a desert *shamal* (northerly wind) can testify.

As for Dubai's expatriate population, it's advisable to dress to suit the occasion. Revealing or tight evening wear is tolerated in clubs, and a bikini is fine on the beach or by the hotel pool, but it's important (and advisable if you want to avoid getting stared at) to be more conservative anywhere in the city: no shorts is a good rule, and women should wear below-the-knee skirts and cover their shoulders. Be aware that Sharjah has 'decency laws', and be sure to dress conservatively on any trips there.

Despite the flagrant exhibitionism of many expatriates, local police are quick to react to any complaints of harassment by men: should the generally harmless spectators at Jumeirah's public beaches become anything more disturbing, it is worth reporting them to the beach patrols.

KEEPING THE FAITH

The call to prayer is likely to greet you upon landing in Dubai; once in the city, you're never more than 500 metres away from a mosque – expect the melodic intonations of the muezzin to define your day and remind you that you're in Arabia. Most mosques are packed for the Friday prayer, which is also broadcast from the minaret via loudspeakers, but Muslims can perform their five-times-daily prayers anywhere, from the side of the road to an office boardroom, as long as they are facing Mecca. Avoid walking in front of anyone praying, and don't stare; public prayer should be viewed as perfectly normal.

IN CONTEXT

Compared to some other Gulf states, the UAE is tolerant and respectful of most other religions – and has a number of temples and churches – but active promotion is frowned upon. Likewise with the consumption of alcohol: although visitors and non-Muslim residents are welcome to buy duty-free products at the airport or have big nights out in clubs and hotel bars, the hard stuff is tolerated rather than celebrated. An important point to remember is that being intoxicated in public is illegal – even if you are behaving perfectly normally. You should therefore use taxis wherever practical, and be as discreet and polite as possible. The nights before religious festivals are usually dry; there is virtually zero tolerance for anyone found driving while drunk. You may see Gulf Arabs, whether local or visiting from Saudi and other strict states, propping up the bar in quieter establishments, but, generally, drinking is the preserve of expatriates.

Other *haram* (religiously forbidden) activities include the consumption of non-halal meat and pork products, which are sold to expatriates but from a separate 'pork shop' in supermarkets. Visitors should also resist public displays of affection between men and women – even holding hands is illegal if you're not married. Also be aware that hand signals (like beckoning with one finger and pointing directly, as well as the internationally recognised rude gestures) are highly offensive, and could lead to arrest and deportation. Displaying the soles of the feet in someone's direction can also be insulting. Don't be fooled into thinking that the common sight of men holding hands is evidence of a burgeoning gay scene, this is merely a sign of friendship.

Although Emiratis are forgiving of blunders, avoid being too informal. For example, wait for a member of the opposite sex to extend a hand before going to shake it. Better yet, place your palm on your heart as a sign of warmth or gratitude. Ask permission before taking a photograph of an Emirati woman and don't snap military sites. The chances are that even if you do blunder, your Emirati hosts will understand.

Dubai taxi.

Sights

Atlantis Hotel. *See p82 & p105.*

THE BIG BUS COMPANY DUBAI

Day Tour!

The Big Bus Company offers you a unique sightseeing experience onboard of a traditional double decker bus. With 21 stops all over Dubai, passengers can design their own itinerary & hop-on / hop-off at any stop of their choice and organize their day the way they want it. Experience the magical city of Dubai with the flexibility to go for a ticket validity of 24 or 48 hours.

* 1hr 45 min City Tour
* 3 hrs Beach Tour
* Free Entrance into Dubai Museum, Sheikh Saeed Al Maktoum's House
* Free daily Arabian Dhow Cruise. Four times a day 11:30, 1:30, 3:30, 5:30pm
* Free Mercato Advantage Booklet (10% to 50% discount at selected outlets)
* Recorded commentary with a choice of 8 different languages
* Unlimited hop on-hop off facility at 21 points around the city of Dubai.

Night Tour!

In addition to the daily hop-on hop-off tour, The Big Bus Company is delighted to announce the launch of its brand new and unique sightseeing experience: the Dubai Night Tour.

Our two hour city tour features live commentary from a fully qualified, and tourist board registered, guide who will point out the magnificence of this sparkling city by night.

The tour departs from Deira City Centre at 7.30pm, returning at 9.30pm, or from Souk Madinat Jumeirah at 8.30pm, returning at 10.30pm.

Tour Highlights:
Deira City Centre, Wafi & Raffles Hotel, Sheikh Zayed Road, Burj Dubai, Dubai Mall, Mall of the Emirates, Atlantis on The Palm, Souk Madinat Jumeirah, Burj Al Arab, Jumeirah Beach Road, Jumeirah Mosque, Al Dhiyafah Street, Downtown Bur Dubai, Dubai Creek side, Al Maktoum Bridge

Night tours operate on Mondays, Wednesdays, Fridays and Saturdays

For more information please call +971 4 340 7709 or email us on to infodubai@bigbustours.com

Double Decker Bus Tours LLC, P.O Box 116250, Dubai, UAE   Web: www.bigbustours.com

Introduction

How to get the most from this unusual destination.

In most other cities, sightseeing might involve roaming through an ancient castle, investigating a historic fort, or wandering round galleries and museums. Things are a little different in Dubai. Although there's a scattering of historic buildings concentrated in the area by the Creek, most visitors to the emirate focus on touring a series of five-star, record-breaking hotels and their restaurants.

Dubai's main attractions were all built in the last ten years and, as with Las Vegas, most visitors aren't interested in exploring history. Instead, they're here to take advantage of every over-the-top service the emirate is so keen to provide. For visitors in search of glamorous nights out and spectacular meals, finding the perfect venue is simply a matter of picking a five-star hotel, but for those few tourists who'd like to discover Dubai's past, culture and traditions, the search for a 'real' Dubai is a search indeed. With a little forward planning and some perseverance, however, you'll find yourself touring impressive historic buildings, revelling in the local culture and experiencing the city's many hidden treasures.

GATEWAY TO THE GULF

Dubai sits on the Gulf, a body of water that is key to the city's success today, and has been a source of food and trade for centuries. Historically, Dubai was two settlements built on either side of the Creek, a 15-kilometre (9.5-mile) inlet around which the city's trade developed. **Deira** is a catch-all term for the area to the north of the Creek, and **Bur Dubai** refers to the south. The terms 'Deira side' and 'Bur Dubai side' are still used to differentiate between the areas north and south of the Creek.

Further along the coast, Bur Dubai merges with **Satwa** and **Jumeirah**, where residential and tourist developments stretch for some 15 kilometres (9.5 miles) southwards, with many of the most prestigious developments lining the arterial **Sheikh Zayed Road**. **Umm Suqeim** is a largely industrial zone, brought into prominence by the many galleries that have opened up in its warehouses and factories. Finally, and furthest south, the **Marina** is home to some of Dubai's most spectacular hotels and the jumping-off point for the road to the **Palm Jumeirah**, the suburb built on sand in the sea. The recommended sights mentioned in these pages are organised by these areas.

When petrodollars began to flow into the emirate in the 1960s, Deira and Bur Dubai developed rapidly, the former becoming the trade centre and the latter the residential area. Today, however, all the major developments in the city (with the exception of Dubai Festival City) are taking place on the Bur Dubai side, with projects such as Dubai Knowledge Village and Dubai Media City springing up alongside Sheikh Zayed Road. Bur Dubai feeds Deira with traffic from Sheikh Zayed Road via five separate crossings: there are four bridges (Garhoud Bridge, named after a district, Al Maktoum Bridge, after the ruling family, the Business Bay Crossing and the Floating Bridge – a temporary structure, as the name suggests), and the Al Shindhaga Tunnel, which runs underneath the Creek at its mouth. When driving from one end of the city to another, Sheikh Zayed Road is a faster if less scenic option than Jumeirah Beach Road.

GETTING AROUND

Dubai's public transport system is definitely on the up. The new **metro system** consists of two lines: the red line, running the length of Sheikh Zayed Road and open from September 2009,

bateaux dubai
A Unique Cruise Experience

A Unique Dinner Cruise Experience

Discover the fascinating modern landmarks and heritage buildings along the Dubai Creek in air-conditioned comfort onboard the luxurious Bateaux Dubai. Cruise into a night of magical proportions where personalised service will enhance your 4-course à la carte dinner, freshly prepared by our Executive Chef.

Bateaux Dubai can also be chartered for private breakfast, lunch, sunset and dinner cruises to celebrate any occasion.

Boarding starts every night at 7.45pm and Bateaux Dubai cruises from 8.30pm to 11pm.

A MEMBER OF

JEBEL ALI INTERNATIONAL
HOTELS

For reservations and more information please call +971 4 399 4994
E-mail: mail@bateauxdubai.com ✪ www.bateauxdubai.com

and the smaller green line, serving Bur Dubai
and Deira, which opened early in 2010. The city
prides itself on this being one of the cheapest
public transport systems in the world, and to
travel the length of the red line – from one end
of the city to the other, a journey of some 50
kilometres (30 miles) – costs around Dhs5.
There are plans for a unified travel system,
with users able to buy a card that entitles them
to the use of the metro, bus and water taxi
system. For areas away from the metro lines,
taxis and buses are fairly cheap and plentiful.

Taxis & cars

For any destinations along the length of Sheikh
Zayed Road, Deira and Garhoud, the metro is
the cheapest form of transport. For anywhere
further afield, taxis are the best way of getting
around. Several years ago, the government
introduced competition into this previously
state-run service, and the effect has been a
dramatic improvement in quality. Drivers are
generally courteous and knowledgeable, and all
cars have meters. A growing number of taxis

accept credit cards. You should have no problem getting a taxi at any major hotel, mall or attraction, but you might face problems in more secluded locations or very late at night – call Dubai Transport (208 0808) to book a taxi.

Choosing to drive yourself means dealing with other road users. Driving in Dubai has been likened to driving dodgems at a fairground, with weaving motorists who drive too fast, then too slow, too close to each other and then space out haphazardly, and rarely if ever indicate anything. You will also need to be aware of Salik – Dubai's toll gate system. All cars in Dubai have a Salik tag, and when a driver crosses a point, Dhs4 is deducted from a prepaid account. Taxis are exempt from Salik fees, and if you have a hire car then the charges are added to your bill at the end.

Street names are not widely used in Dubai for navigation purposes. Instead, when looking for a location, you should first find out a major landmark close to it: a mall, a hotel or a park, for instance. This should help your taxi driver locate it without too much difficulty.

LOOKING BEYOND

What Dubai lacks in historic sites it makes up for in character and ambition. In the shadow of proud hotels and office structures nestle heaving souks and forlorn shipyards, the briefest glimpse of the small fishing village swallowed up by the big city. Although it may be tempting to cling to the beachside splendour of Jumeirah, the Creek is an appealing diversion.

Further afield are unspoiled beaches, wadis and water holes easily explored in a day. Although dune-bashing requires a masterful hand, people not yet skilled can turn to nearly any local tour operator for a 4x4 safari with barbecue and camel rides thrown in for good measure. For weekend excursions, the other emirates are sleepier, but prettier, with opportunities to walk along deserted shores or laze at the feet of cool mountains. There are lots more ideas and informations in the Escapes & Excursions chapter; *see pp242-264.*

SIGHTS

Deira

Where the city began.

It's surprising how little evidence there is in Dubai to suggest that it's ever been anything other than the entertainment playground it is today – and more surprising still when you consider that UAE nationals value tradition and history very highly. However, the government's recent drive to protect the handful of landmarks that remain has given visitors a chance to experience old Dubai. There are a few historic sights scattered across the city – the majority of which can be found in Deira and Bur Dubai, each lying on either side of the Creek. Most of these have been developed in recent decades with tourism in mind. Visiting the sites will give you an idea of how much Dubai has evolved in such a short period of time.

Map p299	**Restaurants &**
Hotels p91	**cafés** p121
	Pubs & bars p144

DEIRA

Broadly speaking, the term Deira is used to describe everything north of the Creek, but in reality it is an amalgam of sub-districts. **Garhoud** has the airport, with a few interesting nightspots and restaurants clustered at the Méridien hotel and around the tennis stadium. Nearby **Festival City** is a relatively new shopping, dining and drinking hub comprising a mall, a marina, and the InterContinental and Crowne Plaza hotels, and on occasion has been converted into a concert venue to host the likes of Queen and Kylie Minogue. For anyone on the history trail, however, the most exciting part is the original Deira alongside the **Creek** – the heart and soul of old Dubai. It is a bustling, chaotic, dusty commercial hub where plate-glass office blocks tower over old souks.

Walk along the Creek, and you'll see old meet new with full force. Five-star hotels such as the Sheraton Dubai Creek and Radisson Blu are just yards away from wharfs that haven't changed in 60 years. On the roads, limousines and 4x4s jostle for space with rickety, multi-coloured pickup trucks, while sharp-suited business folk wait at zebra crossings alongside sarong-clad workers pushing handcarts, and fishermen in work-stained *khanduras*. Traditional dhows still line the wharf and, day and night, goods are unloaded, destined for the many tiny shops that make up Dubai's oldest trading area.

What Deira lacks in refinement it makes up for in atmosphere and character. And to experience it at first hand, all you have to do is walk along the corniche. Walk far enough and you'll stumble across Deira's old **souk** (map p298 H3), sprawling around the mouth of the Creek on the north shore, where the waterway widens at the entrance to the Gulf. The area is best explored during late afternoon or evening, when temperatures are lower and the traders are at their busiest. The entrance to the souk stands under renovated buildings with traditional wind towers. Like most markets, it has evolved into sections defined by the goods sold in each, and crisscrossed by alleyways. The areas are known individually as the **spice souk**, **antique souk** and **textile souk**.

Step into the spice souk and you instantly breathe in the scents of Arabia and the East. Chillis, cardamom and saffron are piled high outside spice shops; ornately decorated, glass-stoppered bottles line shelves in traditional perfume shops; and the sweet aroma of

Abracadabra

What's the best way to cross the Creek?

Dubai's Creek is a significant psychological barrier for many who live in the city. Like Londoners who refuse to go south of the river, or New Yorkers who won't countenance leaving Manhattan Island, many Dubaians are put off heading to 'Deira side'. It's perceived as being a bit low-rent compared to the sparkly towers of Sheikh Zayed Road, the yachty opulence of the Marina, or even the bustle of Bur Dubai. Even for people who realise how worthwhile a trip can be, simply getting there can be offputting. Traffic can often build up on the approaches to the bridges, and the roads of Deira themselves are often congested. The quickest way to get across is to avoid the roads altogether and take to the water. *Abras* chug back and forth for a dirham a time, and a trip on the ramshackle old tugs is an atmospheric and convenient way to get across the Creek. They go from each side of the Bur Dubai textile souk to either Sabkha station (next to the spice souk) or Baniyas (a little further up the Creek).

The new **waterbus** provides an air-conditioned alternative on the same routes, and costs Dhs4 each way. The Road Transport Authority bills these as 'amazingly spacious high-tech boats'. To the uninitiated, they may appear like barges with a greenhouse on top, but they are dry, cool and as quick as the old *abras*. Berths are next to *abra* stations. Another step up the ladder of nautical grandeur is the **water taxi**. These can be called, like road taxis, to come and collect you from the same stations as *abras* and waterbuses. As this book went to print, fees and routes had not been fixed, but the boats can carry up to 11 on a private cruise across the Creek. The cheapest option though, is to go under the water. Down by Shindagha tunnel, near the mouth of the Creek, there is a seldom used **pedestrian tunnel**. It runs from just past the Diving Village on the Bur Dubai side to near the bus station on Baniyas Road on the Deira side. There are views out to the Gulf from each end, and it won't cost you a *fil* to get across.

Souks

SIGHTS

frankincense fills the air. At one time more valuable than gold, frankincense (a gum resin obtained from trees of the genus Boswellia) remains one of Arabia's most prized perfumes and is the base for some of the world's most expensive scents. The original coral-stone shops have been renovated, and much of the dusty charm of the souk has been lost, but it is now a far cleaner place to visit.

Take the time to make your way through the myriad of alleyways to explore the shops selling antiques. Once you reach the antique shops you know that you are approaching the **gold souk**. Its centre is a wide alley covered by a roof and supported by carved wooden pillars, but the souk extends into the adjoining streets. It's worth venturing beyond the main plaza-like area to explore the outer alleys, where many specialist shops trade in silver, pearls and semi-precious stones. Bargaining or haggling is expected in all souks; don't be afraid to leave a shop to try the competition next door if you cannot agree on a price that you consider reasonable. Some shopkeepers will offer tea, coffee or cold drinks while a deal is being made.

SIGHTS & MUSEUMS

🆓 Al Ahmadiya School & Heritage House

Near Gold House building, Al Khor Street, Al Ras (226 0286/www.dubaitourism.co.ae). **Open** 8am-7.30pm Sat-Thur; 3-7.30pm Fri. **Admission** free. **Map** p298 H3.

Established in 1912, this was the first school in Dubai, and was renovated as a museum in 1995. Next door is the Heritage House, a traditional home with interiors from 1890. Guides and touch screens take you through the tour of these two small – and ever so slightly dull – museums.

🆓 Dhow Wharfage

Alongside the Creek. **Map** p299 L4.

Set along the Creek where the National Bank of Dubai building curves over the water, the Dhow Wharfage is a nod to the city's past. The many dhows that dock alongside each other on the Creek, bringing in spices, textiles, and other goods from neighbouring countries, are more than just vessels. In many cases, the seafarers who brave the Gulf and the Indian Ocean live in these colourful wooden beauties.

Bur Dubai

The old centre.

As Dubai was settled, a residential area developed along the sandy southern banks of the Creek and became known as Bur Dubai. It was here that the emirate's rulers made their home, in sea-facing fortifications, and the district remains the seat of the Diwan (the Ruler's Office), Dubai's most senior administrative body. As the city grew, the area became home to embassies and consulates, creating an atmosphere of diplomatic calm, with commercial activity centred on the mouth of the Creek. Today the situation is changing fast and, although the banks of the Creek are still free from development, Bur Dubai has sprawled inland, with tower blocks springing up on practically every available inch of sand.

Map p298	**Restaurants &**
Hotels p86	**cafés** p110
	Pubs & bars p143

FINDING YOUR WAY

As the residential community has grown, so commerce has developed to support local residents. The once tiny **souk** has expanded dramatically, supermarkets and shopping malls have opened, and highways traverse the area. **Dubai Museum** makes a good starting point for exploration of Bur Dubai, and visitors with cars can park in the adjacent space. From the museum, make your way northwards towards the Creek and enjoy the Bur Dubai souk on foot. A curious mixture of old and new, it lacks the traditional charm of Deira's old souk, but does boast a vast array of goods. At worst, this lesser-known area could be described as tacky and cheap; at best it would be fair to say it's a haphazard, market-style collection of shops.

Be sure to pass through the **textile souk**. This is a great place in which to buy traditional Arab clothing, Pakistani and Indian saris and *salwar kameez*, the traditional baggy shirt and trouser outfits worn by women in Pakistan, Afghanistan and, to a lesser extent, India. These can be tailored from the fabric of your choice in a matter of hours. Streets filled with fabric and tailoring shops lead you to the covered area of the **Bastakia souk**, which

is filled with Arabic curios and souvenirs. The best bargains are to be found in the less attractive streets beyond the renovated centre.

A walk through the covered area ends at the *abra* crossing station, where a left turn will lead you to the collection of shops known as the **watch souk**. Hefty doses of caution are essential, but some of the watches on display are genuine, and prices are hard to beat. If you head west from this point, you will reach the **electrical souk**, a great place to buy camera and video equipment or white goods. As with most souks, the boundaries are hazy, but visitors in search of computers, software or games should explore its southern streets.

Bur Dubai sprawls southwards to merge with the coastal development of Jumeirah and westwards to Port Rashid on the coast, but the most rewarding sights are to be found where it all began: along the Creek.

ABRA CROSSING POINT

End of Al Seef Road, close to entrance of Bastakia souk, Dubai Creek.
The cheapest way to view the Creek is by *abra* (traditional wooden water taxis), which cross the Creek day and night. These seemingly

SIGHTS

rickety but watertight boats have been ferrying residents and traders across the Creek since Dubai was first settled; originally they were rowing boats, but today they are powered by smelly diesel engines. Even in the shiny new city that has sprung over the last decade, approximately 15,000 people cross the Creek by *abra* every day. The *abras* are commuter vehicles for manual and low-paid workers, and boarding can be chaotic at peak times, when hundreds of workers jostle for space on the stone steps where the boats pull up. You are likely to find yourself pulled across the decks of several boats by helpful *abra* captains, who are quick to extend welcoming but rather soiled hands to anyone hesitating or looking for a space on the bench seating.

The basic crossing allows you to take in the atmosphere of the Creek, and gives a great insight into how the city operated in the past. For a more comprehensive tour of the Creek it's well worth hiring your own *abra* – simply ask a boat captain and agree a price and the length of the tour before you set out. A journey up and down the Creek should cost no more than Dhs50, but you will have to haggle hard to reach this price.

BASTAKIA

Between Al Fahidi Street & the southern bank of the Creek.
One of Dubai's most picturesque heritage sights, Bastakia is being carefully renovated and turned into a pedestrianised conservation area. The name Bastakia comes from the first people to settle the area, who were traders from Bastak in southern Iran. The ruler of Dubai

encouraged such immigration in the early 1900s by granting favourable tax concessions. Many came and most stayed, which explains why so many Emiratis are of southern Iranian descent. Stepping into the narrow alleyways of Bastakia is to walk into Dubai's past. Many older UAE nationals tell of summers spent in Bastakia, when entire families would gather to sleep outside on raised platforms in order to escape the heat of indoor rooms. Today, Bastakia houses several art galleries, cafés and restaurants, and during the spring it hosts the Bastakia Art Fair. While you're there, don't miss a cool mint and lemon drink at the atmospheric Basta Art Café (*see p113*).

SIGHTS

Abra.

Bastakla. See p69.

Dubai Museum
Al Fahidi Fort, Bastakia (353 1862/www. dubaitourism.co.ae). **Open** 8.30am-8.30pm Sat-Thur; 2.30-8.30pm Fri. **Admission** Dhs3; Dhs1 4-6s; free under-4s. **No credit cards**. **Map** p298 H4.

Dubai's museum is well worth a visit. The Al Fahidi Fort was built in 1787 as Dubai's primary sea defence, and also served as the ruler's residence. In 1970, it was renovated so the museum could be housed within its walls. Inside, the displays are creative and imaginative, allowing you to peek into an Islamic school, walk through a 1950s souk, watch traditional craftsmen at work and even to experience the tranquil beauty of a night in the desert.

Grand Mosque
Close to Dubai Museum. Closed to non-Muslims. **Map** p298 H3.

Although it may look like a historic building that has recently been restored, the Grand Mosque was built only a little over ten years ago. However, it was styled to resemble the original Grand Mosque. Built in around 1900 at the same location, the earlier mosque doubled as a religious school. Sadly, the first Grand Mosque was torn down in the 1960s and replaced by another, smaller one.

FREE Heritage & Diving Village
Al Shindagha (393 7151/www.dubaitourism. co.ae). **Open** 8.30am-10.30pm Sun-Thur; 4.30-10.30pm Fri, Sat. **Admission** free. **Map** p298 G3.

This pleasant 'living' museum by the Creek, staffed by guides, potters, weavers and other craftspeople, focuses on Dubai's maritime past, and depicts the living conditions of the original seafarers, who harvested the waters of the Gulf for pearls and fish to trade. Static but entertaining displays chart the history of Dubai's pearling industry, and a tented village gives a glimpse into the Bedouin way of life that remained unchanged until well into the 20th century. During religious holidays, such as Eid Al Fitr and Eid Al Adha, and throughout the Dubai Shopping Festival (*see p190*), traditional ceremonies are laid on, including sword dancing and wedding celebrations. At such times old pearl divers are often on hand to recount tales of adventure and hardship.

Sheikh Saeed Al Maktoum House
Al Shindagha (393 7139/www.dubaitourism. co.ae). **Open** 7.30am-9pm Sat-Thur; 3-10pm Fri. **Admission** Dhs2; Dhs1 reductions; free under-7s. **No credit cards**. **Map** p298 G3.

Built in 1896 out of coral covered in lime and sand plaster, this traditional house was the home of Dubai's former ruler until his death in 1958, hence its strategic position at the mouth of the Creek. Now restored and converted into a museum, it displays documents, stamps, currencies, and a collection of old photographs of Dubai and its ruling family.

SIGHTS

Heritage & Diving Village.

Satwa, Jumeirah & Sheikh Zayed Road

Home of big villas and bigger skyscrapers.

Just half a century ago, Jumeirah was a fishing village several kilometres outside Dubai. Today, it is one of the most high-profile areas of the city and some Western residents refer to it, with tongue firmly in cheek, as the Beverly Hills of Dubai. A few original villas survive, and are much sought after by expats as beachside homes. The area commonly referred to as Jumeirah – although Jumeirah is only a part of it – stretches along Dubai's southern coast for several kilometres. It is serviced by two main roads: Jumeirah Beach Road, which runs along the coast, and Al Wasl Road, which runs parallel a few blocks inland. A haphazard network of streets lined with luxury villas link the two.

Map p300	Restaurants &
Hotels p100	cafés p127
	Pubs & bars p147

ORIENTATION

Jumeirah developed southwards from Satwa's borders, and the oldest part, known as Jumeirah 1, remains one of the most desirable addresses in Dubai. The first chic malls and coffee shops were here, and it is still popular with people in search of a latte or manicure (the habituées are often called Jumeirah Janes). At this end of the Jumeirah Beach Road, the **Jumeirah Mosque** is one of the city's most picturesque, and the only one to allow non-Muslims to have a peek inside as part of a guided tour.

Along the Jumeirah Beach Road are various shopping malls, the shameful **Dubai Zoo** and several public beaches. The shoreline runs from Jumeirah 1 to the far end of Umm Suqeim, where the Burj Al Arab (*see p101*) and Wild Wadi water park (*see p199*), mark the beginning of the resort strip.

Neighbouring **Satwa** is one of the few remaining parts of Dubai that feels like a 'normal' city, with street life, restaurants and

a mish-mash of nationalities making up the community. Unfortunately, it's not going to be like this for long, as this slice of real estate is to be flattened to make way for another property development; *see below* **The End is Nigh**.

These areas are bordered inland by **Sheikh Zayed Road**. Although this highway runs for hundreds of kilometres, the stretch here, with its skyscrapers set up like giant dominos, is its most famous section. Set back from this main strip is the city's tallest landmark, the **Burj Dubai**. The area around it (known ironically as the **Old Town**) is also becoming an important shopping and social hub.

SATWA & JUMEIRAH
Sights & museums

Dubai Zoo
Jumeirah Beach Road, Jumeirah 1 (349 6444).
Open 10am-5pm Sat-Mon, Wed-Fri. **Admission** Dhs3. **No credit cards**. **Map** p300 C10.

One of a Kind

Independent shops are making their mark along the beach road.

Some of the city's best independent retailers are based on Jumeirah Beach Road, and discerning shoppers flock here. Dubai's myriad of malls is generally fairly unimaginative, with the same big brands predominating; but, for something different, this stretch of calm consumerism between the Jumeirah Mosque and the tumble-down Dubai Zoo is well worth investigating.

First stop is the Village mall, home to **S*uce** (344 7270, *see p176*) one of the most cutting edge fashion retailers in the city – it also has a branch at the Dubai Mall. You'll quite likely salivate over their expensive designs. If your purse convulses at the prices, cross the road to Jumeirah Centre Mall. **S*uce Lite** (344 4391) lives here, and sells last season's leftovers. You're likely to spot cool labels such as Sass & Bide, Antoni & Alison, Citizens of Humanity, See (the Chloé concession) and Johnny Loves Rosie. You can save yourself anything from 40 to 80 per cent by rummaging around. Next door to the original S*uce are sophisticated dresses by Dubai's favourite designer **Ayesha Depala** (344 5378; *see p168*). Also worth a look, in the same mall, is **Luxecouture** (344 7933) for avant-garde labels.

Over at Jumeirah Plaza, **Le Stock** (342 0211) should be your first stop, with Tiger Lily, Matthew Williamson, Joseph, Chloé and Victor&Ralph all on the shelves. **Fleurt** (342 0906; *see p169*) at Mercato Mall, stocks the sort of show-stopping dresses you'd expect the cast of *Sex & the City* to step out in; Betsey Johnson and Dina Bar-El are well represented. If you're expecting, make sure you check out **Mamas & Papas** (344 0981) also in Mercato Mall.

S*uce.

SIGHTS

Seafood, Mediterranean Style...

Dubai Marine Beach Resort and Spa - tel: 043461111 fax: 043453482
Opening Hours: Sunday to Thursday 12:00 - 15:00 and 19:00 - 24:00
Friday and Saturday 12:00 - 24:00

Dubai Zoo.

The animals at the Dubai Zoo are the survivors, and progeny, of a private collection now owned by the Dubai Municipality. The conditions are shabby and animals enjoy little freedom. There are allegedly plans to relocate but, despite many promises over several years, there has been little action. There are lions, tigers, giraffes, bears, reptiles and birds, but it's up to your conscience whether or not you would actually enjoy a visit.

Jumeirah Mosque
Jumeirah Beach Road, Jumeirah 1. **Tours**

10am Sat, Sun, Tue, Thur. **Admission** Dhs10. **No credit cards.** Map p300 D9.
Arguably the most beautiful mosque in Dubai, Jumeirah Mosque stands at the northern end of Jumeirah Beach Road. The Sheikh Mohammed Centre for Cultural Understanding (353 6666, smccu@emirates.net.ae) organises visits (no children under five). You'll walk through the mosque with a small group before putting questions to your guide about the building and the Islamic faith. You must wear modest clothing (no bare legs or arms, and women must cover their heads). *Photo p76.*

SIGHTS

The End is Nigh

The city's coolest, quirkiest, best-loved neighbourhood is about to get flattened.

Satwa is a kooky neighbourhood that mixes Arabic, Indian, Pakistani and Filipino in the heart of Dubai. Its ramshackle buildings and streets (some as much as 30 years old!) are a delightful contrast to the relentless towers and highways through the rest of the city. But it's also prime real estate, and about to be demolished. Any night of the week, the cafés on **Diyafah Street** are worth a stop for a freshly squeezed juice and to watch flash cars cruise by and the area's residents promenade – from young Filipino men done up like surf dudes, to extended Emirati families in search of ice-cream. At the top of this strip, and near Pars Iranian restaurant, are municipal basketball courts

that remain busy even through July and August. You'll find dozens of Filipino, Asian and Arabic men playing, in the kind of community scene not often found in Dubai.
Around the corner from Diyafah is **Al Satwa Road**, which, with its flashes of neon colour, is the heart of an area that is part Manila, part Islamabad, and part 'old' Dubai. But you'll notice that some of the textile shops and tailors now lie empty, tea shops and shisha cafés are slowly being boarded up, and the communities that have made this as close as Dubai can offer to a 'normal' city experience are beginning to move on. Take a stroll around while you still can; it is easily the most vibrant area of the city to walk through.

Jumeirah Mosque. *See p75.*

SIGHTS

Majlis Ghorfat Um Al Sheef

Jumeirah Beach Road, Jumeirah 4; look for brown heritage signposts when nearby (04 394 6343). **Open** 8.30am-1.30pm, 3.30-8.30pm Sat-Thur; 3.30-8.30pm Fri. **Admission** Dhs1. **No credit cards. Map** p302 A15.

Built in traditional style from coral and stone, this building was used by the late Sheikh Rashid bin Saeed Al Maktoum, the founder of modern Dubai, as a summer retreat and place where he could hear the petitions of his subjects. The fact that many of the plans for modern Dubai were probably hatched in such a simple structure, by a man who had known nothing of 20th-century luxury for most of his life, is remarkable. That said, the *majlis* only really merits a fleeting visit.

SHEIKH ZAYED ROAD

★ FREE Dubai Fountain

Next to Dubai Mall, at the foot of the Burj Dubai. **Map** p303 F15.

Powerful nozzles spray water 50 storeys into the air, while 6,600 lights and 50 colour projectors are used to great effect, with various pieces of music playing in the background. The show occurs regularly after dark: our tip is to book a table outside at one of the restaurants in neighbouring Souk Al Bahar, and watch the fountain as you eat.

FREE Gold & Diamond Park Museum

Gold & Diamond Park, Interchange 4, Sheikh Zayed Road (347 7788/www.goldanddiamond park.com). **Open** 10am-10pm Sat-Thur; 4-10pm Fri. **Admission** free. **Map** p304 E2.

The Gold & Diamond Park features examples of Arabian, Italian and Indian jewellery, and conducts guided tours of the manufacturing plant, showing how diamonds are cut and gold is produced. There are lots of opportunities to make purchases, although you'll probably get a better deal at the souks.

Reaching for the Stars

What is in the world's tallest building?

Dubai is an architect's dream, with exciting projects announced daily. Local residents read about crazy new developments with an open jaw, and **Burj Dubai** (translated into English as 'the Dubai tower') has been the most talked about of all. It stands at 818 metres (2,684 feet) – the tallest man-made structure on earth, surpassing the KVLY-TV mast in Dakota, USA. So what's it all about? In a ghastly bout of real estate marketing speak, the tower's website describes it as: 'Monument. Jewel. Icon.' Which means absolutely nothing. In reality it is a mix of shops, bars and restaurants, a hotel and apartments.

The hotel – the world's first Armani Hotel – has 160 rooms on the first floors of the building, two restaurants, a nightclub and a spa. Private apartments occupy floors 17 to 108, and according to the spiel, all 800 units sold within eight hours of going on sale. Floor 78 has the outdoor pool.

There are 144 Armani residences decorated, of course, with the Armani Casa range, and other facilities include four pools, a cigar lounge, a library, residents' room and a gym. Most of the remaining upper floors are offices; the exception is the 124th, which features an indoor and outdoor observatory (it's 442 metres – 1,450 feet – up). The time-poor (and cash-rich) residents and workers can access their swanky addresses via one of the world's fastest elevators (it travels at 18 metres per second, or 40 miles per hour).

The area surrounding Burj Dubai includes the huge Dubai Mall, Souk al Bahar and other hotels and restaurants. Rumours abound that a rival developer, Nakheel, is planning to build an even higher tower. Al Burj, near Ibn Battuta, will be 1,400 metres (4,500 feet) high, but the plans are temporarily on hold due to the global financial situation.

Umm Suqeim

Discover the city's biggest malls, as well as its artistic side.

Umm Suqeim is the stretch of town that runs south along the coast from Al Safa and Jumeirah 3, and along Sheikh Zayed Road to the vast **Mall of the Emirates**. Along the coast here are the Burj Al Arab and Jumeirah Beach Hotel. These were once quite isolated spots, but with the development of Souk Madinat Jumeirah, this part of town has become a social hub. Confusingly, a number of places tag the word Jumeirah onto their name, to try to gain a little cachet from Dubai's most desirable area. To the east runs **Al Quoz** industrial zone, a rather desolate slab of factories, warehouses and worker accommodation. But, in true postmodern style, this industrial wasteland is now becoming a centre for arts in the city.

| **Map** p294 | **Restaurants &** |
| **Hotels** p101 | **cafés** p129 |

Map p294 Hotels p101

ART INDUSTRY

A few years ago, only one or two galleries existed in Dubai, but slowly, a scene is developing. And, in the best traditions of post-industrial creativity, the most interesting shows are to be found in a decrepit, depressing and generally down-at-heel industrial area – Al Quoz, which is just off Sheikh Zayed Road at Interchange 3. **Total Arts** (*see p193*) led the way, setting up shop in 1998. **B21** (*see p191*) and the **Third Line** (*see p192*) opened in 2005. Even a more conservative gallery, **thejamjar** (*see p192*), relocated from a more central location to jump on the kudos bandwagon. If you do head down to thejamjar, you can become an artist yourself by buying a canvas and picking up a brush at one of the art courses the gallery runs. Make sure you book ahead.

Conveniently, many of the best galleries are on the same road. The Third Line is opposite B21 in Al Quoz 3, near the Courtyard and between Marlin Furniture and Spinneys. It's a difficult area for even seasoned taxi drivers to navigate, so if you're planning a visit, make sure you go armed with a gallery map and phone numbe: one commercial unit looks much the same as the next. Alternatively, pick up a free Art Map from one of the bigger galleries, or log on to www.artinthecity.com, which has detailed directions to all the galleries.

For more on art in Dubai, *see pp191-196*.

Art in the City

Where to buy it.

Art is becoming big business in the city, with the likes of Dubai International Financial Centre and Coutts sponsoring shows. If you attend an opening while you're in town, look out for gallery staff putting red 'sold' dots by dozens of the works during the evening. Eclectic artists such as well-known British photographer Martin Parr and colourful mixed media artist Rana Begum have all been to town and exhibited at the Third Line.

Galleries have begun to specialise in certain types of art. You'll find trendy Arabic art at the **Third Line** (*see p192*), Emirati works at the **Flying House** (*see p196*), and Iranian and Middle Eastern canvasses at **B21** (*see p191*).

Third Line. *See p77*.

FREE Antique Museum
*Third interchange, Al Quoz Industrial Area
(347 9935)*. **Open** 9am-8.30pm Sat-Thur;
9am-11.30am, 3.30-8.30pm Fri. **Admission**
free. Map p294 C3.
Although Al Quoz may appear to be a deserted industrial estate, tucked away behind the bleak exteriors
are some of Dubai's best antique haunts. Although
not an actual antique museum, this warehouse is a
diamond in the rough: once past the giant wooden
doors you are transported into a secluded cave of lost
riches. The narrow aisles are packed with a wide
range of handicrafts, shisha pipes, pashmina shawls,
furniture and the odd belly dancing costume.

**INSIDE TRACK
LIVE MUSIC**

JamBase at the Souk Madinat Jumeirah
(*see p225*) is the best venue for nightly
live music in the city, although it's hardly
up against strong competition. The
furniture here is artfully angular, the
decor is calculated art deco chic, and
the food – with dishes inspired by the
southern United States – is surprisingly
tasty too. The in-house jazz and blues
band is one of Dubai's finest.

**INSIDE TRACK
COCKTAILS ON ICE**

Après (*see p149*) is a bar with a view
like no other: you can sip a cocktail in the
warmth, watching the tumbling skiers and
snowboarders on the slopes of Ski Dubai,
the indoor ski slope that is one the city's
most unlikely attractions. Located at Mall
of the Emirates, the snow show is the
perfect way to finish a shopping spree.
The food is reasonably good, too; try
the spectacularly tasty fondue.

The Marina & Around

The newest part of the city.

The **Marina** is the heart of what is referred to, in a somewhat tongue-in-cheek manner, as 'new Dubai' (Old Dubai being the bits around the Creek that sprang up in the 1970s and '80s, and distinct from the Old Town development – due for completion around 2010 – near the Burj Dubai). There's a thriving hub of restaurants and cafés dotted along the promenade near the wharf, where gleaming motor yachts are berthed and scenic dhow trips can be arranged. A stroll around the waterfront pathway surrounding the marina during the evening is particularly lovely.

The Marina is past Mall of the Emirates when driving towards Abu Dhabi, and despite the ongoing construction work, it has forged its own identity and is popular with residents, and websites viewed here aren't subject to the same strict censorship policy seen elsewhere in Dubai.

Map p304	**Restaurants &**
Hotels p103	**cafés** p131
	Pubs & bars p148

SIGHTS

ORIENTATION

The best way to see the Marina, strangely enough, is not from the sea but from on high, so head for **Bar 44** (*see p148*) at Grosvenor House. This lofty perch boasts a near 360-degree vista of the surrounding skyscrapers and portions of the Palm development. From these heights you will be able to spot Le Méridien's ever popular beachside club/restaurant Barasti, where you can soak up the peaceful surroundings of Mina Seyahi Marina with a drink in hand.

Heading further north along the marina, shoppers can visit the newly constructed **Dubai Marina Mall** (*see p159*), which has around 400 stores on four levels and even a Waitrose supermarket. Also nearby is the Marina Yacht Club, its waterfront views making it an idyllic spot for sipping a cocktail while watching the sun set, or an evening meal taken on the terrace restaurant Aquara. The club overlooks the iconic towers of the **Jumeirah Beach Residence** (known by locals as JBR). This collection of some 40

INSIDE TRACK
ART SCENE

The Marina might be better known for its luxury shops and restaurants, but if you venture beneath Marina View Tower, you will find an unexpected outpost of the art world: the **Carbon 12** art gallery (*see p196*), which shows numerous international artists, mainly from the US and Europe. Keep an eye open for Austrian artist Thierry Feuz and some of his bizarre lacquer creations. Art-lovers should also peek into **Boutique 1** (*see p169*), even if the concept of looking at art in a fashion store seems a bit odd. Despite its location, the gallery is determined to prove itself as a dedicated art space in Dubai's burgeoning art arena. **Art Couture** (*see p194*) in Al Fattan Marine Towers also sells art – though the range is largely decorative – created by owner Cynthia Richards and international artists.

Food Chain

Go GM free at one of the few organic restaurants in Dubai.

Organic food is still hard to come by in Dubai, which is why **Az.u.r** (pronounced 'as you are' – see what they did there?), at the Harbour Hotel & Residence, is creating a bit of a stir among the city's foodies (*see p132*). It's newly opened and carries a broad Mediterranean menu – take your pick from paella, tagine or mezze – and there's even plenty of vegetarian options, which is a rarity in a city that caters poorly for them.

The concept behind the restaurant is 'farm-to-fork', a phrase that Chris Baker, Executive Chef at the hotel explains as '…something that I got into a few years ago. It doesn't mean to say that the farmer drives it to you and then you cook it. It's

about knowing the whole process of where it comes from, so if your beef comes from America, which farm in America? What is it fed, is it grass fed or grain fed… how does it get here, is it protected all the way along?'

The restaurant claims that about 75 per cent of the produce it uses is organic, and Baker is quite a strident advocate of good, clean cooking. 'If I wouldn't serve a dish to my wife,' he says, 'why would I serve it to you? I love food and I don't like these chefs around the city that seem to prefer their Montblanc to their knife… you're not the star, your food is.' His attitude, and his food, make a healthy change.

residential buildings constructed along the seafront is home to thousands of expatriates, and along with a handful of five-star hotels nearby, the area has developed a buzzing atmosphere, particularly at the weekends. As the name suggests, you don't have to walk far to get to a strip of sand, as there are several kilometres of open beach. Since the construction of the **Walk** and its dozens of restaurants, boutiques and cafés, the area has sprung to life even more – particularly as it's one of the few pedestrian-friendly areas in Dubai. The new metro system helps connect the Marina to the other areas of the city.

The Walk
Adjacent to beach behind JBR.
With a range of fashion stores like Boutique 1, and Zadig & Voltaire, the Walk is a welcome relief from all the shopping malls in Dubai, as it gives people the opportunity to stroll outdoors, high-street style. There are plenty of restaurants, serving everything from a simple Starbucks latte to an Asian fusion meal at Da Shi Dai or an eggs Benedict at Le Pain Quotidien. Jumeirah Beach Residence also hosts the Covent Garden Market every weekend (except during the summer). Here, you'll find around 75 stalls selling everything from jewellery to local arts and crafts, along with family entertainment.

SIGHTS

The Walk.

Palm Jumeirah

Some built their houses on sand.

Aside from the Burj Al Arab and perhaps the record-breaking Burj Dubai, nothing in the city has grabbed the attention of the world's media quite like the **Palm Jumeirah**, which has broken a few records too. This man-made, palm tree-shaped island must surely rank as one of the most extraordinary engineering feats in modern history. Sand, 94 million cubic metres (21 billion gallons) of it, was poured onto the seabed, eventually creating an area greater than 800 football pitches, and all shaped like a giant palm tree hurled out into the Gulf. The development, the most complete of the newly constructed offshore islands now studding Dubai's coast, has become home to thousands of residents.

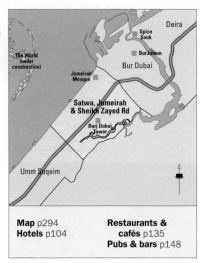

Map p294	**Restaurants &**
Hotels p104	**cafés** p135
	Pubs & bars p148

LIFE IN THE PALM

At the crest of the Palm stands the iconic **Atlantis Hotel** (*see p105*), which opened with a bang – quite literally in this case. Its 2008 opening party was marked by the world's biggest firework display and a special performance by Kylie Minogue, with the likes of Robert de Niro and Lily Allen being paid considerable sums of money to come jetting into town for the occasion. The hotel has 1,376 rooms, 166 suites and the country's premier water park, **Aquaventure**. A visit here is a must, particularly with the 27-metre (90-foot) high, heart-stopping Leap of Faith ride, or the dolphin performances at the adjacent Dolphin Bay. You can also find some of Dubai's hippest dining options at Atlantis such as **Nobu** (*see p135*) or **Ronda Locatelli** (*see p137*). With such extravagance, it goes without saying you can find some of the best (albeit priciest) boutiques at the Palm Strip Mall, including Karen Miller, Escada Sport and Young Designers Emporium. Keep an eye out for the completion of the Palm Mall, which is scheduled to be finished by 2011. It will bring yet more retail, dining and entertainment possibilites to the area.

Palm Monorail
Tickets Dhs 15 single; Dhs25 return.
The Palm was the first place in the Middle East to have a monorail. The 1,000-metre (3,280-foot) railway is fully automatic and driverless, and can carry a maximum of 6,000 people in nine carriages. Though passengers can take in some rather unique views during the ride, it didn't stop a wave of criticism when the prices were released. It costs Dhs15 for a single journey and Dhs25 for return trip, from the foot of the man-made island to the Atlantis hotel. There are plans to extend the monorail to connect to the new metro line.

INSIDE TRACK
SECRET STORES

For beautiful floral arrangements, **Bliss** (430 8501), at Al Shalal between Shoreline Apartments 7 and 8, is a true gem. The designers plan events and arrangements on site and in the shop, and they'll deliver anywhere. For something a bit cheaper, try All Day Mini Mart between Shoreline Apartments 3 and 4 and pick up some gorgeous orchids for only Dhs50.

Palm Jumeirah.

SIGHTS

Atlantis Hotel.

Consume

Boom & Mellow at **Mall of the Emirates**. *See p158*.

Hotels

Getting a room isn't cheap, but your money does go a very long way.

Given that for the most part it's only hotels that can provide licensed restaurants and bars in the city, they are the backbone of the social scene for residents and tourists alike. With the world's tallest tower, Burj Dubai, offering rooms with a view, and the Jumeirah promising 30 or so resorts, it seems that no space on land, sea or air is free from relentless development in Dubai. Competition between hotels means that unless you're visiting during a big event such as the Dubai World Cup, you shouldn't have to pay the 'rack rate'. For the best deals, visit the hotel websites – there's sometimes a discount of up to 50 per cent to be had, particularly during Ramadan and Dubai's sizzling summer months (June to August).

ABOUT THE LISTINGS

The categories indicate the average cost per night of a standard double room in high season (Oct-Apr), including the ten per cent municipal tax and ten per cent service charge. Rates at Dubai hotels vary wildly, and booking a room can be like playing the stock exchange, with huge fluctuations within the space of a few days not uncommon. Don't be scared off by the high prices – bookings through travel agents and websites can be a lot cheaper than the rack rates listed here. Demand is generally high in Dubai, particularly in the winter months, so we recommend booking in advance.

The hotels are rated according to price: Luxury Dhs1,500 and above; Expensive Dhs1,000-Dhs1,499; Moderate Dhs500-Dhs999; Budget below Dhs500.

BUR DUBAI

Luxury

Grand Hyatt Dubai
Al Qataiyat Road (317 1234/www.dubai. grand.hyatt.com). **Rates** Dhs1,224-Dhs1,440 double. **Credit** AmEx, MC, V. **Map** p297 K3 ❶

> ❶ Red numbers given in this chapter correspond to the location of each hotel as marked on the street maps. *See pp294-304.*

With 674 rooms, the Grand Hyatt is an impressive exercise in hotel bombast. It also houses a running track, three outdoor pools, four tennis courts, a spa, 11 busy restaurants and bars, and its very own indoor rainforest with four-tonne dhows hung overhead. Rooms are decorated with contemporary Arabic touches, and bathrooms are smallish, although the massaging shower and colossal tub quickly subdue any spatial quibbles. A great deal of planning has gone into separating the business and pleasure areas, with secluded lounges and executive spaces ensuring the money-minded don't have to contend with children playing leapfrog.
Bars. Business services. Concierge. Gym. Internet (dataport). Parking (free). Pools. Restaurants. Room service (24hr). Spa. TV (satellite).

★ Raffles Dubai
Oud Metha (324 8888/www.dubai.raffles.com). **Rates** Dhs1,020-Dhs-2,460 suite. **Credit** AmEx, MC, V. **Map** p297 J3 ❷
In line with Raffles in Singapore, this is a luxury hotel. The high-ceilinged lobby manages to impress in a city of lobbies, and the opulent, but not ostentatious decor follows through to the suite-only rooms. If you do have time to go for a dip, the tiled floor surrounding the pool has an underwater cooling system so your feet don't get burnt. There's also a massive sun dial where you can tell the time from the amount of lines spurting out of the water feature, and an excellent spa and upmarket shopping centre.
Bars. Business services. Concierge. Gym. Internet (dataport). Parking (free). Pools. Restaurants. Room service (24hr). Spa. TV (satellite).

Expensive

Mövenpick Hotel Bur Dubai

19th Street, Bur Dubai (336 6000/www.
moevenpick-burdubai.com). **Rates** Dhs840-
Dhs1,380 double. **Credit** AmEx, MC, V.
Map p297 J3 ❸
The panorama from the Mövenpick's medium-sized
rooms, which are comfortable without being stuffy,
is inner-city Dubai, but the beds are comfy and the
furnishings adequate. The suites and executive
rooms are a leap up from the standard ones, featuring jacuzzis in the bathrooms. Business facilities are
excellent, and fitness fanatics are well catered to
with a gym and health club. The rooftop has a large
pool deck area and jogging track.
Bars. Business services. Concierge. Gym. Internet
(dataport). Parking (free). Pools. Restaurants.
Room service (24hr). TV (satellite).

Moderate

Arabian Courtyard Hotel

Al Fahidi Street, opposite Dubai Museum
(351 9111/www.arabiancourtyard.com). **Rates**
Dhs615-Dhs750 double. **Credit** AmEx, MC, V.
Map p298 H4 ❹
Set in the very heart of old Dubai, less than a stone's
throw from the Creek and the Souk Al Kabir (Meena
Bazaar), the Arabian Courtyard is so heavily themed
on the heritage angle that you'll be surprised to dis-
cover that in fact it's one of the city's newer hotels.
Spacious bedrooms, many of which have Creek
views, make this a comfortable choice.
Bars. Business services. Concierge. Gym. Internet
(dataport). Parking (free). Pools. Restaurants.
Room service (24hr). TV (satellite).

Arabian Park Hotel

Near Wafi City, opposite Grand Hyatt Dubai
(324 5999/www.arabianparkhoteldubai.com).
Rates Dhs615-Dhs750 double. **Credit** AmEx,
MC, V. **Map** p297 K3 ❺
The Arabian Park Hotel is certainly convenient for
business and leisure travellers, as it is close to the
airport, the World Trade Centre and Wafi City Mall.
Rooms – there are 318 in total – tend to be on the
small side, but they are comfortable. The hotel also
plays host to a decent-sized salt-water pool, a bar
and gym. Additional attractions include a lounge on
each floor complete with plasma TV, mini library
and efficient staff. All in all, this is a good value
three-star option that knocks spots off many of the
city's dated four-star hotels. It's worth knowing that
rates – although not expensive to start with – practically halve during summer.
Bar. Business services. Gym. Internet. Parking
(free). Pool. Restaurants. Room service. TV.

XVA. *See p91.*

CONSUME

Ascot Hotel & Royal Ascot Hotel

Khalid Bin Waleed Road (352 0900/www. ascothoteldubai.com). **Rates** Dhs700-Dhs800 double. **Credit** AmEx, MC, V. **Map** p298 H4 ⑥
The Ascot was the first upmarket hotel to be built in Bur Dubai. Rooms are Georgian in style with refreshing canary yellow walls and although the combination might sound hideous, it actually works. There are a number of restaurants and bars, including the ever-popular pub Waxy O' Conner's. A couple of hundred extra dirhams per night will bag you a more upmarket room at the adjacent Royal Ascot Hotel, the Ascot's new five-star sibling. While neither hotel is likely to blow you away, the Ascot hotels do have an excellent location near the Dubai Museum and Bur Dubai souk.
Business services. Parking (free). Pool. Restaurants. Spa. TV (satellite).

Capitol Hotel

Mankhool Road, Satwa (346 0111/www.capitol-hotel.com). **Rates** Dhs600-Dhs1,200 double. **Credit** AmEx, MC, V. **Map** p300 E7 ⑦
A good alternative to Dubai's garish glitz, the Capitol is a pleasantly basic affair with reasonably sized rooms and huge beds but banal views of

---

Distinguishing by District

Choosing a hotel in Dubai is all about location, location, location.

The first choice you should make when booking your hotel is deciding which part of town you want to stay in. In Dubai, geography dictates style, with prices generally dropping the further you get from the shore.

If it's the classic sun, surf and sand experience you're after, then **Jumeirah** – a loosely-defined area that stretches from the start of Jumeirah Beach Road to just beyond the Burj Al Arab – or the **Marina** area further down the coast, are the districts for you. Ritzy resorts dot Jumeirah Beach Road, but do make sure your wallet is well stocked. The accommodation here is mainly five star (with the exception of the self-styled seven-star **Burj Al Arab**; *see p101*). These hotels are far from cheap, but you'll struggle to find one that doesn't have the wow factor; think stunning views, fine facilities and superlative service. It's worth bearing in mind, though, that when (or if) you tire of soaking up the sun's rays, it's a fair trek to the heritage sights that are mostly clustered around the Creek. The cloud-bothering **Sheikh Zayed Road** has the majority of the city's skyscrapers and hosts the world's tallest building, the Burj Dubai. The main highway to Abu Dhabi is home to the bulk of the city's business hotels. Prices are as staggering as the architecture, but for location (it's strategically positioned between the beach and the Creek) and style, it's hard to beat.

Stretching from Creek to coastline, **Bur Dubai** provides some good value hotels halfway between Jumeirah's polish and Deira's urban delights, and is also home to the **XVA** (*see p91*), one of the city's few genuine boutique hotels. But beware, while pockets of Bur Dubai such as **Bastakia**,

Oud Metha, **Satwa** and **Karama** are some of the most charming in town, the central area is a heaving mass of high-rise towers. Good if you want to feel part of the action, but hardly conducive to a relaxing stay, especially when you factor in the frustrating taxi rides during rush hour.

A colourful mix of souks, skyscrapers and shopping malls, **Deira** is one of the oldest areas of the city and a world away from the shiny new Dubai epitomised by the Marina. Hotels vary from high-class Creek-huggers such as the **Sheraton** (*see p93*) to the cheap and less-than-cheerful establishments that line the rundown areas away from the water. Some way from the shoreline and near the airport, the area tends to be geared more to business than pleasure.

Visitors on a truly tight budget do have options, though not as prominent as the five-star excess dominating the Dubai hotel scene. YHA members would do well to check out the excellent **Dubai Youth Hostel** (*see p96*), and other economy-minded travellers will find that there are a few comfortable and cost-effective options to be had around **Al Fahidi Street** and **Bank Street** (**Khalid Bin Al Waleed Road**) in Bur Dubai. Here you can pick up a clean, albeit pokey room, for a few hundred dirhams, but bear in mind that Bank Street is at the heart of the less salubrious end of Bur Dubai, where it's not unheard of for female tourists to be propositioned while popping into the supermarket in the middle of the day. Across the Creek the neighbourhood around **Al Rigga Street** in Deira is another reasonable hunting ground for cheap beds, but again suffers from less-than-squeaky-clean nocturnal activities.

CONSUME

Satwa. Sadly, the Capitol is let down by its facilities; the rooftop swimming pool is underwhelming, the Chinese restaurant is dismal and the gym is pokey. The hotel is situated close to Satwa's bustling streets and the beach, and nothing is more than a short taxi ride away. As such, it remains a popular choice for leisure travellers, as well as business guests.
Bars. Business services. Concierge. Gym. Internet (dataport). Parking (free). Pools. Restaurants. Room service (24hr). TV (satellite).

Dhow Palace Hotel
Bur Dubai (359 9992/www.dhowpalacehotel dubai.com). **Rates** Dhs700-Dhs900 double. **Credit** AmEx, MC, V. **Map** p301 G6 ❽
This relative newcomer on the block is shaped like a ship, and all the staff wear sailing attire. The 282 rooms are suitably spacious, and furnished in contemporary Arabic decor that doesn't overly assault the senses. Despite being a long way from the beach, the hotel's pool is surprisingly small and suffers from a lack of tanning areas and sun loungers. The gym and other leisure facilities are adequate although hardly five star. Situated in the middle of the concrete jungle of Bur Dubai, the Dhow Palace's location isn't pretty, but it's reasonably close to several Dubai landmarks.
Business services. Internet. Parking (free). Pool. TV.

Four Points by Sheraton
Khalid bin Al Waleed Road (Bank Street), Bur Dubai (397 7444/www.fourpoints.com/burdubai). **Rates** Dhs650-Dhs875 double. **Credit** AmEx, MC, V. **Map** p298 H4 ❾
The Four Points is a small and unremarkable hotel in the centre of town that is geared towards the budget business traveller. With only 125 rooms and basic services, it doesn't draw large crowds, which is great if you're looking for somewhere quiet. The decor of the bedrooms is a tad old-fashioned, but rooms are clean and neat. The communal areas are all a bit library-like, but the Indian restaurant Antique Bazaar and the Viceroy pub are both popular with local residents. All in all, it's not a bad base for exploring Dubai's heritage area.
Business services. Concierge. Gym. Internet (dataport). Parking (free). Pools. Restaurants. Room service (24hr). TV (satellite).

Jumeirah Rotana Dubai
Al Dhiyafah Road, Satwa (345 5888/www. rotana.com). **Rates** Dhs600-Dhs1,200 double. **Credit** AmEx, MC, V. **Map** p300 E8 ❿
The Jumeirah Rotana Dubai is misleadingly named: it's actually found in landlocked Satwa rather than beachy Jumeirah. That said, it has a casual atmosphere and a 50/50 mix of business and leisure guests. The spacious bedrooms have generously sized beds, plenty of wardrobe space and entertaining views over the back streets. There's a shuttle service to a beach club and nearby shopping centres. Guests can enjoy stretching their legs outside on the ever-bustling Al Dhiyafah Road – home to a number of alfresco restaurants – but if you have a romantic escape in mind, look towards Al Sufouh.
Bars. Business services. Concierge. Gym. Internet (dataport). Parking (free). Pools. Restaurants. Room service (24hr). TV (satellite).

Majestic Hotel Tower
Mankhool Road, Bur Dubai (359 8888/www. dubaimajestic.com). **Rates** Dhs800-Dhs1,200 double. **Credit** AmEx, MC, V. **Map** p298 H5 ⓫
This relatively new hotel is well positioned for exploring the Bastakia Quarter and is only a short taxi ride away from Sheikh Zayed Road and Jumeirah. Rooms are spacious enough and Arabian accented – think varnished wooden floors and rich, opulent furnishings. There's also a spacious pool area. Two lifts service 28 floors, so expect to queue and be prepared for it to take ten minutes to reach your room. Note also that the Majestic is quite strict; visitors aren't allowed after 10pm. This aside, the Majestic Hotel Tower is a fine option in Bur Dubai.
Business services. Internet. Parking (free). Pool. Restaurants. Room services. TV.

Ramada Dubai
Opposite Jumbo Electronics, Al Mankhool Road (351 9999/www.ramadadubai.com). **Rates** Dhs540-Dhs925 double. **Credit** AmEx, MC, V. **Map** p298 H5 ⓬
Proud owner of the largest stained-glass window in the Middle East, the four-star Ramada is just outside the more hectic heartland of the Golden Sands area. This and the hotel's inland location mean that most of its clients tend to be business people. The rooms are spacious, although most overlook air conditioning units, building sites or the busy streets below. There's a small pool, which only gets the morning sun. Good service, competitive corporate rates and decent sized rooms make this a sound choice for business guests.
Bars. Business services. Concierge. Gym. Internet. Parking (free). Pools. Restaurants. Room service (24hr). TV (satellite).

Rydges Plaza
Satwa roundabout, Satwa (398 2222/www. rydges.com/dubai). **Rates** Dhs600-Dhs900 double. **Credit** AmEx, MC, V. **Map** p301 F8 ⓭
Occupying a city centre location next to Satwa roundabout, this old-fashioned nine-storey Aussie hotel delivers far more in terms of comfort, style and facilities than its mundane exterior promises. The good position, attentive staff and faux-classical pool area attract a repeat clientele of business travellers and elderly tourists. Bedrooms are spacious, but the furnishings match the dated style of the hotel. Most rooms have a view of the bustling streets below, and there are complimentary beach and airport transfers

CONSUME

to boot. The hotel outlets are popular: Aussie Legends is a good choice if you're after pub grub.
Bars. Business services. Concierge. Gym. Internet (dataport). Parking (free). Pools. Restaurants. Room service (24hr). TV (satellite).

XVA
Al Fahidi Roundabout, Bastakia, behind Basta Art Café (353 5383). **Rates** Dhs650-Dhs800 double. **Credit** AmEx, MC, V. **Map** p298 H4 ⓮
This retro hotel is unique in Dubai. Built more than 70 years ago from coral and clay, it has been restored and re-opened as a triple treat: it's a gallery (don't be surprised if you see an artist working on his canvas), café and boutique guesthouse. Nestled in Bastakia, this is one of a handful of wind tower-topped buildings holding out against the city's lightning modernisation. XVA houses few guests at any time, so book early, particularly if you want to take advantage of the competitive rates. In a city where five-star conformity rules, this place stands out as somewhere special. *Photo p87.*
Concierge. Parking (free). Restaurant.

Budget

Golden Sands Hotel Apartments
Off Bank Street (355 5553/www.goldensands dubai.com). **Rates** Dhs375-Dhs895 double. **Credit** AmEx, MC, V. **Map** p299 J5 ⓯
Comprising a large number of sizeable and fully serviced self-catering flats, these range from one bedroom studios to flats with three and four bedrooms, with additional services such as a gym, sauna and squash courts. Long-term visitors can extend their stay; a one-bedroom studio costs Dhs16,000 and a two-bedroom apartment costs Dhs22,000, per month.
Gym. Room service (24hr). Parking (free). Pool. TV.

President Hotel
Trade Centre Road, Karama (334 6565). **Rates** Dhs400 double. **Credit** AmEx, MC, V. **Map** p301 H7 ⓰
Sat on one edge of the bargain-heavy Karama markets, this 50-room, two-star hotel seems as happy to offer knockdown prices as the traders behind it. The dark and dimly lit hallways lead into similarly gloomy rooms, with views of surrounding buildings and the busy road out front. The beds themselves are quite small, and the tiny bathrooms with their shampoo sachets are just enough to get by on. The President is a fair choice, but you're better off splashing out for the Jumeirah Rotana, Rydges Plaza or, if you can live without a pool, the Ibis.
Bars. Parking (Dhs5-Dhs10). Pools. Restaurants. Room service (24hr). TV (satellite).

Rush Inn
Bank Street (352 2235). **Rates** Dhs350 double. **Credit** AmEx, MC, V. **Map** p298 H4 ⓱

At this well-priced hostelry, the foyer is hung with slightly dismal snapshots of karaoke stars working the plethora of themed in-house bars (one Pakistani, one Filipino and one African), but the rooms are none too shabby. But if you're looking for a tranquil getaway, this place is not for you – the hotel's line-up of nightspots means it can often remain noisy until the wee small hours.
Parking (free). Room service (24hr). TV.

DEIRA
Luxury

★ Park Hyatt Dubai
Dubai Creek Golf & Yacht Club (602 1234/ www.dubai.park.hyatt.com). **Rates** Dhs1,504 double. **Credit** AmEx, MC, V. **Map** p297 K3 ⓲
Too good to leave to golfers, this is also the destination of choice for fashionistas; it's rumoured that Elle Macpherson, Tommy Hilfiger and Giorgio Armani have all stayed. The place oozes calm and luxury – from its white, low-rise Moroccan architecture to the tasteful modern interior – and is one of the best hotels in the city for business travellers who won't miss the lack of a beach. The bedrooms are minimal but inviting, and all have designer bathrooms. The great setting means you can take a stroll along the Creek and look with longing after the boats moored at the marina. *Photo p92.*
Bars. Business centre. Concierge. Gym. Internet (dataport). Parking (free). Pools. Restaurants. Room service (24hr). Spa. TV (satellite).

Expensive

Al Sondos Suites by Le Méridien
Opposite Deira City Centre mall (294 9797/ www.alsondos-lemeridien.com). **Rates** Dh480-Dhs1,320 double. **Credit** AmEx, MC, V. **Map** p297 K2 ⓳
These pleasant suites combine self-catering convenience with five-star service, making the place popular with long-term guests. Handily located opposite the City Centre mall and a short hop from the Creek, Al Sondos will satisfy businessmen, although it is not really suited to the tourist trade, as getting a taxi can be difficult, and you're some way from the beach. There's an impressive burnt-orange lobby and the tiled rooms are clean, spacious and stylishly comfortable. Facilities include daily shoe-shining, turndown services and high-speed internet facilities.
Business centre. Gym. Internet. Parking (free). Pool. Restaurant. Room service (24hr). TV (satellite).

Hilton Dubai Creek
Baniyas Road (227 1111/www.hilton worldresorts.com). **Rates** Dhs1,250-Dhs2,000 double. **Credit** AmEx, MC, V. **Map** p299 L4 ⓴

CONSUME

Park Hyatt Dubai. *See p91.*

One of Deira's classiest hotels, the Hilton Creek was designed by Carlos Ott, the brains behind the Opéra de la Bastille in Paris. The hotel is also home to Gordon Ramsay's award-winning restaurant, Verre, sister restaurant the Glasshouse and some buzzy bars. The rooms are statements in contemporary luxury, and the comfortable beds and ultra-cool black and white bathrooms prove there is substance beyond the style. This Hilton is an excellent choice if you need to stay in Deira.

Bars. Business services. Concierge. Gym. Internet (dataport). Parking (free). Pools. Restaurants. Room service (24hr). TV (satellite).

Hyatt Regency Dubai & Galleria

Deira Corniche (209 1234/www.dubai.regency. hyatt.com). **Rates** Dhs1,499-Dhs1,800 double. **Credit** AmEx, MC, V. **Map** p299 J1 ㉑
Built in 1980, this vast 400-room stalwart sits close to the Creek in downtown Deira. Deal-makers, in particular those from East Asia, are wooed in their droves by the veteran hotel's reputation. The out-of-the-way location – around seven kilometres (four miles) from the city and about as far as you can get from Jumeirah's beaches and restaurants – has created something of a siege mentality, and the hotel has every facility going, including a revolving restaurant, nightclub, cinema, ice rink, mini golf course and its very own shopping centre.

Bars. Business services. Concierge. Gym. Internet (dataport). Parking (free). Pools. Restaurants. Room service (24hr). TV (satellite).

JW Marriott Hotel Dubai

Muraqqabat Street (262 4444/www.jwmarriott. com). **Rates** Dhs1,020-Dhs1,500 double. **Credit** AmEx, MC, V. **Map** p297 K1 ㉒
Keeping in style with the Marriott brand, this is an elegant hotel attached to the Hamarain shopping centre. Rooms are comfortable, offering an old-world formality that's rare in Dubai hotels. The pool and health facilities, aside from the massive gym and training area, are adequate if not incredible, but the daily beach-bound shuttle buses is excellent value as, before leave, passengers are presented with a beach bag that provides towels, water and sun lotion, and on return given cold face towels to calm the sunburn. The location is handy for people sealing deals over at Media City.

Bars. Business services. Concierge. Gym. Internet (dataport). Parking (free). Pools. Restaurants. Room service (24 hr). TV (satellite).

Marco Polo Hotel

Off Al Muteena Street (272 0000/www.marco polohotel.net). **Rates** Dhs1,450 double. **Credit** AmEx, MC, V. **Map** p299 K2/L2 ㉓
This homely hotel has 128 rooms. The Marco Polo does, however, have a smattering of decent dining options, including one of the city's finest Indian restaurants, and a swimming pool and gym, that are

much better than many in this range. Although there is nothing to particularly distinguish this hotel from its competitors, it's nevertheless a relaxed place with no pretensions. For a four-star hotel, we can't help feeling the Polo is a little on the overpriced side, but the consistently high occupancy rates mean they must be doing something right.

Business centre. Parking (free). Restaurants. TV (cable).

Sheraton Dubai Creek

Baniyas Road (228 1111/www.sheraton. com/dubai). **Rates** Dhs1,000-Dhs2,600 double. **Credit** AmEx, MC, V. **Map** p299 K4 ㉔
Stunning from the outside, with its tower and thrusting waterfront extension, the Sheraton is slick but businesslike within. A huge escalator leads the way up to the dimly lit foyer, where a number of restaurants are located. Rooms are comfortable, and although they don't ooze character you can cheer yourself with the fact that they're value for money. The key advantage for the more adventurous tourist is the hotel's location: although the Sheraton is far from the beach, it is close to the *abra* (boat) station, and gold and spice souk.

Bars. Business services. Concierge. Gym. Internet (dataport). Parking (free). Pools. Restaurants. Room service (24hr). TV (satellite).

★ Taj Palace Hotel

Between Al Maktoum Street & Al Rigga Road (223 2222/www.tajpalacedubai.ae). **Rates** Dhs900-Dhs2,000 double. **Credit** AmEx, MC, V. **Map** p299 L3 ㉕
A haven of extravagance in downtown Deira, the Taj Palace Hotel is a mass of glass and steel. In keeping with Muslim practice, no women work past 11pm and it doesn't serve alcohol. These Islamic values have made the Taj popular with visitors from Gulf countries. The rooms are large, combining

Budget Beds

Bijou accommodation on a budget.

Irrepressible entrepreneur Stelios Haji-Ioannou – the man who revolutionised air travel in Europe – is launching **EasyHotel**. From pizzas to insurance and men's toiletries to mobile phones, his range of products has grown in every direction, and he is now set to make his mark on Dubai's hotel industry. His tangerine-tinted, low-cost hotel accommodation is due to hit the Jebel Ali Free Zone in late 2009. As yet, pricing hasn't been confirmed, although insiders anticipate that rooms will start somewhere in the region of Dhs250-Dhs300 per night.

CONSUME

Towers
R⊕tana

Dubai

Towering above all!

Centrally located on the Sheikh Zayed Road, Towers Rotana Dubai is a preferred choice for families and business travellers alike. With 360 guestrooms, suites and Club Rotana Executive Rooms this business friendly hotel offers a variety of award-winning dining outlets including the most popular "Teatro", stylish " Flavours on Two" and talk of the town "Long's Bar". Well known for hosting conferences and meetings, Towers Rotana Dubai offers excellent service, great atmosphere and fitness facilities making it the favourite meeting venue of Dubai's social activities.

P.O.Box 30430, Dubai, U.A.E. T: 971 (0)4 312 2302 F: 971 (0)4 343 5111 towers.dubai@rotana.com.

rotana.com

wooden floors and stylish furnishings. Health facilities are unisex, and the rooftop pool and tranquil spa are deservedly popular. It's a good option for visitors happy to forego location and a glass of wine with dinner. If you do decide to dine in, try their Indian restaurant, Handi.
Business services. Concierge. Gym. Internet (dataport). Parking (free). Pools. Restaurants. Room service (24hr). TV (satellite).

Moderate

Coral Deira
Muraqqabat Street, Deira (224 8587/www.coral-deira.com). **Rates** Dhs850-Dhs1,500 double. **Credit** AmEx, MC, V. **Map** p299 L3 ②
A short drive from the airport, the Coral dominates Muraqqabat Street and is one of only two five-star hotels in Dubai that doesn't serve alcohol (the Taj Palace being the other). As such, the Coral is popular with visitors from Gulf countries, particularly businessmen from Saudi Arabia. Get past the unconvincing purple lights and the hotel is relatively stylish. Modern-day comforts include Villeroy & Boch bathrooms with elongated tubs, as well as two conference rooms and a business centre. The courtesy coach service and travel reservations are handy if you're pressed for time.
Business services. Concierge. Gym. Internet (dataport). Parking (free). Pools. Restaurants. Room service (24hr). TV (satellite).

Metropolitan Deira Hotel
Dubai Clock Tower Roundabout (295 9171/ www.habtoorhotels.com). **Rates** Dhs400-Dhs1,200 double. **Credit** AmEx, MC, V. **Map** p299 L3 ②
This mid-range hotel was built in 1998 and, despite occupying a central position in busy downtown Deira, an air of calm prevails within. The lobby has recently been refurbished yet still looks as though it is desperately in need of a face-lift. The rooms may be comfortable and clean, but they're also slightly tired. Other facilities include a gym and a few restaurants. The Metropolitan's main draw is its location: adjacent to the famous Clock Tower roundabout, it is close to the Creek, corniche and Deira City Centre shopping mall.
Bar. Business services. Gym. Internet. Parking (free). Pool. Restaurants. Room service (24 hr).

Radisson Blu Hotel
Baniyas Road (222 7171/www.radissonsas.com). **Rates** Dhs960 double. **Credit** AmEx, MC, V. **Map** p299 J3 ②
This 1970s monolith was Dubai's first five-star. Although impeccable service, brilliant restaurants and interesting decor still make the Radisson a fine place to stay, you can't escape the feeling that time has taken its toll. On the plus side, recent renovations have updated the place. Stunning views are of either the pool or the Creek. The black marble-walled

executive club is a little cold, but is a popular spot to take in the colourful corniche views. It's a good base for travellers who want to experience the city rather than baste themselves on the beach.
Bars. Business services. Concierge. Gym. Internet (dataport). Parking (free). Pool. Restaurants. Room service (24hr). TV (satellite).

Renaissance Dubai Hotel
Deira (262 5555/www.marriott.com). **Rates** Dhs590-Dhs2,250 double. **Credit** AmEx, MC, V. **Map** p297 K1 ②
The Renaissance is a relatively luxurious hotel in a downtrodden part of town. The rooms are a tad old-fashioned but comfortable, although the suites leave a little to be desired. Although the hotel is pleasant, its location lends itself more to business travellers than visitors in search of sun and sand. However, Deira is an interesting location for people after more than a tan, as the spice, textile and gold souks are all nearby. The facilities are modern and in good condition, but the rates are quite expensive for this part of town, considering what the hotel provides.
Bars. Business services. Concierge. Gym. Internet (dataport). Parking (free). Pools. Restaurants. Room service (24hr). TV (satellite).

CONSUME

THE BEST HOTELS

For sleeping by the beach
Le Méridien Mina Seyahi Beach Resort & Marina (see p103); **Ritz-Carlton Dubai** (see p104).

For celebrity-spotting
Atlantis (see p105).

For guaranteed romance
One&Only Royal Mirage (see p104); **Park Hyatt Dubai** (see p91).

For overwhelming opulence
Burj Al Arab (see p101); **Raffles Dubai** (see p86).

For a taste of Arabia
Jumeirah Bab Al Shams Desert Resort & Spa (see p109); **Mina A'Salam** (see p101).

For sealing the deal
Hilton Dubai Creek (see p91); **Jumeirah Emirates Towers** (see p106).

For bargain beds
Holiday Inn (see p101); **Ibis** (see p109).

For something different
Al Maha Desert Resort & Spa (see p109); **XVA** (see p91).

CONSUME

Sun & Sand Hotel

36A Street, near Dubai Clock Tower, off Maktoum Road (223 9000). **Rates** Dhs350-Dhs1,500 double. **Credit** AmEx, MC, V. **Map** p299 L3 ③

One of the better options in this neck of the woods, this small, reasonably well-equipped hotel includes a pool, gym and shuttle services to the shopping malls, airport and beach. Don't be fooled by the hotel's name, because you're some way from the shore, although you can always soak up the sun by the hotel's rooftop pool. The decor is dated – think gilt-edged sofas and chairs, and marble floors – but the amenities are fair and the staff are friendly. *Business services. Gym. Internet (dataport). Parking (free). Room service (24hr). Swimming pool. TV (satellite).*

Budget

Dubai Youth Hostel

Ousais Road, near Al Mulla Plaza (298 8161/ www.uaeyha.com). **Rates** Dhs230 double. **No credit cards.**

More of an upmarket boarding house than a hostel, Dubai Youth Hostel is deservedly popular with visitors looking for somewhere cheaper to stay in Dubai. Dormitories are provided alongside well-maintained family rooms for travellers with children, and the new wing has single and double rooms. Facilities are good for a hostel – a pool and gym are juxtaposed alongside a jacuzzi, spa, sauna and tennis court. But bear in mind that any dirhams saved on accommodation could quite easily be spent on taxi fares. Make sure you book well in advance and remember that if you're a member of the Youth Hostels' Association you can get a discount. *Gym. Restaurant. Pool. TV.*

Nihal Hotel

Near Clock Tower roundabout (295 7666/www. nihalhoteldubai.com). **Rates** Dhs300-Dhs350 double. **Credit** MC, V. **Map** p299 L3 ③

This cube-shaped, three-star hotel is well positioned in the heart of Deira, making it a good base when it comes to checking out Dubai's heritage areas. It's not the most impressive hotel in the looks department, but at these sort of prices you can't really complain. Although the rooms are basic and there's nothing lavish about the bathrooms, they're clean and comfortable, and possess more character than most in this price bracket. The pool is small, but at least it's there, alongside dilapidated sun loungers. Take advantage of the complimentary shuttle service to Al Mamzar beach park; quite possibly Dubai's best public beach. *Internet. Pool. Restaurants. Room service (24hr). TV.*

InterContinental.

GARHOUD

Expensive

Al Bustan Rotana Hotel

Casablanca Road, Garhoud (282 0000/www. rotana.com). **Rates** Dhs1,850 double. **Credit** AmEx, MC, V. **Map** p297 K2 ③②
Located near Dubai's airport, this Rotana has a reputation as a convenient business hotel. Not that it's all work and no play – the hotel has a swimming pool, an array of restaurants and a well-equipped gym. Standard bedrooms are reasonably sized with huge beds, but wardrobe space is limited and the bathrooms are dated. A handful of rooms come with their own private terraces facing the pool deck. Executive club levels are a distinct improvement with larger rooms, a dedicated check in area, TV lounge, breakfast area and internet access.
Bars. Business services. Concierge. Gym. Internet (dataport). Parking (free). Pools. Restaurants. Room service (24hr). TV (satellite).

InterContinental

Dubai Festival City (701 1111/www.ichotel group.com). **Rates** Dhs750-2,150 double. **Credit** AmEx, MC, V. **Map** p297 L3 ③③
This new and enormous hotel can accommodate up to 500 guests. Situated next to Dubai Festival City (DFC) shopping centre, it's also a fairly good choice if you're staying on business. The hotel has an informal feel to it and the rooms are modern and well designed. And with Reflets – Michelin-starred Pierre Gagnaire's restaurant – added to its roster, the hotel has strong appeal for tourists and residents. There are two golf courses nearby and DFC is close to the airport. The hotel overlooks the Creek with views of the new marina and the old boatyard.
Bars. Business services. Concierge. Gym. Internet (dataport). Parking (free). Pools. Restaurants. Room service (24hr). Spa. TV (satellite).

Le Méridien Dubai

Airport Road, Garhoud (282 4040/www. lemeridien.com). **Rates** Dhs800-Dhs1,200 double. **Credit** AmEx, MC, V. **Map** p297 L2 ③④
A large two-storey hotel near the airport, but away from the flight path, the Méridien caters mainly to shotgun visitors in Dubai for a quick shop or on an en-route layover. Rooms are dated; however, peer outside and you'll be greeted with some pleasant views of the gardens and pool area. Add the health club, terrace balcony rooms and swim-up bar, and this hotel is popular with older American and European tourists, and businessmen. Le Méridien Village is in the grounds, a culinary tour de force with a throng of restaurants set in their own gardens. The place comes alive at night, with people eating and drinking alfresco into the early hours. The steep room rates are a turn-off, although depending on the month of your visit, you might be able to secure a special deal.
Bars. Business services. Concierge. Gym. Internet (dataport). Parking (free). Pools. Restaurants. Room service (24hr). TV (satellite).

Millennium Airport Hotel

Casablanca Road, Garhoud (282 3464/ www.millenniumhotels.com). **Rates** Dhs960-Dhs1,560 double. **Credit** AmEx, MC, V. **Map** p297 K2 ③⑤
As you'd expect from the name, this comfortable crash pad is within spitting distance of Dubai's main airport terminal and attracts a great deal of fleeting business from European suits and airline crew. Kenny G muzak aside, the marble-heavy hotel foyer is elegant and inviting, and the large swimming pool and banks of green grass make it a low-key family favourite. Rooms are large (a twin could easily sleep four adults), airy and have pleasant garden views. Wardrobes and beds are both ample, and a subtle Arabic touch runs throughout the decor and furnishings. The hourly airport bus service makes it a convenient place to stay for business travellers, but leisure visitors will also find the hotel a perfectly comfortable holiday home – although it's a long way from the beach.
Bars. Business services. Concierge. Internet (dataport). Parking (free). Restaurants. Room service (24hr). TV (satellite).

CONSUME

Profile Burj Al Arab

Is it really worth seven stars?

Dubai's most famous hotel is every bit as extravagant and outrageous as you've heard. The tallest hotel in the world when it was built back in 1999, the **Burj Al Arab** appointed itself two stars more than official ratings allow, and watched as the press inches, bookings and room rates rocketed.

The landmark building, whose sail-like structure recalls dhow-trading vessels and is a tribute to the region's seafaring tradition, stands proudly on its own man-made island some 280 metres (920 feet) offshore and is linked to the mainland by a slender, gently curving causeway. Taller than the Eiffel Tower, it has its own helicopter pad on the 28th floor to receive guests who prefer to fly from Dubai's airport rather than ride in one of a fleet of 14 white Rolls-Royces across a bridge that shoots jets of flame to acknowledge the arrival of a VIP.

After the sleek and stylish exterior, the garishly overwrought interior can come as something of a shock; it's definitely not a place for people with egalitarian sensibilities or an aversion to gilding. A triumphant waterfall cascades into the lobby and is flanked by floor-to-ceiling aquariums so vast the staff have to don scuba gear to clean them. Bedrooms are 8,000 square metres of 22-carat gold leaf that covers columns, ceilings, panels and every tap. Huge golden pillars reach up into the atrium: greens, reds and blues all vie for prominence in a reminder that style in Dubai is as much a case of volume as it is of taste.

However, if you have the cash to splash, a night here will earn you unlimited holiday bragging rights – after all, how many people do you know who have stayed in a (admittedly self-appointed) seven-star hotel? Each room at the Burj is a duplex suite and there are 202 in total, including two royal suites on the 25th floor. All are equipped with the latest technology: internet access, a 42-inch plasma screen TV, and, in keeping with the sheer decadence, a remote control allowing you to see who's at the door and let your guests in without having to leave the comfort of your armchair.

The management at the Burj Al Arab prides itself on the hotel's highly personalised

service; there's an entire army of staff (1,200 no less) to tend to your every need. Each suite has its own butler and each floor has its own guest service desk. An unbeatable view of Dubai's coastline can be enjoyed from the Al Muntaha restaurant, which is suspended 200 metres (656 feet) above the Gulf and reached by an express panoramic lift travelling at six metres per second. If you can't afford a bed at the Burj (a standard room will set you back a whopping Dhs6,720 a night) but still want to see the obscene affluence of its interiors for yourself, book yourself in for afternoon tea or cocktails. There's a minimum spend of Dhs250 per person, but the Burj is the closest Dubai has to an Eiffel Tower or an Empire State, so it's just about worth the extravagance.

► For listings, *see p101.*

**INSIDE TRACK
BURJ AL ARAB**

The **Burj Al Arab** (*see right*) is ten
years old in 2009. Keep an eye on
www.jumeirah.com to see if this
means any discount deals at
Dubai's most prestigious hotel.

Moderate

★ Crowne Plaza
*Dubai Festival City (701 2222/www.dubai
hotels.crowneplaza.com).* **Rates** Dhs720-
Dhs1,260 double. **Credit** AmEx, MC, V.
Map p297 L3 ❸❻
This new hotel is well placed if you want to spend
a lot of time at the nearby golf courses., and if you're
a golfing widow, the hotel at least adjoins a new
shopping centre. Predominantly, though, this is a
mid-range business hotel. Rooms are warm and welcoming. The restaurants aren't all open yet, but
there's an all-day dining outlet and a pub. The
Crowne Plaza is slightly cheaper than its sister hotel
next door – the InterContinental – but since it's so
close, you can easily walk over and use the spa and
restaurants there.
*Bars. Business services. Concierge. Gym. Internet
(dataport). Parking (free). Pools. Restaurants.
Room service (24hr). TV (satellite).*

JUMEIRAH
Luxury

Al Qasr
*Al Sufouh Road (366 8888/www.madinat
jumeirah.com).* **Rates** Dhs3,480-Dhs4,560
double. **Credit** AmEx, MC, V. **Map** p304 D1 ❸❼
More ostentatious than its sister Mina A'Salam, Al
Qasr was designed to reflect the royal summer residence and provide the jewel in the crown of the
Madinat resort. The lobby with Arabian lanterns
continues the theme of the Mina A'Salam, although
the bedrooms here are larger than those in its sister
hotel. What makes Al Qasr stand out is its 24-hour
butler service (not quite the Burj – here you share
your Jeeves with 11 other rooms), its two kilometres
of private beach and its proximity to the Talise Spa,
one of the best spas in the Gulf.
*Bars. Business services. Concierge. Gym. Internet
(dataport). Parking (free). Pools. Restaurants.
Room service (24hr). Spa. TV (satellite).*

Dar Al Masyaf
*Al Sufouh Road (366 8888/www.madinat
jumeirah.com).* **Rates** Dhs4,080-Dhs4,380
double. **Credit** AmEx, DC, MC, V.
Map p304 D2 ❸❽

These exclusive summerhouses, which include
seven royal villas named after the seven emirates,
offer the best of both worlds. You get the privacy of
secluded surroundings as well as access to the rest
of the Madinat's extensive facilities. With one pool
to every three villas and 24-hour butler services, the
palatial villas are wonderfully elegant. Assuming
you can stretch to the hefty price tag, the two-
storeyed quarters with their lush, intimate settings
and intricately landscaped gardens will excite even
the most blasé of holidaymakers.
*Bars. Business services. Concierge. Internet
(dataport). Gym. Parking (free). Pools.
Restaurants. Room service (24hr). Spa.
TV (satellite).*

Dubai Marine Beach Resort & Spa
Beach Road (346 1111/www.dxbmarine.com).
Rates Dhs1,800 double. **Credit** AmEx, MC, V.
Map p300 D9 ❸❾
Situated at the beginning of the Jumeirah Beach
Road, the Dubai Marine Beach Resort & Spa is the
beachfront hotel closest to the action. The resort's
great location, small but attractive beach and two
swimming pools make it an ideal leisure venue, and
its proximity to the city gives it the edge for beach-
loving business travellers. Accommodation is scattered in 33 low-rise, villa-style buildings spread
throughout the resort, with each villa containing
only six suites. The complex is a great place in which
to relax before hitting the on-site buzzing bars and
restaurants when night falls.
*Bars. Business services. Gym. Internet (dataport).
Parking (free). Pools. Restaurants. Room service
(24hr). Spa. TV (satellite).*

★ Hilton Dubai Jumeirah
*Al Sufouh Road (399 1111/www.hiltonworld
resorts.com).* **Rates** Dhs1,650-Dhs1,900 double.
Credit AmEx, MC, V. **Map** p304 B1 ❹❶
The Hilton Jumeirah is more package hotel than out-
and-out luxury destination: the rooms are functional
rather than decadent, with cute balconies affording
views of the Gulf. The hotel's large pool has a swim-
up bar with underwater stools on which to sit and
slurp your cocktail. Pleasant terraced gardens lead
down to the sandy beach, where a number of water
sports are available, and there's a decent health club
and gym. If you can get a room for somewhat below
the advertised rack rate then the Hilton really
becomes a bargain for the beachfront.
*Bars. Business services. Concierge. Gym. Internet
(dataport). Parking (free). Pools. Restaurants.
Room service (24hr). TV (satellite).*

Jumeirah Beach Hotel
*Jumeirah Beach Road (348 0000/www.jumeirah
beachhotel.com).* **Rates** Dhs3,100-Dhs3,600
double. **Credit** AmEx, MC, V. **Map** p304 E1 ❹❶
For all the wave-shaped Jumeirah Beach Hotel's
outer grandeur, it's a down-to-earth hotel patronised

in the main by young European families in search of a spot of winter sun. Just across the road lies the Wild Wadi flume park, home to aquatic tomfoolery on an epic scale. Whether you choose to stay in the spacious, colourful rooms of the main hotel or in the refined chic of Beit Al Bahar, you'd be crazy not to turn up at the hotel's dive centre and pay a visit to the man-made coral reef just offshore.
Bars. Business services. Concierge. Gym. Internet (dataport). Parking (free). Pools. Restaurants. Room service (24hr). TV (satellite).

Mina A'Salam
Al Sufouh Road (366 8888/www.madinat jumeirah.com). **Rates** Dhs4,080 double. **Credit** AmEx, MC, V. **Map** p304 E1 ㊷
The Mina was the first hotel completed as part of the Madinat Jumeirah resort. Built around three kilometres (two miles) of Venetian-style waterways filled with *abras* that ferry guests around the resort, the Mina has a more laid-back look than its neighbour – the iconic Burj – and successfully marries Dubai's modern-day opulence with its old-world architecture. With walkways along the harbour, alfresco restaurant terraces, the extremely convivial Bahri Bar and a souk full of lavish boutiques, Mina has a distinctly villagey feel to it – albeit a village full of the affluent.
Bars. Business services. Concierge. Gym. Internet (dataport). Parking (free). Pools. Restaurants. Room service (24hr). TV (satellite).

Budget

Golden Tulip Inn Al Barsha
Al Barsha (341 7750/www.goldentulipalbarsha. com). **Rates** Dhs450 double. **Credit** AmEx, MC, V. **Map** p304 D2 ㊸
The Golden Tulip is near the Mall of the Emirates and is a reasonable place in which to stay. It's small by Dubai standards – 125 rooms – but that means the restaurants aren't particularly wide-ranging. In our experience they're not that good either, so better to head to the mall, which is not exactly short of places to eat. The rooms are somewhat oppressive and you could be staying anywhere, but the roof top pool is pleasant. The hotel is a short taxi ride from Jumeirah Beach Park, but we'd suggest trying Al Manzil (*see p109*) before booking in here.
Bars. Concierge. Internet (dataport). Parking (free). Pools. Restaurants. TV (satellite).

Grand Millennium Hotel
Barsha (429 9999/www.millenniumhotels. com/ae). **Rates** Dhs600-1,200. **Credit** AmEx, Visa, MC. **Map** p304 C2 ㊹
This newly opened five-star hotel is blessed with a great gym. The state-of-the-art equipment includes treadmills, cross trainers, cardio and weight machines, as well as free weight training machines. There are also personal trainers ready to put you

through your paces. The rooms are spacious, with stylish decor and crammed with technology. It's a short trip from here to the Mall of the Emirates.
Bars. Business services. Concierge. Gym. Internet (wireless). Parking (free). Pools. Restaurants. Room service. Spa. TV.

Holiday Inn
Barsha (323 4333/www.holidayinn.com). **Rates** Dhs480-Dhs960 double. **Credit** AmEx, MC, V. **Map** p304 D2 ㊺
Don't turn your nose up just yet – Holiday Inn Dubai is actually a very contemporary, classy affair, with a number of decent restaurants and bars. Located just behind Mall of the Emirates, what the hotel lacks in beach views (you're more likely to see buildings and busy roads), it makes up for in value for money. Popular with businessmen and holidaymakers whose relatives live nearby, this is a very friendly, sparkly new little joint.
Bars. Business services. Concierge. Gym. Internet. Parking (free). Pools. Restaurants. Room service (24hr). Spa. TV (satellite).

UMM SUQEIM
Luxury

★ Burj Al Arab
Off Jumeirah Beach Road (301 7777/www.burj-al-arab.com). **Rates** Suites from Dhs6,720. **Credit** AmEx, MC, V. **Map** p304 E1 ㊻
For review, *see p98* **Profile**.
Bars. Business services. Concierge. Gym. Internet. Parking (free). Pools. Restaurants. Room service (24hr). Spa.

One&Only Royal Mirage. *See p104.*

CONSUME

Address. *See p105.*

THE MARINA
Luxury

★ Grosvenor House West
Marina Beach Dubai
*Dubai Marina (399 8888/www.starwoodhotels.
com).* **Rates** Dhs2,220 double. **Credit** AmEx,
MC, V. **Map** p304 B1 ❼
The lobby to this landmark hotel – the first to open
in the Marina – is small and swish, with dozens of
staff to greet and direct you. With 45 storeys, you're
pretty much guaranteed an excellent view, whether
of the sea or the Dubai skyline. Rooms are spacious,
furnished in a brown and cream colour palette, and
come complete with the essential plasma TV.
Grosvenor House's rooms have high-speed internet
access, and if you want a formal or informal meeting there are plenty of meeting rooms and classy
cafés and bars, which all make it popular with business travellers. There's a small spa, and after
unwinding you can relax even more by heading up
to Bar 44 for an aperitif while watching the sun set
over the Gulf. However, you can't just walk from
your room on to the beach. To feel the sand between
their toes, guests need to take the shuttle to Le Royal
Méridien's beach resort.
*Business services. Gym. Internet (dataport).
Parking (free). Pools. Restaurants. Room service
(24hr). Spa. TV (satellite).*

Habtoor Grand Resort & Spa
*Dubai Marina (399 5000/www.grandjumeirah.
habtoorhotels.com).* **Rates** Dhs1,870 double.
Credit AmEx, MC, V. **Map** p304 B1 ❽
The Habtoor serves beach-bound holidaymakers
and business travellers well, but at rather hefty
prices. There's an impressive stretch of beach, as
well as two floodlit tennis courts and a well-
equipped gym. The rooms are quite conservative,
but the bathrooms are ornate, decked out in green
mosaics and those tiny glass sinks that were fashionable a few years ago. If you fancy some pampering, the Elixir Spa has a good range of treatments
on offer. Like most Dubai hotels, the Grand also
caters for business travellers and tends to get the
details right; if you want a fax machine installed in
your room, flights booked or travel arrangements
confirmed, consider it done.
*Business services. Concierge. Dataport. Gym.
Parking (free). Pools. Restaurants. Room service
(24hr). Spa. TV (satellite).*

Le Méridien Mina Seyahi
Beach Resort & Marina
*Al Sufouh Road (399 3333/www.lemeridien-
minaseyahi.com).* **Rates** Dhs2,610 double.
Credit AmEx, MC, V. **Map** p304 B1 ❾
With a gem of a beach for sun worshippers, the Mina
retains a casual ambience that's at odds with its
rather more formal big brother, Le Royal Méridien.

The Palm Island
Island in the sun.

The **Palm Jumeirah** – one of the three
largest man-made islands in the world,
all of which are under construction off
Dubai's coast – is set to become a major
tourism hotspot, with around 25 hotels
opening over the coming years. Right
now, the hype is all about the **Trump
International Hotel & Tower** (the
centrepiece of the island, due for
completion in 2011), and the 1,539-
room ocean-themed **Atlantis**, which
opened in late 2008. However, other
hotels to take up a tenancy include the
Fairmont Palm Hotel & Resort, due to
open in 2009, the **Taj Exotica Resort
& Spa**, which will boast the biggest spa
in the world and the **Kempinski Hotel
Emerald Palace Dubai**. The latter two
hotels are due open in 2010. With
enough rooms for about 25,000 hotel
guests or one million visitors a year, the
arrival of these Palm pads could and
should go a long way to help meet
Dubai's desperate need for more hotel
rooms. Log on to www.thepalm.ae for the
latest developments on the Palm project.

Rooms are simple but comfortable, with beachside
balconies overlooking the Palm Jumeirah (request a
room with a view when you book). Bathrooms are
fairly ordinary, but include nice little touches like an
in-room radio. It's outside that the Mina really comes
into its own. With over 850m (2,800ft) of golden
sands, the hotel has more beach than any other in
Dubai. And it utilises every inch of it with excellent
water sport facilities (including a PADI-certified
dive centre), a stunning pool area, and one of the best
beach bars in Barasti. The children's facilities,
including the Penguin Club and dedicated pools,
ensure the little ones don't interfere with tan-topping
time, and the glass-fronted gym allows you to look
out to sea while working out.
*Bars. Business services. Concierge. Gym. Internet
(dataport). Parking (free). Pools. Restaurants.
Room service (24hr). TV (satellite).*

★ Le Royal Méridien
*Al Sufouh Road (399 5555/www.leroyalmeridien-
dubai.com).* **Rates** Dhs2,400 double. **Credit**
AmEx, MC, V. **Map** p304 B1 ❺⓿
Roses are a big deal at Le Royal Méridien. In the
rooms are finger bowls of water topped with petals,
rose residue is scattered on the beds, and the bathroom has more blooms than a florist on 13 February.
Such in-your-face opulence is typical of Le Royal

CONSUME

Kempinski Hotel Mall of the Emirates. *See p106.*

Méridien, and the pools, gardens and great stretch of sand have been sculpted in a timelessly classic style. All rooms are sea-facing, large, bright and comfortable, with balconies to enjoy the view down the beach or over the Gulf. Sexy European clients flitter around the upmarket, all-beige coffee spaces and bars, and it is doubtful that the pool has seen a one-piece swimsuit in its life.

Bars. Business services. Concierge. Gym. Internet (dataport). Parking (free). Pools. Restaurants. Room service (24hr). Spa. TV (satellite).

★ One&Only Royal Mirage

Al Sufouh Road (399 9999/www.oneandonly resorts.com). **Rates** Dhs3,200 double. **Credit** AmEx, MC, V. **Map** p304 C1 ⑤

Styled on an Arabian fort, the Royal Mirage is still Dubai's most romantic resort, despite some stiff competition from Madinat Jumeirah. It's composed of three hotels: the Palace, the Arabian Court and the Residence, each one plusher and more expensive than the last. Although many of Dubai's landmarks owe their success to a degree of shock and awe, the Royal Mirage presents an illusion of days gone by with welcome subtlety. The complex's simple low-rise architecture holds sumptuous interiors of rich fabrics and intricate woodwork. Iron lanterns throw patterned candlelight onto sand-coloured walls, and pockets of rooms are interspersed with Moorish arches and verdant gardens. Add the delicate use of gold and warm tones throughout, and the scene is set for the ultimate romantic getaway. The hotel is never more beautiful than at night, when couples emerge to take quiet strolls past the pool and on to the beach before ending the night up on the Roof Top for drinks. Deluxe rooms are sensibly sized and

packed with wonderful examples of attention to detail, from the slippers by the bed to the hand towel artfully folded into the shape of a swan. Every inch of the Royal Mirage seems designed to make you feel good about life; we'd happily hole up here permanently if we had the money. *Photo p101.*

Bars. Business services. Gym. Internet (dataport). Parking (free). Pools. Restaurants. Room service (24hr). Spa. TV (satellite).

Ritz-Carlton Dubai

Al Sufouh Road (399 4000/www.ritzcarlton.com). **Rates** Dhs2,150-Dhs3,500 double. **Credit** AmEx, MC, V. **Map** p304 B1 ⑤

The most classically stylish of Dubai's hotels, the Ritz-Carlton is immaculately presented with a grand marble lobby and gigantic windows offering uninterrupted views of white sands and the lapping Gulf. Rather than following the recent trend for Arabian chic, the hotel emphasises formal European luxury. The wooden-beamed tea lounge is a sophisticated stop-off, and the terrace is a delight at sunset. There's a separate adults-only pool providing peace for couples, and even the family pool is large and languid. Most of the generously sized rooms look out to sea and enjoy private balconies and sumptuous soft furnishings; the bathrooms are an exercise in comfort, with vast, glass-fronted showers and deep baths to lounge in. For a relaxed stay with some old-world charm, the Ritz ticks all the right boxes. Make sure you visit for afternoon tea and check out the in-house spa that provides both Asian and Arabic-inspired treatments.

Bars. Business services. Concierge. Gym. Internet (dataport). Parking (free). Pools. Restaurants. Room service (24hr). Spa. TV (satellite).

CONSUME

Sheraton Jumeirah Beach Resort & Towers
Al Sufouh Road (399 5533/www.starwoodhotels.com). **Rates** Dhs1,500-Dhs1,740 double. **Credit** AmEx, MC, V. **Map** p304 A1 ⓼
Currently the furthest beach hotel from the city, the Sheraton is a stylish resort with a good stretch of sand, decent beach club, spacious gardens and a fine swimming pool. Popular with European package tourists, the hotel blurs five-star lines with the overall feel that's more comfortable than lavish. Rooms are large and overlook either the sea and resort area or the rather less pleasing building sites of the developing Dubai Marina and Jumeirah Beach Residence. Still, it's a good-value place for people looking to escape the trappings of inner-city vacations, which is just as well as a taxi ride into town will set you back a fair whack.
Bars. Business services. Gym. Internet (dataport). Parking (free). Pools. Restaurants. Room service (24hr). Spa. TV (satellite).

Westin
Al Sufouh Road (399 4141/www.westin.com/dubaiminaseyahi). **Rates** Dhs1,150-Dhs12,850. **Credit** AmEx, MC, V. **Map** p304 B1 ⓽
The Westin is a tasteful property overlooking the sea with a small private beach and a few swimming pools. The lobby, with a fancy stained-glass atrium and trendy Murano light fittings hints at the style in the bedrooms. Ask for a room with a balcony and seaview. All the facilities you'd expect from a five-star hotel are present and correct: a couple of restaurants, bars, spa and gym.
Business services. Concierge. Gym. Internet. Parking (free). Pools. Restaurants. Room service (24hr). Spa. TV (satellite).

Expensive

Radisson Blu Hotel, Dubai Media City
Dubai Media City (366 9111/www.dubai.radissonsas.com). **Rates** Dhs1,499 double. **Credit** AmEx, MC, V. **Map** p304 B2/C2 ⓹
The Radisson Blu is a mid-range hotel that is clearly aimed at the business traveller market, although it's not that far from the beach or the Mall of the Emirates. The decor in the rooms is modern with dark wood furnishings, and there's a well-equipped gym and a wellness centre.
Bars. Business services. Gym. Internet (dataport). Parking (free). Pools. Restaurants. Room service (24hr). Spa. TV (satellite).

Budget

Premier Inn
Dubai Investments Park, near the Green Community (885 0999/http://global.premierinn.com). **Rates** Dhs350-Dhs495 double. **Credit** AmEx, MC, V.

The Premier Inn caused quite a stir when it opened but not, for a change in Dubai, because of over-the-top ostentation. Rather it was value for money that caused the talk – there are precious few other places in the city where you can sleep for Dhs450 a night. The company promises that there is a ceiling rate of Dhs650 and this is applied only when there's a major event in the area. In terms of location, it's at the Jumeirah end of town, near Jebel Ali and so not near the airport. Rooms, of which there are 308, are pleasant and feature king-size beds. This Inn is the first of many that are due to be opened in the UAE and Gulf region over the next few years.
Bar. Business services. Internet (dataport). Pool. Restaurant. Room service (24hr). TV (satellite).

THE PALM
Luxury

★ Atlantis
Palm Jumeirah (426 0000/www.atlantisthepalm.com). **Rates** Dhs1,465-Dhs2,165. **Credit** AmEx, MC, V. **Map** p304 C1 ⓾
This aquatic version of Disneyland encompasses 1,373 rooms and 166 suites each designed with the sea in mind. If you've got cash to splash book into the Lost Chambers Suites; you won't be overlooking the ocean, but living in it. Floor-to-ceiling windows give a spectacular view into the Ambassador Lagoon, with marine life gliding by. Outside the hotel, Aquaventure water park and Dolphin Bay attract non-staying guests with the opportunity to swim with dolphins and enjoy some of the park's scariest rides. For foodies, Atlantis brings world-famous chefs Michel Rostang, Giorgio Locatelli, Santi Santamaria and Matsuhisa Nobu to the Emirate. *Photo p107.*
Bars. Business services. Concierge. Gym. Internet. Parking (Dhs50). Pools. Restaurants. Room service (24hr). TV (satellite).

SHEIKH ZAYED ROAD
Luxury

★ Address
Burj Dubai Boulevard, Downtown Burj Dubai (436 8888/www.theaddress.com). **Rates** Dhs1,299-Dhs4,599. **Credit** AmEx, MC, V. **Map** p296 H5 ⓾
Despite opening at the same time as the Dubai Mall, the Address still managed to garner a few headlines. The USP is its modern take on art deco, with everything from the building's shape to its paintings and staff uniforms harking back to the 1920s. But only the look is old-fashioned, everything else is the epitomy of futuristic chic, and walking through its lobby is like walking through the pages of a modern style magazine. Fashionable bar Neos takes full advantage of the hotel's 63 storeys, and the chilled infinity pool that flows over five floors makes up for its slight distance from the beach. *Photo p102.*

Bars. Business services. Concierge. Gym. Internet. Parking (free). Pools. Restaurants. Room service (24hr). TV (satellite).

Al Murooj Rotana Hotel & Suites Dubai

Al Saffa Street, off Sheikh Zayed Road (321 1111/www.rotana.com). **Rates** Dhs1,680 double. **Credit** AmEx, MC, V. **Map** p303 F13 ⑤⑧

Tucked behind the Sheikh Zayed Road and surrounded by a moat-like man-made lake, the Al Murooj Rotana has the convenience of being close to Dubai's main thoroughfare without the traffic noise. The hotel is in the shadow of the rapidly rising Burj Dubai, but with this privilege sadly comes the ongoing drone of construction work, for the time being at least. The rooms are comfortable and contemporary, the pool area pleasant, and there's a well-equipped gym and spa at which to purge your sins. The hotel is mainly directed towards business travellers, with its excellent meeting and conference facilities, but leisure travellers not excited by the beach should be more than happy. One word of warning; avoid the second floor rooms near the perennially busy and noisy Double Decker pub if you're a light sleeper.

Business services. Concierge. Gym. Internet (dataport). Parking (free). Pools. Restaurants. Room service (24hr). Spa. TV (satellite).

Fairmont Dubai

Satwa side (332 5555/www.fairmont.com). **Rates** Dhs1,680 double. **Credit** AmEx, MC, V. **Map** p301 G9/G10 ⑤⑨

An elegant beast of a hotel, the Fairmont juggles the requirements of business and leisure guests with some style. Set directly across from the Trade Centre, it has four illuminated turrets that change colour throughout the week and have taken on a unique place in Dubai's cityscape. At the hotel's centre is a massive foyer graced with groovy velvet sofas and a huge atrium, its walls splashed with every tone of colour to head-spinning effect. Bedrooms are spacious, with large beds, huge windows and well-chosen furnishings – although they suffer from the 'more is more' approach to colour. The minimalist bathrooms, though large, will seem sterile by comparison. A keen eye for detail is evident in the two pool areas on either side of the building – the sunset and sunrise decks – decorated with pretty mosaics to reflect their respective themes. There's an impressive health club, plus the first-rate Willow Stream Spa .

Bars. Business services. Concierge. Internet. Parking (free). Pools. Restaurants. Room service (24hr). Spa. TV.

Jumeirah Emirates Towers

Trade Centre side (330 0000/www.jumeirah emiratestowers.com). **Rates** Dhs2,150 double. **Credit** AmEx, MC, V. **Map** p296 H4 ⑥⓪

The hotel is geared principally to work-trippers and is arguably the best business hotel in the Middle East. A sophisticated lobby lounge, which is an excellent people-watching spot, and acres of atrium dominate the ground floor, and the glass lifts that shoot up and down the 52 storeys are a vertigo-inducing delight. Rooms are sizeable, with attractive dark wood tables, bright, soft furnishings, and panoramas that would blow the socks off the most seasoned of travellers. The Towers has its own large swimming pool, spa, complimentary shuttle and entry to Wild Wadi water park.

Bars. Business services. Gym. Internet (dataport). Parking (free). Pools. Restaurants. Room service (24hr). Spa. TV (satellite).

★ Kempinski Hotel Mall of the Emirates

Mall of the Emirates, Al Barsha Interchange (341 0000/www.kempinski.com). **Rates** Dhs1,730 double. **Credit** AmEx, MC, V. **Map** p304 D2 ⑥①

When you've finished shopping and skiing at the adjoining Mall of the Emirates, you can take some time out at the hotel's wellness centre and spa where the emphasis is on Ayurvedic treatments. If you can't bear to be far from the ski slope for long, you can stay in one of the 15 chalets that overlook the slope. The chalets and hotel rooms come with all mod cons, including flat-screen TVs and DVD players. The decor is homely yet modern, and top class service is guaranteed. *Photo p104.*

Bars. Business centre. Concierge. Gym. Internet (dataport). Parking (free). Pools. Restaurants. Room service (24hr). Spa. TV (satellite).

New Openings

The new players in town.

Dubai's government is aiming to attract ten million tourists by 2010. To cope with the influx, an abundance of new hotels is due to open before the end of 2010, including a **Four Seasons** and the emirate's first **W** hotel. Fashion heavyweights **Armani** and **Versace** are also getting in on the hotel act. Armani's first slumber station (www.armanihotels.com) is due to open by the end of 2009 inside the world's tallest building – the Burj Dubai.

Elsewhere, **Donald Trump** – New York's famous property magnate – is so entranced by the emirate that he has begun developing a 48-storey hotel and apartment block on the Palm Jumeirah, due for completion in 2011; and **Sir Stelios Haji-Ioannou** of EasyJet fame is opening one his EasyHotels here by the end of 2009.

Atlantis. *See p105.*

★ Monarch Dubai

Sheikh Zayed Road (501 8888/www.themonarch dubai.com). **Rates** Dhs2,280 double. **Credit** AmEx, MC, V. **Map** p301 G9 ⑫

Set next to a busy roundabout, the Monarch isn't ideal for leisure travellers, but it's a good choice for business users. Facilities are all present and correct, with a gym, pool, restaurants and a bar lounge. Rooms are modern and masculine, with wood floors and neutral furnishings. Floor-to-ceiling windows allow an excellent view of the city, especially if you're near the top (there are 33 floors). People with huge wads of cash can reserve the Sky suite, which is literally suspended between two towers.

Bars. Business services. Concierge. Gym. Internet (dataport). Parking (free). Pool. Restaurants. Room service (24hr). Spa. TV (satellite).

Palace The Old Town

Burj Dubai (428 7888/www.sofitel.com). **Rates** Dhs2,000 double. **Credit** AmEx, MC, V. **Map** p303 F14 ⑬

The Palace is part of the developments springing up around Burj Dubai, now the tallest building in the world. It's built in an old Arabian style, in contrast to much of the surroundings, but all the construction means that it's a bit noisy if you're lying by the pool or wanting to sit on the terraces or balconies. The restaurants, though, are already proving a hit with locals. For people who need to unwind after a flight, the excellent spa should help. There's easy access from the hotel to the Dubai Mall. *Photo p108.*

Bars. Business services. Concierge. Gym. Internet (dataport). Parking (free). Pools. Restaurants. Room service (24hr). TV (satellite).

Shangri-La Hotel Dubai

Sheikh Zayed Road (343 8888/www.shangri-la.com). **Rates** Dhs2,160 double. **Credit** AmEx, MC, V. **Map** p303 E12/F12 ⑭

The Shangri-La towers above its more established competitors, literally and figuratively. The chic and serene foyer is immaculate and has welcomed many celebrities, and the breathtaking views it provides over the magnificent structures of Sheikh Zayed Road are incomparable. The stylish, spacious standard rooms impress with their minimalist chic, and the Aigner-equipped bathrooms feature separate tub, shower and toilet spaces. Business facilities are state-of-the-art and secluded, and the suites dazzle with their luxurious fittings and Bang & Olufsen entertainment centres. The hotel has several top restaurants, including the wonderful French-Vietnamese establishment, Hoi An.

Bars. Business services. Concierge. Gym. Internet (dataport). Parking (free). Pools. Restaurants. Room service (24hr). Spa. TV (satellite).

Expensive

Crowne Plaza Hotel Dubai

Satwa side (331 1111/www.ichotels.com). **Rates** Dhs1,370 double. **Credit** AmEx, MC, V. **Map** p301 G10 ⑮

Owing to its prime location at the Creek end of Sheikh Zayed Road, guests staying here are a short drive from the beach and the malls. The grand lobby, reached via steep and skinny escalators, has aged well, although the once-swish decor is looking a little tired. Standard rooms are on the small side, and the tiny bathrooms are dated. The views, how-

CONSUME

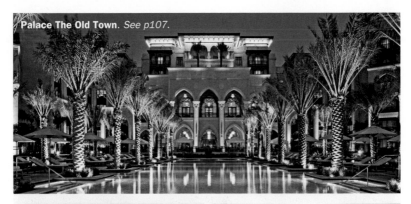

Palace The Old Town. *See p107.*

ever, are as good as any in Dubai. It's the range of facilities that keeps business and leisure tourists loyal to the Crowne Plaza. The health club and pool are spacious and casual.

Bars. Business services. Concierge. Gym. Internet (dataport). Parking (free). Pools. Restaurants. Room service (24hr). TV (satellite).

Dusit Dubai

Trade Centre side (343 3333/www.dusit.com).
Rates Dhs1,200 double. **Credit** AmEx, MC, V.
Map p303 F12 ⑥⑥

The Dusit is a bow-legged colossus of glass and steel that stands out even among the extraordinary buildings lining Sheikh Zayed Road. Its Thai-style decor is evident throughout, from the Asian-chic rooms to the smart sarong-wearing staff. Rooms are lovely, with rich browns and sweeping views. Guests can work out in the well-stocked gym with bird's-eye city views, or laze in the 36th-floor open-air pool, before heading to the mini spa to beautify themselves for a night out on the town. This used to be the closest

you'd get to a high-class bargain on Sheikh Zayed Road, but prices have risen in recent times.

Bars. Business centre. Gym. Internet (dataport). Parking (free). Pools. Restaurants. Room service (24hr). TV (satellite).

Towers Rotana Hotel

Satwa side (343 8000/www.rotana.com).
Rates Dhs1,260 double. **Credit** AmEx, MC, V.
Map p303 F12 ⑥⑦

Although the rooms are only of average size, albeit comfortable, the extraordinary views over Jumeirah compensate. The decor is light and airy, and there's a large pool space and gym situated in a separate wing of the building. Although pitched at business travellers, the Rotana is seconds away from the nightlife of the Sheikh Zayed strip, and should you not wish to stir, Long's Bar is a popular watering hole on site. A good option for holidaymakers who can't afford the lavishness of Jumeirah.

Bars. Business centre. Gym. Internet. Parking (free). Pools. Restaurants.

Moderate

Al Manzil Hotel
Burj Dubai Boulevard (428 5888/www. almanzilhotel.com). **Rates** Dhs780 double. **Credit** AmEx, MC, V. **Map** p296 H5 ⑱

Al Manzil's rooms are decorated in a contemporary Arabic style, and have unusual open-style bathrooms with rainfall showers and huge oval-shaped baths where guests can soak while watching a film on the rotating plasma TV. Days can be spent chilling by the large pool or taking advantage of the complimentary shuttle bus to the beach and shopping malls. A 50-shop souk and various restaurants are scheduled to open adjacent to the hotel, perhaps pushing the price up; but for now this is a gem of a hotel and fantastic value for money.
Business centre. Gym. Internet (free). Parking (free). Restaurants. Room service (24hr). Pool. TV.

Novotel
Behind the World Trade Centre (318 7000/ www.novotel.com). **Rates** Dhs700 double. **Credit** AmEx, MC, V. **Map** p301 G10 ⑲

It may come as a surprise that the no-nonsense Novotel was built to house the World Bank and IMF meetings that were held in Dubai back in 2003. However, it proves that budget need not be boring or basic. The lobby – all dark wood, open space and ordered sophistication – is suitably stylish, and rooms, although small, aren't at all cramped. The hotel holds little appeal for sun-seekers, as it has only a small pool and gym, but it will score highly with business people and those operating along Sheikh Zayed Road. The central location will probably save you a bundle on taxi fares as well.
Bars. Business services. Concierge. Gym. Internet (dataport). Parking (free). Pools. Restaurants. Room service (24hr). TV (satellite).

Budget

Ibis World Trade Centre Dubai
Behind World Trade Centre (318 7000/ www.ibishotel.com). **Rates** Dhs465 double. **Credit** AmEx, MC, V. **Map** p301 G9 ⑳

The ever-popular Ibis is a fuss-free affair: there's no pool and facilities are minimal, but the hotel has invested its time and energy into developing a sophisticated feel for a three star. The lobby is elegant, simple and dotted with Philippe Starck furniture, although the rooms, at 20sq m (215sq ft), are small – and offer pretty drab glimpses of the Dubai World Trade Centre apartments. Nonetheless, it's a sound choice for the shoestring traveller who has no wish for fancy extras and it's excellent value for money – no small achievement in Dubai.
Bars. Internet (dataport). Parking (free). Restaurants. TV (satellite).

CONSUME

Desert Resorts

Time and budget permitting, a stay at one of Dubai's desert resorts is a must.

JUMEIRAH BAB AL SHAMS DESERT RESORT & SPA
Bab Al Shams is a luxury hotel in the middle of the dunes. This grid of low-rise buildings made from pre-scratched, crumbling, mock sandstone is filled with hidden corridors and secret stairwells: rooms open directly on to the sands, and a swimming pool, spa and four restaurants cater to the more usual needs of hotel guests. The range of activities mainly revolves around desert excursions, but there is a well-equipped children's centre that should keep the young ones entertained. At night, enjoy a sunset shisha at Al Sarab bar or try out the Al Hadheerah desert restaurant, which produces a somewhat Disneyfied Arabian experience complete with belly dancer, band and some fairly potent shisha.

Bab Al Shams Desert Resort & Spa
(832 6699/www.jumeirahbabalshams.com).

AL MAHA DESERT RESORT & SPA
Al Maha Desert Resort is set within the single largest conservation area in the country. The perimeter fence stretches around 225 square kilometres (87 square miles) of desert, ringing in and protecting the natural wildlife. You'll be golf-buggied over to your stand-alone tent-roofed suites, all of which have chilled private pools and unrivalled views of dunes dotted with the endangered Arabian oryx.

Few other places in the Emirate provide such an opportunity to get a firsthand experience of Arabian nature. For those looking to restore body and soul, the Jamilah Spa is on hand for to provide rest and relaxation. Whatever you do, don't forget to book in for the sunset camel ride, a deservedly popular 20-minute trip into the gathering dark.

Al Maha Desert Resort & Spa
Between Dubai & Al Ain (303 4222/ www.al-maha.com).

Restaurants & Cafés

Recent immigration has broadened the culinary variety in Dubai.

One of Dubai's most notable features is the diversity of its population. The influx in recent years of Asians, Europeans and Africans has had a huge influence on the eating out scene. Diners with a hankering for rich Indian curries, sushi, Arabic meze or a good, old fashioned plate of fish and chips won't be disappointed, as this is a city designed to cater to the tastes of its many expatriates. And although the ongoing slew of restaurants helmed by Michelin-rated chefs can set the diner back a few hundred dirhams, the streets are full of authentic budget eats. Regardless of how much you want to spend, one thing's certain: the wealth of multicultural offerings should excite the palate.

CONSUME

HOTEL DINING

In most cities, the prospect of dining in a hotel restaurant is dire. In Dubai, it's *de rigueur*. Why? Owing to the rules governing alcohol, hotels and sporting arenas are the only places where you can drink with your meal. Although some of the best eats are still dotted around the city streets, all of Dubai's major restaurants are guaranteed to be located in a hotel chain.

THE ESSENTIALS

There are a handful of restaurants where making a reservation is recommended, if not required. Usually, though, if you show up in person without a reservation, you'll be accommodated. Diners tend to eat a bit later in Dubai, and most restaurants don't start to fill up until 9pm. How you should dress depends on the establishment; at more traditional restaurants (namely, Arabian or Indian eateries outside major hotels), women might feel a little uncomfortable in mini skirts or low-cut tops. At most restaurants, however, the dress code is the same as it would be in the West.

Although most restaurants have a 'smart casual' dress code, and a handful are strict about jackets and evening wear, it is almost

never necessary to dress up for dinner. In some trendier establishments, however, expect to find locals and expats flouting their designer gear.

Note that prices listed are for dinner for two, including three courses and a glass of wine each. We've used the **Dhs** symbol to indicate operations offering particularly good value: restaurants with meals for around Dhs100 or less. The type of cuisine is indicated in blue; **MENA** is short for Middle East/North African.

RAMADAN

During Ramadan, eating, drinking and smoking in public before *iftar* (after sunset, usually around 6.30pm) is against the law, and doing so may incur a fine. Many restaurants that are normally open during the day close during Ramadan, and the few places that remain open either put up curtains to minimise the sight of daytime eating from the street, or force patrons to take the food to a more discreet location for consumption. But every hotel and restaurant in town capitalises on Ramadan by serving large, traditional meals at *iftar*, the time when fasting breaks. It is a good idea to make a reservation, as restaurants really fill up in the evening.

❶ Blue numbers given in this chapter correspond to the location of each restaurant as marked on the street maps. *See pp294-304.*

BUR DUBAI

★ **Aangan**
Dhow Palace Hotel (359 9992). **Open** 12.30-3.15pm, 7pm-12.45am daily. **Average** Dhs300-Dhs400. **Credit** AmEx, DC, MC, V. **Map** p301 G6 ❶ Indian

Wealthy Indian families seem to flock here, and it's no wonder: the food is excellent. An order of fish *moli* is as delicate as anything you'd find in Kerala, and the house speciality, lamb shank cooked in a simmering tomato curry, is a tender and rich concoction that demonstrates how high traditional Indian food can soar. There's an in-house band that belts out traditional Indian tunes. Service is brilliant, if a bit servile, however the music and food tend to distract from the fawning waiters.

Dhs Al Mallah

Al Diyafah Street, Satwa (398 4723). **Open** 6am-4am Sun-Thur; noon-4am Fri; 6am-4am Sat. **Average** Dhs20-Dhs50. **No credit cards**. Unlicensed. **Map** p301 F8 ❷ MENA
An old stalwart on the bustling Al Diyafah Street scene, Al Mallah is the place to go for simple Arabic fast food. Skip the meze (it's better elsewhere) and munch on winning *shawarmas* and falafel sandwiches. The lamb and chicken *shawarmas* are small, but among the tastiest in the city.

Andiamo!

Grand Hyatt Dubai (317 1234/www.dubai. grand.hyatt.com). **Open** 12.30-3pm, 6-11.30pm daily. **Average** Dhs350-Dhs450. **Credit** AmEx, DC, MC, V. **Map** p297 K3 ❸ Italian
There's nothing particularly innovative about Andiamo!, which makes its overly enthusiastic punctuation seem a little unnecessary. What it does is serve passable Italian fare at a reasonable price. The classics are the best: the beef *carpaccio*, which is tender and pinkly fresh, is a solid opener, and the fish makes a solid bet for a main course. Still, if you're looking for authentic Italian fare, some other venues deliver better.
▶ *For more information about the Grand Hyatt Dubai, see p86.*

Asado

The Palace, Old Town (428 7888). **Open** 7-11.45pm daily. **Average** Dhs500-Dhs600. **Credit** AmEx, DC, MC, V. **Map** p303 F14 ❹ Latin American
This Argentinian gem is the only spot in Dubai where you can feast outside on a whole roasted goat and look up at the mighty Burj Dubai. There may be no place in town that better relishes the city's incongruity. As it's South American in focus, steak is the house speciality, and the knowledgeable waiters let you see the cuts before you buy. It's an ideal place for that all-important business meeting, even if you do conduct it with a roasted goat leg in hand.

Asha's

Wafi (324 0000). **Open** noon-3pm, 7-11pm daily. **Average** Dhs300-Dhs350. **Credit** AmEx, MC, V. **Map** p297 J3 ❺ Indian
Singers sing, they don't generally know that much about the restaurant business. But Asha Bosle, Bollywood diva and the voice behind a thousand film soundtracks, is different, and her eponymous eaterie is surprisingly good. The quality of produce is high, with fresh, colourful ingredients making the flavours and smells all the more potent. It's perhaps better to stick to the traditional Indian dishes on the menu, where the homely produce truly shines.

Awtar

Grand Hyatt Dubai (317 1234). **Open** 12.30-3pm, 7.30pm-2am Sun-Fri. **Average** Dhs350-Dhs450. **Credit** AmEx, DC, MC, V. **Map** p297 K3 ❻ MENA
Beautifully draped ceilings, cream furnishings and large open windows create a light and tranquil space. The service is immaculate, barely allowing a crumb to hit the table before it is swept up. Lebanese staples are well done, especially the *shish taouk,* which

Bombay Chowpatty. *See p113.*

CONSUME

WE KEEP IT STYLISH, SIMPLE AND SUMPTUOUS.

Seasoned with distinctive flair and a dash of creativity, Courtyard by Marriott Dubai Green Community offers an international range of culinary experiences for all connoisseurs of good taste.

Unforgettable dining experiences await you in the tranquil surroundings of The Pine Grill restaurant and cosy Italian kitchen – Cucina.

Or you could escape to the Rendezvous Lounge overlooking the mesmerising crystal blue lake; sit back and savour a freshly brewed cup of coffee.

If you're looking for tasty snacks, an impressive menu of drinks and a great atmosphere in which to meet and make friends, The Bar above Cucina is your first choice.

Last but not least, on a warm sunny day, you'll discover the pleasure of lounging by the pool, sipping a frosty beverage from Aquamarine.

For reservations or more information please call 04 885 2222 or log onto www.marriottdiningatcy.ae

Courtyard by Marriott
Dubai Green Community
Dubai Investment Park,
P.O.Box 63845
Dubai, UAE
T: +971 4885 2222
F: +971 4885 2525

DUBAI
GREEN COMMUNITY

Terms & Conditions apply

comes with succulent chicken and fluffy bread. You may find cheaper Lebanese food elsewhere, but if you love the cuisine, it's worth splashing out.

Basta Art Café

Al Fahidi Street, Bastakiya, Bur Dubai (04 353 5071). **Open** 8am-10pm daily. **Average** Dhs100-Dhs200. **No credit cards**. **Map** p298 F8 **7** Café
Hugged in the friendly branches of the Narra tree and surrounded by greenery and blossoming pot plants, this leafy courtyard café makes you feel you're a million miles away from the hustle of Bur Dubai. The venue makes an ideal spot for lazing in the sunshine with friends, and there are books, artwork and various handicrafts for sale. Sandwiches and salads are massive, fresh and reasonably priced, and with an extensive assortment of fresh juices, teas and beautifully served Arabic coffee, there are few better spots to soothe away the madness of Dubai.

Bastakiah Nights

Bastakiah Nights, Bur Dubai (353 7772). **Open** 11am-11pm Sat-Thur; 2-11pm Fri. **Average** Dhs250-Dhs350. **Credit** AmEx, DC, MC, V. Unlicensed. **Map** p298 H3 **8** MENA
The outdoor courtyard, oversized coffee pots and chorus of wailing evening prayers resonating from the mosques around Dubai creek certainly give Bastakiah Nights the atmospheric edge, luring many a wide-eyed tourist eager for a taste of 'real' Arabia. Unfortunately, the quality of food doesn't match the serene setting. Lebanese staples are lacklustre. It's really the decor and location that make the place a first stop for many tourists in town.

Bateaux Dubai

Al Seef Road, opposite the British Embassy (399 4994). **Open** Boarding at 7.45pm, cruise from 8.30pm-11pm. **Average** Dhs550-Dhs650. **Credit** AmEx, DC, MC, V. **Map** p299 J3 **9** International
The meal aboard this dinner-cruise ship isn't worth a postcard home, but then again, it's not the food that attracts dozens of tourists, but the views of Dubai's ever-expanding coastline. The menu, of vaguely international bent, offers a choice with little to intrigue or excite. Still, food aside, it's not a bad way to spend two and a half hours on a clear evening.

Dhs Bombay Chowpatty

Karama, behind Trade Centre Road (396 4937). **Open** 8.30am-11.30pm Sat-Wed; 8.30am-12.30am Thur, Fri. **Average** Dhs20. **No credit cards**. Unlicensed. **Map** p299 K2 **10** Indian & Pakistani
As the name suggests, this hole-in-the-wall street stand specialises in Bombay-style street food. It's an insanely popular hideaway, in no small part because it's insanely cheap. Fill up on *puris, parathas, dosas* and any number of fried numbers for the grand total of Dhs5 a pop. *Photo p111.*

Dhs Calicut Paragon

Opposite Lulu supermarket, Karama (335 8700). **Open** 11.30am-4.30pm Sat-Thur; 1-4.30pm Fri. **Average** Dhs50. **No credit cards**. Unlicensed. **Map** p297 J3 **11** Indian & Pakistani
For a cheap humble curry that could easily have arrived off a plane from Kerala, you could do no better than the tasty concoctions for sale at Calicut Paragon. Fish and coconut curries are a speciality, and the polite staff are happy to make recommendations if you're not sure what to order.

Coconut Grove

Rydges Plaza, Satwa (398 3800). **Open** 7pm-12.30am daily. **Average** Dhs250-Dhs350. **Credit** AmEx, DC, MC, V. **Map** p301 F8 **12** Indian & Pakistani
Amid the lurid pink walls, dense palm fronds and mismatched dark wooden furniture, you'll find one of the most original curry houses in Dubai. Serving excellent, authentic coastal dishes from Sri Lanka, Kerala, Malabar and Goa, the menu is as varied as it is long. It may not have the suave decor of some of Dubai's other Indian restaurants, but neither does it have the prices. Coconut Grove is unique in its quirkiness, and the slightly eccentric staff just add to the establishment's charm. *Photo p114.*

Elia

Majestic Hotel, Mankhool Road, Bur Dubai (359 8888). **Open** noon-midnight daily. **Average** Dhs400-Dhs500. **Credit** AmEx, DC, MC, V. **Map** p298 H5 **13** European
Walking into Elia, you won't notice anything palpably Greek, but this is part of its appeal. It's understated, simple and intimate. Starters like the beef meatballs or cabbage *dolma* make it clear why head chef Yannis Baxevanis is nicknamed 'the aroma magician' of Greek cuisine. Plucked from his homeland to head up a kitchen of four Greek chefs, Yannis is fanatical about fresh produce and herbs.

Ewaan

The Palace, Old Town (428 7888). **Open** noon-3pm, 6pm-midnight daily. **Average** Dhs450-Dhs550. **Credit** AmEx, MC, V. **Map** p303 F14 **14** MENA
In a place that seems so Arabic, with its tents and lanterns and piped-in oud music, it is surprising to see a joint of beef swimming in barbecue sauce and a chicken stir fry on the buffet. Still, while the food might seem a little confused, it is consistently tasty. Feast on the exhaustive selections of cold meze (particularly the rough and punchy *mutabbal*) while gaping up at the Burj Dubai.

Fire & Ice

Raffles Dubai, Oud Metha (314 9888). **Open** 7pm-midnight daily. **Average** Dhs500-Dhs600. **Credit** AmEx, MC, V. **Map** p297 J3 **15** Steakhouse

CONSUME

Coconut Grove. *See p113.*

Fire & Ice has a mighty reputation in the city, and its prices are set to match, but it's also known for its tasty steaks. The fillet is, as expected, exquisite, although perhaps not worth the outlay. There are definitely better cuts in Dubai for fewer dirhams, but the atmosphere and charm go some way to softening the pricey experience.

▶ *Raffles Dubai is one of the city's top hotels. For more about it, see p86.*

Fish Basket
10th Street, Oud Metha (336 7177). **Open** 10am-1am daily. **Average** Dhs250-Dhs350. **Credit** AmEx, MC, V. Unlicensed. **Map** p297 J3 ⑯ **Seafood**
At Fish Basket, diners can either choose their own fish from the market or be guided by the knowledgeable staff. Either way, it's clean, cheap and guaranteed to hit the spot. It's not the place for a long lingering lunch or date, but dirham for dirham, the Fish Basket is a great bet.

Dhs Gazebo
Trade Centre Road (359 8555). **Open** noon-3.15pm, 7-11.45pm daily. **Average** Dhs100-Dhs200. **Credit** AmEx, MC, V. Unlicensed. **Map** p301 G6 ⑰ **Indian & Pakistani**
Although not a romantic dining spot, Gazebo still manages to fuel passions. Fans of the intimate, independently owned establishment hail it as the city's best Indian restaurant. Whether it truly reigns supreme is debatable, but one thing is for certain: Gazebo dishes up some brilliant curries. As the food focuses on dishes from Lucknow and Hyderabad, you'd be better off skipping the well-worn *sag paneers* and opting instead for the *achari gosht*, made up of buttery chunks of lamb in a tamarind, fennel and sun-dried tomato sauce.

Govinda's
Behind Regent Palace Hotel Karama (396 0088). **Open** noon-3pm, 7pm-midnight Sat-Thur; 1.30-3pm, 7pm-midnight Fri. **Average** Dhs50. **Credit** AmEx, MC, V. Unlicensed. **Map** p299 J5 ⑱ **Indian & Pakistani**
This Indian vegetarian restaurant has branches around the world, adhering to staunch practices that ensure culinary purity. Such is the popularity of this Karama favourite, you'll need to battle with the city's Indian community to get a table. Don't expect much when it comes to decor, but do expect great food. Try the yellow dhal with spinach; it's satisfyingly wholesome. The ice-cream is also good– sugar free and 100 per cent natural.

Hukama
The Address, Burj Dubai Boulevard, Downtown Burj (436 8888). **Open** 5pm-midnight daily. **Average** Dhs550-Dhs650. **Credit** AmEx, MC, V. **Map** p296 H5 ⑲ **Chinese**
Hukama's design is so immaculate it feels like you're inside an architect's blueprints. This is thanks in no small part to a window that presents one of the city's most spectacular views of the Burj Dubai. The Chinese waitresses float along in beautiful silk gowns and many of the dishes are delightful. Hukama fills several of the city's niches. It has the view and, although there are a few upmarket Chinese restaurants that compete on the food front, not many are as reasonably priced.

▶ *For more on the Address, see p105.*

Dhs Iranian Club
Oud Metha Road (336 7700). **Open** 12.30-3.30pm, 8-10pm daily. **Average** Dhs100-Dhs200. **Credit** AmEx, MC, V. Unlicensed. **Map** p297 J3 ⑳ **MENA**

CONSUME

Outside Persia, you can't get more Tehran than this. As evidence, consider the dramatic sounds of the *kamancheh* (a stringed instrument) and the requirement that all women don a provided veil. The food is just as authentic, as its popularity among Iranians testifies. The salad buffet opener is a must, with some of the best houmous in Dubai.

Iz

Grand Hyatt Dubai (317 1234/www.hyatt.com). **Open** 12.30-3pm, 7pm-2am daily. **Average** Dhs500-Dhs600. **Credit** AmEx, MC, V. **Map** p297 K3 ㉑ **Indian**
Iz does high-end Indian tapas in fashionable, modern surroundings. One strong example of the Iz concept is the prawn masala, a smouldering, cumin-infused gravy coating plump prawns. Most dishes are baked in the tandoor, allowing the meat and vegetables to breathe. Individual dishes do feel expensive for their portion size, but this is an excellent opportunity for fans of Indian food to mix and match flavours.

★ Keva

Al Nasr Leisureland, Oud Metha (334 4159). **Open** 11am-3am daily. **Average** Dhs300. **Credit** AmEx, MC, V. **Map** p297 J3 ㉒ **Indian**
Diners arriving at Keva are presented with a single page of judiciously selected Punjabi gems by enthusiastic staff who praise the virtues of each dish. The selection of starters is limited, but the mains are excellent, and encourage overindulgence, and the atmosphere is buzzy. Highly recommended.

★ Khan Murjan

Wafi, Oud Metha (324 4555). **Open** 10am-11.30pm daily. **Average** Dhs250-Dhs350. **Credit** AmEx, MC, V. Unlicensed. **Map** p297 J3 ㉓ **MENA**
Khan Murjan strives for authenticity and nine times out of ten, it achieves it. Set in a 14th-century themed indoor souk – the folks at Wafi have done an excellent job of evoking an ancient Baghdad bazaar – the place is a regular hangout for locals. Be prepared for huge portions and Arabic charm aplenty. Arabic music, played by three Syrian musicians, helps create the atmosphere that makes the Khan Murjan Restaurant a great dining destination.

Khazana

Al Nasr Leisureland, Oud Metha (336 0061). **Open** 12.30-2.30pm, 7-11.30pm daily. **Average** Dhs300-Dhs400. **Credit** AmEx, MC, V. **Map** p297 J3 ㉔ **Indian & Pakistani**
Celebrity chef Sanjeev Kapoor's Khazana is a great family restaurant thanks to its mild but tasty curries. The cane furniture creates a relaxed atmosphere and the waiters are a friendly bunch. The Masala popadoms are a cracking start to a delicious meal, in which hints of chilli in the dishes are more a friendly pat on the back than a weighty punch.

Dhs Lan Kwai Fong

Opposite Mövenpick Hotel, Oud Metha (335 3680). **Open** 11.30am-3.30pm, 6.30-11.30pm daily. **Average** Dhs100-Dhs200. **Credit** AmEx, MC, V. Unlicensed. **Map** p297 J3 ㉕ **Chinese**
Lan Kwai Fong's setting, not far from the Mövenpick Hotel, is a far cry from its namesake, the busy area of Hong Kong famous for its bars and rowdy spirit. From the outside it doesn't look like much – a dark canteen at a guess – but inside, it appears authentic and a largely Chinese clientele suggests this doesn't end with the decor. The half crispy duck is a shrewd bet.

Latino House

Al Murooj Rotana (321 1111). **Open** 7-11.30pm daily. **Average** Dhs500-Dhs600. **Credit** AmEx, MC, V. **Map** p303 F13 ㉖ **Latin American**
Latino House has an intimate setting away from the construction and everyday hustle of the city, and the food and service are equally impressive. Request a table outside on the terrace and you can look up at the stars. Mexican staples such as tacos and burritos are available, but it might be better to kick things off with the tapas selection. The chilli shrimp is an excellent main course.

Dhs Lemongrass

Oud Metha (334 2325). Taxi: next to Lamcy Plaza. **Open** noon-11.15pm daily. **Average** Dhs100-Dhs200. **Credit** AmEx, MC, V. Unlicensed. **Map** p297 J3 ㉗ **Southeast Asian**
Lemongrass is one of the city's most popular Thai restaurants. The place has a welcoming, casual ambience, making it a good choice for lunch and dinner. The restaurant has the air of a cosy café, with wicker chairs, black and white photos of Thai countryside and multilevel seating, allowing diners privacy even when the place is packed – as it regularly is. Fortunately, the staff seem used to this and don't forget about you. *Photo p117.*

Mango Tree

Souk Al Bahar, Downtown Burj Dubai (426 7313). **Open** 12.30pm-midnight daily. **Average** Dhs550-Dhs650. **Credit** AmEx, MC, V. **Map** p296 H5 ㉘ **Southeast Asian**

INSIDE TRACK
TIPPING

Most restaurants in Dubai add a ten per cent gratuity to the bill. As a result, it is not necessary to add anything when you pay. However, it is considered polite, especially in upscale restaurants, to add an extra five to ten per cent if the service has been good.

Palatable

Spoil your taste buds with a treasure chest of dining options at **Kempinski Hotel Mall of the Emirate**
Dabble in a collage of treats and snacks at **Aspen**, or take your appetites on a joyride with **Sezzan**
colourful cuisine. If elegance and fine dining are what your palates crave, look no further than t
impeccable menu at **K Grill***. A trinity of tantalising experiences, **Mosaic Chill**, **Evory Lounge** and **1897 B**
offer you mellow settings along with premium delicacies and beverages.

*Opening Summer 2009

P.O. Box 120679 • Dubai • United Arab Emirates
Tel +971 4 409 5999 • Fax +971 4 341 4500
restaurants.mallofeemirates@kempinski.com • www.kempinski-dubai.com

global hotel alliance   KEMPINSKI - A COLLECTION OF INDIVIDUALS

With competition from the Address hotel, restaurants at Souk Al Bahar tend to be empty. As a result, the staff tend to hover over your every move. Although the hovering can be exhausting, it's still a likeable place. The decor is seriously hip: the middle of the room has a giant Buddha statue, and the long, winding restaurant culminates in a massive room housing 1,000 bottles of wine. The restaurant also serves up a mean, green free-range chicken curry.

Manhattan Grill
Grand Hyatt Dubai (324 4445). **Open** 12.30-3pm, 7-11.30pm Sat-Wed; 12.30-3pm, 7pm-1am Thur, Fri. **Average** Dhs1,000-Dhs1,500. **Credit** AmEx, MC, V. **Map** p297 K3 ㉙ **Steakhouse**
Wander past the indoor rainforest in the Grand Hyatt, and you'll find a classy, sedate restaurant serving up some of the most succulent steaks in town. There's not a lot of atmosphere, but it has appeal thanks to its friendly, attentive staff. Steak is the main attraction, although there are fish and vegetarian options as well. Meat-eaters can choose from various cuts, including the esteemed wagyu, and tailor it to their specification by selecting a piquant sauce, creamy mash or crunchy chips.
▶ *The Grand Hyatt Dubai really is pretty grand. For more, see p86.*

★ Dhs Manvaar
20B Street, Karama (336 8332). **Open** noon-3pm, 7pm-midnight daily. **Average** Dhs100-Dhs200. **Credit** AmEx, MC, V. Unlicensed. **Map** p297 J3 ㉚ **Indian & Pakistani**
Manvaar isn't simply good, it's downright amazing. The restaurant is a dark, intimate room, plastered with intricately embroidered linens. It specialises in Rajasthani food – a region of Indian cuisine that is underrepresented in Dubai. The menu challenges you to take risks, and you should, as each new flavour proves a revelation.

Medzo
Wafi (324 4100). **Open** 12.30-3pm, 7.30-11.30pm daily. **Average** Dhs650-Dhs850. **Credit** AmEx, MC, V. **Map** p297 J3 ㉛ **Italian**
The setting at Medzo is rich and moody – soft leather chairs and trendy fittings grace the interior, and pergolas and Wafi-style hieroglyphics await outside. Service is easygoing but slick, and the menu is engaging without being long-winded. The antipasti here are worth lingering over. Pasta and mains are thoroughly dependable; highlights include langoustines with pork belly confit and monkfish wrapped in pancetta.

Dhs Mezza House
Yasoon Building, Downtown Burj Dubai (420 5444/www.mezzahouse.com). Taxi: opposite the Address. **Open** noon-1am daily. **Average** Dhs200-Dhs300. **Credit** AmEx, MC, V. **Map** p303 F15 ㉜ **MENA**
Mezza House is worth seeking out for outstanding Levantine cuisine. The restaurant has a casual, neighbourly vibe and it's staffed by some of Dubai's friendliest waiters. Your mind may boggle at the array of dishes native to Jordan, Syria, Lebanon and Palestine, but the waiters are more than happy to explain what each entails. Meze staples are done extremely well, and the specialities are even better. Bear in mind that if you want to order a Palestinian-Jordanian *mashawi* main course, you need to phone and order it the day before.

Mizaan
Monarch Dubai, Sheikh Zayed Road (501 8888). **Open** 6.30-11am, noon-3pm, 6-11pm daily. **Average** Dhs250-Dhs350. **Credit** AmEx, MC, V. **Map** p301 G9 ㉝ **MENA**
Prices are high at this Arabic staple, serving an international à la carte menu and range of buffets, yet all dishes are artfully presented and expertly delivered by attentive staff. Highlights include the

CONSUME

Lemongrass. *See p115.*

Ravi Restaurant.

Organic Food & Café
The Greens, Sheikh Zayed Road (361 7974).
Open 8am-8pm daily. *Store* 8am-9pm daily.
Brunch 11am-3.30pm Fri, Sat. **Average**
Dhs200-Dhs300. **Credit** AmEx, MC, V.
Unlicensed. **Map** p304 C2 **36** Café
The setting, a tag-on to the organic supermarket,
may not be the most glam in Dubai, but it doesn't
matter. The food speaks for itself and the owner's
passion for healthy, organic chow shines through in
succulent meats, fresh veg and nutritious salads.
The brunch buffet is an excellent opportunity to
sample a bit of everything. From all-day breakfasts,
including a huge brie and apple omelette, to a variety of organic pizzas, this is a boon for the health
conscious and people who appreciate real food.
Other locations Satwa (368 9410).

Dhs Pars Iranian Restaurant
Satwa (398 4000). Taxi: behind Satwa
roundabout, beside Rydges Plaza. **Open**
7pm-1am daily. **Average** Dhs200-Dhs300.
Credit AmEx, MC, V. Unlicensed. **Map**
p301 F8 **37** MENA
Though there are branches of Pars throughout the
city (including a new fast food variant at the Dubai
Mall), the original Satwa outpost is particularly
magnetic. The all-outdoors venue may be a bit chal-
lenging during the summer months, but for the rest
of the year, the semi-private carpeted platforms give
the place a certain romance. Once you've settled into
your elevated cubbyhole, it's time to dine on some
of the best kebabs in town.
Other locations Beside Al Mullah Plaza
(296 8990); Dubai Mall (no number); Mall of
the Emirates (341 1666); Trade Centre
Roundabout (398 8787).

Dhs Ravi Restaurant
Satwa (331 5353). Taxi: near Rydges Plaza.
Open 5am-3am daily. **Average** Dhs1-Dhs50.
No credit cards. Unlicensed. **Map** p301 F8 **38**
Indian & Pakistani
Ravi Restaurant is best visited in the early hours,
when the wipe-clean outdoor tables are bustling
with boisterous groups. The menu is long and
includes many familiar generic Punjabi dishes, but
there are some treats: try the *haleem,* a slow-cooked
dish of wheat, lentils and meat (usually lamb) with
the consistency of porridge, or the *nihari,* slow-
cooked beef so tender it falls from the bone. It's popular with a range of people from Pakistani cabbies
to wealthy NRIs (non-resident Indians) shouting at
each other in American accents. Best of all, the cooking is excellent, and the prices low.

Switch
Dubai Mall (04 339 9131). **Open** 10am-10pm
Sun-Wed; 10am-midnight Thur, Fri. **Average**
Dhs350. **Credit** AmEx, MC, V. Unlicensed.
Map p296 H5 **39** **International**

pumpkin soup and a main of moist chicken strips,
surrounded by artichokes and onions. The restaurant opens out into the sophisticated main lobby and
although it suffers the same difficulty as dozens of
restaurants in Dubai in the same situation – its
atmosphere gets sucked out into the reception area's
high ceilings – the food makes up for it.

★ Noble House
Raffles Dubai (314 8888). **Open** 7-11.30pm daily.
Average Dhs1,200-Dhs1,300. **Credit** AmEx,
MC, V. **Map** p297 J3 **34** Chinese
Noble House is one of the most original Chinese dining concepts we've seen, and it serves some of the
best food in the city. However, it also produces some
rather plain, overpriced dishes. Granted, black truffle dumplings, a wagyu pancake and some of the
most succulent lamb ribs we've ever tried warrant
paying a few hundred dirhams, but the same can't
be said for average stir-fry noodles and lacklustre
lobster. Still, the setting is amazing, and there's a
definite sense of ceremony that comes with the meal.

Options
World Trade Convention Centre (329 3293).
Open noon-3pm, 7-11.30pm daily. **Average**
Dhs350-Dhs450. **Credit** AmEx, MC, V. **Map**
p301 G9 **35** **Indian & Pakistani**
Options, Indian celebrity chef Sanjeev Kapoor's
Dubai HQ, serves up posh curry in giddily decorated
surroundings. But the food is the main reason to visit,
and the presence of so many Indian diners is testa-
ment to its quality. Try the spinach kofta stuffed
with *malai paneer* (balls of rubbery Indian cheese).
It's the gravy that gives the dish a distinctive flavour,
as honey sweetness meets tomato tang.

CONSUME

There's no doubt that Switch's interior is breathtaking – would you expect any less from a restaurant designed by Karim Rashid? The smooth, undulating plastic wall is worth a trip to the Dubai Mall alone. Unfortunately, the food doesn't really inspire as much as the decor. Still, for a juice and a coffee, and a peek at some of Dubai's most interesting interior design, it's worth popping in to Switch.

Thiptara

The Palace, The Old Town (428 7961). Taxi: Downtown Burj Dubai. **Open** 7pm-midnight daily. **Average** Dhs500-Dhs600. **Credit** AmEx, MC, V. **Map** pp303 F14 ④ **Southeast Asian**

A walk across the Palace hotel's breathtaking grounds leads you to Thiptara. 'The magic at the water' overlooks the hotel's swimming pool at the base of the mighty Burj Dubai. The dishes' price tags are equally awe-inspiring – unless you go for the set menu, at around Dhs250 per person. Lay down the gauntlet, and plate after bowl will arrive – filled with increasingly satisfying fare.

Troyka

Ascot Hotel (352 0900). Taxi: Bank Street, Bur Dubai. **Open** 12.30-2.45pm, 8pm-2.45am daily. **Average** Dhs300-Dhs400. **Credit** AmEx, MC, V. **Map** p298 H4 ④ **Russian**

This is a great place for a big group of friends to go for a lively night out. Just don't bother arriving much before 11pm, as the restaurant will be empty, and the entertainment – which comes in the form of a hilarious Russian cabaret – starts at around 10.30pm. Forget ordering a glass of house wine, as your table will be sharing a bottle of vodka. Don't expect culinary delights – just expect an entertaining show and you'll leave happy.

XVA Café

Bur Dubai, Al Fahidi Street (353 5383). Taxi: Bastakia historic quarter. **Open** 9am-7pm Sat-Thur. **Average** Dhs50-Dhs150. **Credit** AmEx, MC, V. Unlicensed. **Map** p298 H3/H4 ④ **Café**

XVA Café is worth a visit for its tranquil, old-world charm, the galleries off to the side and a glass of its

Zuma. *See p121.*

Brought to you by Raymond Visan, The creator of Buddha-Bar

AN EXPERIENCE IN ITSELF

Soak in the opulent ambience, enjoy the delicious flavors of an asian fusion bistrot, relax to the rhytmic sounds of the karma kafe collection performed by our resident DJ Ralph K., and be wowed by one of the world's largest fountains

TIMING
Weekdays
Sat - Wed 12:00 noon till 2:00 am
Weekends
Thu - Fri: 12:00 noon till 3:00 am

Souk Al Bahar,Level 3, Downtown Burj Dubai
For Reservations, contact +971 4 423 09 09 - Fax:+971 4 423 09 90
website: www.karma-kafe.com / email: info@karma-kafe.com

famously refreshing mint lemonade. It can get busy with shoppers and amblers from the nearby Souk Al Bastakia flea market (open during the winter on Saturdays), which, unfortunately, can lead to a jostle for tables. The freshly-made houmous deserves special mention. If you can put up with the bad service, it makes for a very pleasant afternoon indeed.

★ Zuma

DIFC, Gate Village 6 (425 5660). **Open** noon-3pm, 7pm-midnight daily. **Average** Dhs700-Dhs800. **Credit** AmEx, MC, V. **Map** p296 H4 ❹ **Japanese**

At the ultra-hip Zuma, the modernist brass tones, and chilled out trance all seem stamped with the words, 'Exclusive: hoi polloi, do not enter'. You would assume the staff would be the pinnacle of snootiness, and yet they're warm and unpretentious. Alongside its contemporary Japanese fare, Zuma offers the staples like sushi and tempura. The bill is high, but for fine dining it isn't tear-inducing. *Photo p119.*

DEIRA

Ashiana

Sheraton Dubai Creek Hotel & Towers (228 1111). **Open** 12.30-3.30pm, 7.30pm-1.30am Sat-Thur; 7.30pm-1.30am Fri. **Average** Dhs200-Dhs300. **Credit** AmEx, MC, V. **Map** p299 K4 ❹ **Indian & Pakistani**

One of the best Indian restaurants in the city. The staff are attentive, knowledgeable and have personality – something often lost in hotel restaurants. The food is superb: perfectly cooked meat, creamy yet spicy sauces, fragrant rice and buttery naans.

Aquarium

Dubai Creek Golf & Yacht Club (295 6000). **Open** noon-3pm, 7pm-midnight daily. **Average** Dhs500-Dhs600. **Credit** AmEx, MC, V. **Map** p297 K3 ❹ **Seafood**

A visit to Aquarium remains a delight. A starter of crab cakes is light and delicate, another of scallops is fresh and yielding. Round things off with the trio of crème brûlée correctly prepared with the requisite firm, sugary crust and unctuous interior.

Bistro Madeleine

InterContinental, Al Rebat Street, Dubai Festival City (701 1111). **Open** 8am-midnight daily. **Average** Dhs400-Dhs500. **Credit** AmEx, MC, V. **Map** p297 L3 ❹ **Café**

This tiny bistro serves excellent – if simple – food. Unfortunately, the restaurant can be inconsistent. One evening might produce an expertly cooked grilled salmon, but on another night the same fish is a tad dry. The French toast breakfast may have you in raptures on one visit; go back the next week, and it might be cut too thickly and served without accoutrements. Still, by and large, the cooking here is good, and so are the prices.

Bombay

Marco Polo Hotel (272 0000). **Open** 12.30-2.30pm, 7.30pm-12.30am daily. **Average** Dhs200-Dhs300. **Credit** AmEx, MC, V. **Map** p299 K2 ❹ **Indian & Pakistani**

The service at this out-of-the-way Indian restaurant is attentive, though the decor has a shabby 1970s feel to it. The food is good, but not the best in Dubai. Fish is a speciality, and highlights include the *lahsooni* fish tikka – thick chunks of soft, tandoori-baked hammour coated in a garlic marinade. Portions are large, so you're not likely to have room for dessert, which is just as well since the sweets are fairly standard. Good value for money.

★ Café Chic

Le Méridien Dubai (282 4040). **Open** 12.30-2.45pm, 8-11.45pm daily. **Credit** AmEx, MC, V. **Average** Dhs600-Dhs700. **Map** p297 L2 ❹ **French**

The bourgeois decor smacks of France and the food could rival any café in Paris. The attentive – at times overly so – waiters spring into action. Dishes are served with true Gallic sass: silver domes unveil wafts of crustacean jus, frog's legs and snails. The roasted guinea fowl is divine, and the succulent *sole meunière* is enough to transport diners to the meandering alleys of Montmartre.

China Club

Radisson Blu Hotel, Deira Creek (205 7333). **Open** 12.30-3.30pm, 7-11.30pm daily. **Average** Dhs400-Dhs500. **Credit** AmEx, MC, V. **Map** p299 J3 ❹ **Chinese**

The China Club's interior has a sort of world-worn charm, and the homely food is excellent. Although it's perfectly acceptable to dine out at this bastion of traditional Chinese fare in the evening, the daytime *yum cha* is where the restaurant makes its mark. The *yum cha* is served every day, but on Fridays the vibe is more convivial.

★ Dhs China Sea

Al Maktoum Street, Deira (295 9816). **Open** 11am-1am daily. **Average** Dhs250-Dhs350. **Credit** AmEx, MC, V. Unlicensed. **Map** p299 K3 ❺ **Chinese**

Chinese expats rave about China Sea, and so when you enter the large café you will expect the moon on a chopstick. The descriptions next to each dish are vague, so you're better off pointing to various plates and seeing what the cooks come up with. The results are mesmerising. One word of warning: the portions at China Sea are big, and meant for sharing, so it's best to come with a large group.

Epicure

Desert Palm, Al Awir Road, International City (323 8888). **Open** 7am-11pm daily. **Average** Dhs400-Dhs500. **Credit** AmEx, MC, V. **International**

CONSUME

Finding Epicure is like biting into a delicious chocolate and finding an even tastier caramel centre. The setting – alongside polo pitches and palm trees – is everything most of central Dubai is not: relaxing, verdant and tasteful. The food demonstrates that Epicure's expertise extends beyond the realms of the New York deli: sweet red snapper is admirably moist, and the delicious authenticity of a Singaporean staple of flat-fried noodles on a menu characterised by geographical cherry picking confirms the chef's skill.

Focaccia

Hyatt Regency Dubai (209 1234). **Open** 12.30-3.30pm, 7-11.30pm daily. **Average** Dhs250-Dhs350. **Credit** AmEx, MC, V. **Map** p299 J1 (51) **Italian**

The mezzanine level of the Hyatt Regency is not the first place you would think to find an authentic Italian restaurant, but the food here is surprisingly good, and there's an uninterrupted view over the creek to boot. The interior of Foccacia is a touch too faux Italia, but it doesn't detract from the deliciousness of well-made pasta dishes like gnocchi, veal tortellini and crispy ciabatta, served with roasted garlic.

Glasshouse

Hilton Dubai Creek (227 1111). **Open** 7am-midnight daily. **Average** Dhs400-Dhs500. **Credit** AmEx, MC, V. **Map** p299 L4 (52) **International**

Perhaps the link to its fine-dining, Gordon Ramsay-owned neighbour Verre has influenced the food for the better. Given the high quality of the food at Glasshouse, the bill at the end of the night is surprisingly low. The mussels make a hearty and comforting main course. Lovers of pork belly are also in for a treat, as the variant here is meltingly delicate. Friday brunches are also a popular option, as are the Monday drink deals (Dhs10 per drink when you order two courses).

Golestan

Hilton Dubai Creek (227 1111). **Open** 7am-midnight daily. **Average** Dhs400-Dhs500. **Credit** AmEx, MC, V. **Map** p299 J1 (53) **MENA**

Stuck in backstreet Garhoud, Golestan deserves more attention than it gets. It might feel a bit like a cave in the banquet-hall back room, but this is some of the cheapest and most flavourful Persian food around. Popular with locals and Iranian expats, the back room has a persistent shisha haze. The thick, almost meaty *mirza ghasemi* stands out as some of the city's finest – chunks of tasty aubergine flamed with a steamy medley of tomatoes: mopped up nicely with bread fresh from the tandoor.

Kiku

Le Méridien Dubai (282 4040). **Open** 12.30-2.30pm, 6.30-11pm daily. **Average** Dhs350-Dhs450. **Credit** AmEx, MC, V. **Map** p297 L2 (54) **Japanese**

There's always a healthy contingent of Japanese businessmen in attendance at Kiku. Follow their lead when it comes to choosing from the extensive menu. We're big fans of the seafood salads and bowls of soup. The marinated cod is small but good, full of flavour and light as a feather.

More Café.

Kisaku

Al Khaleej Palace Hotel, Deira (223 1000).
Open noon-2.30pm, 7-11pm daily. **Average**
Dhs400-Dhs500. **Credit** AmEx, MC, V. **Map**
p299 K3 ⑤ **Japanese**
Kisaku is one of Dubai's best Japanese restaurants.
The grey, mirrored bistro is a whirl of activity,
packed with animated Japanese businessmen drinking sake and having a great time while sumo competitions play on TV. As far as the food is concerned,
the Don menu of assorted sashimi is a great place to
start. Seven fat pieces of nigiri come gorgeously gar-
nished with spring onions and ginger, and taste
heavenly. The hotate scallops lord it over the teppanyaki menu, and the well-textured bean curd salad
is full of tasty vegetables.

Handi

Taj Palace Hotel, Deira (223 2222). Taxi:
between Al Maktoum Street & Al Rigga Road.
Open noon-3.30pm, 7-11.30pm daily. **Average**
Dhs250-Dhs350. **Credit** AmEx, MC, V. **Map**
p299 L3 ⑤ **Indian & Pakistani**
Handi serves up tasty northern-Indian cuisine, but
unless you live in Deira it's no longer worth facing
the Dubai traffic for. People who live nearby will
find a tabla player and singer at work, and a slightly
disjointed layout. Take a table by the open kitchen,
however, and you'll feel like the place has a bit of a
buzz. Order the dhal Handi with black lentils, a buttery dish, and the fresh okra masala, both great as
an accompaniment or for vegetarians.

JW's Steakhouse

JW Marriott Dubai, Deira (607 7977). **Open**
12.30-3.30pm, 7.30-11pm daily. **Average**
Dhs500-Dhs600. **Credit** AmEx, MC, V.
Map p297 K1 ⑤ **Steakhouse**
This distinguished steakhouse is a Dubai institution. Everything about the restaurant screams old-
fashioned quality. Freed of the need to innovate or
deliver a modern twist on old classics, JW's serves
simple steaks and baked potatoes to a very high
standard. The masterstroke, however, is that it manages this without becoming stuffy or snobbish.

Miyako

Hyatt Regency Dubai (317 2222). **Open** 12.30-
3.30pm, 7.30pm-midnight daily. **Average**
Dhs350-Dhs450. **Credit** AmEx, MC, V.
Map p299 J1 ⑤ **Japanese**
Humming with devotees until the wee hours, this
intimate Japanese restaurant is, without doubt, the
genuine article. The exhaustive menu is filled with
authentic specialities not offered in many other
Dubai restaurants. A highlight among the starters,
the tasty chilled spinach comes in a tower, basking
in tempura-style sauce. But Miyako made its name
in sushi. The rainbow roll, a six-piece circle of tuna,
salmon and hammour wrapped over coils of barbe-
cued eel, jumps with texture and taste.

Eating on the Cheap

Food without an expense account.

Foreigners associate Dubai with over-the-
top decadence, and although it's true
that a lot of the eating out scene takes
place in hotels, some of the city's best
restaurants are tucked away on side
streets in bustling neighbourhoods like
Bur Dubai and Deira. In these areas, it's
possible to feast for as little as Dhs10.
For some excellent, inexpensive curries,
head to **Ravi Restaurant** (*see p118*) for
the *haleem*, a slow-cooked dish of wheat,
lentils and meat (usually lamb) the
consistency of porridge. For something
on the go, head to Diyafa Street in Satwa
for a *shwarma*, Dubai's answer to street
food. For Dhs5, you can feast on a
drooling lamb sandwich from **Al Mallah**
(*see p111*). Or you could join the rank
of Indian expats, and pop into **Bombay
Chowpatty** (*see p113*) to experiment
with Indian snack food (the *puris* –
fried bread – are the way to go here).

For a slightly more upmarket (yet no
more bank busting) dining foray, many of
the restaurants lining Karama Park have
excellent, cheap Indian food. **Calicut
Paragon** (*see p113*), which specialises in
the cuisine of Kerala in India's south,
has a rich, inexpensive, fish curry. In the
cooler months, **Pars Iranian Restaurant**
(*see p118*) is a wonderfully atmospheric
spot for grilled fish and Persian kebabs.

Some inexpensive restaurants aren't
just as good, but better than their more
expensive counterparts. **Lemongrass**
(*see p115*) is touted by some as the
best Thai in the city, and **China Sea**
(*see p121*), a Deira-based Chinese
restaurant that draws a large crowd,
easily has the freshest, most authentic
food this side of Beijing.

More Café

Gold & Diamond Park, near Mall of the
Emirates, Sheikh Zayed Road (04 323
4350/www.morecafe.biz). **Open** 7am-11pm
daily. **Average** Dhs200-Dhs300. **Credit**
MC, V. Unlicensed. **Map** p304 E2 ⑤ **Café**
The eggs Benedict is superb here, and the salads and
sandwiches do the trick. The pumpkin, feta and
spinach salad is a favourite with vegetarians and
comes dripping in a thick and nicely tart dressing.
The fillet steak with peppercorn sauce is always
good. Alternatively, try one of the enormous sandwiches, or a vat of soup with thick crusty bread. Be

CONSUME

warned, however, that More really does live up to its name – all of the portions, from starters to main courses to desserts, are huge.

Other locations Al Marooj Rotana (343 3779); Garhoud (283 0224).

★ Quattro
Four Seasons Golf Club, Festival City (601 0101). **Open** 7pm-midnight Tue-Sun. **Average** Dhs800-Dhs900. **Credit** AmEx, MC, V. **Map** p297 L3 ⑥⓪ **Italian**

Setting, service and food combine to create a genuine sense of occasion at Quattro, a restaurant determined to maintain its standing near the pinnacle of Dubai's food scene. Quattro is surrounded by a swathe of green space, courtesy of the Four Seasons Golf Club and its huge artificial lake. Although mostly from the north of Italy, the food on offer is wide-ranging, and often inspired.

★ Rare
Desert Palm (323 8888). **Open** 6.30pm-midnight daily. **Average** Dhs900-Dhs1,000. **Credit** AmEx, MC, V. **Steakhouse**

Rare is an exemplary haven for aficionados of steak. From the offset things look promising, as you're ushered through the cool, dark and minimalist interior of the dining area and out onto the balcony with a view of polo fields. It's also refreshing to see a restaurant specialise in game (pigeon and guinea foul make for excellent starters). The place is beautifully conceived, just like everything else about this restaurant.

Rare.

★ Reflets Par Pierre Gagnaire
InterContinental, Dubai Festival City (701 1111). **Open** 7-11pm daily. **Average** Dhs1,900-Dhs2,000. **Credit** AmEx, MC, V. **Map** p297 L3 ⑥① **European**

Reflets is the latest restaurant in a string of international hits by six-time Michelin-starred French chef Pierre Gagnaire. Blanketed with lush purple carpet, and with pink chandeliers flanking mirror-lined walls, it's like the inside of a jewellery box. Gagnaire is heavily involved with the menu, and it shows. The food is some of the best in Dubai, and though it's a pricey restaurant, you do get your money's worth.
► *For more on the InterContinental, see p97.*

Rivington Grill
Souk Al Bahar, Downtown Burj Dubai (423 0903). **Open** noon-11pm daily. **Average** Dhs500-Dhs600. **Credit** AmEx, MC, V. **Map** p296 H5 ⑥② **Steakhouse**

Step into Rivington Grill and you will have the strangest sensation that you have accidentally stumbled through a portal; one that drops you slap bang in the middle of London. The restaurant's philosophy is simple: seasonal British fare, served well and without pomp. A knowledgeable staff member is always a nod away from meeting any request or

CONSUME

Al Mahara.

CONSUME

answering any question. Even with the Burj Dubai glistening a stone's throw away, Rivington Grill is one of the best escapes in the emirate.

Sakura
Taj Palace Hotel, between Al Maktoum Street & Al Rigga Road, Deira (223 2222). **Open** 11.30am-2.30pm, 7pm-midnight daily. **Average** Dhs250-Dhs350. **Credit** AmEx, MC, V. **Map** p299 L3 ❻ **Japanese**
The interior at Sakura – minimalist design and comfortable furniture – serves as a welcome relief to the traffic in Deira. The food, too, is lovingly prepared and beautifully presented. Sushi and sashimi dishes are made in front of you by a skilled chef and the miso soup starters are as you'd expect – rich, flavoursome, and reasonably sized too.
Other locations Crowne Plaza, Sheik Zayed Road (800 276963).

Shabestan
Radisson Blu Hotel, Dubai Deira Creek (222 7171). **Open** 12.30-3pm, 7-11pm daily. **Average** Dhs350-Dhs450. **Credit** AmEx, MC, V. **Map** p299 J3 ❻ **MENA**
Shabestan is one of the best Iranian restaurants in Dubai. Kick things off with a couple of shared starters. The *nargesi* is outstanding – thinly chopped and entwined spinach that falls onto your fork and has a wholesome yet spicy flavor. Mains are fairly typical Persian kebabs, but the *kebab e soltani* – fillets of tangy lamb served with some of the finest mast we've tasted – is excellent, and comes with generously saffroned rice.

Sukhothai
Le Méridien Dubai, Garhoud (217 0000). Taxi: Airport Road. **Open** 12.30-2.45pm, 7.30-11.45pm daily. **Average** Dhs400-Dhs500. **Credit** AmEx, MC, V. **Map** p297 L2 ❻ **Southeast Asian**
Tucked away within the Méridien Airport's yellow brick road of restaurants, Sukhothai first impresses with its wood-heavy Asian oasis of an interior, and then even more so with the quality of its food. Although the menu initially appears overwhelming, the four set menus offer an easy and economical route out of the confusion. Our favourite is the 'royal Thai', which comprises a combination of seafood, vegetarian and meat dishes, including a particularly juicy mushroom dish and a scrumptious mango and sticky rice pudding.

Thai Kitchen
Park Hyatt Dubai Creek (602 1234). **Open** 7pm-midnight Sat-Thur; noon-4pm, 7pm-midnight Fri. **Average** Dhs400-Dhs500. **Credit** AmEx, MC, V. **Map** p297 K2/K3 ❻ **Southeast Asian**
Thai Kitchen is one of Dubai's most stylish Thai restaurants. It's in the chic creek-side Park Hyatt, and its relatively out-of-the-way location may mean you have only a handful of fellow diners during the week. But the thing that really sets Thai Kitchen apart is its sizzling open-plan kitchen – or, more specifically, the food that comes out of it. Served in petite bowls that emphasise their contents' delicate flavours, the cuisine is consistently light and tasteful.

Traiteur
Park Hyatt Dubai (602 1234). **Open** 12.30-3.30pm, 7pm-midnight daily. **Average** Dhs600-Dhs700. **Credit** AmEx, MC, V. **Map** p297 K2/K3 ❻ **European**
Overlooking the creek and nestled in beneath the Park Hyatt, Traiteur is a feast for the eyes. The menu – cleverly divided into all the major food groups – is quite ballsy in its approach, with blue fin tuna vying for attention with beef tenderloin and seafood platters offering every mollusc under the sea. Although Traiteur has been the reserve of business folk in the past, this kitsch hub – there's something 1980s New York about it – is fast becoming a spot for Dubai's bright young things.

★ Verre
Hilton Dubai Creek (227 1111). **Open** 7pm-midnight daily. **Average** Dhs1,000-Dhs1,200. **Credit** AmEx, MC, V. **Map** p299 J1 ❻ **European**
It's lucky people come to Gordon Ramsay's restaurant for the food, as the staid surroundings are at best functional, at worst offputting. The French fare, though, is good enough to continue pulling in the crowds. Ramsay-trained executive chef Matt Pickop definitely has talent, and the service, like the food,

remains thoroughly competent. Melt-in-the-mouth duck and a refreshing mint crème brulee are particular high points, although many other dishes can render you speechless.

Vivaldi
Sheraton Dubai Creek Hotel & Towers, Deira (207 1717). **Open** 6.30-10.30am, noon-3pm, 7-11.30pm daily. **Credit** AmEx, MC, V. **Map** p299 K4 ❻ **Italian**
Vivaldi may be on the wrong side of the creek, but there are few better places to spend the evening than on the terrace of this long-serving Italian restaurant. Twinkling dhows glide past, pedestrians promenade on the waterfront below, and you get to enjoy some consistently competent Italian cuisine. Stand-out starters include pan-fried foie gras with roasted figs, and lashings of Jabugo ham sprinkled with rocket.

Yalumba
Le Méridien Dubai (282 4040). **Open** 5.30am-10.30am, 12.30-3pm, 7.30-11pm daily. *Brunch* 12.30-3.30pm Fri. **Average** Dhs200-Dhs300. *Brunch* Dhs429 including champagne and wine. **Credit** AmEx, MC, V. **Map** p297 L2 ❼ **International**
This Aussie restaurant reflects the cuisine of Down Under very well; part Southeast Asian, part seafood, part steakhouse. It's true to Australia in other ways too, as the sheen of urbane sophistication gives way to giddy young hoons dancing on table tops, usually by about 3pm. Good food, à la carte options and freely flowing bubbly.

JUMEIRAH

Al Mahara
Burj Al Arab (301 7600). **Open** 12.30-3pm, 7pm-midnight daily. **Average** Dhs1,500-Dhs1,600. **Credit** AmEx, MC, V. **Map** p304 E1 ❼ **Seafood**
The jewel in the Burj Al Arab's culinary crown is a combination of style and kitsch. For kitsch is the only word that can be applied to a dinner that begins with a ride in an 'underwater submarine'. The dining room, on the other hand, is sleek and inviting, starched tablecloths and plush seating set around a central, cylindrical floor-to-ceiling aquarium. Sadly, the food doesn't measure up. It's not that it's bad, it's just that, with a sweep of new restaurants headed up by internationally renowned chefs opening across Dubai, this venue has quite simply been outclassed.

Al Muntaha
Burj Al Arab, Jumeirah (301 7600). **Open** 12.30-3pm, 7pm-midnight daily. *Brunch* 10am-4pm Fri. **Average** Dhs1,900-Dhs2,000. **Credit** AmEx, MC, V. **Map** p304 E1 ❼ **European**
The ultimate in Dubai-style splurging has to be wolfing down Dhs595 wagyu steak on the 27th floor of the Burj Al Arab. It's hard to justify the prices.

Still, the service is superb and the decor is luxurious, if garish. The evening is consequently one of pure, unashamed decadence. Each dish is a masterpiece. However, like many works of art, these masterpieces can be bizarre. Damien Hirst would be impressed with the chef's tasting menu.

Beachcombers
Jumeirah Beach Hotel (406 8999). **Open** 7.30am-midnight daily. *Brunch* 12.30-4.30pm Fri. **Average** Dhs350-Dhs450. *Brunch* Dhs225 with Pimms; Dhs185 food only; Dhs60 children. **Credit** AmEx, MC, V. **Map** p304 E1 ❼ **Southeast Asian**
A roving magician and a children's den (PlayStations, DVDs, books, toys) ensure that this is a popular family spot. Arrive early to claim a table on the beachside terrace facing the Burj Al Arab. Indoors, the vibe's a little confused, with Polynesian beachshack decor, a band playing Latin sounds and cuisine hailing from Southeast Asia. But, somehow, it all falls together. *Photo p128.*

Michelin Parade

Haute cuisine in Dubai.

Gordon Ramsay was foresighted when he opened **Verre** (*see p126*), his first restaurant outside England and Dubai's first fine dining venture. In recent years, other celebrity chefs have joined him. Vineet Bhatia, the first Michelin-starred Indian, has elevated Indian cuisine with **Indego** (*see p135*). Of course, Gary Rhodes couldn't allow Ramsay to reign over Dubai's dining scene solo, so he came in 2007 and attached his name to **Rhodes Mezzanine** (*see p137*), bringing with him the best bread and butter pudding in Dubai.

Last year, with the opening of Atlantis on the Palm Jumeirah, four celebrity chefs joined the ranks: Japan's Nobu Matsuhisa (*see p135*), Spain's Santi Santamaria (*see p136*), Italy's Giorgio Locatelli (*see p137*) and France's Michel Rostang (*see p137*). However, French culinary mastermind Pierre Gagnaire stole the show with **Reflets Par Pierre Gagnaire** (*see p125*). The venue proved so elegant, and the food so awe-inspiring, that *Time Out Dubai* dubbed it the best restaurant in all of Dubai in the 2009 restaurant awards. In the next few years, Michel Roux, Jamie Oliver and Jean-George Vongerichten are all rumoured to be opening up their own establishments.

CONSUME

Beachcombers. *See p127.*

CONSUME

Flooka

Dubai Marine Beach Resort & Spa, Jumeirah Beach Road, Jumeirah (346 1111). **Open** 12.30-2.45pm, 7.30-11.45pm Sun-Thur; 12.30-11.45pm Fri, Sat. **Average** Dhs400-Dhs500. **Credit** AmEx, MC, V. **Map** p300 D9 **74** Seafood

With the stylish decor and a delicious array of seafood, you could almost pretend you're sailing aboard a luxury yacht. And it's not hard to imagine, thanks to all the pine decking, rope and the idyllic sea-view terrace. The people behind Flooka have done a fine job preparing seafood with a fresh, flavoursome Mediterranean twist: things like baby octopus, fat prawns and lime-drenched *samke nayeh*. Mop it all up with flatbread and Lebanese staples like houmous drizzled in olive oil and coarsely chopped tabbouleh, and you'll be singing a sea shanty in no time.

La Maison d'Hotes

Jumeirah 1, Street 83B (344 1838). **Open** 12.30-3.30pm, 8pm-midnight daily. **Average** Dhs100-Dhs200. **No credit cards**. Unlicensed. **Map** p302 C12 **75** European

La Maison d'Hotes is oddly sat in a guesthouse tucked away among a series of villas. In a city full of five-star hotels, it is surreal to come across a European-style bed-and-breakfast, complete with a restaurant, café and a quaint little gift shop. It's no wonder that La Maison holds such allure for the French nationals who frequently eat here. There are à la carte options and prix fixe dinners, meaning all three courses come out on the same tray – kind of like an upscale ready meal.

★ La Parrilla

Jumeirah Beach Hotel (348 0000). **Open** 6.30pm-midnight daily. **Average** Dhs900-Dhs1,000. **Credit** AmEx, MC, V. **Map** p304 E1 **76** Latin American

There's only one real reason people should come to La Parrilla, and that's for the steaks. A weighty slab of Angus beef tenderloin cooked medium-rare to perfection is no problem for the chefs, with the blackened, smoked exterior that slices open with ease to reveal tender pink flesh within. Service is also excellent; be sure to chat to Margarita, the warm and welcoming hostess. The chilli shrimps and crab meat gratinare two excellent starters, and the dark chocolate praline cake or Spanish-style coconut crème brûlée round things off nicely.

▶ *Just across the road from the Jumeirah Beach Hotel is the Wild Wadi waterpark; see p199.*

Lime Tree Café

Jumeirah Beach Road, near Jumeirah Mosque (349 8498). **Open** 7.30am-6pm daily. **Average** Dhs100-Dhs200. **Credit** AmEx, MC, V. **Map** p300 D9 **77** Café

This expat haunt is almost as iconic as the Burj Al Arab. The staples of the menu are famous – from the filling wraps, unique salads and delicious juices and smoothies to the notorious desserts (the huge chocolate brownie and carrot cake are enough to keep punters returning time and time again). The grub is a substantial cut above other cafés. All the ingredients are wholesome, tasty and imaginative, and palpably fresh.

Other locations Ibn Battuta Mall (366 9320).

Majlis Al Bahar

Burj Al Arab (301 7600). **Open** 12.30-2pm,
7pm-midnight daily according to weather.
Average Dhs700-Dhs800. **Credit** AmEx,
MC, V. **Map** p304 E1 **⑰ European**

A meal at the Burj Al Arab's beach restaurant is like
something torn from the pages of a Harlequin
romance novel, so it's a place worth saving for someone you want to impress. If he or she doesn't look at
you favourably after the beef fillet that disintegrates
on the tongue or the creamy tiramisu then you may
as well give up, the relationship isn't going anywhere. Still, if that's the case, at least it won't have
cost you nearly as much as the other restaurants in
the Burj Al Arab.
▶ *For more about the Burj Al Arab, see p101.*

Dhs Maria Bonita's Taco Shop

Um Al Sheif Street, Umm Suqeim (395 5576).
Open noon-11.30pm daily. **Average** Dhs50-
Dhs150. **Credit** AmEx, MC, V. Unlicensed.
Map p294 C2 **⑲ Latin American**

Maria Bonita's is one of those Dubai secrets that
only expats who have been here for years seem to
know about. It's not licensed, but order an alcohol-
free pina colada, take a seat outside, and chat to the
two caged parrots while munching on tortilla chips
and salsa. All of the tried and tested Mexican staples are here – tacos, burritos and quesadillas – and
they are all very good, well presented, with helpings
of salad, salsa, sour cream and refried beans, coupled with a homely kind of feel.
Other locations Green Community, near the
Courtyard Marriott (885 3188).

Marina Seafood Restaurant

*Jumeriah Beach Resort, below 360 nightclub
(348 0000).* **Open** 6pm-1am daily. **Average**
Dhs1,200-Dhs1,300. **Credit** AmEx, MC, V.
Map p304 E1 **㉚ Seafood**

It is a confident chef who knows when to meddle
with his ingredients and when to leave well alone,
which makes dining at Marina a pleasure. It also
goes a long way to make up for the dated decor.
Seafood is fresh, cooking inventive and service
immaculate. But a posh meal out (and at these prices,
that's what you're expecting) is about the whole
experience. Sadly, Marina falls a little short.

MJ's Steakhouse

Al Qasr, Madinat Jumeirah (366 6730). **Open**
7-11.30pm daily. **Average** Dhs1,000-Dhs1,200.
Credit AmEx, MC, V. **Map** p304 D1 **㉛
Steakhouse**

Expensive, but the steaks are great, if not quite up
to what you'd expect for the dirhams. The cavernous
interior, all high ceilings and wooden floors, somewhat kills the ambience. Steaks on offer range from
Aberdeen Angus to cuts from New Zealand, but it's
the Australian wagyu that stands out. Elsewhere on
the menu are burgers, chicken and fish.

Organic Foods & Café

Dubai Mall (434 0577). **Open** 8am-8pm daily.
Brunch 11am-3.30pm Fri, Sat. **Average** Dhs200-
Dhs300. *Brunch* Dhs95; Dhs65 children. **Credit**
AmEx, MC, V. **Map** p296 H5 **㉜ Café**

The anti-brunch, if you will. Pile your plate high –
only this time with healthy, wholesome fare like

CONSUME

Maria Bonita's Taco Shop.

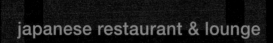

spicy red cabbage salad, tangy tomato soup with quinoa bread, vegetarian lasagne and crunchy wild, brown rice. Your stomach will thank you.
Other locations The Greens (361 7974).

Pachanga
Hilton Dubai Jumeirah (399 1111). **Open** 6.30pm-midnight daily. **Average** Dhs800-Dhs900. **Credit** AmEx, MC, V. **Map** p304 B1 ❸❸ **Latin American**
There's some fine Latin American fare on offer at this restaurant, especially if you are a fan of steak. The atmosphere is enlivened by a three-piece band, and the venue is also known for the occasional tango and samba night. But the food is so good, you won't be tempted to leave your seats. Kick off the meal with Mexican olive bread and dips. For the main, be sure to order the churrasco-style meat, brought to your table on a skewer fresh from the grill.

Signatures
Jebel Ali Hotel, Jebel Ali (804 8604). **Open** 7-11pm Tue-Sun. **Average** Dhs650-Dhs750. **Credit** AmEx, MC, V. **European**
Signatures is a lovely, but lonely, restaurant. In a bid to get more customers than, well, none, it relaunched the wine list and menu at the beginning of 2009, making it strictly organic. The chicken is free-range, the beef is Argentinian grass-fed, and the fish is line caught – the chef even sources produce from a garden out the back. It is the ingredients, not the dishes themselves, that make Signatures stand out. When something is naturally beautiful, garnish isn't necessary to make it a showstopper, and this is something the cooks understand.

Dhs Smiling BKK
Al Wasl Road (349 6677). Taxi: next to Jumeirah Post Office. **Open** 11am-midnight daily. **Average** Dhs100-Dhs200. **Credit** AmEx, MC, V. Unlicensed. **Map** p300 D9 ❸❹ **Southeast Asian**

**INSIDE TRACK
BRUNCH**

Friday brunch is an institution. This four-hour meal tends to fall in to one of two categories: drunken binges or elegant midday meals. Either way, they're always all-you-can-eat affairs, and the most popular ones sport bottomless glasses. It's definitely not a ritual you want to miss out on. Try the brunches at **Beachcombers** (*see p127*), **Yalumba** (*see p126*) and **Organic Foods & Café** (*see p128*). All the restaurants at **Al Qasr** open their doors for a completely over-the-top hotel brunch (*see p100*).

Smiling BKK.

Smiling BKK boasts real charm and absurdity. The menu looks like a bored teen has been at it, renaming all the dishes with names such as 'Billy Jean's not my lover' (steamed fish with basil, lemon and chilli) or 'Fook yu' (noodles in Thai gravy with meat or seafood). On certain nights of the week you're invited to sing for your supper. But what sort of dinner should you expect? An extremely reasonably priced, albeit average one.

Zheng He's
Mina A'Salam, Madinat Jumeirah (366 8888). **Open** 12.30-3pm, 7-11.30pm daily. **Average** Dhs600-Dhs700. **Credit** AmEx, MC, V. **Map** p304 E1 ❸❺ **Chinese**
Zheng He's joins ranks with Dubai's classiest Chinese restaurants, but manages to do so without pomp. The decor is traditional and serene and, although the menu boasts haute ingredients like caviar, truffles and wagyu, it's only to augment delicious and classical Chinese fare. The Beijing duck is expertly prepared and is highly recommended, as do the scallops with black truffle and white asparagus. The service is as spot on as at any five-star venue, though the restaurant is tucked away under the Mina A'Salam.

THE MARINA

22/55 Café Bistro
Dubai Marina Yacht Club (362 7900). **Open** 7am-11pm daily. **Average** Dhs400-Dhs500. **Credit** AmEx, MC, V. **Café**

CONSUME

CONSUME

25/55 Café Bistro stands out for being well thought out and well priced. The decor hits the right notes, too. Outside, tables overlook the marina, which in the evening produces a beguiling view. The interior is nothing to be sneezed at, though; it's romantic without being overly fussy. The food is pleasingly good, with a plump fillet of snapper oozing with natural juices and a grilled rump of lamb similarly drooling and served butter-soft.

Az.u.r
Harbour Hotel & Residence, Dubai Marina (319 4000). **Open** noon-11pm daily. **Average** Dhs550-Dhs650. **Credit** AmEx, MC, V. **Map** p304 B2 ⑧⑧ **European**
'Farm to fork' implies, in many parts of the world, that the food is from a nearby organic farm. It seems az.u.r. (pronounced 'as you are') uses the term more loosely: the food is not local, but it is organic and cooked from scratch on the premises. A nice aspect of az.u.r. is that the kitchen doesn't mind accommodating your wishes, within reason. If you want extra coriander in your soup, for example, the folks at az.u.r. are more than happy to oblige.

Beach Bar & Grill
One&Only Royal Mirage, the Palace (399 9999). **Open** noon-3.30pm, 7-11.30pm daily. **Average** Dhs700-Dhs800. **Credit** AmEx, MC, V. **Map** p304 C1 ⑥⑦ **International**
With its romantic beach setting, this spot is popular so booking is wise. Most people choose to sit outside, where a split-level wooden verandah allows views of the beach, sea and the Palm. The menu has plenty of options, with seafood, steaks and a wide range of vegetarian options. It's not cheap – with mains invariably costing more than Dhs100 and starters weighing in at Dhs70. But you get what you pay for: the food is well presented and tasty, and the service attentive.

Bice
Hilton Dubai Jumeirah, Dubai Marina (399 4444). **Open** 8.30am-1.30am daily. **Average** Dhs550-Dhs650. **Credit** AmEx, MC, V. **Map** p304 B1 ⑧⑧ **Italian**
Bice plays on the theme of an Italian restaurant in an international setting, from, 'Buona sera' uttered by Asian waiting staff, to set-pieces such as giant pepper mills and trolley loads of olive oil. Any suspicions about the speedy appearance of dishes are soon allayed; lobster carpaccio with caviar and artichoke heart – one of the signature dishes – makes a wonderful starter, and the pasta dishes are inventive too. Bice remains one of the city's safest bets for a good Italian dining experience.

Bombay by the Bay
Rimal, Plaza Level, Jumeirah Beach Residence (04 429 7979). **Open** 11.30am-11.30pm daily. **Average** Dhs200-Dhs300. **Credit** AmEx, MC, V. **Map** p304 B1 ⑧⑨ **Indian**

As a neighbourhood, Jumeirah Beach Residences tends towards an array of characterless restaurants. Bombay by the Bay is an exception. The billowing interior, complete with cushy private rooms and flowing curtains, makes for a relaxed way to have dinner. Add to this the polite, eager-to-please waiters and juicy, delectable curries, and you have a real gem of a restaurant.

Buddha Bar
Grosvenor House (399 8888). **Open** 8pm-2am daily. **Average** Dhs800-Dhs900. **Credit** AmEx, MC, V. **Map** p304 B1 ⑨⓪ **Southeast Asian**
It's neither new nor unique, but Buddha Bar's enduring popularity is well deserved. Following the format of sister branches throughout the world, its interior oozes sophistication, with low-level lighting and DJs spinning house. The super-pricey menu is a slightly puzzling affair, with endless pages of sushi followed by a large variety of hot and cold starters (the punchy beef tataki salad is a hit). The main courses that follow are, for the most part, disappointingly middle-of-the-road. Booking ahead is a must, as this place is packed every night of the week.

Bussola
Westin Dubai Mina Seyahi (399 4141). **Open** noon-2.45pm, 7-10.45pm daily. **Average** Dhs500-Dhs650. **Credit** AmEx, MC, V. **Map** p304 B1 ⑨① **Italian**
This attractive restaurant has an interesting menu and an easygoing vibe. The pasta options are some of the best in the city: if you feel daring, try spaghetti cooked in sea water with mullet roe and sea urchins; or to hit the spot every time, bucatini with pancetta, onion and tomatoes. Thoughtful combinations occur through the entire menu, with fruit put to effective and flavoursome use in many of the main courses. Definitely a restaurant to try.

Certo
Radisson SAS, Dubai Media City (366 9111). **Open** noon-3.30pm, 7-11.30pm Sun-Fri; 7-11.30pm Sat. **Average** Dhs500-Dhs600. **Credit** AmEx, MC, V. **Map** p304 C2 ⑨② **Italian**
Certo stands out for its consistently fine food and reasonable prices. Try as it might, the somewhat dramatic decor can't brush off the business hotel vibe, but it is a very good option for lunching suits. The cannellini bean soup with rosemary, garlic and basil oil is outstanding – unshowy but packed with flavour. Meanwhile the 'artisan' pasta pairs well with parma ham and porcini mushrooms. For atmosphere and service, there are better places, but Certo is certainly up there with its more expensive rivals.

Dhs Counter Culture
Harbour Hotel & Residence, Al Sufouh Road, Dubai Marina (319 4000). **Open** 24 hrs daily. **Average** Dhs100-Dhs200. **Credit** AmEx, MC, V. Unlicensed. **Map** p304 B2 ⑨③ **Café**

Nobu. *See p135.*

CONSUME

THE AVIATION CLUB

Bhi craic agus ceol againn

TOBACCONIST

THE IRISH VILLAGE

...irrepressibly Irish

music & entertainment in a traditional Irish setting

04 282 4750

The menu at Counter Culture isn't particularly enticing for a dinner time jaunt: it suggests a soup-and-sandwich shop. But if you hunger for more, head to the counter. Fresh salads, massive pies, and grilled mains will satisfy most food cravings. It's simple but satisfying fare. The prices all hover around the Dhs30 mark, and the venue is open 24 hours.

Eau Zone
One & Only Royal Mirage (399 9999). **Open** noon-3.30pm, 7-11.30pm daily. **Average** Dhs600-Dhs700. **Credit** AmEx, MC, V. **Map** p304 C1 ❾ **Southeast Asian**
Eau Zone is the epitome of romance. The warm glow of candlelight envelops the seating on the wooden jetty by a lagoon-like pool. The menu has a small selection of delicious-sounding dishes combining European fare with Asian, Thai and Chinese twists. There's a good choice for vegetarians and fans of seafood. The flavours are superb, although the textures are slightly tough. There's no denying, however, it's very good nosh and beautifully presented.

Hunter's Room & Grill
Westin Dubai Mina Seyahi Beach Resort & Marina (399 4141). **Open** noon-2.30pm, 6-11pm daily. **Average** Dhs800-Dhs900. **Credit** AmEx, MC, V. **Map** p304 B1 ❾ **Steakhouse**
This marina steakhouse is an excellent restaurant (albeit a pricey one). In the menu, descriptions of the food are interspersed with the adventures of 19th-century British military engineer, artist and hunter, Captain William Cornwallis Harris. The restaurant's sleek contemporary layout, the dozen or so choices of water and multiple selections of salt (yes, salt), continue the theme of luxury. And the food doesn't disappoint. The main attraction – a chargrilled US 20oz Porterhouse corn-fed steak – is tender and bursting with rich flavours.

Indego
Grosvenor House (399 8888). **Open** 7.30pm-midnight Sun-Fri. **Average** Dhs600-Dhs700. **Credit** AmEx, MC, V. **Map** p304 B1 ❾ **Indian**
Diehard fans of Indian cuisine might be affronted by Indego's European/haute take on subcontinental fare. But whether or not you're willing to concede that the food is, in fact, Indian, you'll still find it brilliant. It is the brainchild of celebrity chef Vineet Bhatia, the restaurant's consultant chef and the first Indian to receive a Michelin star. Although Indian food traditionalists may turn up their noses at the idea of a chocolate samosa dessert, that just means there's more for everyone else.

Magnolia
Al Qasr Hotel, Madinat Jumeirah (366 6730). **Open** noon-3pm, 7-11.30pm daily. **Average** Dhs400-Dhs500. **Credit** AmEx, MC, V. **Map** p304 D1 ❾ **International**

Vegetarians can be hard done by at most restaurants in Dubai, so Magnolia, which caters primarily for them, will come as a relief. The menu is creative, and tasty enough to tempt carnivores, particularly since it deliberately and carefully eschews preservatives, pesticides and other contaminants. The wine list is organic and the water list is just as extensive, although somewhat less expensive.

Maya
Le Royal Méridien Beach Resort & Spa (399 5555). **Open** 7.30pm-midnight Mon-Sat. *Bar* 6.30pm-2am Mon-Sat. **Average** Dhs600-Dhs700. **Credit** AmEx, MC, V. **Map** p304 B1 ❾ **Latin American**
Consultant chef Richard Sandoval fuses traditional Mexican ingredients with ideas from Europe and Asia, just as he has done with Maya restaurants in New York and San Francisco. If you want to try something different in this city, you'll definitely find it here. Grab some excellent guacamole, made by the table, and move on to the lamb chipotle, which is tender and juicy. With such a diverse menu, there is something for everyone.

Nina
One&Only Royal Mirage (339 9999). **Open** 7-11.30pm daily. **Average** Dhs400-Dhs500. **Credit** AmEx, MC, V. **Map** p304 C1 ❾ **Indian & Pakistani**
Nina is more cool Bollywood than hot-and-earthy Delhi, and – if you can get past the snooty reservations line – it's worth booking in for a taste of Indian fine dining. With its lofty surroundings and chilled-out ambient beats, it feels like some super-hip members' only club. If you can't decide what to go for, opt for the taster menu – offering smaller versions of nine à la carte dishes, including the famously good tomato butter chicken, and a delicate lamb with celery and mint.

Nobu
Atlantis, the Palm (426 2626). **Open** 7pm-midnight daily. **Average** Dhs850-Dhs950. **Credit** AmEx, MC, V. **Map** p304 C1 ❿ **Seafood**
As an international chain, albeit a fine dining one, the food at Nobu is pretty predictable, though no less

---

THE BEST CURRIES

For a mean lamb curry
Aangan. *See p110.*

For high-end fare
Indego. *See above.*

For Rajasthani cuisine
Manvaar. *See p117.*

CONSUME

Pai Thai

CONSUME

excellent. Nobu classics, like the black cod and rock shrimp tempura, are served, and the chef doesn't disappoint. As is true at Nobu's 15 other outlets, the food is mighty expensive, and the staff can be pretty pushy. But order right, and you're guaranteed a lovely meal. *Photo p133.*

Ottomans
Grosvenor House, West Marina Beach (399 8888). **Open** 8pm-12.30am Mon-Sat. **Average** Dhs400-Dhs500. **Credit** AmEx, MC, V. **Map** p304 B1 European
If you're searching for a refined, Middle Eastern atmosphere, make a beeline for Ottomans. As you sip wine on the romantic terrace, you might even forget to pay attention to the food. But you should, because it's superb. With such a fabulous array of dishes adorning the menu, you might struggle to decide what to order. The attentive and friendly staff can help answer your queries; you may do well to pick a few starters, such as pistachio-encrusted prawns.

Ossiano
Atlantis, the Palm (426 2626). **Open** 7pm-midnight daily. **Average** Dhs1,900-Dhs2,000. **Credit** AmEx, MC, V. **Map** p304 C1 Seafood
Dining at three-star Michelin chef Santi Santamaria's first restaurant outside Spain is a momentous occasion. This is made all the more true when you take your seat in the large, tranquil expanse, hemmed in by Atlantis's aquarium. After nibbling on warm bread and a tray full of amuse bouches, try out the tasting menu. The procession of food is a work of art, the flavours growing stronger with each new sequence. It's pricey, but worth it.

P2
Madinat Jumeirah (366 6730). **Open** noon-3pm, 7-11.30pm daily. **Average** Dhs600-Dhs700. **Credit** AmEx, MC, V. **Map** p304 E1 Seafood
P2 is the upstairs brasserie to Pisces, the seafood restaurant. P2 is a tad more informal, and its menu a bit more French than its parent. Alongside plentiful seafood options, there is tasty beef tartare, a delicious duck confit and, for dessert, a light and fluffy crème brûlée. It's all very good, and the terrace is lovely. A good choice if you haven't got the dirhams for Pisces and like some French flair with your fish.

★ Pai Thai
Al Qasr Hotel, Madinat Jumeirah (366 6730). **Open** 7-11.30pm daily. **Average** Dhs400-Dhs500. **Credit** AmEx, MC, V. **Map** p304 D1 Southeast Asian
Pai Thai is tremendously romantic. Beginning with the *abra* cruise over to the Al Qasr eaterie, there's good reason for it being seen as one of Dubai's top places to take a date. It has it all: candles, terrace seating, live music. The food is excellent, if maybe not the most authentic Thai in town. Still, the setting makes the place.

★ Pierchic
Madinat Jumeirah (366 8888). **Open** noon-2.30pm, 7-11.30pm daily. **Average** Dhs900-Dhs1,000. **Credit** AmEx, MC, V. **Map** p304 E1 Seafood
The food at Pierchic is superb. From the freshly shucked oysters and the melting yellowfin tuna, right through to the decadent valhrona chocolate fondant, the kitchen doesn't put a step wrong. But what makes dinner at this most romantic of restaurants a truly exceptional experience is the fairytale setting. It has a fine view of the Burj Al Arab.

Pisces
Madinat Jumeirah (366 8888). **Open** 7-11.30pm daily. **Average** Dhs900-Dhs1,000. **Credit** AmEx, MC, V. **Map** p304 E1 Seafood
A longtime favourite for locals and expats alike, if for no other reason than the pristine Madinat setting the restaurant. Food, however, can be a bit hit and miss given the high price. Tuna carpaccio and pan seared scallops may sing only to be let down by lacklustre mains. Although the atmosphere makes it a worthwhile stop, there is better seafood in town.

Prego's
Media Rotana Barsha, Al Barsha Road (435 0000). **Open** 7-11.30pm daily. **Average** Dhs350-Dhs450. **Credit** AmEx, MC, V. **Map** p304 D2 Italian

The menu at Prego's boasts a fantastic assortment of Italian cured meats. Watching chef Mauro Cereda haul fat rounds of dismembered shoulder and thigh, and slice them as thin as sheets of paper, is almost as mesmerising as letting each delicate slice melt on the tongue. The waiting staff are knowledgeable and unobtrusive, and you'd be wise to take the recommendation of tiramisu.

★ Rhodes Mezzanine

Grosvenor House, Dubai Marina (399 8888). **Open** 7.30-11.30pm Mon-Sat. **Average** Dhs1,000-Dhs1,250. **Credit** AmEx, MC, V. **Map** p304 B1 ⓲ European

The all-white decor at Rhodes Mezzanine has the look and feel of a lounge in the afterlife. The food is of especially high quality thanks to the helping hand of consultant chef Gary Rhodes. The theme is elevated British classics. Rhodes's take on jam roly poly, jaffa cake, and bread and butter pudding make a decadent finish. Although a pricey meal out, dining at Rhodes feels like a proper event, and the staff fill you up to the gills.

Ronda Locatelli

Atlantis, Palm Jumeirah (426 0750). **Open** noon-midnight daily. **Average** Dhs600-Dhs700. **Credit** AmEx, MC, V. **Map** p304 C1 ⓲ Italian

Michelin-star Italian chef Giorgio Locatelli's Dubai restaurant has not escaped Atlantis's theme park touches: as you dine under a large, mushroom-shaped wood-burning oven, you feel as if you have followed Alice down a rabbit hole. Great care is taken to make every dish stand out, but there's no fussiness. It's good old fashioned rustic food – pizzas, pastas and steaks – elevated to the heavens.

Rostang, the French Brasserie

Atlantis, the Palm (426 2626). **Open** noon-3.30pm, 6-11pm daily. **Average** Dhs600-Dhs700. **Credit** AmEx, MC, V. **Map** p304 C1 ⓲ European

Diners hoping to experience Michelin-rated chef Michel Rostang at his Dubai restaurant will likely be disappointed by the food. It's not really up to his standard, and the service leaves something to be desired as well. Although some items, such as the lobster salad and scallops, are pleasant, they're not really worth the high price, especially when you consider the poor service.

Royal Orchid

Marina Walk (04 367 4040). **Open** noon-11.30pm daily. **Average** Dhs200-Dhs300. **Credit** AmEx, MC, V. **Map** p304 B2 ⓲ East Asian

When it comes to food, the Dubai Marina is a better spot to find an outlet run by a Michelin-rated chef than a relaxed cheap and casual meal. Royal Orchid is one of the few places that serves up reasonable, if predictable, pan-Asian fare in this neighbourhood. Ambitiously covering China, Thailand and Mongolia, rather than focusing on a single territory, the Royal Orchid could easily have slipped out of focus, but despite a couple of minor hitches, it continues to serve good value Asian food.

Tang

Le Méridien Mina Seyahi Beach Resort & Spa (03 399 3333). **Open** 7-11pm Sun-Fri. **Average** Dhs700-Dhs800. **Credit** AmEx, MC, V. **Map** p304 B1 ⓲ European

There's something rather irksome about the Alice in Wonderland chairs and fussy decor, yet the menu offers a glittering array of refreshingly experimental dishes, which are served in the style of molecular gastronomy greats Heston Blumenthal and Ferran Adrià. If you've eaten at either chef's signature restaurant, the dishes at Tang will seem oddly familiar. That said, it's a great spot for a taste of something out of the ordinary – foie gras with strawberry meringue, anyone?

SHEIKH ZAYED ROAD

Dhs Almaz by Momo

Harvey Nichols, Mall of the Emirates (409 8877). **Open** 10am-midnight Sat-Thur; 10am-1.30am Fri. **Average** Dhs250-Dhs350. **Credit** AmEx, MC, V. Unlicensed. **Map** p304 D2 ⓲ MENA

Though shoved at the back of Harvey Nichols, this restaurant manages to throw together good food with enough kitsch touches to feel unique and un-mall like. Don't let the absence of alcohol sway your judgement, the place is still lively. There are some unusual and inspired things on the menu, from pigeon pastilla to lamb tagine. All in all, a good place for Moroccan grub.

Al Nafoorah

Jumeirah Emirates Towers (319 8088). **Open** 12.30-3pm, 8pm-midnight daily. **Average** Dhs400-Dhs500. **Credit** AmEx, MC, V. **Map** p304 C1 ⓲ MENA

INSIDE TRACK
SERVICE

Europeans may be slightly taken aback by the obsequious service in many restaurants, especially as basics, like delivering the bill in timely fashion, often tend to be overlooked. It is best not to get offended by how over-the-top the waiters can seem at time. Keep in mind that many locals and expats have come to expect this type of service, so it's best not to let it get to you. The waiters are only acting according to their training.

CONSUME

This Financial Centre haunt is hugely popular. Lunch and dinner are packed with a crowd of business people tucking into the first-rate food. Go for the *baba ganoush* – it's unbeatably fruity and as rough and tasty as true *ganoush* should be. Also, grab a plate of *jergier* with your meze; this is crisp and fresh rocket leaf that glistens with oil and sparks with punchy onions.

Amwaj
Shangri-La Hotel (405 2703). **Open** 7pm-midnight Sun-Fri. **Average** Dhs700-Dhs800. **Credit** AmEx, MC, V. **Map** p303 F12 **115** Seafood

Service is as sleek and subtle as the nautically-themed decor, and the food is of a consistently high quality, rounding up all the usual suspects of seared scallops, whole dover sole and so on – a kind of 'Seafood Greatest Hits'. Although the decor recalls a hotel lobby, the quality of the food makes up for any deficiencies in atmosphere.

Dhs Bento-Ya
Behind Sketchers shoe shop, Sheikh Zayed Road (343 0222). **Open** noon-3.30pm, 6.30-11.30pm Sun-Thur; 5.30-11pm Fri; noon-3pm, 6.30-11.30pm Sat. **Average** Dhs100-Dhs200. **Credit** AmEx, MC, V. Unlicensed. **Map** p301 G10 **116** Japanese

'Simple' and 'genuine' sum up this diminutive Japanese joint, which has enough Japanese clientele to quell any fears about authenticity. With walls plastered with 'know your sushi' and 'fish of the UAE' posters, diners will be greeted by a chorus of 'welcome' from a friendly choir of staff, and plied with mugs of green tea. The sushi and sashimi are particularly decent. If you need meat, go for the *yakiniku* bento box.

Cavalli Club
Fairmont Dubai (04 332 9260). **Open** 7.30pm-2am daily. **Average** Dhs1,000-Dhs1,300. **Credit** AmEx, MC, V. **Map** p301 G9/G10 **117** International

People who love the designs of Roberto Cavalli will adore this restaurant. The decor is decked out in Swarovski crystals and his signature animal prints (not even the chef's uniform is spared a splash of multi-coloured zebra print) and the food is treated with the same sense of flash and grandeur. Almost every dish on the menu is accompanied with some combination of truffles, fois gras and caviar (in some case, these added value items improve the food, but mostly they're just there for boasting rights). Shortly after it opened, the restaurant proved a hot spot with the city's socialites, who packed the place out. Definitely a place to see and be seen, but foodies can find better fare in town for the same, or lower, price.

CONSUME

Okku. *See p141.*

CONSUME

Al Hadheerah. *See p142.*

Empire

Monarch Dubai (501 8888). **Open** 6-11pm daily. **Average** Dhs1,000-Dhs1,100. **Credit** AmEx, MC, V. **Map** p301 G9 **118** **European**
The name could very well describe the city's aspirations and the dishes are served with the sheen and gloss usually reserved for the town's major developments. There's even the dichotomy between modernity and tradition: a manly colour scheme (chrome and burgundy) and a menu with crêpes suzette as a nod to old-fashioned French fare, although entrées buried in foam and canapés served in illuminated blocks of ice betray a cooking philosophy that is forward-thinking, albeit somewhat gimmicky.

★ Exchange Grill

Fairmont (332 5555). **Open** 7pm-midnight daily. **Average** Dhs700-Dhs800. **Credit** AmEx, MC, V. **Map** p301 G9/G10 **119** **Steakhouse**
The meat at the Fairmont's signature steakhouse is some of the tastiest in town – perfectly cooked, appealing looking and served in style. The service stands out in this joint, if you'll pardon the pun, from the friendly greeting to the knowledge of all things meaty. The decor is second to none, as is the wine list; there is also a great range of non-steak options for the less carnivorous diner. If you're prepared to shell out, this is one posh spot that's well worth a visit.

Hoi An

Shangri-La Hotel (405 2703). **Open** 7pm-1am daily. **Average** Dhs600-Dhs700. **Credit** AmEx, MC, V. **Map** p303 F12 **120** **Southeast Asian**
Ornate screens, paper lanterns and warm, low-level lighting blend with a buzzy atmosphere. The set menu is a good way to explore Vietnamese cuisine, and at Dhs280 a pop, it's fairly good value. The 'hue' menu is a particularly attractive option, kicking off with a mixed starter, that includes coconut and lobster ravioli. Fresh fruit and a scoop of coconut ice-cream await those who have room.

Marrakech

Shangri-La Hotel (405 2703). **Open** 7pm-1am Sat-Thur. **Average** Dhs350-Dhs500. **Credit** AmEx, MC, V. **Map** p303 F12 **121** **MENA**
Marrakech isn't one of the city's best-known restaurants – perhaps because its modern take on traditional Moroccan cuisine caters to more of a niche market. Still, it offers a decent meal. The pigeon pastilla scores highly for starters. The mountainous couscous royal is golden, perfectly steamed and packed with carrots, swede, hunks of super-soft lamb, veal and a disintegrating chicken drumstick.

Nezesaussi

Al Manzil Hotel (428 5927). **Open** 6pm-2am Sun-Thur; noon-2am Fri, Sat; special opening hours during sports events. **Average** Dhs250-Dhs350. **Credit** AmEx, MC, V. **Map** p296 H5 **122** **Bar food**
Nezesaussi has great grub, but, aesthetically, it is an odd restaurant. The bar has the TV screens, cheesy memorabilia and middle-aged, glassy-eyed punters of a standard sports bar, but also a fancy open cooking station and sizeable wine rack. Still, if you get past the confused decor, you'll find a lot to recommend the place. The staff are prompt and the food, which is a mix of South African and Australian-themed dishes, is, on the whole excellent, if a little highly priced.

Nineteen

Montgomerie Clubhouse (390 5600). **Open** 7pm-midnight Sun-Wed; noon-3.30pm, 7pm-midnight Thur-Sat. **Average** Dhs700-Dhs800. **Credit** AmEx, MC, V. **Map** p304 B2 **123** **European**
You are likely to get pangs of lifestyle envy while driving past villas in the plush Emirates Hills, but you can have a slice of the residents' lives by dining at Nineteen, the Montgomerie Clubhouse's restaurant. The service is friendly and efficient, the decor classy and the food exquisite. Seafood mains like monkfish and halibut are superb and bursting with flavour. The view of water and rolling greens from the terrace adds to the feeling of contentment.

Okku

Monarch Dubai (501 8888). **Open** 7pm-3am daily. **Average** Dhs600-Dhs700. **Credit** AmEx, MC, V. **Map** p301 G9 **124** **Japanese**
Okku is packed with skinny girls in short skirts and men in business suits. Bartenders dressed in black prepare Dhs50 cocktails near an expansive aquarium sporting iridescent jellyfish imported from Japan. Despite the restaurant claims to be 'innovative' and 'unique', the menu's offerings of miso black cod, rock shrimp tempura and yellowtail carpaccio, ring Nobu-shaped bells. Although Okku may not be the most original dining concept in town, the food is still excellent. *Photo p139.*

Ruth's Chris Steak House

Monarch Dubai (501 8666). **Open** 6.30pm-11.30pm Sat-Wed; 6.30pm-midnight Thur, Fri. **Average** Dhs1,100-Dhs1,200. **Credit** AmEx, MC, V. **Map** p301 G9 **125** **Steakhouse**
Ruth's Chris does giant slabs of American beef exceedingly well. They have a very specific cooking

CONSUME

THE BEST ARABIC EATS

For a desert vibe
Al Hadheerah. *See p142.*

For a whirling dervish with your mezza
Khan Murjan. *See p115.*

For a Persian kebab
Shabestan. *See p126.*

technique, which staff are keen to explain. The steaks are broiled at 1,800F, and then served on plates that are warmed to 500F. The plates have a thick pool of sizzling butter, with your meat in the middle – it's sure to leave your arteries clogged just from looking at it, but it's worth it.

Shang Palace
Shangri-La Hotel (343 8888). **Open** 12.30-3pm, 8pm-midnight daily. **Average** Dhs600-Dhs700. **Credit** AmEx, MC, V. **Map** p303 F12 **126** Chinese

Dining at Shang Palace is a regal affair – until you peer over the balcony to the bustling lobby below. The restaurant has basically been crowbarred into a corner of the hotel, but to its credit, it pulls it off well. The test of any Chinese restaurant is always the Beijing duck. Here, they carve the meat instead of shredding it, and the slices are neat and tender. It is the highlight dish on a menu of staples which offers a solid selection of favourites.

Spectrum On One
Fairmont Hotel (332 5555). **Open** 6.30pm-1am daily. **Average** Dhs600-Dhs700. **Credit** AmEx, MC, V. **Map** p301 G9/G10 **127** International

Dinner at Spectrum on One is a mixed affair. Chinese spare ribs are sticky and succulent, but an expensive steak is bland and overcooked. However, it is the Friday brunch that really makes this place. The international selection (you can slop Goan curry and sushi on the same plate) and flowing champagne make it a regular brunch haunt for expats.

Teatro
Towers Rotana Hotel (343 8000). **Open** 6pm-2am daily. **Average** Dhs350-Dhs450. **Credit** AmEx, MC, V. **Map** p303 F12 **128** International

Diners certainly don't go to Teatro for the third-floor views of Sheikh Zayed Road. But they do go, in droves, for the excellent food, great service and stylish decor. There is definitely a strong Oriental flavour; throw yourself into it by enjoying, in particular, the crispy and tasty Asian sampler starter. The East-meets-West theme is also reflected in the decor, with the reds and golds of the Orient punctuated by Roy Lichtenstein-esque theatre posters from the '60s.

Tokyo@TheTowers
Jumeirah Emirates Towers (319 8088). **Open** 12.30-2.30pm, 7.30-11.30pm Sat-Thur; 1-3.30pm, 7-11.30pm Fri. **Average** Dhs400-Dhs500. **Credit** AmEx, MC, V. **Map** p296 H4 **129** Japanese

Teppenyaki chefs are entertainers, and the ones at Tokyo@TheTowers are no exception. Dinner time is enlivened by a circus-like whirlwind of party tricks. Meat and seafood are flung around in front of you, along with props like salt and pepper shakers and worryingly sharp knives. Although teppanyaki is the main draw, other Japanese food is

available, like warming bowls of miso soup, salads of green leaves and seaweed, shrimp, crunchy tempura and sashimi from the sushi bar.

Vista
Holiday Inn Express, Internet City (427 5500). **Open** 5pm-1.30am daily. **Average** Dhs350-Dhs450. **Credit** AmEx, MC, V. **Map** p304 C2 **130** International

With its divine grub, tasteful decor and Burj Al Arab terrace views, Vista ticks a number of important boxes. And although there's a stigma of eating in a Holiday Inn, the food is surprisingly good, with fish and chips and crab linguine making for fine mains. The menu is of international bent, yet despite the odd range in food served, this place makes a relaxed spot for a good meal out.

Vu's
Jumeirah Emirates Towers (319 8088). **Open** noon-3pm, 7.30pm-midnight Sat-Thur; 7.30pm-midnight Fri. **Average** Dhs800-Dhs900. **Credit** AmEx, MC, V. **Map** p296 H4 **131** European

With fantastic views of Sheikh Zayed Road, slick decor, great service and sophisticated fare, Vu's is a high point – literally, being on the 50th floor of Emirates Towers – of dining out in Dubai. The atmosphere can be slightly stiff, but the food does merit reverence. The portions are small, but the quality of taste and texture ensure you are more than satisfied.

OUT OF TOWN

Al Hadheerah
Jumeirah Bab Al Shams Desert Resort & Spa, Dubailand (809 6100). **Open** 7-11.30pm daily. **Average** Dhs400-Dhs500. **Credit** AmEx, MC, V. MENA

Al Hadheerah is built to resemble a fortified Arabian desert village. The rustic-looking buildings are illuminated by Islamic stained-glass lanterns, making for a romantic setting. The lavish outdoor buffet has a dozen food counters serving scores of carefully created Arabic dishes, including Emirati food. A band plays Arabic music on stage while a belly dancer wiggles, and later there are camel rides and a tunic-twirling Sinbad appears. A great place to take visitors for a Disney-esque taste of Arabia. *Photo p140.*

Le Pizzeria Dune
Jumeirah Bab Al Shams Desert Resort & Spa, Dubailand (809 6100). **Open** 6-11.30pm Sun-Thur; 12.30-4pm, 6-11.30pm Fri; 12.30-3pm, 6-11.30pm Sat. **Average** Dhs400-Dhs500. **Credit** AmEx, MC, V. Italian

Le Pizzeria Dune is very romantic thanks to its quiet, tucked-away setting. Around half-an-hour's drive from Dubai, this Italian restaurant is perfect for an intimate encounter. Fresh toppings and tasty tomato paste form the basis of these simple, crispy pizzas, laden with mozzarella and herbs.

Pubs & Bars

Surprise – you can get a drink here after all.

Many visitors to the UAE are surprised to discover that the country has a drinking culture, but given the numbers of British, Irish and Australian expats out here it should come as no surprise. In fact, the city has a wide range of bars, from the ultra-chic and exclusive to down 'n' dirty faux-British pubs (since all venues must be connected to hotels, there are no genuine public houses here, just hotel bars in drag). There really is something for every occasion, although the decentralised, pedestrian-unfriendly nature of the city means that it's a good idea to plan ahead when going out. For nightclubs and live music venues, *see pp220-226.*

CONSUME

BUR DUBAI

Boston Bar
Jumeira Rotana Hotel, Al Dhiyafah Road (345 5888/www.jumeirarotana.com). **Open** noon-2.30pm daily. **Credit** AmEx, MC, V. **Map** p300 E8 ❶
Based on the bar in *Cheers*, the Boston is an unpretentious expat boozer that's full of Brits. It can get very lively during football matches, and dancing on the bar frequently breaks out on the ladies' nights.

Elegante
Royal Ascot Hotel (355 8500). **Open** 10pm-3am daily. **Credit** AmEx, MC, V. **Map** p298 H4 ❷
Elegante does its best to project an image of class in an area better known for its seedy clubs. Get past the no-nonsense doormen and you'll find yourself surrounded by a mixed crowd of dressed-up, arms-up clubbers, particularly on the popular R&B nights.

★ Ginseng
Pyramids, Wafi City, Oud Metha Road (324 8200/www.ginsengdubai.com). **Open** 7pm-1am Sat-Mon; 7pm-2am Tue-Fri. **Credit** AmEx, MC, V. **Map** p297 J3 ❸
A cosy Asian-themed venue that can't work out whether it's a bar, a restaurant or a club. Ginseng has a large array of fierce cocktails, and although it's stylish, it's not too pretentious. *Photo p144.*

Rock Bottom Café
Regent Palace Hotel, World Trade Centre Road (396 3888/www.ramee-group.com). **Open** noon-3am daily. **Credit** AmEx, MC, V. **Map** p299 J5 ❹
Although it's officially a bar and restaurant rather than a club, Rock Bottom only comes alive when other bars kick out. Something of a cattle market, RBC nevertheless pulls in an impressive crowd with its proven blend of bullfrogs (a highly potent cocktail that utilises all the white spirits plus Red Bull) and the resident DJ and live band, who pump out the pleasers until closing time. There's even an in-house *shawarma* joint for dancers with the munchies.

Vintage
Pyramids, Wafi City, Oud Metha Road (324 4100/www.wafi.com). **Open** 5pm-2am daily. **Credit** AmEx, MC, V. **Map** p297 J3 ❺
There's something about Vintage's chic interior and stupendous cellar that soothes the soul. The wine bar is constantly buzzing with sophisticated chatter, and there's a good cheeseboard at hand to help you soak up the excess alcohol.

**INSIDE TRACK
LADIES' NIGHTS**

Drinks promotions for ladies are offered so frequently in bars that it's possible for the fairer sex to obtain free drinks on any given night if you plan ahead. For the latest deals and promos, pick up *Time Out Dubai* or visit www.timeoutdubai.com

---

❶ Green numbers given in this chapter correspond to the location of each bar as marked on the street maps. *See pp294-304.*

CONSUME

Waxy O'Conner's

*Ascot Hotel, Khalid Bin Al Waleed Road
(Bank Street) (352 0900/www.ascothoteldubai.
com).* **Open** noon-1.30am Sat-Wed; noon-3am
Thur; noon-2am Fri. **Credit** AmEx, MC, V.
Map p298 H4 ⑥

In no way affiliated to the popular UK chain, Waxy's
is a bustling Irish pub on the frantic Bank Street. The
reason for the sun-starved pint pit's success is simple: the proprietors have lined up a deluge of deals to
entice the budget-conscious boozer. The biggest bargain is the Friday brunch, which will get you a full
Irish breakfast, five drinks and a second buffet further down the line for less than Dhs100. *Photo p147.*

DEIRA

★ Belgian Beer Café

Crowne Plaza Hotel, Festival City (701 2222).
Open 5.30pm-2am daily. **Credit** AmEx, MC, V.
Map p297 L3 ⑦

Clad in wood and covered in trinkets, the Belgian
Beer Café stands in stark contrast to the pseudo-deco
swirls of its parent hotel – and is all the better for it.
Shame the balcony overlooks big swathes of nothing, but this is one of the few places in Dubai that
breaks out of the Fosters/Heineken/Guinness tri-
umvirate: the 'café' purveys imported beers such as
the excellent Kwak and the more familiar
Hoegaarden. It's no wonder, then, that it fills to
bursting point nearly every weekend – especially
after a concert at the nearby Festival Centre.

Dubliner's

*Le Méridien Dubai, Airport Road, Garhoud
(282 4040).* **Open** noon-2am daily. **Credit**
AmEx, MC, V. **Map** p297 L2 ⑧

An intimate Irish bar serving decent pub grub and
some of the biggest pies in town, the Dubliner's is a
jovial place for a pint. The decor incorporates dark
wood, the obligatory Guinness posters and the back
end of a truck, alongside acres of Celtic paraphernalia attempting to convince patrons that they're not
really on the edge of a desert. It's a good, if raucous,
place to come to watch televised sports, and its proximity to the airport makes it worth a punt if you have
only got a few hours in town and aren't feeling particularly adventurous.

★ Irish Village

*The Aviation Club, Garhoud (282 4750/
www.irishvillage.ae).* **Open** 11am-1am daily.
Credit AmEx, MC, V. **Map** p297 K3 ⑨

Although the Irish Village hardly stands out from
any of the billion other Irish hooch houses from
Dubai to Derby, it's a great option if you're looking
for a pint, a nibble and a crowd to enjoy them with.
The major draw during winter months is the fantastic outside terrace that stands alongside a duck
pond. But the vast assortment of draught beers
available – including old favourites such as
Guinness and Kilkenny – keep people flooding in all
year round. So too do the frequent gigs by stars of
yesteryear, including Bob Geldof, who turns up like
clockwork every St Patrick's Day. *Photo p148.*

Ginseng. *See p143.*

Authorised Alcohol

The local laws on drink and drinking.

The sheer number of bars and clubs might suggest otherwise, but the UAE is a Muslim country, and the consumption of alcohol by non-Muslims is tolerated rather than encouraged or celebrated. Here's the low-down on legal drinking.

BRINGING IT IN
It is fine to bring alcohol into the UAE – indeed, once you're through passport control the first thing you'll see is a duty-free shop. At present you're limited to four items per person. After leaving Dubai Duty Free, it's advisable to keep your purchases bagged up until you reach your destination.

BUYING IT HERE
Dubai residents can buy alcohol from one of the city's two suppliers, MMI (424 5000) and A&E (222 2666), providing they have a valid alcohol licence. Licences can be picked up from MMI and A+E stores, throughout the city. However, the application process is a complicated one, requiring visa photocopies and multiple signatures. As a result, it's not uncommon for expats to skip the licence altogether and hope that the police never have reason to enter their houses.

Only one licence is awarded per household, and the amount you can purchase is dependent upon your salary. People with Muslim names may find themselves being turned down flat irrespective of their actual religious beliefs.

PUBLIC HOUSES
The law demands that all bars be attached to hotels or private clubs, although many establishments will have their own entrances away from the hotel lobby. Technically, residents must have alcohol licences to drink in hotel bars and pubs, but this law is only very rarely applied, mostly during the occasional police crackdown. A more noticeable aspect of alcohol laws for most visitors is the large tax placed on alcoholic beverages – finding a pint for less than Dhs28 in the city is a challenge.

DRUNK AND DISORDERLY
Public displays of drunkenness are frowned upon, and there is zero tolerance when it comes to the city's strict under-age drinking and drink-driving laws. You must be 21 to purchase or consume alcohol, and many bars will require photo ID before they serve baby-faced boozers. Drive with the faintest whiff of alcohol on your breath, and you can expect to do some time in one of Dubai's prisons, as well as pay a small fortune in punitive fines. It is worth bearing this in mind the morning after a heavy night: stay off the road until the last traces are out of your system. Dubai isn't really geared up for walking from pub to pub, so opt instead for one of the city's taxis, which can generally be found swarming around nearby hotels and malls.

DRY DAYS
Certain days may be deemed by the government to be dry days, during which alcohol is restricted from 7.30pm the previous night to 7.30pm that day. Some, like prophets' birthdays, happen regularly each year. Others are declared on an ad hoc basis to mark major events, such as the death of a member of the royal family. Generally, the more important the deceased, the longer the dry period – some have gone on for 40 days.

RAMADAN
Although Ramadan is based around fasting and strict adherence to Muslim teachings, expats are still welcome to drink alcohol after sundown, when the blanket ban on public consumption of all kinds of drink and food ends. Although certain restaurants may continue to serve food behind closed doors and obscured windows, it will be impossible to get alcohol until the sun has set.

When that happens, however, you can expect the city's bars and pubs to become livelier than in the rest of the year. Since there is a total ban on loud music and live non-traditional music through the Ramadan period, the city's nightclubs all close for the duration, moving the city's party animals to the normally quieter drinking spots.

Based on the lunar calendar, Ramadan lasts for approximately 30 days, and moves back by ten days on the Gregorian calendar each year: in 2009 it will begin on August 21, in 2010 it will begin on August 11, and so on. For more about Ramadan rules, *see p186.*

Dubai Mall
Ground Floor
Grove Carnival Street
T. +97143399131
resto@meswitch.com
www.meswitch.com

★ QD's

*Dubai Creek Golf & Yacht Club, Garhoud Road
(295 6000/www.dubaigolf.com).* **Open** 6pm-2am
daily (closed summer). **Credit** AmEx, MC, V.
Map p297 K3 ⑩

Nestled in the grounds of Dubai Creek Golf & Yacht
Club, QD's is a must-visit during the winter months.
A classy open-air affair, this wood-decked bar has
superb views across the Creek, pizzas cooked by a
wood-burning oven, and all the shisha you can
smoke. The regular DJs can be a bit of a hit and miss
affair, but if you can block out the occasional musical mistake, watching the sun crash down beyond
the Creek with a cocktail in your hand is almost as
good as it gets in Dubai.

Warehouse

Le Méridien Village (217 0000). **Open** 5pm-3am
daily. **Credit** AmEx, MC, V. **Map** p297 L2 ⑪

One of the newest venues in Dubai, the Warehouse
is also one of its nicest and most baffling. Despite
the name, it is in fact a large, rather swish-looking
marble-clad bar and restaurant, with patios at the
front and rear and a large balcony area to accommodate as many people as possible. It also has a small
and rather underwhelming club area that sits
uncomfortably alongside the refined decor in the rest
of the place. Still, it's definitely worth swishing by
for a glass of wine. *Photo p149.*

JUMEIRAH

Agency

*Souk Madinat Jumeirah (366 8888/
www.madinatjumeirah.com).* **Open** 7pm-2am
daily. **Credit** AmEx, MC, V. **Map** p304 D1 ⑫

A much more attractive proposition than its
Emirates Towers twin, this branch of the Agency
boasts an equally impressive – and expensive –
selection of wines, and its food is largely excellent.
However, it is also massively popular with the area's
well-heeled business types, and finding a spare table
will prove very tricky indeed.

BarZar

*Souk Madinat Jumeirah (366 6197/www.
madinatjumeirah.com).* **Open** 5pm-2am Sat-
Thur; noon-2am Fri. **Credit** AmEx, MC, V.
Map p304 D1 ⑬

BarZar's languid waterside terrace is one of the most
popular drinking spots in the city. Set in the
Madinat's bustling souk, the bar pulls in punters
with a variety of drinks deals and promotions. The
place is large, with two indoor floors, an upstairs balcony and the aforementioned patio. Big-screen TVs
play a mix of muted MTV and sports events, while
variable bands play over the top. It gets horren-
dously packed at weekends, though, so be prepared
for queues at the bar.

Dhow & Anchor

*Jumeirah Beach Hotel (348 0000/www.
jumeirahbeachhotel.com).* **Open** noon-1am daily.
Credit AmEx, MC, V. **Map** p304 E1/E2 ⑭

Falling somewhere between an old-fashioned British
boozer and a Mediterranean taverna, Dhow &
Anchor is a lively place where residents and tourists
throw back drinks and talk nonsense at an increasing volume. However, beyond the whorls of cigarette
smoke is a snug dining room and a lovely open terrace where decent Anglo-centric pub fare can be
sampled reasonably cheaply.

CONSUME

Waxy O'Conner's. *See p144.*

Left Bank
Souk Madinat Jumeriah (368 6171/www.
mmidubai.com). **Open** noon-2am daily.
Credit AmEx, MC, V. **Map** p304 D1 **15**
Neon lighting, low seating and minimalist decor is
the order of the day here, in distinction to the far
superior – and rather classier-looking – sister bar in
Souk Al Bahar. Left Bank's All Bar One-esque interior won't be to everyone's taste, but the bar's waterside terrace is worthy of a visit – if you are able to
get a seat, that is.
▶ *For more about that sister bar in Souk Al*
Bahar, see p151.

★ Malecon
Dubai Marine Beach Resort & Spa, Beach
Road (346 1111/www.dxbmarine.com). **Open**
7pm-3am daily. **Credit** AmEx, MC, V. **Map**
p300 D8 **16**
In no way affiliated to its famous overseas name-
sakes, Malecon is a funky salsa spot with an in-
house Latino troupe and blue walls that have been
completely covered in graffiti. It's a restaurant in the
early evening, while the later hours see the dance
floor get some serious action as a regular collective

of merengue maniacs cut some rug. The stylised
decor has also made it a popular spot for local bands
to play occasional gigs.

Sho Cho
Dubai Marine Beach Resort & Spa, Jumeriah
Beach Road (346 1111/www.dxbmarine.com).
Open 7pm-1am daily. **Credit** AmEx, MC, V.
Map p300 D8/D9 **17**
With a gorgeous terrace overlooking the Gulf and
manga movies projected on the fish tank-studded
walls, Sho Cho is a super-hip Japanese-themed bar.
Sophisticated, classy and dead trendy, this is where
the beautiful people go to play, pose and look pretty:
you will not see an ounce of spare body fat in the
place. Tuesday and Sunday night tend to be heaving, so it's best to telephone ahead for reservations
or to arrive as a couple as the door policy is notoriously tough on single males.

Skyview Bar
Burj Al Arab (301 7777). **Open** 7pm-2am daily.
Credit AmEx, MC, V. **Map** p304 E1 **18**
Skyview Bar is certainly not the place to come for a
swift one (there's a minimum spend of Dhs275 per
person, reservations are essential and the strict dress
code's definitely not open to discussion), the
Skyview's position atop the famous seven-star hotel
ensures its popularity. The bar's decor is garish to
say the least – chameleon-with-an-identity-crisis carpets and broken Casio calculators on the wall – but
the views are superb, and the bragging rights on
your return home help to justify the cost.
▶ *For more about Dubai's most famous hotel,*
see p98 Profile.

THE MARINA

Bar 44
Grosvenor House, Dubai Marina (04 317 6871/
www.grosvenorhouse-dubai.com). **Open** 12.30pm-
2am Fri-Wed; 12.30pm-3am Thur. **Credit** AmEx,
MC, V. **Map** p304 B1 **19**
There's a plethora of classy and expensive venues
in Dubai, but the vertiginous Bar 44 – so called
because it's located on the 44th floor of Grosvenor
House – has plenty to elevate its standing even further. The views across new Dubai are exceptional,
while the exquisite cocktail menu will have you
revisiting the bar time and time again. Add efficient
and knowledgeable service – nearly any cocktail can
be engineered to your taste – and you have a classy,
albeit expensive, bar that is head and shoulders
above the majority of its competitors.

★ Barasti Bar
Le Méridien Mina Seyahi Beach Resort &
Marina, Al Sufouh Road (318 1313/www.
lemeridien-minaseyahi.com). **Open** 11am-2am
Sat-Wed; 11am-3am Thur, Fri. **Credit** MC, V.
Map p304 B1 **20**

Irish Village. *See p144.*

Warehouse. *See p147.*

Permanently packed, this wood-decked, sun-drenched beach bar almost doubled in size during its 2006 refit, but even with the additional space you'll still struggle to find a table, particularly at the weekend. Alongside the usual alcoholic treats, the bar does a nice sideline in shisha pipes, and offers the perfect setting for a puff over-looking the sea. Despite being set in one of the more touristy locations, Barasti still has a cheery local ambience. *Photo p150.*

★ Buddha Bar

Grosvenor House, Dubai Marina (399 8888/www.buddha-bar.com). **Open** 8pm-2am Sat-Wed; 8pm-3am Thur, Fri. **Credit** AmEx, MC, V. **Map** p304 B1 ㉑

Despite the somewhat incongruous decor – a large statue of a monk who may or may not be the Buddha himself – and a bar serving countless concoctions, Buddha Bar is a chic and only slightly pretentious bar-cum-lounge club that also serves good, albeit expensive, Asian food.

Roof Top

Arabian Court, One&Only Royal Mirage, Al Sufouh Road (399 9999/www.oneandonlyresorts.com). **Open** 5pm-1am daily. **Credit** AmEx, MC, V. **Map** p304 C1 ㉒

A sedate sipping station, the Roof Top remains one of the most magnificent drinking venues in the city. The views, which take in the serene Gulf and the bizarre Palm Jumeirah, can't be beaten, and the soundtrack of commercial chilled beats peppered with the odd classic is perfectly judged. Drinks certainly aren't cheap, though. The Roof Top is an excellent launch pad for a special romantic evening. Don't confuse it with the Madinat Rooftop (*see p225*).

SHEIKH ZAYED ROAD

Agency

Jumeirah Emirates Towers, Sheikh Zayed Road (319 8780/www.jumeirah.com). **Open** 6pm-1am Sat-Wed; 6pm-2am Thur; 5pm-1am Fri. **Credit** AmEx, MC, V. **Map** p296 H4 ㉓

An upmarket wine bar, the the Agency attracts affluent, well-dressed, well-behaved thirtysomethings looking to drink away the stresses of the day. The bar's chilled-out interior – a blend of dark wood and crimson velvet furniture – is made for conversation. It's a crying shame then that the exterior is so uninspiring: sat on patio furniture and flanked by potted plants, you gaze out towards a pair of escalators. If it's alfresco ambience you're after, the branch at Souk Madinat Jumeirah is a better bet, although it's often impossible to get a seat there.

Après

Mall of the Emirates (341 2575/www.mmidubai.com). **Open** noon-1am daily. **Credit** AmEx, MC, V. **Map** p304 D2 ㉔

Après is a place that tries to mix alpine ski lodge and stylish nightspot aesthetics, but ends up looking like a mad interior designer's dream. Armed with every conceivable drink under the sun, the staff claim to be able to make a cocktail to suit anyone's tastes – and with connoisseur choices made from ingredients as diverse as cucumber, tobacco-infused rum, sage and coriander, the fussiest of taste buds should be tickled. The food is reasonably good, too – especially the spectacularly tasty fondue. The sight of cartwheeling skiers on the other side of the large slope-facing windows, along with the barmen's impressive juggling, should keep you entertained.

CONSUME

CONSUME

Barasti Bar. *See p148.*

Blue Bar

Novotel, Sheik Zayed Road, behind the Dubai World Trade Centre (332 0000). **Open** 2pm-2am daily. **Credit** AmEx, MC, V. **Map** p301 G10 ㉕

Blue Bar once carved itself a bit of a live music niche with its regular weekend jazz nights, but managerial interference has seen it move more towards a more mainstream jazz-blues-rock sound. Located on the ground floor of the business-like Novotel hotel, the place combines chilled-out vibes and an unusually good selection of draught Belgian beers to potent effect. On normal nights, TV screens churn out the usual MOR pap and the place resembles the hotel bar it is, but it's still a nice enough place to go for a quality lager or two.

Cin Cin

Fairmont Dubai, Sheikh Zayed Road, (332 5555). **Open** 6pm-2am daily. **Credit** AmEx, MC, V. **Map** p301 G9/G10 ㉖

Curved around an enormous central pillar, this horseshoe-shaped wine-pusher is a favourite among the office crowd. The floor-to-ceiling wine racks house over 250 different varieties, and the sporadic use of lighting, languid soundtracks, and adjoining cigar bar all impress. A bar for grown-ups, with the prices set to match.

Double Decker

Al Murooj Rotana Hotel & Suites Dubai, Defence Roundabout, near Dusit Dubai (321 1111/www.rotana.com). **Open** noon-3am daily. **Credit** AmEx, MC, V. **Map** p303 F13 ㉗

Double Decker is an unashamed Anglophile of a bar. From the grandiose coats of armour adorning the walls to the hordes of sunburnt punters parading around, it's a home away from home for the expat crowd. It might not have the most adventurous atmosphere, but with excellent service and a resident DJ armed with party tunes, it's frequently packed to the gunnels.

★ Fibber McGee's

Behind Crowne Plaza on Sheikh Zayed Road, between rears of Crowne Plaza & Fairmont Hotel (332 2400/www.fibbersdubai.com). **Open** 8an-3am daily. **Credit** MC, V. **Map** p301 G9 ㉓

Fibber McGee's is unusual in not being in a hotel. This back-street boozer is tucked away off Sheikh Zayed Road, and is not one for people wanting to sample a glass of chilled white wine while mulling over the latest developments on the Dubai Financial Market. A lack of windows means the place isn't the sunniest of venues, but the closed-in feeling helps create a great atmosphere, especially when football or rugby matches are being shown on the big-screen televisions that line the walls. Also worth checking out is the excellent Easy Tiger Quiz Night on Tuesdays – easily the best of its kind in the city.

Harry Ghatto's

Jumeirah Emirates Towers, Sheikh Zayed Road (330 0000/www.jumeirahemiratestowers.com). **Open** 8pm-3am daily. **Credit** AmEx, MC, V. **Map** p296 H4 ㉙

People can be split into two camps: those who love karaoke, and those who hate it but secretly wish they had the nerve to get up on stage and start crooning 'Suspicious Minds'. If you have accepted your inner diva, Harry Ghatto's is the best place in Dubai to belt out a few classics. The bar nestles in the back room of the Tokyo@The Towers and is a cosy little space, serving expensive imported Japanese beer and sake. The staff will help any nervous performers unsure about how to join in.

★ Left Bank

Souk Al Bahar, Old Town, near Burj Dubai (368 4501). **Open** noon-1am daily. **Credit** AmEx, MC, V. **Map** p303 F14 ㉚

Not to be confused with the darker, more 'urban' Madinat Jumeirah branch of Left Bank, this deceptively large bar, which is nestled in the Souk Al Bahar mall near the Burj Dubai, is a much classier affair. With a fine selection of spirits, snug seating and a pleasingly intimate ambience, it's a perfect spot for everything from quiet conversation to office outings. But beware – the bar can get incredibly busy on weekend nights. *Photo p152.*

Long's Bar

Towers Rotana Hotel, Sheikh Zayed Road (312 2231/www.rotana.com). **Open** noon-3am daily. **Credit** AmEx, MC, V. **Map** p303 F12 ㉛

Long's is one of those places ruddy-faced expats refer to with a crinkly grin as being a 'Dubai institution'. Certainly, some of the punters here could do with being removed to a facility of some sort, but the reason it's such a longstanding favourite is because it's a fairly authentic reproduction of a spit 'n' sawdust British pub. Expect TV football, good value drinks and predictable albeit tasty food.

Lotus One

World Trade Centre, near Novotel, Sheikh Zayed Road (329 3200). **Open** noon-2am daily. **Credit** MC, V. **Map** p301 G9/G10 ㉜

INSIDE TRACK
GREAT OUTDOORS

Enjoy the warm climate and sip a cocktail or two outside. **Barasti Bar** (*see p148*) is one of the most popular beach bars in the city, and the decking is packed at weekends. For panoramic views of the Gulf, head to **360** (*see p223*). If you're planning a late one, try **Chi** (*see p220*) nightclub, which has an outdoor garden.

CONSUME

A swanky Thai fusion restaurant-bar-club, Lotus One is a popular weekend hangout. Occasionally slow bar service and plenty of knocks and nudges from sunglass-toting posers can make it a little frustrating, but with suspended decks and chairs, cow-print leather cushions and a glass floor showcasing a river and rubble scene underneath, there's plenty to keep your eyes busy.

Neos

The Address, Downtown Burj Dubai (436 8927). **Open** 5pm-2am daily. **Credit** AmEx, MC, V. **Map** p303 F15 ③

Located on the 63rd floor of the Address hotel (strangely, the lift doesn't stop on floor 62), Neos provides spectacular views of Sheikh Zayed Road and Dubai Mall's mega-fountain – which is good news, because the astronomical menu prices and chrome-heavy interiors aren't particularly enticing. Still, the faux-1920s ambience, complete with bow-tied waiters, is (if you can excuse the chrome) pleasant, and there's always a high chance of glimpsing a Bollywood star or two – they flock to the place like glamorous moths to lamplight. Beware, though – there's a shirts-only policy on the door.

Scarlett's

Jumeriah Emirates Towers, Sheikh Zayed Road (330 0000/www.jumeriahemiratestowers.com). **Open** noon-3am Sat-Thur; 4pm-3am Fri. **Credit** AmEx, MC, V. **Map** p296 H4 ③

Another of Dubai's three-in-one specials, Scarlett's is a popular bar-restaurant-nightclub with a Dixieland theme. It has become a bit of a Dubai institution with its young, mostly affluent and invariably well-dressed crowd, which spends time drinking and attempting to strike up conversations with members of the opposite sex. It follows that Tuesday's ladies' night is particularly popular.

Trader Vic's

Crowne Plaza Hotel Dubai, Sheikh Zayed Road (331 1111/www.tradersvics.com). **Open** 12.30-3pm, 6.30-11.30pm daily. **Credit** AmEx, MC, V. **Map** p301 F10/G10 ③

Trader's combination of a jolly Polynesian-style band and some of the most potent cocktails in the UAE creates a wonderfully carefree atmosphere. Seating is limited and the bar is often crowded, so arrive early if you want to take the weight off your feet and make the most of the happy hours (when prices drop from astronomical to merely expensive). **Other locations** Souk Madinat Jumeriah (366 5646).

Vu's Bar

Jumeriah Emirates Towers Hotel, Sheikh Zayed Road (330 0000/www.jumeirahemiratestowers. com). **Open** 6pm-3am daily. **Credit** AmEx, MC, V. **Map** p296 H4 ③

Laid-back elegance at premium prices has well-heeled punters heading up to this swanky 51st-floor bar, which boasts one of Dubai's finest views. Arrive early in the evening to watch the sun go down and the lights come on across the city – an experience made all the sweeter thanks to the bar's mouth-watering cocktail list. Wear a collar and shoes, or the fashion police at the doors won't let you in. A change in hotel policy means that you can no longer enjoy the spectacularly speedy glass elevator ride from the lobby to the bar (now only available to the fortunate few with room keys).

Left Bank. *See p151.*

Shops & Services

Consumption is entertainment in Dubai.

Dubai is all about the three Ss: sun, sea and shopping. Tourists flock to the sandy city to see if the rumours are true – are there really over 100 shopping malls? Well, yes and no. The sizzling heat of half the year means that the environment isn't conducive to stores in the open air. To pull in the punters, top shops amalgamate in the air-conditioned safety of the malls, where you can also find all manner of entertainment – there's a ski slope at Mall of the Emirates (*see p158*), and an Olympic-sized ice rink and shark-filled aquarium at Dubai Mall (*see p157*). But don't expect every

shopping centre to be a hotbed of great labels and well-known brands; there are around a dozen malls (*see pp154-159*) worth jumping in a taxi for; the others serve day-to-day needs and have only basic stores on offer.

THE SHOPPING SCENE

In terms of variety and colour, the shopping experience is a long way off New York's Fifth Avenue, but Dubai is upping the ante year after year, introducing more great outlets and opening bigger malls (such as Dubai Mall, *see p157*). And, thanks to changes in legislation, independently-owned boutiques are flourishing (*see p173* **Going It Alone**). When it comes to souks (*see p160*), this may be the Middle East, but if you have vivid images of bustling thoroughfares similar to those in Egypt or Syria, you'll be surprised – most are covered markets – but you can still haggle and walk away with glittering gold, beautiful silks and bags of

fragrant spices. Haggling is a tradition in the souks, and it really is rare to pay the full price on the tag – if there is one. The trick to haggling is to take your time, be polite and to decide what you are happy to pay for the item. Bargaining isn't common practice in malls, although it doesn't hurt to ask for a discount, especially if you're paying cash.

Frittering money away is a national sport in the UAE, there's even a Shopping Festival, so you can splash your hard-earned cash late into the night. Typical shop opening hours are from 10am until midnight, with stores opening up later on Fridays, usually at around 2pm. Visitors used to the generous return, exchange and refund policies found in Europe and the United States should be aware that consumers don't have as many rights in Dubai. When exchanges are available, rather than having weeks to take your purchase back, the norm here is between three to seven days. To avoid unwanted stress, be sure to ask what a store's policy is before making your purchase.

INSIDE TRACK
DUBAI OUTLET MALL

It might be in the middle of pretty well nowhere (way out on the Dubai-Al Ain road), but the **Dubai Outlet Mall** (*see p157*) is worth the trip. It might be last season's gear, but with big name labels at bargain prices, why not stand out from the crowd? Brands on offer include Adidas, Calvin Klein, Esprit, Guess, Mango, Massimo Dutti, Nike, Nina Ricci, Nine West, Paris Gallery, Puma, Reebok, Rodeo Drive and Tommy Hilfiger.

General

DEPARTMENT STORES

Bhs
BurJuman Centre (352 5150/www.bhs.co.uk).
Open 10am-10pm Sat-Thur; 2-10.30pm Fri.
Credit AmEx, MC, V. **Map** p299 J5.

Although not exactly an exclusive haunt in its native Britain, Bhs does a roaring trade in Dubai. Cheap prices with plenty of wardrobe basics make it a one-stop shop for families. Unlike its sister stores in the UK, here you'll find the focus on children's wear rather than adult clothing.
Other locations Al Ghurair City (227 6969); Ibn Battuta Mall (368 5404); Lamcy Plaza (335 8334).

Bloomingdales

The US department store famous for its large, medium and small brown bags is set to open in Dubai Mall in February 2010. *See right* **Dubai Mall**.

Debenhams

Mall of the Emirates (340 7575/www.debenhams. com). **Open** 10am-midnight daily. **Credit** AmEx, MC, V. **Map** p304 D2.
The Dubai branch of Britain's popular department store won't disappoint and stocks a comprehensive range of goods from cosmetics to homewares. Concessions are this store's forte, and you can find fashion from collections by John Rocha, Jasper Conran, Matthew Williamson and Pearce Fonda. The lingerie section is particularly strong and includes lines by Triumph, Chantelle and Freya.
Other locations Deira City Centre (294 0011); Ibn Battuta Mall (396 5900).

Harvey Nichols

Mall of the Emirates (409 8888/www.harvey nichols.com). **Open** 10am-midnight daily. **Credit** AmEx, MC, V. **Map** p304 D2.
This store represents Harvey Nichols' third venture onto foreign soil, after Riyadh and Hong Kong, and it fills a big gap in Dubai's shopping market. With high-end brands, luxury accessories and the cult cosmetic haven Fushi, the department store is unsurprisingly sleek, with a clientele to match.

Jashanmal

Wafi City Mall (324 4800/www.jashanmal-uae.com). **Open** 10am-10pm Sat-Wed; 10am-midnight Thur, Fri. **Credit** AmEx, MC, V. **Map** p297 J3.
The UAE's answer to the UK's John Lewis, this store has a fine selection of well-kitted out departments. The household section is particularly strong: you'll find everything from Disney sandwich boxes to kettles, vacuum cleaners, Le Creuset pans, bedding and crockery items.
Other locations Al Ghurair City (227 7780); Mall of the Emirates (347 1715).

★ Marks & Spencer

Waterfront Centre, Dubai Festival City (206 6466/www.futtaim.com). **Open** 10am-10pm daily. **Credit** AmEx, DC, MC, V. **Map** p297 L3.
Dubai's largest branch of the British high street favourite stocks plenty of family-friendly clothing essentials and off-the-peg suits, and is home to a fantastic lingerie department. The health and beauty section is particularly well stocked, and there's also a food department that stocks frozen meals, freshly baked goods and plenty of crisps and nuts.
Other locations near Al Ghurair City, Deira (222 2000); Wafi City Mall (324 5145).

★ Saks Fifth Avenue

BurJuman Centre (351 5551/www.saksfifth avenue.com). **Open** 10am-10pm Sat-Thur; 2-10pm Fri. **Credit** AmEx, MC, V. **Map** p299 J5.
The epitome of New York chic, this store has lost none of its sassiness in its transplant to the Middle East. On two levels you'll find an array of top-end labels including Prada, Alberta Ferretti and Dior. You can also splurge on Manolo Blahnik. *Photo p161.*

Salam

Wafi City Mall (324 5252/www.salams.com). **Open** 10am-10pm Sat-Wed; 10am-midnight Thur; 2.45pm-midnight Fri. **Credit** AmEx, DC, MC, V. **Map** p297 J3.
With D&G, Moschino, Escada and Lacoste all in supply, this department store will have your whole family decked in designer gear, the children's section has plenty to choose from too. *Photo p158.*

MALLS

Bur Dubai

Al Ghazal Mall

Al Dhiyafah Road (345 1434). **Open** 10am-10pm Sat-Thur; 4-10pm Fri. **Map** p300 F8.
It's not one of the city's hottest shopping haunts, but this quiet mall is ideal for a laid-back roam, with its decent cross-section of stores. There's a well-stocked La Senza and a handful of quirky independent brands such as Pilgrim and Dethar.

BurJuman Centre

Trade Centre Road (352 0222/www.burjuman. com). **Open** 10am-10pm Sat-Thur; 4-10pm Fri. **Map** p299 J5.
Much improved after an extension, BurJuman is a subdued, chic mall with plenty of designer barns, including Burberry, Donna Karan, Christian Lacroix and Tiffany & Co, as well as a good selection of high

---

THE BEST MALLS

For the most square feet
Dubai Mall. *See right.*

For gimmicky decor
IBN Battuta Mall. *See p159.*

For ski fanatics
Mall of the Emirates. *See p158.*

CONSUME

A World of Its Own

Size certainly matters at Dubai's biggest mall.

At 440,000 square feet, Dubai Mall is the emirate's largest shopping haven. That's the equivalent of 50 soccer pitches. The most-talked about attractions in this mini city of a mall are the Olympic-sized ice rink and the shark-filled aquarium. The former features 'learn to skate' programmes and is designed to host international ice hockey contests and double up as a concert arena.

The aquarium, meanwhile, holds an almost unfathomable 10 million litres of water, and boasts the world's biggest viewing panel at 32.8 metres wide and 8.3 metres high. In true Dubai style, it's one of the largest tanks on the planet and there are plans for it to eventually be filled with more than 33,000 animals, including 400 sharks and rays (shark feeding currently takes place at 4pm every day). You can gaze at the fishes for free, but there's a fee to enter the walk-through glass tunnel (Dhs20 for children, Dhs25 for adults). A 'lunar-cyclic' lighting system will change the ambience of the tank depending on the time of day. There's also an underwater zoo, which for Dhs50 (the price includes entry to the tunnel) brings you face to face with piranhas, a giant catfish, otters, a penguin colony and seals. Keen scuba divers can also pay a fee to dive with the sharks.

But that's not all Dubai Mall has to offer. The Grove part of the mall is a pleasant open-air streetscape with trees, walkways, cafés and a retractable roof that slides open in winter and lets in lots of sunlight in summer. There's also the world's largest gold souk, with 220 retailers and traditional Arabic architecture, including bronze horse, palm tree and camel statues. Even the food court is the biggest in Dubai, with 40 outlets, water fountains and outside terraces to take the sun.

For bookworms, a trip to Japanese chain **Kinokuniya** (*see p162*) is essential. The region's first, its cavernous interior stocks all manner of page-turners, including a sizeable graphic novel section. For all your food shopping needs, the first **Waitrose** (*see p179*) store outside the UK (an upmarket supermarket chain) covers almost the entire bottom half of the lower ground floor. For some really serious retail therapy, US department store **Bloomingdales** opens in 2010, and will be spread over four levels.

For children, there's **Sega Republic**, which has an indoor spin-coaster and one of the largest selections of arcade and gaming machines in the world. You can find **Hamleys** on level two, and **Kidzania**, a city scaled down to children's size where kids can role play in 70 different professions, from doctors to chefs.

All in all, you could easily spend a day in Dubai Mall and not get bored. Maybe make that a long weekend.

▶ For contact details, see p157.

CONSUME

Dubai Festival City.

street stores such as Zara, Mango, Diesel and Massimo Dutti. Saks Fifth Avenue makes it stand out from the crowd. There are plenty of upmarket cafés to rest at in between splurges.

Lamcy Plaza
Oud Metha (335 9999/www.lamcyplaza.com). **Open** 9am-midnight Sat, Thur, Fri; 9am-10pm Sun-Wed. **Map** p297 J3.
Seemingly abandoned in a strange time warp, Lamcy Plaza certainly doesn't strive to keep up with the other malls' obsession with cutting-edge modernity. The interior is dated, there's a bizarre and tacky replica of Tower Bridge, and an unrealistic-looking waterfall. But if you're looking for bargains this might just be the perfect mall. Stock up on cut-price clothes from Fashion Factory and handy Dhs5-Dhs10 knick-knacks at the extraordinary Japanese discount store Daiso. Before you go, grab a cheap curry at Thai Express.

Burj Dubai

★ Dubai Mall
Financial Centre Road (437 3200/www.the dubaimall.com). **Open** 10am-10pm Sun-Wed; 10pm-midnight Thur-Sat. **Map** p303 F13.
This is the city's biggest mall, complete with Olympic-sized ice rink and shark-filled aquarium. *See p155* **Dubai Mall**.

Deira

Al Ghurair City
Al Rigga Road, Deira (222 5222/www.alghurair city.com). **Open** 10am-10pm Sat-Thur; 2-10pm Fri. **Map** p299 K3.
This veteran mall, actually the oldest in Dubai, combines Arabic decor with modern design. Popular outlets here include Nine West and Paris Gallery. The mall itself is a bit of a maze, spread over two floors, with corridors branching out at all angles, but it's worth persevering; tucked in the alleyways are excellent speciality stores selling everything from Arabic jewellery and rugs to South African beauty products.

Deira City Centre
Deira/Garhoud area (295 1010/www.deiracity centre.com). **Open** 10am-10pm Sat-Thur; 2-10pm Fri. **Map** p297 K2.
Once the jewel in Dubai's shopping crown, Deira City Centre has had to work hard to fight off competition from the likes of Mall of the Emirates and Ibn Battuta Mall. It's putting up a good fight, and having introduced a whole flood of new titles to its portfolio, including Club Monaco, H&M and New Look, it's still a shopping heavyweight. There's also a massive branch of French hypermarket Carrefour, the amusement centre Magic Planet and a multiplex cinema.

★ Dubai Festival City
Deira/Garhoud area (375 0505/232 5444/www. dubaifestivalcity.com). **Open** 10am-10pm Sun-Wed; 10am-midnight Thur-Sat. **Map** p297 L3.
These connected centres opened in early 2007 to a cavalcade of hype. No wonder, really, as they contain a whopping 500 stores and have a fantastic location by the water. The corridors are bathed with natural light and several good restaurants are scattered along the waterfront. Few malls offer so much variety – there's Marks & Spencer, Kenzo, Lacoste, Mark Jacobs, Calvin Klein and a huge Ikea. The picturesque Festival Square at the heart of the venue offers a regular programme of entertainment too.

Dubai-Al Ain Road

Dubai Outlet Mall
Dubai-Al Ain Road (Route 66) (423 4666/ www.dubaioutletmall.com). **Open** 10am-10pm Sun-Wed; 10am-midnight Thur-Sat.
Last season's gear at bargain prices. *See p153* **Inside Track**.

International City

Dragon Mart
Next to International City (368 7070/www. dragonmart.ae). **Open** 10am-10pm Sat-Wed; 10am-11pm Thur; 2-11pm Fri.
For bargains on clothes, hardware and furniture, a stop here is essential. *See below* **Inside Track**.

Jumeirah

Jumeirah Centre
Jumeirah Beach Road, Jumeirah (349 9702/ www.gmgdubai.com). **Open** 10am-9pm Sat-Thur; 4-9pm Fri. **Map** p300 D9.
This attractive mini-mall is popular with local residents and has compact outlets spread over its two floors. Benetton, the Nike Store and the Body Shop

---

INSIDE TRACK
DRAGONMART

For shoppers who have a nose for a bargain, **Dragon Mart** (*see above*) is the way forward. Here, haggling is par for the course and you can find all kinds of crazy kitsch. Take Sun Flower, a fake plant shop, with beautifully sculpted lilies for Dhs5, bunches of roses for Dhs40 and life-size palm trees at Dhs100-Dhs600 a pop. And there's no missing the garish signs for Zheijian Yiuan Optoelectronics, a neon haven selling all manner of light-up signs ('Open' and 'Cocktails' are particular highlights) for as little as Dhs160.

CONSUME

all feature, as well as Blue Cactus, which sells discounted designer gear. At the handicraft store Sunny Days, you can splash out on beautiful textiles and Persian rugs. Alternatively, sit back in one of the alfresco cafés with a cappuccino and relax.

Jumeirah Plaza

Jumeirah Beach Road, Jumeirah (349 7111).
Open 10am-10pm Sat-Thur; 5-10pm Fri.
Map p300 D9.
There are no big brands here, but this pretty centre is home to several smaller outlets, including gift

shop Susan Walpole and the excellent second-hand bookshop House of Prose. For creatives types there is a T-shirt design shop, and for interior fanatics, a few well-stocked craft shops upstairs.

★ Mall of the Emirates

Interchange 4, Sheikh Zayed Road (409 9000/ www.malloftheemirates.com). **Open** 10am-midnight Sat, Thur, Fri; 10am-10pm Sun-Wed.
Map p304 D2.
Staggeringly big and horrifically busy at weekends, this mall is Dubai's main hive of shopping activity,

Salam. *See p154.*

CONSUME

bringing together designer, high street, boutique and craft outlets under one enormous roof. The ground level is lined with high street names and a huge Carrefour, and the upper level caters for the exclusive brands. Take time out and catch a movie at the multiplex or cool off after all that window-shopping by getting on the piste at the ski dome. There are also oodles of cafés and restaurants – some licensed to serve alcohol – to keep you well fuelled. And thanks to the arrival of the Dubai Community Theatre & Arts Centre, on some nights you can catch a bit of live entertainment too. *Photo p166.*

Mercato Mall

Jumeirah Beach Road, Jumeirah (344 4161/ www.mercatoshoppingmall.com). **Open** 10am-10pm Sat-Thur; 2-10pm Fri. **Map** p302 C12.

Italian designed and inspired, Mercato is a light and airy mall decorated with stonewash murals and alleys. Although there is not quite the choice you'll find in bigger malls, there's a good mix of stores, including Mango, Massimo Dutti, Virgin Megastore and Topshop. There are also a few little boutiques worth checking out, including funky swimwear and lingerie store Moda Brazil, and the *Sex and the City*-inspired Fleurt.

Palm Strip

Jumeirah Beach Road, Jumeirah (346 1462). **Open** 10am-10pm Sat-Thur; 4-10pm Fri. **Map** p300 D9.

Set by the beach, this whitewashed mall is one of the very few open-air shopping strips in the city. Shops are set back from the road and arranged over two levels. The lower level is dominated by restaurants, including Starbucks and Japengo Café, in addition to a well-stocked branch of Zara Home. Upstairs you can opt for a bit of preening in the N.Bar nail salon, browse through a few home stores and check out a great haunt for mothers, Favourite Things Mother & Child.

★ Souk Madinat Jumeirah

Al Sufouh Road (366 6546/www.madinat jumeirah.com). **Open** 10am-11pm daily. **Map** p304 D1.

One of Dubai's most popular spots, the Madinat's souk has been made to resemble a traditional Arabian marketplace. With its maze of dimly lit identical corridors, it's easy to find yourself walking in circles while meandering past colourful outlets selling arts, crafts, homeware, jewellery and plenty of souvenirs. Although there is a handful of major branded stores including Bonpoint and Ounass, the majority of shops here cater mainly for tourists, and prices are accordingly high. Connected to a huge hotel complex, the mall has plenty of licensed bars and restaurants, which means it's always bustling with bags of atmosphere. Head to the man-made waterways to dine alfresco and people-watch under the eye of the Burj Al Arab.

Town Centre

Jumeirah Beach Road, Jumeirah (344 0111). **Open** 10am-10pm Sat-Thur; 5-10pm Fri. **Map** p302 C12.

Nestled next to Mercato Mall, this boxy centre seems slightly dated. At least Feet First offers top-notch reflexology, the S.O.S. salon provides affordable beauty treatments and Kaya Skin Clinic is a high-tech centre that will help tackle any skin woes. Visiting families should check out the innovative Café Céramique, where you can paint your own crockery while snacking on healthy food.

Village

Jumeirah Beach Road, Jumeirah (342 9679/ www.thevillagedubai.com). **Open** 10am-10pm Sat-Thur; 4-10pm Fri. **Map** p300 D9.

Attracting boutiques rather than high street outlets, the Village is an avant-garde shopper's dream. S*uce is a girly fashionista's treasure, Luxecouture is packed with New York's finest designer pieces and Ayesha Depala's boasts some lovely chichi designs.

Sheikh Zayed Road

Boulevard at Emirates Towers

Sheikh Zayed Road (330 0000/www.jumeirah emiratestowers.com). **Open** 10am-10pm Sat-Thur; 4-10pm Fri. **Map** p296 H4.

Nestled at the base of the Jumeirah Emirates Towers office block, this swanky mall offers a sophisticated spread of designer stores on its two floors. Gucci, Giorgio Armani, Yves Saint Laurent and Bottega Veneta dominate the ground floor, and upstairs you'll uncover Jimmy Choo.

Dubai Marina Mall

Dubai Marina, off Sheikh Zayed Road (436 1000/www.dubaimarinalmall.com). **Open** 10am-10pm daily; *Waitrose supermarket* open 8am-11pm daily. **Map** p304 B1.

Located in the Dubai Marina, this mall features 155 stores on four levels. With its Waitrose supermarket, it's more a convenience stop for residents of the Marina and Jumeirah Beach Residence, but there is also a food court, and the Favourite Things store has a supervised play area where you can drop off the children while you shop.

★ Ibn Battuta Mall

Between Interchange 5 & 6, Sheikh Zayed Road (362 1900/www.ibnbattutamall.com). **Open** 10am-midnight Sat, Thur, Fri; 10am-10pm Sun-Wed. **Map** p304 A2

Inspired by the adventures of the intrepid Arab traveller Ibn Battuta, this mall is one of the most eclectic in town. It's divided into six themed courts, each with corresponding architecture: Andalusian, Tunisian, Egyptian, Persian, Indian and Chinese. There are streams of great shops; so check out the Apple Centre and the vast branch of Debenhams. *Photo p170.*

CONSUME

CONSUME

SOUKS

Dubai's markets provide a lively commercial lifeline for local traders. You won't find the colourful bazaars seen in some Arabian cities, but prices for some goods can be cheaper than those in the malls.

Fish market

Deira, opposite Hyatt Regency Dubai & Galleria. **Open** 9am-1pm, 4-10pm Sat-Thur; 4-10pm Fri. **Map** p298 H2.

An army of men in blue uniforms rush around boxing, weighing and carving up the day's catch in this huge hall with stall upon stall of fish. While splashing your path past the stalls – this is not a place for flip-flops – expect to see black hammour, koffer, kingfish, safi, shark and plenty of brawny king prawns.

Fruit & vegetable souk

Deira, opposite Hyatt Regency Dubai & Galleria. **Open** 9am-1pm, 4-10pm Sat-Thur; 4-10pm Fri. **Map** p298 H2.

If you enter here from the adjoining meat market, it's like dying and being reborn. Bright, colourful and fragrant with an upbeat atmosphere, it's a fun place to look around even if you have no intention of stocking up on fresh goods. Pick up some ice-cold coconut water to keep you refreshed as you ogle everything from bog standard bananas to more intriguing buys, including bitter gourds, custard apples, dragon fruits and mangosteens.

Meat market

Deira, opposite Hyatt Regency Dubai & Galleria. **Open** 9am-1pm, 4-10pm Sat-Thur; 4-10pm Fri. **Map** p298 H2.

It's unlikely that you'll want to invest in half a lamb carcass while on holiday, but for people with an interest in food, Dubai's meat market is fascinatingly repulsive. Duck behind the enormous carcasses that swing from intimidating meat hooks while butchers busy themselves by hacking away at cow heads – watch out for flying jaws as fragments are thrown into various buckets. If that hasn't put you off, meat-eaters can find plenty great bargains here.

THE BEST SOUKS

For an unforgettably pungent experience
Fish market. *See above.*

For the cheapest ingredients
Fruit & vegetable market. *See above.*

For the most atmosphere
Spice souk. *See above.*

★ Spice souk

Between Al Nasr Square and the Creek, near Gold Souk, Deira. **Open** times vary, usually 8am-1pm, 4-9pm Sat-Thur; 4-9pm Fri. **Map** p298 H3.

Postcard-pretty sacks of aromatic ingredients line the small shop fronts at this colourful souk. Expect to find frankincense, nutmeg, cardamom, star anise, vanilla pods and saffron imported from Iran. This is one of the most atmospheric souks in town and gives you a glimpse into the old Dubai, but don't expect a leisurely stroll – getting through the area without being lured into several shops is hard work.

Textile souk

Al Fahidi Street, Bur Dubai. **Open** 9am-1pm, 4-10pm Sat-Thur; 4-10pm Fri. **Map** p298 H4.

The shops on this street house an enormous range of designs from the simple to the intricately elaborate. The majority of the material comes from the Indian subcontinent and at most stores you're free to haggle for a great price. If you intend to get something made up by a tailor, it's worth asking them how much material you will need to avoid any unnecessary revisits. Rivoli (352 5448) comes highly recommended; it's split into men's and women's floors, and you can find a good selection of materials here.

Specialist

ANTIQUES & CURIOS

Antique Museum

Third interchange, Al Quoz Industrial Area (347 9935). **Open** 9am-8.30pm Sat-Thur; 9-11am, 3-8.30pm Fri. **Credit** AmEx, MC, V. **Map** p304 E3.

Although Al Quoz may appear to be a deserted industrial estate, tucked away behind the bleak exteriors are some of Dubai's best antique haunts. Although not an actual antique museum, this warehouse is a diamond in the rough: once past the giant wooden doors you are transported into a secluded cave of lost riches. The narrow aisles are packed with a wide range of handicrafts, shisha pipes, pashmina shawls, furniture and the odd belly dancing costume.

Creative Art Centre

Behind Choithram supermarket, Jumeirah Beach Road, Jumeirah (344 4394). **Open** 8am-6pm Sat-Thur. **Credit** AmEx, MC, V. **Map** p300 D10.

Spanning two pristine villas, this centre brings together souvenirs, art and antiques. As a result, it's a haunt for people who want to add a splash of panache to their homes as well as a great spot for visitors to find some interesting keepsakes from their trip. Among the array of Arabic knick-knacks are several collector's items including wooden chests, old Omani doors turned into coffee tables and plenty of Bedouin silver.

Saks Fifth Avenue. *See p154.*

CONSUME

★ Gallery One

Mall of the Emirates (341 4488). **Open**
10am-midnight daily. **Credit** AmEx, MC, V.
Map p304 D2.
With its beautiful bold prints and one-offs, this compact exhibition space is rapidly gaining popularity among the art lovers of Dubai. The outlet features an eclectic mix of oil prints and photography, including limited edition original prints of the Beatles, Bob Marley and Jimi Hendrix among others.

Kani Home

Ibn Battuta Mall (368 5408). **Open** 10am-midnight Thur-Sat; 10am-10pm Sun-Wed.
Credit AmEx, MC, V. **Map** p304 A2.
Kani Home stocks Kashmiri goods, including handmade silver jewellery, brightly dyed silk kaftans, elaborate bedspreads, genuine pashminas, beautifully detailed rugs and antique Jamava shawls.

Majlis Gallery

Al Fahidi Roundabout, Bastakia, Bur Dubai (353 6233/www.majlisgallery.com). **Open**
9.30am-1.30pm, 4.30-8pm Sat-Thur. **Credit**
AmEx, MC, V. **Map** p298 H4.
With its appealing location in Bastakia, Dubai's old town, this is a great place to stop off for a coffee and a bit of shopping as you wander the winding alleyways. Step back in time through the chunky wooden doorway to find yourself in a serene courtyard surrounded by a series of exhibition rooms displaying work from local and international artists. Small sculptures and Arabian ornaments are often on display and if you don't mind paying top dirham, the gallery has a deserved reputation for its original on-canvas creations.

Showcase Antiques, Art & Frames

Jumeirah Beach Road, Jumeirah (348 8797).
Open 9am-8pm Sat-Thur. **Credit** AmEx, MC, V.
Map p304 E2.
Three storeys of antiques, artefacts and art make Showcase a store well worth a visit. There are plenty of items from Oman – you can pick up a rosewood chest from around Dhs1,800 and 19th century firearms from Dhs900. The beautiful Arabic pots that line the stairs are hard to resist and will set you back around Dhs700 a piece. A range of framed tribal jewellery, knives and *khanjars* dating back 100-odd years will appeal to customers looking to purchase a small slice of history.

Total Arts

The Courtyard, between Interchange 3 & 4, Sheikh Zayed Road, Al Quoz (228 2888/ www.courtyard-uae.com). **Open** 8am-1pm, 4-8pm Sat-Thur. **Credit** AmEx, MC, V. **Map** p304 E3.
A welcome surprise in the middle of dreary Al Quoz, the Courtyard is a self-enclosed street reminiscent of New York's Soho district. It offers a hotchpotch of impressive art stores and cafés. Tribal weavings and rugs from Iran are also available, and every piece is clearly labelled with details of age and origin.

BOOKS

Censorship laws mean that all books coming into the country are checked. Off-limits subjects include Israel and Judaism, gay and lesbian interest, alcohol, drugs and sex, and nudity and anything controversial regarding Islam is also likely to be blacklisted. International magazines are painstakingly leafed through and anything deemed indecent is blacked out using a marker pen. Although books are sold at roughly the UK/US price, imported magazines can double in price by the time they've reached Dubai's shops.

Book Corner
Al Dhiyafah Road (345 5490/www.book corner.ae). **Open** 10am-10pm Sat-Thur; 2-10pm Fri. **Credit** AmEx, MC, V. **Map** p300 F8.
A sleek, modern affair, with an exceptional selection of non-fiction. The cookery section upstairs is also one of the best in town, and on the lower level you'll find fantastic books on subjects such as interior design, architecture and art.

Book World
Plant Street, Karama, behind Pizza Inn (396 9697). **Open** 9am-1pm, 5-9.30pm Sat-Thur; 4.30-9.30pm Fri. **Credit** AmEx, MC, V. **Map** p301 F7.
Crammed with over 45,000 used books and thousands of magazines, this store operates on a pile-them-high-sell-them-cheap policy. Everything from gluts of Ian Rankin to the odd Khaled Hosseini is available, and few items cost over Dhs25.
Other locations Al Hudaiba Street, Satwa (349 1914).

Borders
Mall of the Emirates (341 5758/www.borders stores.com). **Open** 10am-midnight daily. **Credit** AmEx, MC, V. **Map** p304 D2.

Borders opened with a bang in November 2006, offering perhaps the widest selection of titles in town. The range of fiction is second to none in Dubai, and the children's section and choice of Arabic-language books are also extremely impressive.

House Of Prose
Jumeirah Plaza, Jumeirah Beach Road, Jumeirah (344 9021). **Open** 10am-10pm Sat-Thur; 5.30-8pm Fri. **Credit** AmEx, MC, V. **Map** p300 D9.
This Dubai institution has a simple policy: you buy any one of its reasonably priced books, read it, and then keep it or return the book and get 50 per cent of your money back. The books stay in circulation, you save money and you get to see what the bookworms of Dubai are reading. Rummage for long enough and you'll discover there's something for everyone.
Other locations Ibn Battuta Mall (368 5526).

Jashanmal
Mall of the Emirates (266 5964/ www.jashanmal-uae.com). **Open** 10am-10pm Sat-Thur; 2-10pm Fri. **Credit** AmEx, MC, V. **Map** p304 D2.
Meticulously neat and well stocked, Jashanmal outlets make an effort to stock all the new releases available in the region. The biography section is excellent too, and there's a well-stocked children's area. The store holds regular events, including in-store appearances by well-known authors.
Other locations Village Mall (344 5770).

Dubai Festival City. *See p157.*

CONSUME

★ Kinokuniya
Dubai Mall (434 0111/www.thedubaimall.com).
Open 10am-10pm Sun-Wed; 10am-midnight
Thur-Sat. **Credit** AmEx, DC, MC, V.
Map p303 F13.
This massive store in Dubai Mall stocks more than
half a million books and a thousand magazines in
English, Arabic, Japanese, French, German and
Chinese at any given time. *See p155* **A World of
Its Own**. *Photo p172.*

★ Magrudy's
*Jumeirah Plaza, Jumeirah Beach Road (344
4193/www.magrudy.com).* **Open** 10am-10pm
Sat-Thur; 2-10pm Fri. **Credit** AmEx, MC, V.
Map p300 D9.
A Dubai institution, Magrudy's now has shops
throughout the city, although this original outlet on
Jumeirah Beach Road remains its spiritual home.
The chain has had to improve to keep up with the
globally popular likes of Borders and Virgin, but it's
holding its own with particularly impressive educa-
tion, business and children's sections and a good
selection of audio books.
Other locations BurJuman Centre (295 3323);
Deira City Centre (295 7744); Ibn Battuta
(366 9770).

Virgin Megastore
Mall of the Emirates (341 4353/www.virgin.com).
Open 10am-midnight daily. **Credit** AmEx, MC,
V. **Map** p394 D2.

Virgin may specialise in DVDs and CDs, but its
range of books is impressive too. New releases, best-
sellers and self-help titles dominate the shelves, but
you'll also find a large collection of art, design and
photography books, Arabic-language titles and
Penguin classics. Virgin's range of contemporary fiction is second to none.
Other locations Deira City Centre (295 8599);
Mercato Mall (344 6971).

ELECTRONICS

The malls in Dubai are full of major chain
stores such as Jacky's, Jumbo Electronics and
Plug-ins, but for the best deal in town on
electronics, head to **Computer Street**, a
flurry of shops just off Khalid Bin Al Waleed
Road (Bank Street) in Bur Dubai.

Just a blip away on your GPS system lies
Electrical Street, which shares space with
the textile souk on Al Fahidi Street. In the
evenings its shop fronts blaze with fluorescent
and flashing lights. There's a vast range of
electrical goods from which to choose, and
over-eager shop assistants will do their best
to entice you in. On the whole, prices on most
goods are very competitive, owing to the
number of places offering the same or similar
products, so you should be able to pick up a
bargain DVD player, digital camera or stereo
if you haggle hard. However, if you're planning
to take your item back home with you, be sure

to check that you're buying a model that will operate in your home country. Televisions are set to operate at different frequencies in different parts of the world, and DVD players are restricted to play discs from a certain region, so what works in Dubai won't necessarily work in London and Lahore.

★ Carrefour
Deira City Centre, Garhoud (295 1600/ www.carrefouruae.com). **Open** 9am-midnight Sat-Thur; 10am-midnight Fri. **Credit** AmEx, MC, V. **Map** p297 K2.

A supermarket may not seem the ideal place to pick up electronics, but Carrefour has a bin full of bargains waiting to be snapped up. Alongside the cameras and music systems are plenty of cheap, high-quality household items. The staff may not be as knowledgeable as those working in specialist stores, but you're almost certain to get the best price in town here, if you're prepared to deal with the queueing and the crowds.

Other locations Mall of the Emirates (409 4899).

CompuMe
Near Dubai Tennis Stadium, Zalfa Building, Garhoud (282 8555/www.compume.com). **Open** 9am-9pm Sat-Thur; 4-10pm Fri. **Credit** AmEx, MC, V. **Map** p297 K3.

CompuMe includes a PC clinic, where repairs and upgrades are carried out while you wait, and sells specialist software programs, computing magazines and books. You'll also find good-value laptops, cheap and cheerful PCs, pocket-sized PDAs and photo-quality printers. HP, IBM, Dell and Toshiba are among the brands on sale.

Other locations Mall of the Emirates (341 4442).

Jacky's
Deira City Centre (294 9480/www.jackys.com). **Open** 10am-10pm daily. **Credit** AmEx, MC, V. **Map** p297 K2.

One of the giants of the electrical scene in Dubai, Jacky's has come a long way since opening its first store in 1988. Now with seven outlets in the emirate, the city centre location goes head-to-head with fellow superpower Jumbo Electronics next door. A vast selection of fridges, freezers, washers and dryers is complemented by an assortment of kitchen and household essentials such as blenders, toasters, kettles and irons.

Other locations Al Mankhool Road, Bur Dubai (352 3555); BurJuman Centre (352 1323); Mall of the Emirates (341 0101); Wafi City Mall (324 2077).

★ Jumbo Electronics
Deira City Centre (295 3915/www.jumbo corp.com). **Open** 10am-10pm Sat-Thur; 2-10pm Fri. **Credit** AmEx, MC, V. **Map** p297 K2.

This popular shop is one of the largest Sony distributors in the world, and has 16 outlets scattered around the city. The shop also has an enviable supporting cast of all the other leading international brands. The store layout is very customer-orientated and aims to be interactive, meaning that you can road test potential buys, like the PlayStation3 or the PlayStation Portable (PSP).

Other locations Al Mankhool Road, Bur Dubai (352 3555); BurJuman Centre (352 1232); Mall of the Emirates (341 0101); Wafi City Mall (324 2077).

LG Digital Centre
Al Sayegh Brothers Building, Port Saeed Road, Deira (262 2770/www.lgcommercial.com). **Open** 8.30am-1.30pm, 2-6.30pm Sat-Thur. **Credit** AmEx, MC, V. **Map** p297 K2.

Given its location in a part of the city where hagglehard, sell-it-quick traditions still pervade, this electrcial store is a welcome haven from the bustle outside its doors.

★ ProMac Store – Apple Centre
China Court, Ibn Battuta Mall (366 9797/ www.apple.com). **Open** 10am-noon Sat, Thur, Fri; 10am-10pm Sun-Wed. **Credit** AmEx, MC, V. **Map** p304 A2.

Make sure you have your sunglasses at the ready before entering this gleaming sheen of whiteness. The very latest products are available and the staff are well trained in computing know-how. As well as the likes of the 15-inch MacBook and the TVMicro there are G5s, iMacs and plenty of iPods, plus audio speakers and natty little optical mice.

VV & Sons
Al Fahidi Street, Bur Dubai (352 2444/www. vvsons.com). **Open** 9am-1pm, 4.30-9.30pm Sat-Thur; 4.30-9.30pm Fri. **Credit** AmEx, MC, V. **Map** p298 H4.

This is the shop for the serious audiophile. A vast range of speakers is displayed at the back of the store, catering for anything from home cinema to outdoor gigs. Upstairs there's a selection of high-quality DVD players and amps for heavy-duty home cinema. In terms of names, lesser-known brands such as Jamo and Sherwood Electronic Labs sit next to international favourites like JBL.

Other locations Nasser Square, behind HSBC bank, Deira (221 8077).

FASHION
Beachwear

★ Aqua Beachwear
Al Ghazal Mall, Dhiyafah Road (345 3490/ www.aquabeachwear.com). **Open** 10am-10pm Sat-Thur; 4-10pm Fri. **Credit** AmEx, MC, V. **Map** p300 F8.

Dubai Outlet Mall. *See p157*

Finding a bikini that flatters your figure can be a truly infuriating process, but Aqua Beachwear comes to the rescue, with its wide selection of styles to suit all shapes and sizes. The brightly coloured designs are eye-catching, and you'll be able to match them with handy accessories such as sarongs, bags and towels.

Goldenpoint

Mall of the Emirates (341 0834/www.
goldenpointonline.com). **Open** 10am-midnight Sat-Thur; noon-10pm Fri. **Credit** AmEx, MC, V. **Map** p304 D2.

Sporty labels from Speedo and Rip Curl are stocked here which means that, as well as more frivolous styles, avid swimmers can pick up costumes that won't get ripped off in the crashing waves.

Heat Waves

Town Centre Mall, Jumeirah Beach Road,
Jumeirah (342 0445). **Open** 10am-midnight Sat-Thur; 5pm-midnight Fri. **Credit** AmEx, MC, V. **Map** p302 C12.

For straightforward swimsuits and bikinis in a range of plain and flattering colours, head to Heat Waves. Most of the swimwear on offer leans towards the conservative end of the market, but if you're prepared to have a root through, you'll come across some more fashionable styles.
Other locations Jumeirah Plaza (344 9489).

Moda Brazil

Mercato Mall, Jumeirah Beach Road, Jumeirah
(344 3074/www.modabrazil.com). **Open** 10am-midnight Sat-Thur; 2-10pm Fri. **Credit** AmEx, MC, V. **Map** p302 C12.

This lush Latino boutique stocks one of the widest selections of fashionable beachwear in town, from racy cut-out swimsuits to tropical-coloured bikinis. Sizes are on the small side, but designs are cutting-edge and will make you feel as if you've just stepped off the catwalk.

★ Praias

Mall of the Emirates (341 1167). **Open** 10am-midnight Sat-Thur; noon-10pm Fri. **Credit** AmEx, MC, V. **Map** p304 D2.

The fashion-conscious will love this store. With the sexiest bikinis in town, there is much for the confident. But it's not just for model-esque figures, since a good handful of the bikinis are underwired and offer excellent support.

Children's wear

★ 1/2 Pint

Organic Foods & Café, Mankhool Road, Satwa
(398 6889). **Open** 8.30am-6.30pm Sat-Thur; 10.30am-3pm Fri. **Credit** MC, V. **Map** p301 F8.

1/2 Pint sells handmade casual clothes for children aged up to eight. The range is designed by Mariam

Mall of the Emirates. *See p158.*

El-Accad, who only uses natural fabrics to create practical and comfortable clothes.

Armani Junior
Mercato Mall (342 0111/www.armanijunior. com). **Open** 10am-10pm Sat-Thur; 2-10pm Fri. **Credit** AmEx, MC, V. **Map** p302 C12.
Armani Junior boasts a colourful range of children's clothing that caters to boys and girls from the ages of two to 14. As well as T-shirts, hats and jeans, denim separates for girls are available along with trousers and jackets for cooler climes. For the label-conscious young man, a range of trousers, hoodies and trainers completes the collection.

Bambu Beach
Ibn Battuta Mall (368 5214). **Open** 10am-10pm Sun-Wed; 10am-midnight Thur-Sat. **Credit** AmEx, MC, V. **Map** p304 A2.
This Dubai-based label was created with the UAE lifestyle in mind and sells fashion for the whole family. Children from three to 12 are catered for with linen, cotton and silk separates, swimwear and accessories all available. Think butterfly prints and polka dots for girls and brightly patterned shorts for boys.

B Bush
Souk Madinat Jumeirah (368 6212). **Open** 10am-11pm daily. **Credit** AmEx, MC, V. **Map** p304 D1.

Aspiring surfers and boarders will feel at home here. It stocks a range of clothes including sweatshirts, trousers, shorts and T-shirts, providing the sort of kit that keeps up with the coolest kids on the block.

★ Bonpoint
Souk Madinat Jumeirah (368 6212/www. bonpoint.com). **Open** 10am-11pm daily. **Credit** AmEx, MC, V. **Map** p304 D1.
A store with its finger firmly on the fashion pulse, Bonpoint has cornered a niche market showcasing a children's collection inspired by high fashion and celebrity culture. Thoughtfully laid out, Bonpoint's collection features cute, yet terribly chic outfits.

★ Favourite Things Mother & Child
Dubai Marina Mall (434 1984/www.favourite things.com). **Open** 9am-9pm daily. **Credit** AmEx, MC, V. **Map** p300 D9.
With a safe indoor play area, a party room and a coffee shop for mums, this all-encompassing shop is bound to keep mother and child entertained for hours. The novelties boutique is great for finding original birthday gifts, and they'll even cater for parties.

Iana
Ibn Battuta Mall (368 5518). **Open** 10am-midnight daily. **Credit** AmEx, MC, V. **Map** p304 A2.
Devotees of casual chic Italian garb need look no further than Iana for colourful, pint-sized and laid-back attire. The chain's brand of no-nonsense, candy-coloured cottons are aimed at babies to pre-teens.

I Pinco Pallino
Wafi City Mall (324 4944/www.ipincopallino.it). **Open** 10am-10pm Sat-Thur; 5pm-midnight Fri. **Credit** AmEx, MC, V. **Map** p297 J3.
This Italian brand's formal range includes gowns in luxurious natural fibres with coordinated accessories, clothes for babies and casual wear. But I Pinco isn't cheap, and Park Avenue princesses-to-be can expect to shell out a small fortune.

★ Osh Kosh B'gosh
Mall of the Emirates (341 3040/www. oshkoshbgosh.com). **Open** 10am-midnight daily. **Credit** AmEx, MC, V. **Map** p304 D2.
This cute store offers everything a preppy little New Englander could want, with a vast selection of cords and shirt combos for boys, as well as precious embroidered dresses, skirts and hats for mini madams.

Patchwork
Mercato Mall (349 6060). **Open** 9am-10pm Sat-Thur; 2-10.30pm Fri. **Credit** AmEx, MC, V. **Map** p302 C12.
Patchwork perfectly illustrates that you are never too young for a bit of bling. Top names such as GF Ferré, Miss Sixty and Energie are all stocked, with sizes to fit children aged four to 14 years.

CONSUME

Tape à l'Oeil

Mall of the Emirates (341 0480). **Open**
10am-10pm Sat-Thur; 2-10pm Fri. **Credit**
AmEx, MC, V. **Map** p304 D2.
If your children fancy themselves as Monte Carlo
high rollers, then this fashion brand from France is
the perfect choice to suit their wishes. The clothes
stocked here are all colourful, fun and trendy.
Other locations BurJuman Centre
(352 3223).

Designer

Ayesha Depala

The Village, Jumeirah Beach Road (344 5378).
Open 10am-10pm Sat-Thur; 4-10pm Fri.
Credit MC, V. **Map** p300 D9.
This talented young Indian designer's first boutique
in Dubai is awash with silk, chiffon, tulle and lace,
all in soft, serene colours. Her collections are the epitome of femininity – as is the store itself. With lilac

---

Celebrate Consumerism

There are discounts aplenty at Dubai's annual celebration of shopping culture.

Started in 1996, the Dubai Shopping
Festival is growing every year, with bigger
and better offers and seemingly every Tom,
Dick and Harry of the retail world jumping
on board. The city comes to life with nearly
every mall, store and souk taking part in
the events, with eye-catching displays,
discounts, promotions and competitions.
Big stores often slash their price tags by
up to 75 per cent, and if you turn up early
on in the festival, you'll definitely find
bargains. The festival also brings together
music shows, art exhibitions, dancers and
plenty more to spice up your Dubai visit.

People less inclined to part with cash
might be more interested in **Global Village** –
the festival's most bizarre element. It's a
celebration of cultural diversity, and of the
UAE population's addiction to spending
money, with displays of dance, handicrafts
and music. The concept is admirable, but
it's always been a hit-and-miss affair; for
every gem you'll unearth from the markets of
Afghanistan or Yemen, you'll find countless

examples of global tat – vegetable peelers,
teddies and numerous dubious weight-loss
devices. 2009 saw it host a record-breaking
bid for the biggest biryani, so it's worth a
visit for the strangeness factor too.

It's refreshing that the festival makes use
of Dubai Creek, which remains one of the
city's most beautiful backdrops, and
yet is woefully underused. There's a Night
Souk on Al Seef Street, complete with
funfair and floating restaurants. Weekends
also see spectacular firework displays.
Jumeirah Beach Residence, one of
Dubai's newest and most successful
developments, is also alive with the
shopping festival. Here you can view work
by a host of international artists, drop the
little 'uns off at the children's corner and
take in one of the many fashion shows.

The festival usually attracts more than
three million visitors, a figure that is set to
rise significantly. You can discover all about
the stores taking part, and the events and
exhibitions taking place, at www.mydsf.com.

walls, sparkling chandeliers and a chic chaise longue, browsing is a treat. From long evening gowns, baby-doll dresses and delicate cardigans, each garment is beautifully cut and timelessly stylish.

★ Boutique 1

The Boulevard at Jumeirah Emirates Towers (330 4555). **Open** 10am-10pm Sat-Thur; 3-10pm Fri. **Credit** AmEx, DC, MC, V. **Map** p296 H4.
Formerly known as Villa Moda, Boutique 1 stocks over 150 brands, from established names like Missoni and Chloé to emerging designers. There's a bountiful supply of jeans and evening wear, plus everything in between.

Burberry

BurJuman Centre (351 3515/www.burberry.com). **Open** 10am-10pm Sat-Thur; 2-10pm Fri. **Credit** AmEx, MC, V. **Map** p299 J5.
At Burberry, customers can wander across acres of plush carpet to lay their hands on cashmere scarves, desirable updates on the classic trench coat, and plenty of tartan on bags, skirts and accessories.

Carolina Herrera

Mall of the Emirates (341 5095). **Open** 10am-10pm Sun-Wed; 10am-midnight Thur-Sat. **Credit** AmEx, MC, V. **Map** p304 D2.
What with all the scented candles scattered around, this store feels like a chic living room. Herrera's gowns are popular on the red carpet and, should you have the funds, are well worth investing in.
Other locations Dubai Festival City (232 6030).

Chanel

Wafi City Mall (324 0464/www.chanel.com). **Open** 10am-10pm Sat-Thur; 5-10pm Fri. **Credit** AmEx, MC, V. **Map** p297 J3.
This shop is the epitome of chichi French chic and has a small but select range of the label's latest collections. There are classy suits, evening wear and a good selection of affordable accessories.

Christian Lacroix

BurJuman Centre (352 7755/www.christian-lacroix.fr). **Open** 10am-10pm Sat-Thur; 2-10pm Fri. **Credit** AmEx, MC, V. **Map** p299 J5.
This hoity-toity designer range has a small but wildly elegant selection in its Dubai branch. With plenty of eccentric pieces, it is the place for people who view fashion as art.

★ Donna Karan

BurJuman Centre (351 7554/www.donna karan.com). **Open** 10am-10pm Thur-Sat; 2-10pm Fri. **Credit** AmEx, MC, V. **Map** p299 J5.
At Donna Karan's first-floor BurJuman outlet you'll find many of her signature tailored pieces, as well as plenty of sumptuous coats and to-die-for red dresses. For dressed down – and more affordable – clothing, look at the ground floor DKNY diffusion range.

★ Fleurt

Mercato Mall (342 0906). **Open** 10am-10pm Sat-Thur; 2-10pm Fri. **Credit** AmEx, DC, MC, V. **Map** p302 C12.
A selection of the highly desirable and glam Dina Bar-El dresses, colourful leather handbags and stylish modern jewellery is on sale at this sassy little store. We defy you to leave empty-handed.

Giorgio Armani

The Boulevard at Jumeirah Emirates Towers (330 0447/www.armani.com). **Open** 10am-10pm Sat-Thur; 4-10pm Fri. **Credit** AmEx, MC, V. **Map** p296 H4.
A slick store that oozes style thanks not only to the fashion but also to the minimally decked-out surroundings. Sparkling black marble floors, dark walls and spotlights draw you to the colourful rails of clothes. Women will find a mind-boggling range of flattering skirts, smart jackets and funky party pieces, and men will leave in perfectly fitting suits.

Gucci

Al Maktoum Street, Deira (221 5444/www.gucci.com). **Open** 10am-11pm Sat-Thur; 5-9.30pm Fri. **Credit** AmEx, MC, V. **Map** p299 L3.
Gucci has long been synonymous with high-octane glamour and sex appeal, and this has been maintained despite Tom Ford's departure a few years back. You'll find the best of the best in this two level outlet. The womenswear, menswear and accessory departments are all brimming with luxurious buys.
Other locations The Boulevard at Jumeirah Emirates Towers (330 3313); Mall of the Emirates (341 0669).

Hermès

BurJuman Centre (351 1190/www.hermes.com). **Open** 10am-10pm Sat-Thur; 2-10pm Fri. **Credit** AmEx, MC, V. **Map** p299 J5.
Liberally sprinkled in the credits of all the major fashion magazines, Hermès has become known as a long-standing symbol of Gallic elegance and style. Push through the somewhat intimidating doors and you'll find scarves of every hue and design, a great range of glamorous tote bags and purses made from the skins of a variety of deceased exotic animals.

Hugo Boss

Mercato Mall (342 2021/www.hugoboss.com). **Open** 10am-10pm Sat-Thur; 2-10pm Fri. **Credit** AmEx, MC, V. **Map** p302 C12.
Among the more expensive brands out there, Hugo Boss shirts do give you real quality for the extra cost. Boss has branched out from formal attire and now makes some of the softest and most comfortable jeans around, as part of the casual Boss Orange label collection. The Boss Green collection is the sportier side of the brand. Great for top-class hoodies and sportswear that you won't want to get dirty by actually playing sports in.

CONSUME

Other locations BurJuman Centre (355 7845); Deira City Centre (295 5281); Mall of the Emirates (341 0630).

Max Mara
BurJuman Centre (351 3140). **Open** 10am-10pm Sat-Thur; 2-10pm Fri. **Credit** AmEx, MC, V. **Map** p299 J5.
If there is one thing Max Mara does well, it's coats. Not wildly flamboyant ones, but simply good quality classics. The Italian fashion house has a long-standing reputation for creating couture lines. You'll also find SportMax stocked here, a slightly cheaper line of knits and outdoor wear.

INSIDE TRACK
CHEAP TAILORING

Head over to the Bur Dubai souk and you'll find a maze of shops all selling material fairly cheaply, and a wealth of tailors willing to turn it into your garment of choice. A fitted shirt can cost around Dhs100, and to get a full suit made can cost around Dhs750 (with material on top). Much cheaper than bespoke clothing back in a European city, and if you haggle, you can knock off a little extra.

★ Ounass
Souk Madinat Jumeirah (368 6167/www. altayer.com). **Open** 10am-11pm daily. **Credit** AmEx, MC, V. **Map** p304 D1.
The best thing about Ounass is the fact it brings together an eclectic mix of labels and styles from Hale Bob and Juicy Couture, alongside sleek lingerie, pretty dresses and a great footwear selection.

★ Tiger Lily
Wafi City Mall (324 8088). **Open** 10am-10pm Sun-Thur; 5-10pm Fri. **Credit** AmEx, MC, V. **Map** p297 J3.
Shopping here is akin to rummaging through a stylish celebrity's wardrobe. Rails filled with flowing, feminine dresses vie for your attention, and kitsch accessories catch the eye. Look for pieces by Australia's hottest exports sass & bide as well as UK favourite Julian MacDonald.

Versace
Al Maktoum Street, Deira (355 1845/www. versace.com). **Open** 10am-10pm Sat-Thur. **Credit** AmEx, MC, V. **Map** p299 L3.
Figure-hugging dresses, the skinniest of trousers, leather jackets and lashings of fur and gold are the order of the day at this Versace store. Alongside the ostentatious creations is a good range of very wearable clothes.
Other locations BurJuman Centre (351 7792); Wafi City Mall (324 7333).

Ibn Battuta Mall. *See p159.*

Yves Saint Laurent

Mall of the Emirates (341 0113). **Open** 10am-10pm Sun-Wed; 10am-midnight Thur-Sat. **Credit** AmEx, DC, MC, V. **Map** p304 D2.

YSL's modern collection ranges from expensive jackets to reasonably priced dress shirts, and although it's not cheap, remember that in 1999 Gucci bought the YSL brand, so the standards will be high, but the prices are cheaper than its parent company. **Other locations** The Boulevard at Jumeirah Emirates Towers (330 0445).

High street

Benetton

Mall of the Emirates (341 4646/www.benetton.com). **Open** 10am-10pm Sun-Wed; 10am-midnight Thur-Sat. **Credit** AmEx, DC, MC, V. **Map** p304 D2.

The '80s knitwear giant is still going strong: the famous sweaters and cute Ts in a hue of rainbow colours are still in store, and have been joined by lingerie, loungewear and sleepwear. The store also stocks some great basics for a working wardrobe. **Other locations** Deira City Centre (295 2450); Jumeirah Centre (349 3613).

Bershka

Mercato Mall (344 8645/www.bershka.com). **Open** 10am-10pm Sat-Thur; 2-10pm Fri. **Credit** AmEx, MC, V. **Map** p302 C12.

Bershka produces an exciting collection of funky casual clothes and sassy going out gear. Thumping trance accompanies customers around the store and gets them in a foot-stomping festival mood. **Other locations** Deira City Centre (295 8440); Mall of the Emirates (341 0223).

★ Blue Cactus

Jumeirah Centre, Jumeirah Beach Road, Jumeirah (344 7734). **Open** 10am-9pm Sat-Thur; 4.30-9pm Fri. **Credit** AmEx, DC, MC, V. **Map** p300 D9.

Quality not quantity is what's on offer at Blue Cactus. The store may be small, but the stock consists of top-notch chain-store labels and designer womenswear. Expect to find Kay Unger dresses, Prada short-sleeve shirts and entire outfits by DKNY at a fraction of their usual retail price.

Club Monaco

Deira City Centre (295 5832/www.clubmonaco.com). **Open** 10am-midnight Sat-Thur; 10am-10pm Sun-Wed. **Credit** AmEx, MC, V. **Map** p297 K2.

Two decades after its birth, Club Monaco has finally reached the Middle East. This store is home to chic essentials aimed at urban men and women. With plenty of A-list fans, Club Monaco's a great alternative if you can't afford high fashion labels. Colours tend to be subdued, so you won't find any garish creations here.

★ Diesel
BurJuman Centre (351 6181/www.diesel.com).
Open 10am-10pm Sat-Thur; 2-10pm Fri.
Credit AmEx, MC, V. **Map** p299 J5.
Chock-full of hipster must-haves that ooze attitude, this is a veritable warehouse of *du jour* jeans and accessories. Well-cut jeans and retro tops will leave you looking too cool for Dubai.
Other locations Deira City Centre (295 0792); Mall of the Emirates (341 1395); Mercato Mall (349 9958).

Fashion Factory
Lamcy Plaza, Oud Metha (336 2699). **Open** 9am-10pm Sun-Wed; 9am-midnight Thur-Sat.
Credit AmEx, DC, MC, V. **Map** p297 J3.
Don't let Fashion Factory's location deter you from visiting. Lurking at the back of Lamcy Plaza, it's easy to miss, but with nearly every item in the store priced at under Dhs100, make it your mission to seek it out. There are bargains to be had on major high street brands, including Monsoon, Camaïeu and more.

★ H&M
Mall of the Emirates (341 5880). **Open** 10am-midnight Sat, Thur, Fri; 10am-10pm Sun-Wed.
Credit AmEx, DC, MC, V. **Map** p304 D2.
H&M has opened three shops in Dubai. If you like jumble sales, you'll love H&M, which sells cheap clothes across the age/sex spectrum, as well as cosmetics, accessories and underwear. This is the place to pick up serviceable basics for a snip.
Other locations Deira City Centre (295 7549); Ibn Battuta Mall (364 9819).

Kinokuniya. *See p162.*

iSell
Sultan Business Centre, Karama (334 2494).
Open 10am-7pm Sat-Thur. **No credit cards**.
Map p297 J3.
The cheapest and best vintage second-hand wares in town. *See right* **Going It Alone**. *Photo p174.*

Mango
BurJuman Centre (355 5770/www.mango.com).
Open 10am-10pm Sat-Thur; 2-10pm Fri. **Credit** AmEx, MC, V. **Map** p299 J5.
Dubai's Mango outlets are as well stocked and as reasonably priced as those in Europe. Along with the usual range of carefully chose, stylish clothes, expect some bejewelled and flowing styles to fit in more with local tastes.
Other locations Deira City Centre (295 0182); Mall of the Emirates (341 4324); Mercato Mall (344 7195).

Massimo Dutti
Deira City Centre (295 4788/www.massimo dutti.com). **Open** 10am-midnight Sat, Thur, Fri; 10am-10pm Sun-Wed. **Credit** AmEx, MC, V.
Map p297 K2.
Stacks of sophisticated suits, crisp cotton shirts, rugged leather jackets, ultra-glam evening wear, well-finished accessories and catwalk-savvy shoes make Dutti one of the city's most popular shops. The store is a boon for men and women of all ages – the clothes effortlessly exude class and don't have sky-high price tags.
Other locations BurJuman Centre (351 3352); Mall of the Emirates (341 3151); Mercato Mall (344 7158).

Mostafawi
Jamal Abdul Nasser Square, Deira (352 4222).
Open 8am-1pm, 4.30-9pm Sat-Thur. **Credit** MC, V. **Map** p299 J3.
For the cheapest authentic branded jeans in town, it pretty much has to be Mostafawi. *See p173* **Going It Alone**.

★ New Look
Deira City Centre (295 9542/www.newlook.co.uk).
Open 10am-10pm Sun-Wed; 10am-midnight Thur-Sat. **Credit** AmEx, DC, MC, V.
Map p297 K2.
This huge shop opened its doors in 2006, and has been a destination for bargain-loving fashionistas ever since. The season's top trends are always on offer, as well as all the basics such as jeans and T-shirts. Head to the back of the store and you're surrounded by endless rows of pumps and points. The lingerie and accessories departments are also fantastic.

New Yorker
Dubai Festival City (232 9744). **Open** 10am-10pm Sun-Thur; 10am-midnight Fri, Sat.
Credit MC, V. **Map** p297 L3.

Going It Alone

The emirate's top independent shops uncovered.

In such a shop-happy city, one doesn't have to look for long to find a little retail therapy. But it's worth going beyond the obvious to find some truly unique trinkets, and at bargain prices too. **Mostafawi** (*see left*) offers the cheapest authentic branded jeans in town, with boot cut Wranglers a steal at under Dhs100. It's so cheap you can overlook the fact that half the stock is painfully out of date, the staff are surly and the changing room is tiny.

Talking of cheap chic, there's a horde of fashion devotees who would like to keep **iSell** (*see left*) under wraps. The reason? It's packed with the cheapest – and best – vintage and second-hand wares in town, including battered leather bags, granny-inspired frocks and old Converse trainers. Whether it's knackered trilbies or antiquated jewellery, no visit to Dubai would be complete without a scour of iSell.

If you're after some authentic decorations for the house, you can't go far wrong with **O'De Rose** (*see p181*). It has a garden area where you can sip tea and displays an array of global trinkets. There are suzani-embroidered sofas, ottomans from Bokja in Lebanon, and *mezze* trays. For cheaper souvenirs hit, um, **Gifts &**

Souvenirs (*see p180*), which displays a comprehensive, if unexpected range of bargain deals. Think His Highness Sheikh Mohammed Bin Rashid Al Maktoum crockery sets, incense burners and carved wooden caskets inlaid with mother-of-pearl.

For quirky gems that'll let you stand out among Dubai's in-crowd, head to **S*uce** (*see p176*). Crammed to its pink, sweet-as-sugar ceilings with sass & bide, Amuzi & David, Isabella Capeto and Laura Lees, it's a definite stop for anyone worth their weight on the social circuit.

How about something for book worms? The aptly named **Book World** (*see p162*) is a literary lover's paradise. On our visit, the store stocked the complete set of David Niven's autobiographies, Gabriel Gárcia Marquez's *Of Love And Other Demons*, and Mills & Boon's *Summer of Love* – at less than Dhs50 for the lot. There's also a great selection of second-hand magazines, including the first edition of *Time Out Dubai*.

When you're done shopping for yourself, it's time to find some presents. There's no better place to rummage around for bizarre gifts than **Classic City** (*see p180*). The mosque alarm clocks and Mr Lover Lover eau de cologne are cases in point.

CONSUME

O'De Rose.

We're always a little dubious of shops named after cities, but we're big fans of the whole cheap and cheerful ethic of New Yorker. On par with the nooks and crannies of H&M, there's a raft of apparel for under Dhs100 that's colourful, wearable and, most importantly, durable. From slogan T-shirts to electric blue jeans, and trilby hats to Converse-esque pumps, you could pick up an entire ensemble for less than Dhs250.

Paul Frank

Dubai Festival City (232 5915/www.paulfrank. com). **Open** 10am-10pm Sun-Thur; 10am-midnight Fri, Sat. **Credit** AmEx, MC, V. **Map** p297 L3.

Ah, good old Julius the monkey. You either love him or hate him. Personally, we're a big fan. But there is more to Paul Frank than just that cheeky little monkey. Over the years, Paul Frank Industries (PFI) has rolled out several lines of apparel and accessories; men's and women's sportswear, kids clothing, swimwear, eyewear, watches, and even home furnishings – all of which you'll find here.

Promod

BurJuman Centre (351 4477/www.promod.com). **Open** 10am-10pm Sat-Thur; 2-10pm Fri. **Credit** AmEx, MC, V. **Map** p299 J5.

This Spanish store's vibe is definitely bohemian. There's a vast range of daywear and covetable extras like beaded necklaces, bangles, hats, scarves and bags. With Promod's casual rather than dressy clothes, you can rejuvenate your wardrobe without breaking the bank.

Other locations Deira City Centre (295 7344); Mall of the Emirates (341 4944); Mercato Mall (344 6941).

★ Reiss

Mall of the Emirates (341 0515/www.reiss.co.uk). **Open** 10am-10pm Sun-Wed; 10am-midnight Thur-Sat. **Credit** AmEx, MC, V. **Map** p304 D2.

This is a gorgeous shop where the clothes have a designer feel. There are full and pleated skirts with unusual stitching details and abstract patterns in the weave, plus cotton tops in contemporary shapes and plenty of well tailored suits. It's more expensive than your average chain, but worth the extra splurge.

Stradivarius

Deira City Centre (295 1221). **Open** 10am-midnight Sat, Thur, Fri; 10am-10pm Sun-Wed. **Credit** AmEx, MC, V. **Map** p297 K2.

The majority of this store's stock is suited to teenagers. Big on bright colours, Lycra, short skirts and funky extras, it's certainly an eye-catching space. The shoe and bag selection is impressive too.

Other locations Mall of the Emirates (341 3999).

★ Topshop

Mercato Mall (344 2677). **Open** 10am-10pm Sat-Wed; 10am-11pm Thur, Fri. **Credit** AmEx, DC, MC, V. **Map** p302 C12.

Leggings, stretch minis, layered day-glo tops, leg warmers, plastic jewellery, vest dresses, boob tubes, studded belts, coloured court shoes, neon fishnets, lashings of bling – the high street darling of the fashion pack has got it all. The collection changes with the whimsical speed of high fashion, but you'll always be sure to find a wide range of cheeky underwear.

Other locations Deira City Centre (295 1010); Ibn Battuta Mall (368 5948).

iSell. *See p172.*

CONSUME

Twisted
*Times Square Centre Mall (341 8746/www.
twistedco.com).* **Open** 10am-10pm Sat-Wed;
10am-midnight Thur, Fri. **Credit** AmEx, MC, V.
Map p294 C3.
This is a great place to go to for jeans and T-shirts
and it won't cost you a fortune. T-shirts cost Dhs55
and jeans are Dhs149; plus, all the accessories are
designed in-house, making everything unique.
Army-green T-shirts and shirts fill the racks for both
men and women. The fabrics have been washed to
give that worn-in look and there are also some rock
chic belts, and cool leather and canvas bags.

Vintage 55
*Dubai Festival City (232 6616/www.vintage
55.com).* **Open** 10am-10pm Sun-Wed; 10am-
midnight Thur-Sat. **Credit** AmEx, MC, V.
Map p297 L3.
Hollow black wooden boxes are stacked to the ceiling, displaying items like quirky T-shirts, cute white
capri pants embellished with the words 'Jackie O',
striped vests featuring the words 'First Lady', well-
cut jeans and cool, comfy shorts. There are also
kitsch ornaments along with cult books like Marlo
Brando's biography.
Other locations Wafi (327 9786).

Lingerie

There are plenty of shops selling luxury lingerie
in Dubai, but expect lots of frilly numbers with
little erotic flair. Nonetheless, the following
stores fight the good fight against mediocrity.

Agent Provocateur
*Inside Saks Fifth Avenue, BurJuman Centre
(351 5551/www.agentprovocateur.com).*
Open 10am-10pm Sat-Thur; 4-10pm Fri.
Credit AmEx, MC, V. **Map** p299 J5.
Agent Provocateur serves up decadent sauciness
without descending into sleaze. As a brand, it's a
well-executed and well-oiled machine, from the
packaging and perfume to the lingerie itself. Also a
good place at which to pick up stockings.

Inner Lines
Deira City Centre (295 0627). **Open** 10am-
midnight Sat-Thur; 10am-10pm Wed-Sun.
Credit AmEx, MC, V. **Map** p297 K2.
At Inner Lines you'll find a small but attractive
selection of Calvin Klein underwear, encompassing
knickers and bras in every colour of the rainbow.
Other brands stocked include BodySlimmers and
the Princesse Tam Tam range, which supports and
flatters the fuller figure.

Nayomi
Mercato Mall (344 9120/www.nayomi.com).
Open 10am-10pm Sat-Thur; 4-10pm Fri.
Credit AmEx, MC, V. **Map** p302 C12.

One of the leading Middle Eastern retailers of quality lingerie, Nayomi stocks lacy dressing gowns and
rather less sexy nightdresses for around Dhs300.
Other locations Al Ghurair City (227 3887);
Ibn Battuta Mall (366 9832); Mall of the Emirates
(341 4377).

Sportswear

Adidas
BurJuman Centre (359 0995/www.adidas.com).
Open 10am-10pm Sat-Thur; 4-10pm Fri. **Credit**
AmEx, MC, V. **Map** p299 J5.
Adidas is one of the rare sports brands that also suc-
ceeds as street fashion, and at their Dubai stores you
can find old-school styles alongside gym essentials.
This store boasts a massive range of trainers, track-
suits, shorts and T-shirts, and a selection of watches.
Other locations Adidas Factory Shop (282
5868); Al Ghurair City (228 9733); Deira City
Centre (295 0261); Ibn Battuta Mall (366 9777);
Mall of the Emirates (347 7007).

★ Golf House
BurJuman Centre (351 9012). **Open** 10am-10pm
Sat-Thur; 4-10pm Fri. **Credit** AmEx, MC, V.
Map p299 J5.
Catering for the flourishing golf scene in Dubai, Golf
House is a good stop-off before you hit the green.
With top-of-the-range clubs, clothes and all the
essentials, there is plenty to keep the novice and the
seasoned professional happy.
Other locations Deira City Centre (295 0261);
Ibn Battuta Mall (366 9895); Lamcy Plaza (334
5945); Mall of the Emirates (341 0511).

Go Sport
Ibn Battuta Mall (368 5344). **Open** 10am-
midnight daily. **Credit** AmEx, MC, V.
Map p304 A2.
This French megastore include clothing and equipment for almost every sport you can think of, including biking, riding, golf, weights, boxing and fishing.

Nike
BurJuman Centre (351 5376/www.nike.com).
Open 10am-midnight Sat-Thur; 2-10pm Fri.
Credit AmEx, MC, V. **Map** p299 J5.
This sizeable Nike store ticks all the right boxes,
thanks to well-stocked shelves and helpful staff.
Besides the latest tracksuits, trainers, sports and
gym clothing, this outlet boasts an excellent collec-
tion of sunglasses and futuristic-looking watches.
Other locations Al Ghurair City (227 5758);
Ibn Battuta Mall (366 9777); Mall of the Emirates
(341 0933).

★ Rage
Mall of the Emirates (341 3388). **Open**
10am-midnight daily. **Credit** AmEx, MC, V.
Map p304 D2.

CONSUME

Rage has the best selection of skateboards in the city. The place is full of personality; expect punk tunes and smashed-up boards on the ceiling. Whether you're after a pair of Etnies trainers, a bikini or the latest Flip skateboard, you won't leave disappointed.
Other locations Dubai Festival City (336 9007).

Sun & Sand Sports
Khalid Bin Al Waleed Road (Bank Street), Bur Dubai (3516222/www.sunandsandsports.com). **Open** 10am-10pm Sat-Thur; 2-10pm Fri. **Credit** AmEx, MC, V. **Map** p298 J5.
One of the biggest sports shops in Dubai, this store stocks everything from tennis gear to gym equipment. Prices are reasonable, and although you won't find the best selection of footwear in town, the sheer quantity of everything else makes up for it.
Other locations BurJuman Centre (351 5376); Deira City Centre (295 5551); Ibn Battuta (366 9777).

FASHION ACCESSORIES
Bags

Coach
Jumeirah Emirates Towers (330 1020/www. coach.com). **Open** 10am-10pm Sat-Thur; 2-10pm Fri. **Credit** AmEx, MC, V. **Map** p296 H4.
There's certainly plenty to choose from. There's the Slim Tote, a sleek bag trimmed in embossed alligator skin, or the Carly, Slim Flap, Shoulder Bag and Satchel, each studies in Legacy canvas. There is, of course, the small matter of cost. You won't usually be able to buy a Chloé or Louis Vuitton bag for less than Dhs4,500, but you could buy a small Coach bag for around Dhs2,000. Other items like wallets, scarves and sunglasses will set you back about Dhs1,000.

Radley
Wafi (324 2620). **Open** 10am-10pm Sat-Wed; 10am-midnight Thur; 2pm-midnight Fri. **Credit** AmEx, MC, V. **Map** p297 J3.
According to creative director and founder Lowell Harder, Radley is not a fashion-led brand. The only concession they make to passing fads is identifying seasonal colour trends. The handbags are simply designed, oversized, bling bling totes that you're likely to find adorning the arm of the average fashionista. The luggage and wallets line is the epitome of minimalism. There are only two big drawbacks, the first of which is the price. The average bag will set you back something upwards of Dhs1,300.

Jewellery

★ Accessorize
Mall of the Emirates (341 0479/www.monsoon. co.uk). **Open** 10am-midnight Sat, Thur, Fri; 10am-10pm Sun-Wed. **Credit** AmEx, MC, V. **Map** p304 D2.

This high street accessories chain is an offshoot of Monsoon. It's a haven for boho fans, the store offers plenty of beaded, bobbled and embroidered goodies.
Other locations Ibn Battuta Mall (341 3993); Lamcy Plaza (335 7375).

Cartier
The Boulevard at Jumeirah Emirates Towers (351 3332/www.cartier.com). **Open** 10am-10pm Sat-Thur; 5-10pm Fri. **Credit** AmEx, MC, V. **Map** p296 H4.
This branch of Cartier is packed to the brim with dazzling charms, links and delicate paves.
Other locations BurJuman Centre (355 3533).

Damas
Deira City Centre (295 3848/www.damas jewel.com). **Open** 10am-midnight Sat, Thur, Fri; 10am-10pm Sun-Wed. **Credit** AmEx, MC, V. **Map** p297 K2.
The most advertised and popular jeweller in the Middle East prides itself on its high-quality gold creations – and there's not a knuckleduster in sight. Damas caters for women of all ages, and the Lebanese singing sensation Nancy Ajram is currently the face of the brand.
Other locations Al Ghurair City (296 0063); The Boulevard at Jumeirah Emirates Towers (330 3262); Ibn Battuta Mall (366 9944); Lamcy Plaza (335 5177); Mercato Mall (349 8833); Souk Madinat Jumeirah (344 0111); Wafi City Mall (323 4555).

Dazzle
Al Ghazal Mall, Dhiyafah Road (345 3163). **Open** 10am-10pm Sat-Thur; 4-10pm Fri. **Credit** AmEx, MC, V. **Map** p300 F8.
Subtlety isn't Dazzle's strength. From huge chandelier ear adornments to chunky rings Mr T would blush at, the small boutique shamelessly revels in attention-seeking accessories. Look closely and you will uncover some pretty and more delicate dazzle with which to lift your outfit.

Glitter
Ibn Battuta Mall (368 5582). **Open** 10am-midnight Thur-Sat; 10am-10pm Sun-Wed. **Credit** AmEx, MC, V. **Map** p304 A2.
You don't have to blow your budget to get seriously fashionable; just take a trip to Glitter and check out the Crislu collection of crystal rings and pendants. With the platinum-coated bands ranging in price from Dhs750 to Dhs1,000, you'll still have dirhams in your purse to splash out on the elegant pendants at Dhs500.
Other locations Al Ghurair City (229 3978); Deira City Centre (295 4012).

S*uce
The Village Mall, Jumeirah (344 7270). **Open** 10am-10pm Sat-Thur; 4.30-10pm Fri. **Credit** AmEx, MC, V. **Map** p300 D9.

CONSUME

S*uce.

If it's pure gems you're after, with enough quirks to set you apart from Dubai's crowds, S*uce is your stop. *See p173* **Going It Alone**.

★ Tiffany & Co
Deira City Centre (295 3884/www.tiffany.com). **Open** 10am-midnight Thur-Sat; 10am-10pm Sun-Wed. **Credit** AmEx, MC, V. **Map** p297 K2.
The aura of Audrey Hepburn's glamour will always linger around Tiffany's. This outlet may be small in comparison to the New York branch, but it still squeezes in a flabbergasting selection of classy jewellery, chic accessories and gift items. Be sure to check out the highly coveted engagement rings and signature heart chains. It's worth asking for a discount if you're buying something expensive – it may just save you a dirham or two.
Other locations BurJuman Centre (359 0101); Mall of the Emirates (341 0655).

Shoes

Aldo
BurJuman Centre (359 3375/www.aldoshoes. com). **Open** 10am-10pm Sat-Thur; 2-10pm Fri. **Credit** AmEx, MC, V. **Map** p299 J5.
This Canadian shoe emporium is hard to beat for sheer choice, boasting a dazzling array of styles for men and women at surprisingly cheap prices. Aldo is pretty hot on the heels of the latest trends, and a selection of bags, belts and beads is also available.
Other locations throughout the city.

Converse
Dubai Festival City (232 5906/www.converse. com). **Open** 10am-10pm Sat-Thur; 11am-11pm Fri. **Credit** MC, V. **Map** p297 L3.
There are cool, coloured Converse trainers displayed on all the walls; but the service is terrible. For the kids, a pair of kicks will cost around Dhs90, whereas grown-ups will get a pair for Dhs155. Your shopping experience may leave a lot to be desired, but at least you'll walk out with some pretty special trainers.

★ Jimmy Choo
The Boulevard at Jumeirah Emirates Towers (330 0404/www.jimmychoo.com). **Open** 10am-10pm Sat-Tue; Wed-Fri 4-10pm. **Credit** AmEx, MC, V. **Map** p296 H4.
The king of shoemaking has a swanky branch in the sleek Jumeirah Emirates Towers. You can load up on ornate sandals, strappy kitten heels, spectacular evening shoes and leather boots.

Nine West
Deira City Centre (295 6887/www.ninewest.com). **Open** 10am-10pm Sat-Thur; 2-10pm Fri. **Credit** AmEx, MC, V. **Map** p297 K2.
For basics, Nine West consistently delivers the goods. It's also one of the few shoe shops in Dubai to offer large sizes, and prices are reasonable.
Other locations Al Ghurair City (221 1484); BurJuman Centre (351 6214); Ibn Battuta Mall (368 4097); Mall of the Emirates (341 0244); Mercato Mall (349 1336).

Classic City. *See p180.*

CONSUME

★ Pretty FIT
Mercato Mall (344 0015/www.prettyfit.com).
Open 10am-10pm Sat-Thur; 2-10pm Fri.
Credit AmEx, MC, V. **Map** p302 C12.
This is a reliable shop selling shoes in all styles.
Some, adorned with stripes, polka dots, checks or
flowers, may not be to everyone's taste, but there are
some beautifully simple options too. Prices are an
absolute bargain.
Other locations Deira City Centre (295 0790);
Mall of the Emirates (341 3666).

Vincci
BurJuman Centre (351 7246). **Open** 10am-10pm
Sat-Thur; 2-10pm Fri. **Credit** AmEx, MC, V.
Map p299 J5.
This upmarket store stocks one of the city's finest
ranges of footwear. Delicate pumps sit alongside
suede slouch boots and glam sky-high heels. All are
excellent quality.

FOOD & DRINK

Cacao Sampaka
Dubai Mall (434 1427). **Open** 8.30am-midnight
daily. **Credit** AmEx, MC, V. **Map** p303 F13.
Cacao Sampaka is a Spanish chocolatier and veritable heaven for chocoholics. It stocks a gastronomic
innovation collection with anchovy, curry, parme-
san cheese and black olive chocolates, and row upon
row of pots of tomato chocolate jam.

Jeff de Bruges
*Mall of the Emirates (341 0960/www.jeff-de-
bruges.com).* **Open** 10am-midnight daily.
Credit AmEx, MC, V. **Map** p304 D2.

Chocolate lovers will worship the scrumptious offerings here. With the finest Belgian chocolates on sale
this side of Wallonia, the place is chock-full of truffles, marzipan, fruit jellies, ganaches and pralines.

Oil & Vinegar
*Harvey Nichols (409 8961/www.oiland
vinegar.com).* **Open** 10am-midnight Sat, Thur,
Fri; 10am-10pm Sun-Wed. **Credit** AmEx, MC, V.
Map p304 D2.
Ordinary bottles of oil and vinegar might suit you
fine, but if you've got a fine taste in condiments,
you'll find solace here. Situated on the top floor of
Harvey Nichols, Oil & Vinegar offers an elaborate
selection of oils from olive to truffle.
Other locations Madinat Jumeirah (368 6178).

Patchi
*Souk Madinat Jumeirah (368 6101/www.patchi.
com).* **Open** 10am-10pm daily. **Credit** AmEx,
MC, V. **Map** p304 D1.
Renowned for its selection of high quality choco-
lates, Patchi, a Lebanese brand, is undoubtedly the
Rolls-Royce of chocolates in the region.
Other locations Mercato Mall (349 1188); Wafi
City Mall (324 4030).

Wafi Gourmet
Wafi City Mall (324 4433). **Open** 9am-1am
daily. **Credit** AmEx, MC, V. **Map** p297 J3.
At the centre of this Egypt-themed mall, Wafi
Gourmet is a temple of temptations for any food-
loving pharaoh. The shop is filled with Arabian
cheeses, sweets, olives, truffles and dates. There's a
café in the corner, so you can enjoy your purchases
from the deli counters before you even get home.

Waitrose
Dubai Mall (434 0700). **Open** 8am-midnight daily. **Credit** AmEx, MC, V. **Map** p303 F13.
The UK supermarket chain has opened its first store outside Blighty. *See p155* **Dubai Mall**.

HEALTH & BEAUTY
Cosmetics & perfume

Ajmal Perfumes
Deira City Centre (295 3580/www.ajmalperfume. com). **Open** 10am-10pm Sat-Wed; 10am-midnight Thur, Fri. **Credit** MC, V. **Map** p297 K2.
Ajmal is a swanky Arabian perfumer at which you can pick up strong scents from the region. A word of warning to the uninitiated – Arabian scents are much headier and spicier than Western perfumes.
Other locations BurJuman Centre (351 5505).

Arabian Oud
Souk Madinat Jumeirah (368 6586/www. arabianoud.com). **Open** 10am-10.30pm daily. **Credit** AmEx, MC, V. **Map** p304 D1.
This Saudi perfumer's Eastern ambience is balanced by its contemporary interior and an unlimited range of authentic oils and potions. You can create your own mix and then choose the intricate bottle it will end up in. A popular destination for the uninitiated as well.
Other locations BurJuman Centre (352 6767); Ibn Battuta Mall (368 5638).

Areej
Mall of the Emirates (340 5223/www.altayer. com). **Open** 10am-midnight daily. **Credit** AmEx, MC, V. **Map** p304 D2.
As well as plenty of designer names including Dior and Chanel, you'll find funkier labels like Smashbox at branches of Areej. New fragrances tend to arrive here very promptly, meaning you're bound to find the latest products.
Other locations The Boulevard at Jumeirah Emirates Towers (330 3340); Ibn Battuta Mall (366 9985); Mercato Mall (344 6803).

★ Body Shop
BurJuman Centre (351 1335). **Open** 9.30am-10pm Sat-Thur; 2-10pm Fri. **Credit** AmEx, MC, V. **Map** p299 J5.
The Body Shop continues to sell divine products that have been going for years, like the brazil nut body butter and excellent Amlika leave-in conditioner, alongside their newer cranberry and orange ranges. Shoppers with a conscience will be pleased to know that even in Dubai you can take any of your old products in for recycling and that along with having a fair trade policy, the Body Shop continues to champion animal and human rights issues.
Other locations Al Ghurair City (228 9494); Deira City Centre (295 0701); Jumeirah Centre

(344 4042); Ibn Battuta Mall (368 5456); Mall of the Emirates (341 0551); Wafi City Mall (324 5435).

★ Boots
Ibn Battuta Mall (368 5936/www.boots.com/ www.alshaya.com). **Open** 10am-10pm Sun-Wed; 10am-midnight Thur-Sat. **Credit** AmEx, MC, V. **Map** p304 A2.
When this famous British healthcare and pharmaceuticals brand announced it was spreading its wings to the Middle East, there was a collective jump for joy among British expatriates. Fill your basket with items from the No7 make-up range, pamper your complexion with creams from Skin Kindly and Botanics, and for something to help you unwind, check out the Sanctuary's excellent product range.
Other locations Mall of the Emirates (340 6880); The Village (349 9112).

Faces
BurJuman Centre (352 1441). **Open** 10am-10pm daily. **Credit** AmEx, MC, V. **Map** p299 J5.
Beauty magazines come to life when you step inside this shop. With a mixture of designer fragrances, cosmetics and mid-range brands like Bourjois, Urban Decay, Hard Candy, Pout and Benefit, it's a favourite with twenty- and thirtysomething women.
Other locations Dubai Festival City (232 5747); Ibn Battuta Mall (368 5594); Mall of the Emirates (347 1225).

★ MAC
Deira City Centre (295 7704/www.mac cosmetics.com). **Open** 10am-10pm Sun-Wed; 10am-midnight Thur-Sat. **Credit** AmEx, MC, V. **Map** p297 K2.
MAC is used by professional make-up artists around the globe, and it's no wonder, with its plethora of foundations, glosses and beauty tools, and showstopping bright and glitter eye shadows. The staff are helpful and on hand to give you a makeover and make-up tips.
Other locations BurJuman Centre (351 2880); Ibn Battuta Mall (368 5966); Mall of the Emirates in Harvey Nichols (409 8931); Mercato Mall (344 9536); Wafi City Mall (324 4112).

Paris Gallery
Deira City Centre (295 5550/uae-parisgallery. com). **Open** 10am-midnight Sat, Thur, Fri; 10am-11pm Sun-Wed. **Credit** AmEx, MC, V. **Map** p297 K2.
This stalwart of the UAE's beauty industry invokes the ambience of a Parisian boudoir. Staff can be over eager, but most international brands are stocked, with products tantalisingly displayed on carousels. There's also a spa on the upper level.
Other locations Al Ghurair City (221 1166); BurJuman Centre (359 7774); Ibn Battuta Mall (368 5500); Lamcy Plaza (366 2555); Wafi City Mall (324 2121).

CONSUME

INSIDE TRACK
GIFT VILLAGE

In a land where there's Healthcare City, Humanitarian City and Global Village, it seems fitting that there's a **Gift Village** slapped in the mix. Nestled behind Deira City Centre, in it you can find some decent mens and ladies clothing if you dig around, and there's some inspired tat – a mounted movie poster of *There's Something About Mary* in German, for Dhs2, is a particularly good example. There's a great children's aisle too, packed with Spongebob Square Pants paraphernalia and a sea of Spider-Man toys.

★ Pixi
Mall of the Emirates (341 3833/www.pixi beauty.com). **Open** 10am-midnight Sat, Thur, Fri; 10am-11pm Sun-Wed. **Credit** AmEx, MC, V. **Map** p304 D2.
A treasure trove of cosmetic variety, Pixi is bursting with rainbow-coloured make-up, natural skincare and all the beauty tools you need to keep immaculately groomed.

Rituals
Deira City Centre (294 1432/www.rituals.com). **Open** 10am-midnight Sat, Thur, Fri; 10am-10pm Sun-Wed. **Credit** AmEx, MC, V. **Map** p297 K2.
The face, body and hair ranges at Rituals are a little more expensive than your regular toiletries, but the quality is superb.

GIFTS & SOUVENIRS

Classic City
Satwa Street, Satwa (349 1012). **Open** 8.30am-1am Sat-Thur; 9am-midnight Fri. **Credit** MC, V. **Map** p301 F9.
There's no better place than Classic City to rummage for quirky and potentially hilarious gifts. *See p173* **Going It Alone**. *Photo p178.*

Gifts & Souvenirs
Karama Central Market, Karama (337 7884). **Open** 9am-10pm Sat-Thur; 4-10pm Fri. **Credit** MC, V. **Map** p297 J3.
This aptly named souvenir hub boasts a comprehensive, albeit unexpected range of cheap items. *See p173* **Going It Alone**.

Rugs

Dubai offers a vast range of rugs, from antique to new, contemporary to traditional, and cheap to expensive. They come from a number of countries, including Iran, Turkey, Pakistan and Central Asia. If you're planning on buying an antique rug, you should check its reverse side. The more knots there are on the underside, the better the rug's quality and the longer it's likely to last. On the whole, silk is more expensive than wool, and rugs from Iran are generally more expensive than the equivalents from Turkey or Kashmir. Be sure to visit the Dubai Shopping Festival (*see p168*) for Afghan, Iraqi and tribal designs at low prices at Global Village.

HEALTH & BEAUTY
Opticians

Most malls have an optician; eye tests are often free if you buy glasses or contact lenses.

Al Jaber Optical Centre
Deira City Centre (295 4400). **Open** 10am-10pm Sat-Thur; 2-10pm Fri. **Credit** AmEx, MC, V. **Map** p297 K2.
At Al Jaber you'll find shades by practically every luxury brand under the sun, although the glasses section is a little skimpy. Featured brands include Montblanc, Hugo Boss, Giorgio Armani, Cartier, Oakley, Burberry and Nike.

Bahrain Optician
Wafi City Mall (324 2455/www.bahrainoptics. com). **Open** 10am-10pm Sat-Thur; 4.30-10pm Fri. **Credit** AmEx, MC, V. **Map** p297 J3.
Not only does this store make an effort to stock the latest designs and changes its collection each season, but the service is also quick and reliable. You can go from eye test to final fitting in a couple of days.

Barakat Opticals
Beach Centre, Jumeirah Beach Road (329 1913). **Open** 10am-10pm Sat-Thur; 4.30-10pm Fri. **Credit** AmEx, MC, V. **Map** p300 D10.
A good option for a quick optical fix, Barakat Opticals is a straightforward opticians with a reasonable if unexciting spread of frames. The service is friendly and efficient.

Bavaria Optics
Al Dhiyafah Road, Satwa (345 1919). **Open** 9am-1pm, 5-9.30pm Sat-Thur; 5-9.30pm Fri. **Credit** AmEx, MC, V. **Map** p301 F8.
One of a number of fine opticians on the Al Dhiyafah Road (the equally good Yateem Opticians is just down the road; 04 345 3405), Bavaria Optics sells a great range of specs and the eye tests are thorough.

Salons

★ Franck Provost
Burj Al Arab (301 7249/www.franckprovost-dubai.com). **Open** 10am-10pm daily. **Credit** AmEx, MC, V. **Map** p304 E1.

It's hard to get a booking at this salon for two very good reasons: the stylists actually know what they're doing, and when you have an appointment, you get to go into the Burj Al Arab without the usual hassle. Considering the location, prices are surprisingly affordable (Dhs300 for a cut). They also offer great packages of cut, colour and blow-dry combos, with prices starting at Dhs550.
Other locations Dubai Marina (362 9865); Dubai World Convention Centre (331 0801); Mall of the Emirates (341 3245); Ritz-Carlton Dubai (318 6141).

N.Bar
Ibn Battuta Mall (339 4801). **Open** 10am-10pm daily. **Credit** AmEx, MC, V. **Map** p304 A2.
N.Bar is light and airy with white walls and chrome fittings, although it stops just short of being clinical. The staff are friendly, helpful and efficient. Treatments include waxing, massage, manicures, pedicures, acrylic, silk, gel and fibreglass nail enhancements, plus a number of luscious-sounding treatments for pampered hands and feet.
Other locations Al Ghurair City (228 9009); The Boulevard at Jumeirah Emirates Towers (330 1001); BurJuman Centre (359 0008); Dubai Internet City (390 9535); Grosvenor House (399 9009); Palm Strip Mall (346 1100).

Toni&Guy
Jumeirah Emirates Towers (330 3345/www.toniguy.com). **Open** 10am-10pm Sat-Thur; 4-8pm Fri. **Credit** AmEx, MC, V. **Map** p296 H4.
Don't expect to find bog-standard hairdressers at Dubai's Toni&Guy branches; these people are no less than hair technicians, and each one has worked his or her way up through the T&G ranks. A visit here is not cheap (a wash, cut and blow-dry will cost you between Dhs195 and Dhs275), but you know you are in safe hands.
Other locations Grand Hyatt Dubai (324 4900).

HOUSE & HOME

Ikea
Dubai Festival City (263 7555/www.ikea dubai.com). **Open** 10am-10pm daily. **Credit** AmEx, MC, V. **Map** p297 L3.
Ikea has flat-packed itself all the way to the Middle East with its huge outlet offering miles and miles of inspiration to nest-builders. Expect self-assembly kitchen, bedroom and bathroom furniture and accessories in abundance, designed to Scandinavian standards and tastes. Clean minimalist lines and homely wooden frames are the order of the day.

Kas Australia
Mercato Mall (344 1179/www.kasaustralia.com.au). **Open** 10am-10pm Sat-Thur; 2-10pm Fri. **Credit** AmEx, MC, V. **Map** p302 C12.
Kas Australia is a master purveyor of the soft, the fluorescent and the frilly. Citrus-coloured pillows plump up against extravagantly textured throws and brightly coloured fabrics in this snug Aussie outlet.
Other locations BurJuman Centre (349 0503); Ibn Battuta Mall (366 9386).

O'De Rose
Al Wasl Road, Umm Suqeim 2 (348 7990). **Open** 10am-8pm Sat-Thur; 4-8pm Fri. **Credit** AmEx, MC, V. **Map** p294 C2.
A boutique stocking global trinkets, complete with tea garden. *See p173* **Going It Alone**.

★ One
Jumeirah Beach Road, Jumeirah (345 6687). **Open** 9am-10pm Sat-Thur; 2-10pm Fri. **Credit** AmEx, MC, V. **Map** p300 D9.
This Dubai company is almost as famous for its colourful ad campaigns and frequent publicity stunts as it is for its frequently splendid contemporary furniture. The secret to its success is its design-led product range, which neatly marries ethnic

CONSUME

Ohm Records. *See p182.*

accessories (think incense burners, Buddha heads and textured photo frames), with bold, contemporary items of furniture that wouldn't look out of place in any budding interior designer's home.
Other locations BurJuman Centre (351 4424); Mall of the Emirates (341 3777); Wafi City Mall (324 1224).

Zara Home
Mall of the Emirates (341 4184/www.zarahome. com). **Open** 10am-10pm Sun-Wed; 10am-midnight Thur-Sat. **Credit** AmEx, MC, V. **Map** p304 D2.
Just like the clothing range, Zara Home caters for fans of hip urban chic, with a country twist. There is a mix of styles to suit every design taste, from ethnic animal print and vibrant Indian batik to kitsch paisley and modern cream hues.
Other locations BurJuman Centre (359 9988).

MUSIC & ENTERTAINMENT

JS Music
Ibn Battuta Mall (366 9715). **Open** 10am-midnight daily. **Credit** AmEx, MC, V. **Map** p304 A2.
Whether you are looking to crash and burn as the next Keith Moon or strum-diddley-dum your hippy tunes, you should find the appropriate instrument in here. There's a good range of instruments in store, and all the additional bits of kit that you'll need to start you on your way to Carnegie Hall.

Music Chamber
Crowne Plaza Shopping Centre (331 6416). **Open** 10am-11pm Sat-Thur; 5-10pm Fri. **Credit** AmEx, MC, V. **Map** p298 G10.
The concept of the Music Chamber is 'musicians, not merchants'. This philosophy means that prices are kept low on instruments, from handmade guitars to pianos, and that all the little bits of kit that Dubai's musicians have traditionally had to order over the internet (sax, reeds, trumpet oil, guitar strings) are now all to hand. There are also 15 practice rooms that you can hire to play the piano or rehearse with your band. Lessons are also available: choose from violin, percussion, singing, sax, flute, trumpet, piano, oud, kanoun and guitar, and pay Dhs540 for four one-hour lessons, plus a one-off registration fee of Dhs100.

★ Ohm Records
Opposite BurJuman Centre (397 3728/www. ohmrecords.com). **Open** 2-10pm daily. **Credit** AmEx, MC, V. **Map** p299 J5.
Ohm Records was the first record shop in the Middle East to sell vinyl shipped in from overseas. It prides itself on introducing the masses to innovative electronic music, and all its records come from independent labels, with not a mainstream tune in sight. Professional and bedroom DJs gather at the weekends to play on the decks. The shop also sells record bags, streetwear, as well as processors and turntables.

Virgin Megastore
Mall of the Emirates (341 4353/www.virgin.com). **Open** 10am-midnight daily. **Credit** AmEx, MC, V. **Map** p304 D2.
Virgin's vast range of music, movies, multimedia, games, computers, mobile phones, consumer electronics and books is the most impressive in town, although the selection focuses on the mainstream. There's also an in-store café, a game zone for PlayStation2 and Xbox fanatics, as well as the store's ever-popular listening stations.
Other locations BurJuman Centre (351 3358); Deira City Centre (296 8599); Mercato Mall (344 6971).

SPORTS & FITNESS

★ Al Boom Diving Club
Le Méridien Mina Seyahi Beach Resort (399 2278/www.alboomdiving.com). **Open** 9am-5pm daily. **Credit** AmEx, MC, V. **Map** p304 B1.
Al Boom offers diving lessons and all the equipment you'll need to get started. It provides unbeatable facilities (including a swimming pool for beginners), a full range of PADI courses, full equipment rental and a shop stocking the latest from the top brands in diving equipment.

Al Boom Marine
Ramool showroom, before Mirdif, turn right at the Coca-Cola sign (289 4803/www.alboom marine.com). **Open** 8am-8pm Sat-Thur; 4-8pm Fri. **Credit** AmEx, MC, V. **Map** p297 L3.
Stockists of the coolest beach and outdoor clothing in Dubai, Al Boom is the exclusive distributor for brands such as Bombardier, Oakley, O'Neill, Rip Curl and Hurley, so this is the place to head to for boards, bikinis and beanies, as well as respectable brands of surf- and wakeboards.
Other locations Al Bahar showroom, Jumeirah 3, Jumeirah Beach Road (394 1258).

Dubai Desert Extreme
Beach Centre, Jumeirah Beach Road (344 4952/ www.dubaidesertextreme.com). **Open** 10am-8pm Sat-Thur. **Credit** AmEx, MC, V. **Map** p300 D10.
This is where the skate kids get their decks, trucks and wheels. If you're looking for some skate fashions, this is a good bet, with T-shirts from Shorty's and Independent the pick of the bunch.

Picnico
Al Bahr Marine, Jumeirah Beach Road (394 1653). **Open** 9am-9pm Sat-Thur; 4.30-9pm Fri. **Credit** AmEx, MC, V. **Map** p302 C11.
Picnico is an eclectic camping emporium located on Jumeirah Beach Road (on the edge of the petrol station forecourt). It's better suited to seasoned rather than inexperienced campers, specialising in GPS systems as well as tents, sleeping bags, gas stoves and barbecue sets.

CONSUME

Arts & Entertainment

Dubai Aquarium. *See p200.*

Calendar

Massive sport, cultural and music events all year round.

It's hard to believe that a couple of decades ago, a person moving to Dubai would have qualified for a hardship allowance from his or her employer – financial compensation for having to live and work in such a hot, boring place. The climate is as inhospitable as ever, but Dubai's calendar is now packed with festivals and events to lure in visitors and hopefully persuade them to stay. The **Dubai Rugby Sevens** and **Dubai World Cup** are among the biggest sporting events, the **Dubai Shopping Festival** attracts millions of shoppers each year looking for bargains, and **Dubai Desert Rock** is a haven for the region's headbanging collective (yes, it exists). Most events tend to take place either side of the summer; not much happens between June and September when the weather is too hot. Also, there are generally no sporting or music events during Ramadan, but this religious event provides an altogether different experience for visitors to the city.

THE LOWDOWN

We've selected an eclectic haul of things to do, but if you're already in town, *Time Out Dubai* magazine is invaluable for late announced events and up-to-date details of the major events; www.timeoutdubai.com is great for last-minute research before you leave. If you're planning your trip around a particular event – or going out of your way to attend one – be sure to confirm the details in advance; we've thoroughly checked the information here, but dates and programmes change, and events can be cancelled without notice.

SPRING

Barclays Dubai Tennis Championships

Dubai Tennis Stadium, Aviation Club, Garhoud Road (282 9166/www.barclaysdubai tennischampionships.com). **Date** mid Feb-early Mar. **Map** p297 L3.
Why miss a chance to see what Roger Federer does best in a laid-back, sun-drenched venue? The Dubai Open is a fantastic opportunity to see the world's top players, such as court superstars Rafael Nadal and Maria Sharapova, slamming it out at the Aviation Club, home to the Irish Village pub, where strawberries and cream are served for the event.

Dubai International Jazz Festival

Dubai Media City, off Sheikh Zayed Road (391 1196/www.dubaijazzfest.com). **Date** late Feb-early Mar. **Map** p304 B2.
It's hardly Montreux, but the Dubai International Jazz Festival has been a huge crowd puller since the first event in January 2003. The pleasant outdoor setting helps create a good vibe. In the past it has been able to attract James Blunt, David Gray, Jamie Cullum, Stanley Jordan and Mike Stern. Not exactly cutting-edge jazz, but pleasant nonetheless.

Dubai Desert Rock

Venue varies (333 1155/www.desertrock festival.com). **Date** early Mar.
This rock festival of extreme proportions is the most important event on any respectable headbanger's calendar. The 2007 gig featured Iron Maiden, for the fifth anniversary in 2008, 28,000 fans turned up to see Marky Ramone, Velvet Revolver and Muse, and Motörhead headlined in 2009.

Dubai International Boat Show

Dubai International Marine Club, next to Le Meridien Mina Seyahi, Dubai Marina (www.boatshowdubai.com). **Date** early Mar. **Map** p304 B1.
Even if you're not planning to splash out yourself, drop in to see some beautiful boats and Dubai's elite snapping up yachts left, right and centre.

Art Dubai

Madinat Arena, Madinat Jumeirah, next to Wild Wadi on Jumeirah Beach Road (366 8888/ www.artdubai.ae). **Date** mid Mar. **Map** p304 D1.
The first major international art fair in Dubai came to fruition in 2007 as the Gulf Art Fair, and was re-named Art Dubai for 2008. A number of big names in the art world come to the city to show off their latest works, and there's always a strong turnout from all the local galleries.

Bastakia Art Fair

Bastakia, Bur Dubai (www.baf.ae). **Date** Mar. **Map** p298 H3.
This satellite to Art Dubai has also been going since 2007 (it was originally called the Creek Art Fair) and is going from strength to strength. Both local and regional galleries exhibit in the charming old buildings of Bastakia, many of which are not open to the public for the rest of the year.

Chill Out Festival

Various venues (397 3728/ www.ohmrecords.com). **Date** Mar.
A relaxed music event that since it first took place in 2007 has attracted DJs along the likes of Richard Dorfmeister, Andy Smith of Portishead fame and Talvin Singh. Local bands and musicians are also well represented.

Dubai World Cup

Meydan Racecourse (327 0077/www.dubai worldcup.com). **Date** late Mar. **Map** p295 F4.
The Dubai World Cup is the richest horse race in the world and draws in thousands of enthusiasts every year. But it's not just a sporting event – it's the biggest date in the city's social calendar. All facets of UAE society attend, in all manners of dress, and the atmosphere in the free stands can be pretty electric. The cup takes place at the newly-built Meydan Racecourse, and the prize money for the main race has been increased to US$10 million.

Taste of Dubai

Dubai Media City (www.tasteofdubai09.com). **Date** mid Mar. **Map** p304 B2.
'The best taste festival in the world,' is how celebrity chef Gary Rhodes summed up the 2009 event, according to the Taste of Dubai website. And with many of the city's top restaurants gathering in one place (including Rhodes' Mezzanine), allowing visitors to sample their finest cuisine, who could argue? The chef's theatre and cookery schools should help you brush up on your skills in the kitchen.

SUMMER

Sir Bu Na'air Traditional Sailing Race

Various venues (www.dimc-uae.com). **Date** May.
Dozens of traditional dhow sailing boats race each other over the Persian Gulf. A joy to watch or photo.

Dubai Summer Surprises

Various venues (www.mydsf.com). **Date** mid June-mid Aug.
A three-month effort to draw in the crowds over Dubai's stifling summer, Dubai Summer Surprises (DSS) features the odd bargain and an endless stream of free children's entertainment, which mainly takes place in the city's shopping malls. DSS is presided over by the irksome Modhesh, a bright yellow cartoon character that appears in 'person' in the various malls, at his Modhesh Fun City HQ, and in effigy at every street corner and roundabout.

Hopfest

Irish Village, Aviation Club, Garhoud (www.irish village.ae). **Date** early Aug. **Map** p297 K3.

Dubai World Cup.

ARTS & ENTERTAINMENT

Ramadan

Dos and don'ts.

Ramadan is Islam's holiest month, one of prayer, self-restraint and fasting. Accordingly, there are a few things visitors should keep in mind during this time:

● Make sure you don't eat, drink or smoke in public after sunrise and before sunset, the period when Muslims are required to fast. This includes chewing gum and eating anything in your car or a taxi.

● Dress conservatively throughout the month and public displays of affection are a definite no-no.

● Don't swear in public.

● At the *iftar* table, Muslims are allowed to break their fast at the sound of the *adhan*, or call to prayer. If you're invited to an *iftar* meal, you shouldn't eat before that time.

● Don't play loud music or keep your television volume high, particularly during times of prayer, and loud behaviour in public is frowned upon.

● Don't try to convince a Muslim to break the fast, and never buy a Muslim alcohol. The latter is legally forbidden at all times of the year, and enforced with graver consequences during Ramadan.

● Don't walk on a prayer mat or pass in front of a Muslim who is praying, and always ask permission before entering a mosque.

● Don't photograph or point and stare at Muslim or Emirati women.

Iftar at Ritz Carlton.

Normally held over three days in marquees at the Irish Village, the event introduces the public to over 100 international beers that you usually don't find in Dubai. There's a DJ and live bands, and like most events at the IV, as it's locally known, it is a buzzy and busy affair.

Ramadan

Various venues. **Date** 22 Aug-21 Sept 2009 & 11 Aug-9 Sept 2010 (exact date depends on the lunar calendar).

The Muslim holy month is dedicated to the practice of fasting from sunrise to sunset, an imperative extended to non-Muslims in public settings. But as soon as the sun goes down and the imam calls for prayer, the calm is replaced by a lively and elaborate cultural event. The major attraction for tourists here is the *iftar* feast, something most restaurants and five-star hotels take full advantage of. Expect to be offered an array of plump dates and milk, a common way to break the day's fast, followed by *Arabian Nights*-worthy samplings of some of the region's most popular cuisine. If you're not lucky enough to be a guest at an Emirati family's *iftar* dinner, catch the Ramadan experience by trying an *iftar* buffet dinner at the popular Lebanese restaurant Al Nafoorah at Jumeirah Emirates Towers, the Iranian set menu at the Radisson SAS Hotel's Shabestan in Deira, or one of the many shisha-serving Ramadan tents across the city. It is important that tourists behave respectfully throughout this month; drinking alcohol in public is unacceptable, and live or loud music is considered offensive.

AUTUMN

Eid Al Fitr

Various venues. **Date** 21-23 Sept 2009 and 10-12 Sept 2010 (exact date depends on the lunar calendar).

As Ramadan comes to a close, excitement starts to build as Muslims wait for a lunar sign that it's time for Eid Al Fitr – 'Feast of Breaking the Fast'. The three days after the month-long fast are among the most vibrant in the Islamic calendar, with celebrations culminating in an elaborate daily show of fireworks, traditional music and festivities.

UAE Desert Challenge

Various venues (www.uaedesertchallenge.com). **Date** mid Oct-early Nov.

One of the largest motor sport events in the Middle East, the Desert Challenge pits the world's finest endurance riders and cross-country drivers against each other. The drive lasts several days, starting in Abu Dhabi, cutting through Liwa, and on to the finish line in Dubai.

Gitex Shopper

Airport Expo, near Dubai Airport (www.gitex shopperdubai.com). **Date** mid Oct. **Map** p297 L2.

UAE Desert Challenge.

Dubai Rugby Sevens.

It's hard to believe that an entire city might get excited by the prospect of a discounted laptop or a reduced MP3 player, but the Gitex Shopper is big news in Dubai. The road to the Airport Expo gets jam-packed with cars, as eager drivers wait to get inside and see what Dubai's biggest electronic stores are discounting this year, with everything from cameras to computers to MP3 players available at their stands. The show is paired with another Gitex show at the Trade Centre, just for the industry, where companies such as Panasonic and Sony display their latest technological wares.

Camel racing
Nad Al Sheba camel racetrack, off the Dubai-Al Ain Road (338 2324). **Date** Oct-Mar. **Map** p295 D3.
Whether it's the 'sport of kings' connotation or the ungainly efforts of the 'ships of the desert' that grab you, a visit to a camel race is an interesting cultural experience; the contests attract all the different strata of United Arab Emirates society plus a fair number of visitors. The season's races usually take place on Thursdays and Fridays at around 7am; you can watch training sessions most mornings at around 10am, and later from 2pm to 5pm. The season reaches its peak in March, with prize races attended by the ruling families. If you're worried about exploitation, robot jockeys are used these days instead of the child jockeys of old.

Horse racing
Nad Al Sheba horse racecourse, off the Dubai-Al Ain Road (336 3666)/www. nadalshebaclub.com). **Date** *Nov-Mar* 7pm Thur. **Map** p295 D3.
Horse racing is such a major part of Emirati society that many smaller towns and villages have their own racetracks. The country's principal venue for the sport is in Dubai at Nad Al Sheba, where local and international steeds and their jockeys compete through a winter season that culminates with the Dubai World Cup in March (at which point the city's racing scene will also move to its new venue, the state-of-the-art Meydan racecourse). In accordance with the tenets of Islam, gambling is not allowed, although various competitions, such as the 'pick six' race card, have cash prizes.

Dubai World Championship
Jumeirah Golf Estates, off the Emirates Road (375 2222/www.dubaiworldchampionship.com). **Date** early Nov.
From 2009, the Dubai World Championship serves as the finale to the European Tour's season-long Race to Dubai. Replacing the previous Order of Merit, the Race to Dubai will help decide the world's top 60 players, who then go head to head on the Jumeirah Golf Estates Earth course (designed by Greg Norman) to compete for a total prize of US$20 million – the richest prize in golf.

Red Bull Flugtag

Dubai Creek (www.redbullflugtag.ae). **Date** mid Nov. **Map** p299 J3.

Teams build flying machines and launch them over the Creek. 'Flugtag' means 'flying day' in German, although most craft crash straight into the water.

WINTER

Dubai Rugby Sevens

The Sevens, Al Ain Road (www.dubairugby7s. com). **Date** late Nov.

The IRB World Sevens Series features 16 world-class international teams and large numbers of local and regional players competing for a variety of trophies over three days. The tremendously popular event is one of the highlights of the city's calendar.

National Day Festival

Various venues. **Date** 2 Dec.

The UAE's Independence Day sees the whole country turn into one jammed street, packed with noise, toys, beautiful cars and enough silly string to cover the Palm Jumeirah. All the major monuments and tourist attractions are open to the public, and in the evening there are firework displays and concerts.

World Offshore Powerboat Championship

Dubai Marine Club, Le Méridien Mina Seyahi Beach Resort & Marina, Al Sufouh Road, Jumeirah (399 4111/www.class-1.com). **Date** early Dec. **Map** p304 B1.

The UIM Class 1 World Offshore Powerboat Championship takes place over two days in

Get Out of Town

There's further fun to be found just a short drive away.

Although Dubai may tend to hog a lot of the global headlines, its neighbour Abu Dhabi is gathering pace, with a number of high-profile events. On 1 November 2009, the first **Abu Dhabi Grand Prix** – the final one of the year's F1 season – takes place on the newly built Yas Marina Circuit (www.yasmarinacircuit.ae). It's sure to be a fixture again for 2010, but dates had not been confirmed when we went to press.

The **FIFA Club World Cup** is set to take place at the city's Zayed Sports City Stadium in December 2009. Pitting the winners from each of the international football championships against one another in a knockout tournament, the competition could see past winners like Manchester United and AC Milan taking part. For many years this competition has taken place in Japan, but it has now found a new home.

Zayed Sports City is also home to the **Capitala World Tennis Championship** (www.capitalaawtc.com), which takes place every January, seeing six of the world's top male tennis players compete for a US$250,000 purse. The prize pales against the US$2 million offered for the winner of the **Abu Dhabi Golf Championship**, twice won by Paul Casey, which has taken place every January since 2006 at the Abu Dhabi Golf Club. See www.abudhabigolfchampionship. com for details of the next event.

A firm favourite on the Abu Dhabi calendar for many years has been the **Red Bull Air Race**, which takes place every April

(www.redbullairrace.com). It's free to watch, just stand on the city's Corniche and enjoy the antics high above.

Big names from the world of art and culture also flock to Abu Dhabi; in the summer of 2008 it was Picasso, with a huge exhibition dedicated to the Spanish painter set up at Emirates Palace (a big exhibition like this is planned each year). **ArtParis-AbuDhabi**, taking place each October (www.artparis-abudhabi.com), is another addition, displaying an array of modern and contemporary works. And in November, movie buffs can enjoy the **Middle East International Film Festival** (www.meiff.com), with a wide variety of films from around the world and a guest list of Hollywood greats. But perhaps the biggest coup came in April 2009, when the city staged its first **WOMAD** festival (www.womadabudhabi.ae). The concerts were free to watch, with performances by artists of the calibre of Youssou N'Dour and Robert Plant. We await news that it will return.

But if you're looking for events slightly off the beaten track and away from the major cities, you would be wise to plan your visit toward the start of the year. That way you can visit the **Al Ain Aerobatic Show** in January (www.alainaerobaticshow.com) to see all manner of flying craft take to the skies for a number of stunts, or maybe even the **RAK International Half Marathon** in Ras Al Khaimah (www.rakmarathon.org) – which has the biggest cash prize for any half marathon in the world.

ARTS & ENTERTAINMENT

December and is part of the international championships, which take place in the Mediterranean and the Gulf. Top teams from around the world compete for a place on the podium in 42-foot, five-tonne powerboats that travel at 250kmph (160mph).

Dubai International Film Festival
Various venues (www.dubaifilmfest.com).
Date early Dec.
Although Dubai cinemas rarely stray from a popular mix of Hollywood blockbusters and corny action flicks, the increasingly popular DIFF showcases cinema that is otherwise impossible to see in the UAE. Expect gala screenings, local film, and the arrival of many celebrity guests: previous years have attracted the likes of Nicholas Cage, Morgan Freeman and George Clooney.

Eid Al Adha
Various venues. **Date** 26 Nov 2009 & 16 Nov 2010 (exact date depends on lunar calendar).
The second Eid takes place on the tenth day of the last month of the Islamic calendar, Dhul-Hijjah. The Festival of the Sacrifice, marking the period after the pilgrimage to the holy city of Mecca, begins with Muslims gathering for the Eid prayer. Although only the pilgrims in Mecca can participate fully, other Muslims across the world join in by also celebrating on the correct days. In Dubai there is a four-day holiday. No alcohol is served on the day that precedes Eid Al Adha.

Dubai Marathon
Various venues (www.dubaimarathon.org).
Date mid Jan.

Ethiopian running legend Haile Gebrselassie is one of the many athletes who have competed for the US$2 million prize in the annual Dubai Marathon and in fact he won a rain-soaked race in 2009 in a time of 2hrs, 5mins and 29secs, the eighth fastest in history. It's an early start, and there are also 10km and 3km competitions.

Dubai Shopping Festival
Various venues (www.mydsf.com).
Date mid Jan-mid Feb.
This is a month-long festival of bargain hunting, with various bits of shopping-related entertainment thrown in. Started in 1996, it's responsible for attracting a large proportion of the tourists who visit the city annually, and thus usually produces an increase in traffic, and makes hotel rooms impossible to find. Expect discounts of up to 80 per cent in some stores, with competitions and giveaways daily. There are regular firework displays over the Creek, mini events such as food festivals and fashion shows, and carnivals, parades and shows.

Dubai Desert Golf Classic
Emirates Golf Club, off Interchange 5, Sheikh Zayed Road (380 1777/www.dubaidesert classic.com). **Date** late Jan. **Map** p304 B2.
Every winter the Emirates Golf Club welcomes the finest golfers in the world to its pristine greens to compete for an impressive prize purse of US$2.5 million. Rory McIlroy of Northern Ireland won the event in 2009, and Tiger Woods has won it twice (in 2006 and 2008). South African Ernie Els is the most successful competitor in the competition's history, however, with three victories to his name.

Dubai Desert Golf Classic.

Art Galleries

Art is still booming in Dubai.

Art from the Middle East is hot right now. But while Charles Saatchi was buying, it was Dubai that was selling. The city has become a showcase, allowing regional artists international recognition. Gone are the days when a handful of galleries would struggle to get a full opening night: nowadays, art parties pile them in, there are fairs and biennials, a roaring social scene, and the galleries have become the place to see new indie cinema, hear lectures and snap up some champers.

Although the art scene stretches the length of the city, its real heart lies in Al Quoz, the city's industrial area. This anomaly of dust and factories among Dubai's sheen may not be pretty, but its warehouses are becoming the city's answer to London's East End or New York's DUMBO district. Then there's Bastakia, the heritage quarter, which is home to a handful of illustrious galleries; DIFC's Gate Village, an unlikely arts hub in the financial district; and even a few galleries down in the Marina. Thought you knew what Dubai's art scene was about? Look, look, then look again.

ARTS & ENTERTAINMENT

AL QUOZ

1x1 Contemporary
WH No.1, Plot No.3642223, Al Quoz Industrial Area 1 (348 3873/www.1x1artgallery.com). **Open** by appointment. **No credit cards.** **Map** p294 C3.
This dominating gallery in the backstreets of the industrial quarter has a rotating selection of shows specialising in all things new, daring and slightly scary that come out of the Indian art scene. As so many of India's artists turn a scathing eye on the future of the subcontinent, a strange, almost toxic aesthetic has developed, and 1x1 Contemporary captures that in this huge, ex-warehouse.

Artsawa
Exit 43 Sheikh Zayed Road, Road 323, Al Quoz, opposite Shirawi Equipment (340 8660/www. 1x1artspace.com). **Open** 10am-7pm Sun-Thur. **Credit** MC, V. **Map** p294 C3.
Artsawa opened in mid 2008 at the height of the Dubai art boom, and has since shown a varied roster of artists that leans towards North Africa. The gallery is split-level, with an impressive mezzanine that reflects the building's warehouse past, and has a layout that changes in line with the mixed media and huge installation works the shows tend towards.

★ Ayyam Gallery
Alserkal Avenue, Street 8, Exit 43 of Sheikh Zayed Road, Al Quoz 1 (323 6242/www.ayyam gallery.com). **Open** 10am-8pm Sun-Thur. **Credit** AmEx, MC, V. **Map** p294 C3.
The Damascus art scene is booming. To reflect that, the Dubai branch of this Syrian art gallery opened in 2008 to a huge response. Despite their contemporaneity, sculpture and painting are still the focus among Syria's artists, perhaps due to the palpable sense of the past that pervades Damascus. Note the emulation of the texture of centuries-old walls in some of the paintings. An incredible space.

★ B21 Art Gallery
Al Quoz 3, near the Courtyard, opposite Spinneys warehouse (340 3965/www.b21gallery.com). **Open** 11am-7pm Sat-Thur. **No credit cards.** **Map** p294 B3.
This is a small but invigorating space with an Iranian slant in its shows. Daring art is prime B21 territory and its roster includes the likes of Ramin and Rokni Haerizadeh (both picked up by Charles Saatchi), Reza Aramesh and Nadine Kanso.

About the author
Chris Lord *hails from the UK and is the Art listings editor of the weekly* Time Out Dubai *magazine.*

★ Meem Gallery
Umm Suqeim Road, heading towards Arabian Ranches from Interchange 4, taking a U-turn at the third traffic light next to Marina Interior Design warehouse and halfway on main road, next to Pressotto (04 347 7883/www.meem.ae). **Open** 11am-7pm Sat-Thur. **Credit** MC, V. **Map** p304 D2.
Meem offers an authoritative and ambitious programme of Middle Eastern and Arabic art, and boasts a well-stocked art library with occasional lectures; it also prvides helpful advice and information. Shows tend towards painting and sculpture, and allow the visitor to research some of the big names in Middle East art history.

★ Thejamjar
Street 17a, Al Quoz, behind Dubai Garden Centre on Sheikh Zayed Road (341 7303/ www.thejamjardubai.com). **Open** 10am-9pm Sat-Thur; 2-9pm Fri. **Credit** MC, V. **Map** p304 E2.

Thejamjar provides a massive exhibition space that doubles as a forward-thinking gallery and arts centre. Aside from regular shows by international artists, there are painting workshops, DIY painting days with access to all the necessary materials and events for children. This refreshingly novel approach has made thejamjar a player in Dubai's art scene. Oh, and don't miss one of its opening parties, they can be a bit raucous.

★ Third Line
Al Quoz 3, near the Courtyard, between Marlin Furniture and Spinneys (341 1367/ www.thethirdline.com). **Open** 11am-8pm Sat-Thur. **Credit** AmEx, MC, V. **Map** p294 B3.
The Third Line was one of the first big hitters to open in the city, and it has continued since then in its commitment to the most contemporary of Middle Eastern artists. Youssef Nabil, Fouad Elkoury, Amir H Fallah and Laleh Khorramian have all shown here, and if you're talent-spotting it's a great place to see the up-and-comers from the region. *Photo p194.*

Thejamjar.

the Fairmont Hotel, but this new address has served it well. The roster continues to grow and includes several strong Saudi Arabian artists.

★ Cuadro
Gate Village Building 10, DIFC (04 425 0400/ www.cuadroart.com). **Open** 10am-8pm Sun-Thur; noon-6pm Sat. **Credit** AmEx, MC, V. **Map** p296 H4.
The galleries in Dubai are big, but few quite top the sprawl of Cuadro, which incorporates five decently sized spaces for exhibitions, and is virtually a museum if you judge such a thing by size alone. Seeing is believing in this contemporary space with a dynamic curatorial team.

★ Empty Quarter
Gate Village, DIFC (04 323 1210/www.theempty quarter.com). **Open** 9am-10pm Sun-Thur; 3-10pm Fri. **Credit** AmEx, MC, V. **Map** p296 H4.
This is Dubai's only gallery dedicated solely to photography. It has a huge space, variable according to need, with a superb selection of photography books.

Farjam Collection Gallery
Gate Village 4, DIFC (04 323 0303/www.farjam collection.com). **Open** 10am-8pm Sun-Thur; noon-8pm Sat. **No credit cards**. **Map** p296 H4.
Tired of installations? Bored with the new? Then come here. The Farjam Collection shows exquisite Islamic antiquities, including carpets, illuminated manuscripts, wood and lacquer pieces, and paintings from the early Islamic centuries onwards.

Opera Gallery
Gate Village Building 3, DIFC (04 323 0909/ www.operagallery.com). **Open** 10am-8pm Sun-Thur; noon-8pm Sat. **Credit** AmEx, MC, V. **Map** p296 H4.
Things must be good (and lucrative) in Dubai if Opera has a base here. Split into two, jet black spaces, the gallery has a steady rotation of shows up front, and a number of masters downstairs. Everything is from outside of the region, with China and South America the main players.

Total Arts at the Courtyard
Off Sheikh Zayed Road, between junctions 3 & 4 (04 347 5050/www.courtyard-uae.com). **Open** 10am-1pm, 4-8pm Sat-Thur. **Credit** AmEx, MC, V. **Map** p294 C3.
The Courtyard is an arts and cultural centre that has made a name for itself in Dubai. Within that overall area, Total Arts has use of a large space which is dedicated to artists from the region, and shows works by some of the Middle East's more established names. After some hard browsing, head downstairs to the Arabic style Courtyard café.

DIFC

ArtSpace
The Gate Village, Level 2, DIFC (04 323 0820/www.artspace-dubai.com). **Open** 10am-8.30pm Sat-Thur. **Credit** AmEx, MC, V. **Map** p296 H4.
ArtSpace is a sleek, contemporary gallery, and one of Dubai's most established names. It used to be in

ARTS & ENTERTAINMENT

INSIDE TRACK
ARTMAP

Things might be booming on Dubai's art circuit, but the biggest hindrance to visitors is finding half of the galleries, particularly those tucked away in some old warehouse. Fear not; nip into one of the bigger galleries like **Ayyam Gallery** (*see p191*) or the **Third Line** (*see p192*) and pick up a free Art Map or see www.artinthecity.com, which provides detailed directions to all the city's spaces.

Third Line. *See p192.*

BASTAKIA

Majlis Gallery
*Al Fahidi R/A, Bastakia, Bur Dubai (04
353 6233/www.themajlisgallery.com).* **Open**
9.30am-8pm Sat-Thur. **Credit** MC, V. **Map**
p298 H4.
The Majlis Gallery is set in one of Bastakia's traditional Arabic courtyards, and appropriately it tends
towards more traditional watercolours and paintings, often displaying foreign artists who reflect on
the experience of the Middle East. A relaxing spot
and a stalwart on the Dubai scene.

★ XVA Gallery
*Bastakia, behind the Majlis Gallery (353 5383/
www.xvagallery.com).* **Open** 9am-9pm Sat-Thur.
Credit AmEx, MC, V. **Map** p298 H4.

XVA Gallery has become even bigger and better
now that it has incorporated next door's Ave
Gallery. This beautiful art space in the heart of old
Dubai combines traditional Arabic architecture and
pleasing old-world charm with all the style, panache
and 21st-century convenience that one would expect
of a contemporary gallery. And they do a mean
lemon-mint juice too. *Photo p196.*

MARINA

Art Couture Gallery
*21 Al Fattan Marine Towers, JBR (399 4331,
www.artcoutureuae.com).* **Open** 10am-9pm
Sat-Thur; 2-9pm Fri. **Credit** AmEx, MC, V.
Map p304 B1.
Art Couture is a sophisticated gallery tucked away
in a rather strange mall that seems to be full of

Boom or Bloom?

The unlikely rise of Dubai's art market.

When news that art was becoming Dubai's next big thing hit the press, many people were mystified. After all, this is Dubai, land of seven-star luxury and fake islands: there'd be no market there for an art scene. Recent years have shown how wrong all that eyebrow raising was. What might have seemed like a passing blip on the artworld's radar has instead become something more sustainable, with many of the elements that make up art scenes in other parts of the world.

The annual **Art Dubai** fair (www.artdubai.ae) may be the biggest symbol of how strong things are. International galleries clamour to exhibit here every March, as the fair brings their wares to a whole new market with a taste for the contemporary. As a further sign of its success, Art Dubai has sparked spin-off events like the **Bastakia Art Fair** (www.baf.ae), a fringe event that happens in the heritage quarter at the same time. Taken together, these shows have turned the world's attention on to the possibilities for art in the Middle East.

At street level too, things are looking strong, and you'll be hard pressed to find a section of the city that hasn't got a gallery tucked away somewhere. To tap into the gallery scene, begin at **Thejamjar** (*see p192*) in Al Quoz, which is a hub for the city's creative movements. The opening nights may be big and lavish, but there are also DIY painting workshops nearly every day and a programme of film screenings. Still in Al Quoz, the **Third Line** (*see p192*) is one of the city's stalwarts and, aside from a constantly changing line-up of artists, the gallery has set about documenting what's happening here.

Bastakia, once a sleepy heritage quarter, has been transformed. Wander around the area every Saturday and see the place come alive with **Souk Al Bastakia** (which runs from 10am until sunset), a weekly market integrated with local galleries like **XVA Gallery** (*see p194*) and **Majlis Gallery** (*see p194*).

One of the main gripes about the art scene was that it was too geared towards getting art into the hands of rich buyers, with not enough focus on the local level. A number of galleries have since tried to discover Emirati artists, and it's been an enlightening process. **Elementa** (*see p196*) has exhibited a number of local artists, with shows curated by Emirati artists. To see the backbone of Emirati art, however, a trip to the **Flying House** (*see p196*) is in order. The converted villa-cum-installation by this Emirati collective really gives some idea of the way that Emirati artists are thinking right now, with works by Hassan Sharif and Mohammed Kazam among others.

But these are all just elements building the art scene here. The artworld, having seen Dubai's pavilion at Venice Biennale 2009, is rapidly getting wise to the unlikely happenings in the desert.

ARTS & ENTERTAINMENT

Art Dubai.

XVA Gallery. *See p194.*

Lebanese barber shops and Russian-orientated gold outlets. While artist Cynthia 'Reta' Richards often exhibits (Art Couture Gallery does belong to her, after all), this small but attractive space often brings in impressive international and locally based artists. The works on show tend towards the pleasingly decorative, and it's perfectly possible to pick up a few small pieces at an affordable price.

★ Carbon 12

Marina View Towers, Dubai Marina, opposite Radisson, Dubai Marina (050 873 9623/ www.carbon12dubai.com). **Open** noon-7pm Sun-Thur; by appointment Sat. **No credit cards. Map** p304 B2.

Walking into Carbon 12 is like descending into a vault, as it's in the basement of one of the Marina's defining towers. However, lest claustrophobia repel, remember that this space provides an international roster of artists, and has a brash, bright approach to curatorial direction. Well worth the trip.

ELSEWHERE

Elementa

Gallerie 88 FZCO, LIU: K-05, Dubai Airport Free Zone (299 0064/www.galleryelementa.com). **Open** noon-8pm Sat-Thur. **No credit cards. Map** p297 L2.

This is a modern and contemporary art gallery that features work by established and emerging artists from around the world. Elementa has shown a marked interest in displaying works by young Emirati artists and students based in Dubai. A bit out of the way, but worth the trip nonetheless.

Flying House

House no.18, Street 25, Al Safa (050 651 9935/www.the-flyinghouse.com). **Open** by appointment. **No credit cards. Map** p296 G5.

Run by a collective of Emirati artists, this converted villa has been made into one huge installation, showcasing the works of Mohammed Kazam, Abdul Raheem-Sharif and Hassan Sharif. An exciting insight into contemporary art from the Emirates.

Traffic

Saratoga Building, behind Tamweel, near Mall of the Emirates (341 8494/www.viatraffic.org). **Open** 10am-8pm Sat-Thur. **Credit** MC, V. **Map** p304 D2.

Traffic is Dubai's premium gallery for contemporary design, and its in-house design team has a lot of creative input in the city itself, with involvement in fairs and the UAE pavilion at 2009's Venice Biennale. There's a good selection of design from around the world, with some unusual contemporary pieces from the Middle East.

Children

Big fun for little travellers.

Visiting Dubai with children can be as easy as plonking them on the beach and setting them to work on a mini replica of the Burj Al Arab. However, there's a whole lot more on offer than sun, sea and sandcastles in this manic, dusty city. Arabic culture reveres childhood, and consequently every kind of kid is catered for here, from water parks and skiing lessons for sporty tots, to aquariums, and arts and crafts sessions for deep thinkers. Glitzy options are certainly on offer if you have the budget, but thankfully there's also plenty of free stuff out there if you know where to look. To keep up to date with all the latest family events, make sure you buy *Time Out Dubai Kids*, on the shelves every month.

ACTIVE

Aquaventure
Atlantis, Palm Jumeirah (426 0000/www. atlantisthepalm.com). **Open** 10am-6pm daily. **Admission** Dhs285 adults; Dhs220 children under 1.2m. Price includes access to private beach. **Credit** AmEx, MC, V. **Map** p294 A2.
The city's newest, shiniest water park boasts the Ziggurat, a towering central structure from which spring slides of all shapes and sizes. The most scream-inducing is the Leap of Faith, a 27.5-metre (90-foot) near-vertical drop through a shark-infested lagoon (although you are safely encased in a tunnel). If you actually want to see the sharks then there's a winding, tube-based slide that goes through the same pool at a fraction of the speed. Smaller children are also catered for with the thoroughly soaking Splashers' zone. *Photo p198.*

Dreamland
Emirates Road, exit 103, Umm Al Quwain (06 768 1888/www.dreamlanduae.com). **Open** *Jan-Mar* 10am-6pm daily. *Apr-May* 10am-7pm daily. *June* 10am-7pm Sun-Wed; 10am-8pm Thur-Sat & public holidays. *July-Aug* 11am-9pm daily. *Sept-Dec* 10am-6pm daily. *Ramadan* 10am-4pm daily. **Admission** Dhs100 adults; Dhs70 children under 1.1m tall; free children under 1m tall and under-3s. **Credit** AmEx, MC, V.

About the author
*British-born writer **Ele Cooper** is assistant editor of the monthly* Time Out Dubai Kids *magazine.*

It might not be strictly in Dubai, but the 45-minute drive to Umm Al Quwain's Dreamland is worth it if you've got very young water babies. Having been refurbished in 2009, it's much more peaceful than Dubai's water parks, meaning shorter queues (if any at all) and a massively reduced chance of losing over-eager tots. Parents can join little ones in the Aqua Play area – complete with water bouncers, see-saws and water bikes – while older children are catered for with scarier slides. Outdoorsy types will be interested to know that you can also camp overnight.

Dubai Autodrome
Motor City (367 8700/www.dubaiautodrome. com). **Open** times vary. **Admission** *Indoor karting* (15 mins) Dhs100. *Laser quest* (15 mins) Dhs80. *Both* Dhs160. Annual registration fee of Dhs10. **Credit** MC, V. **Map** p294 B4.
Anyone aged seven and above can try their hand at go-karting on the 500-metre (1,640-foot) indoor track at Motor City (there's also a 1.2km – 0.75mile – outdoor track for adults only). This, combined with laser quest, an in-the-dark shooting game (involving light beams rather than bullets), makes it a summer favourite for young action junkies. There's also a small café for when hunger strikes.

FREE Dubai Creek & souks
Deira/Bur Dubai. **Map** p298 H3.
The busiest, most historic part of Dubai is a must-see for any visitor hoping to instill a sense of the city's culture in their children. It's been a trading hub since the early 20th century, and traditional dhows (wooden fishing boats) still dominate the waterways

Time Out Dubai **197**

Aquaventure. See p197.

ARTS & ENTERTAINMENT

and, at Dhs1, crossing the creek in an *abra* remains many people's preferred mode of Deira-Bur Dubai transport (and let's face it, children love boats). Older offspring might find the hustle and bustle of the surrounding textile, gold and spice souks exciting, but those areas are probably best avoided if you've got babies or children who don't like crowds.

FREE Dubai Heritage & Diving Village
Al Shindagha, Bur Dubai (393 7151/www. dubaitourism.ae). **Open** 8.30am-10pm Sat-Thur; 4.30-11pm Fri. **Map** p298 G3.
Sitting at the mouth of the creek, the setting of this educational centre is lovely and surprisingly big, but it's something of a ghost town in the summer. However, go on a winter evening – particularly during Eid, National Day or Dubai Shopping Festival (*see p190*) – and it's buzzing. There are history tours round the heritage village with palm-frond-weaving and bread-making displays, and children can take a camel ride and visit the farm. The diving village focuses on the lives of coastal people, has a very small aquarium, and occasionally shows traditional dhow building. There are also various stalls selling touristy bits, and three restaurants.

Dubai Ice Rink
Dubai Mall (437 3111/www.dubaiicerink.com). **Open** 10am-noon, 12.15-2.15pm, 2.30-4.30pm, 5.45-7.45pm, 8-10pm Sun-Wed; 11.15am-1.15pm,

1.30-3.30pm, 5-7pm, 7.30-9.30pm, 9.45-11.45pm Thur-Sat. **Admission** Dhs50. **Credit** AmEx, MC, V. **Map** p303 F13.
The only Olympic-sized facility in Dubai and handily for ice-shy parents, it's slap bang in the middle of one of the world's biggest malls. This is guaranteed to keep little ice bunnies occupied for hours, or for as long as the slightly bizarre opening times will allow, anyway. Rumour has it that ice discos will be starting up later in the year, so it would be worth giving the venue a call or checking on its website to see if you can strut your stuff on the ice.

★ Full Moon Desert Drumming
Gulf Ventures Desert Camp (050 659 2874/ www.dubaidrums.com). **Prices** Dhs175; Dhs75 5-14s; free under-5s. **Credit** AmEx, MC, V in advance at www.timeouttickets.com, otherwise **no credit cards**.
A truly unique experience: you are driven into the pitch black desert, and then led down a path lit with flaming torches to veritable feast of rhythmic activity. Rows of cushions and *djembe* (African drums) await visitors, and a troupe of professional drummers from all over the world leads the group through various improvisations. On our last visit, the children couldn't get enough of it. There's also a cracking Arabic buffet dinner and alcoholic drinks are available at just above cost price. The site is about 30 minutes' drive from Dubai.

Ski Dubai

Mall of the Emirates (409 4000/www.
skidubai.ae). **Open** 10am-11pm Sun-Wed;
10am-midnight Thur; 9am-midnight Fri; 9am-
11pm Sat. **Admission** *Snow park* Dhs80 over-
13s; Dhs75 0-12s. *Two hours on slope* Dhs180
over-13s; Dhs150 0-12s. *Ski slope day pass*
Dhs300 over-13s; Dhs240 0-12s. **Credit**
AmEx, MC, V. **Map** p304 D2.
Where better to cool down than the Middle East's
first indoor ski resort? At a whopping 400 metres
(1,300 feet) long, it's certainly a sight to behold, and
as well as the serious pursuits of skiing and boarding, there's fun to be had tobogganing, bobsledding
and tubing. Little Christmas visitors will also enjoy
meeting Frostbite, the slope's mascot polar bear. All
clothing except hats and gloves is provided.
▶ *There's lots more to do at the Mall of the*
Emirates; see p159 for further ideas.

★ Wild Wadi

Jumeirah Beach Hotel (348 4444/www.wildwadi.
com). **Open** *Nov-Feb* 10am-6pm daily. *Mar-May*
10am-7pm daily. *June-Aug* 10am-8pm daily. *Sept-*
Oct 10am-7pm daily. **Admission** *All day* Dhs195
over 1.1m; Dhs 165 under 1.1m. *Sun downer*
Dhs165 over 1.1m; Dhs135 under 1.1m.
Credit AmEx, MC, V. **Map** p304 E1.
This Dubai stalwart remains a firm favourite with
us. It may be a little rougher round the edges than
its baby sibling Aquaventure (*see p197*) but it also
has more character and is arguably more family-
friendly, with less emphasis on white knuckle terror
rides (although there are still some pretty scary
slides) and more on chilling out (its lazy river is 360
metres long, and so gentle you could almost fall
asleep while drifting along it). *Photo p200.*

ANIMALS AND NATURE

FREE Animal Sanctuary & Petting Farm

At the end of Dubai Bypass Road (E611) on
the Ajman/Sharjah border (050 273 0973/
www.poshpaws.com). **Open** 10am-5pm daily.
Admission free.
An unfortunate side effect of Dubai's high population turnover is the vast quantity of unwanted pets
departing expats leave in their wake. Luckily, this
not-for-profit organisation provides a home for them,
currently housing cats, dogs, turtles, snakes, horses
and parrots, among other things. At the time of
going to press, they were expecting a baby baboon,
abandoned by a family who bought it in a souk (yes,
really). Children can pet the animals while learning
how they should really be cared for.

★ Dolphin Bay

Atlantis, Palm Jumeirah (426 1030/www.
atlantisthepalm.com). **Open** daily 10am-
sunset. **Admission** Dhs845 for shallow water
interaction; Dhs1,030 for deep-water (3m)

Dubai Ice Rink.

ARTS & ENTERTAINMENT

interaction (over-12s only). *Observer pass* Dhs385; Dhs320 3-7s. Includes entrance to Aquaventure & private beach. **Credit** AmEx, MC, V. **Map** p294 A2.

Swimming with the dolphins is on most children's wish lists (and adults too if we're honest), and Dolphin Bay certainly treats its residents well, with 4.5 hectares of salt water lagoons for them to swim in. Both shallow-water and deep-water interaction sessions involve an hour of instruction on dry land followed by 30 minutes in the pool with the dolphins. Visitors who would rather watch from the comfort of sun loungers can buy the observer pass – although it still doesn't come cheap.

▶ *See p105 for more on the Atlantis hotel.*

Dubai Aquarium & Discovery Centre

Dubai Mall (437 3155/www.thedubai aquarium.com). **Open** 10am-10pm Sun-Wed; 10am-midnight Thur-Sat. **Admission** *Aquarium tunnel* Dhs25; Dhs20 3-16s; free under-3s. *Aquarium tunnel & underwater zoo* Dhs50. **Credit** MC, V. **Map** p303 F13.

Few children can resist a visit to Dubai Aquarium, particularly since it has the world's largest viewing panel and a walk-through tunnel with 270-degree field of vision (there are few things more surreal than sharks and stingrays floating above your head). It holds around 33,000 creatures, including penguins and water rats, as well as the usual fishy suspects. Check the website for feeding times.

▶ *For more on Dubai Mall, see p155.*

Wild Wadi. See p199.

Lost Chambers

Atlantis, Palm Jumeirah (426 0000/www. atlantisthepalm.com). **Open** 10am-11pm daily. **Admission** Dhs100; Dhs70 under-13ss. **Credit** AmEx, MC, V. **Map** p294 A2.

An impressive aquarium built around the legend of Atlantis, with a maze of different rooms decorated in line with the underwater explorer theme which children will love. Although it does make for a fun trip out, visitors on a budget would do well to note that the Ambassador Lagoon, a huge tank containing 250 species including sharks, can actually be seen for free from the hotel's corridors.

▶ *See p105 for more on the Atlantis hotel.*

INDOOR ENTERTAINMENT

Café Ceramique

Mall of the Emirates (04 341 0144/www.cafe-ceramique.com). **Open** 9am-midnight daily. **Prices** From Dhs35 for ceramic item, paint and materials. **Credit** AmEx, MC, V. **Map** p304 D2.

Café Ceramique's unique selling point is the fact that it will keep children quiet for a fabulously long time. The concept is simple: choose your ceramic item (in our opinion, nothing beats a good mug), sketch a design, paint it, leave it for the staff to glaze and collect it seven days later. Oh, and try to remember to bubble wrap it so it survives the journey home...
Other locations Town Centre, Jumeirah (04 344 7331).

★ Children's City

Creekside Park (04 3340 808/www.dubai childrencity.ae). **Open** 9am-8.30pm Sat-Thur; 3-8.30pm Fri. *Ramadan* 9am-4pm Sat-Thur; 3-6.30pm Fri. **Admission** Dhs15; Dhs10 2-15s; Dhs40 family. **No credit cards.** **Map** p297 K3.

Fantastic indoor fun for when it gets too hot outside, this is like a playground for little and big kids alike. Touchy-feely educational exhibits vie for space with a life-size cockpit (great for wannabe pilots) and a newly refurbished planetarium. There's also a great toy shop in the downstairs area.

Dubai Museum

Al Fahidi Fort, Bastikiya (353 1862/www. dubaitourism.ae). **Open** 8.30am-8.30pm Sat-Thur; 2.30-8.30pm Fri. *Ramadan* 9am-5pm Sat-Thur; 2-5pm Fri. **Admission** Dhs3; Dhs1 under-7s. **No credit cards.** **Map** p298 H4.

Housed in Al Fahidi fort, a very cool-looking building dating from 1787, Dubai Museum is packed to the rafters with life-size models of all sorts of traditional Arabic sights that could be seen before the discovery of oil: souks, houses, pearl diving, date farms, mosques and, of course, desert. There's also a good array of artefacts recovered from graves from the third millennium BC.

ARTS & ENTERTAINMENT

Café Ceramique.

★ Favourite Things

Dubai Marina Mall (434 1984/www.favourite things.com). **Open** 9am-9pm daily. **Admission** 1st hr Dhs80; Dhs20 additional hours. **Credit** AmEx, MC, V. **Map** p304 B2.

Having recently moved from its original location in Jumeirah, this spruce play centre (including soft play area, castle-themed jungle gym, fancy dress room, cooking/science room and sand room) keeps children happy for hours on end. There's also a bright, airy café, a novelty boutique – great for original gifts – and a hair salon. It's also renowned for being one of the cleanest places in the city. *Photo p202.*

Kidzania & Sega Republic

Level 2, Dubai Mall (04 8003 8224 6255/ www.thedubaimall.com). **Open** 10am-10pm Sun-Wed; 10am-midnight Thur-Sat. **Credit** MC, V. **Map** p303 F13.

A veritable haven for little people, Kidzania is a mini city, complete with buildings and streets, where children can dress up as doctors, chefs and car mechanics, and sample life in their desired roles. Sega Republic, for the older ones, is an indoor, game theme park with areas such as Sports Zone, Speed Zone, Redemption Zone (a games arcade, not a place to confess sins), plus a rollercoaster and other high-adrenaline motion-simulator rides.

Magic Planet

Mall of the Emirates (341 4444) & Deira City Centre (04 295 4333). **Open** *Mall of the Emirates* 10am-midnight daily; *Deira City Centre* 10am-10pm Sun-Wed; 10am-midnight Thur-Sat. **Admission** free but all rides and games require money to be put on a swipe card. **Map** p304 D2.

Whizzing, buzzing and whirring, Magic Planet is possibly the noisiest place in Dubai, and is absolutely heaving most nights. There are all sorts of arcade games as well as some theme park-style rides, cosmic ten-pin bowling, bumper cars, pool and billiards. If that's not enough to convince you, Magic Planet is so fun that two fully-grown members of the Time Out team have held birthday parties there in the past year.

Stargate

Gate 4, Za'abeel Park (04 325 9988/www. stargatedubai.ae). **Open** 10am-10pm Sat-Wed; 10am-midnight Thur, Fri. **Admission** free. *Rides* Dhs-Dhs30. **Credit** MC, V. **Map** p301 H9.

A spacecraft on a quest for fun has crash-landed in Dubai's Za'abeel Park. At least, that's the concept behind Dubai's latest thrill-packed zone for children. Hi-tech, educational and packed with excitement, the mammoth Dhs400 million project is spread over five space-themed domes – Earth, Lunar, Saturn, UFO and Mars – and connected with tunnels on three floors. Adventure rides for kids aged four to 14 years include an indoor-outdoor rollercoaster, gigantic soft

> ## INSIDE TRACK
> ## BURJ AL ARAB
>
> You probably don't want to fork out a fortune for a jaunt inside the Burj Al Arab, so it's lucky that the highlight of the building is actually the view from the outside. Grab an ice-cream, sit yourself down on the public beach at Umm Suqeim and watch the hotel's light show as the sun sets.

play area, the latest in 3D entertainment, a lunar ice
rink and a go-karting and dodgem area. Computer
games, shops and a multi-cuisine food court complete the experience.

PARKS AND BEACHES

★ Al Mamzar Park
*Al Mamzar Creek, near Sharjah border (296
6201).* **Open** 9am-6pm daily. Wed ladies' day.
Admission Dhs5. **No credit cards.**
Al Mamzar is a great place to go if you want a quiet
spot during the week. As well as three golden
beaches, the park provides barbecue sites, a swimming pool, food kiosks, a lagoon, a large wooden
fort, a scenic train, an amphitheatre regularly stag-
ing family shows, and many children's play areas.
Lifeguards keep watch.

Al Safa Park
Sheikh Zayed Road (349 2111). **Open** 8am-11pm
daily; ladies' day Tue. **Admission** Dhs3. **No
credit cards. Map** p296 G5.
This is one of Dubai's oldest and largest green
spaces, and it has an organic feel. It takes a good couple of hours to explore all the nooks and crannies,
and there is a small lake with boats, waterfall and a
random hill with shady trees. There's also a train,
four-seater bicycles, children's amusement park and
a café selling decent snacks. The slightly rundown
but ludicrously cheap tennis courts are handy, and
in the winter there's a flea market every first
Saturday of the month (see www.dubai-
fleamarket.com for details). There's a separate area
solely for women.

Creekside Park
*Between Maktoum & Garhoud Bridges (336
7633).* **Open** 8am-11pm daily. **Admission**
Dhs5. **No credit cards. Map** p297 K3.
In our opinion the best park in Dubai, Creekside has
expansive grassy areas, cable cars offering amazing
views of the city, botanical gardens, four-person covered bikes, three-person tandem bikes, fishing, an
amphitheatre, fantastic water views and weird fig-
urines based on '90s Jim Carrey movie *The Mask.*
The only downside is the lack of parking.

Jumeirah Beach Park
*Jumeirah Beach Road (050 858 9887/349
2555).* **Open** 8am-11pm daily; ladies' day Mon.
Admission Dhs5; Dhs20 for cars. **No credit
cards. Map** p302 A15.

Favourite Things. *See p201.*

Creekside Park.

Bordering the beach and always busy, Jumeirah Beach Park is a nice place for a picnic if you don't want sandy sarnies. It has tables, barbecue sites, small play areas for children, volleyball, showers and swimming facilities with lifeguards. You can also rent sun loungers and frequent the fast food cafés if you can't be bothered with the exhausting preparation a picnic entails.

RESTAURANTS

★ Beachcombers
Jumeirah Beach Hotel (406 8999/www.
jumeirah.com). **Open** 7.30am-midnight daily.
Main courses Dhs100-Dhs 150. **Credit**
AmEx, MC, V. **Map** p304 E1.
Don't let the slightly naff interior fool you – this is a cracking place for families (and the beautiful Burj Al Arab views from the outside terrace more than compensate for the Polynesian beach shack theme indoors). Usually serving up a combination of top quality Indian, Thai, Malaysian and Japanese cuisines, there are live cooking stands and one of the best dessert tables in town. Head there on a Friday or Saturday, and children can eat brunch (involving unlimited food and drink) for only Dhs35. There's a staffed games room with PlayStations, DVDs and toys, although a roving magician and live band will keep at-table children amused.

Benihana
Al Bustan Rotana, Casablanca Road,
Garhoud (282 0000/www.rotana.com).
Open 7pm-midnight daily. **Credit** AmEx,
MC, V. **Map** p297 K2.
The theme nights here make for an unforgettable family dining experience. Sit at high stools around the teppan grill as mischievous chefs cook up a storm while simultaneously entertaining their audi-

ences with knife-juggling and cheeky jokes, cooking relentlessly until you beg for mercy. Save some room though – the pudding table's green tea chocolate fountain is something else. The theme nights (Saturday and Tuesday are sushi nights, Sunday is devoted to teppanyaki) cost Dhs159 per person, including unlimited food and alcoholic drink.

Chili's
Mall of the Emirates (www.chilis.com). **Open**
11am-11pm Sat-Wed; 11am-midnight Thur;
1.30pm-midnight Fri. **Main courses** Dhs40-
Dhs70. **Credit** AmEx, MC, V. **Map** p304 D2.
Chili's is something of a Dubai institution, even if the semi-posh fast food it serves may not rate highly on the healthy stakes. However, sometimes you want to binge, and then it never fails to hit the spot. A good range of Mexican nosh like *fajitas* and *que-sadillas* sits alongside American staples like burgers and not-so-healthy salads (the chicken Caesar option contains more calories than a cheeseburger), but no matter what you opt for, you can be sure that the portion will be huge. Children's menus come printed on the back of an activity sheet which should keep them quiet for, er, three minutes.
Other locations throughout the city.

Coconut Grove
Rydges Plaza, Satwa Roundabout (398 2222).
Open noon-3pm, 7pm-midnight daily. **Main
courses** Dhs50-Dhs70. **Credit** AmEx, MC, V.
Map p301 F8.
It's one of the best budget joints in town, with fine southern Indian and Sri Lankan cuisine paired with sterling service. Staff are unfailingly welcoming and helpful, and it's usually packed with Indian and Western families. It's also licensed. Stand out dishes include a tikka masala laden with juicy chunks of hammour and a tasty aubergine dish that goes by

the tongue-twisting moniker of *kathrikai kara
kozhambu*. Nans and rice come in huge portions,
ensuring appetites are more than adequately sated.

Irish Village

*Aviation Club, Garhoud (282 4750/www.theirish
village.ae).* **Open** 11am-1am Sat-Wed; 11am-2am
Thur, Fri. **Main courses** Dhs40-Dhs60. **Credit**
AmEx, MC, V. **Map** p297 K3.
Is there a city on earth that does not have at least
one Irish-themed pub? Dubai certainly has its fair
share, and the Irish Village is the jewel in the big
green novelty crown. It serves up reliable pub grub
and is a dream for parents whose children's bottoms
have an aversion to remaining still, on a seat, for
more than five minutes: it's surrounded by lots of
grass and a lake containing ducks and turtles.
Service is generally pretty surly, but if you can get
past the scowls that greet you, you're in for a pleasant afternoon in the sun.

Johnny Rockets

*Mall of the Emirates (04 341 2380/www.johnny
rockets.com).* **Open** 11am-midnight daily. **Main
courses** Dhs50-Dhs80. **Credit** AmEx, MC, V.
Map p304 D2.
Johnny Rockets delivers the 1950s family diner experience with aplomb – just check out the dancing staff
at the Marina branch. Serving arguably the best
burgers in town (the key is the fresh ingredients),
the salubrious, child-friendly joint proudly grills
fresh beef right in front of your nose, and tosses it
up into a mean burger with whopping slices of
tomato and onion. Not one for herbivores.
Other locations Dubai Marina; next to Village
Mall in Jumeirah.

Lime Tree Café

*Jumeirah Beach Road, next to Spinneys (04 349
8498/www.thelimetreecafe.com).* **Open** 7.30am-
6pm daily. **Main courses** Dhs30-Dhs40. **Credit**
AmEx, MC, V. **Map** p300 D9.
One of the best cafés in Dubai, and a firm favourite
with expat yummy mummies and their designer
buggies. Just go to the counter, select your grub from
the mouth watering display of wholesome, tasty and
imaginative options and, if it's the weekend, prepare
to fight for a table. If you're in a savoury mood you
can't beat the vegetable tortilla stack and the sweet

potato salad, but the sweet of tooth should make a
beeline for the carrot cake, which has achieved leg-
endary status in Dubai.
Other locations Ibn Battuta Mall, China Court
(04 366 9320).

★ More

*Al Garhoud, behind Welcare Hospital (04 283
0224).* **Open** 8am-10pm daily. **Main courses**
Dhs40-Dhs70. **Credit** MC, V. **Map** p297 K2.
A firm *Time Out* favourite, More's distinctive interiors, which combine decadent Cadbury-purple
walls and industrial steel pipes, are second only to
its enormous portions and achingly delicious strawberry and balsamic juice in the 'what makes it stand
out' stakes. The friendly staff welcome children like
long-lost friends and the almost embarrassingly
extensive menu means that even the fussiest little
diners will find something they like. From sarnies
to curries to full-on meaty extravaganzas, you can
be sure that More has it covered.
Other locations Al Murooj Rotana (04 343
3779); Gold & Diamond Park (04 323 4350);
Dubai Mall (no phone).

On the Border

The Walk, Jumeirah Beach Residence (423 0627).
Open 11am-midnight daily. **Main courses**
Dhs40-Dhs70. **Credit** AmEx, MC, V. **Map**
p304 B2.
Dubai has many Mexican/American restaurants,
but none better than On The Border. For starters,
the guacamole live! (their exclamation mark, not
ours) is an entertaining option for kids, as the server
brings all the ingredients to your table and prepares
the avocado mush in front of you. Children's menus
are covered with jokes and activities, with healthy
options like grilled chicken and sautéed vegetables
there for parents who are strong-willed enough to
shun the cheese-packed 'big beef borduritto'.
Other locations Festival City (232 8112).

Organic Foods & Café

The Greens, off Sheikh Zayed Road (361 7974).
Open 8am-8pm daily (store open 8am-9pm).
Main courses Dhs40-Dhs70. **Credit** MC, V.
Map p304 C2.
If great value grub bursting with fresh, wholesome
flavours and goodness is your thing then look no
further. The setting may not be the most glam in
Dubai, but it doesn't matter. The food here speaks
for itself and the owners' passion for healthy,
organic chow shines through in succulent meats,
fresh veg and crisp, nutritious salads. From all-day
breakfasts, including a huge brie and apple omelette,
to a variety of organic pizzas with fresh toppings,
all the way to a mound of fragrant steaming Thai
fish curry, this is a boon for the health-conscious and
people who appreciate real food. The Dubai Mall
branch also has a kids' play area.
Other locations Dubai Mall (434 0577).

Film & Theatre

Filmgoing is a social event in Dubai but one dominated by multiplexes.

Filmgoing is extremely popular in Dubai. But despite the diverse nature of Dubai audiences, Western films remain most popular, with mainstream Hollywood blockbusters filling auditoriums for weeks on end. A glance at a week's listings will reveal a decided taste for lowbrow comedies, inoffensive rom-coms, and an endless parade of horror flicks. This lowest common denominator approach occasionally irks residents, but still keeps cinemas packed all year long. There is no real art-house scene to speak of, apart from a few dedicated individuals who hold free screenings around town in clubs and galleries. This could all change, though, as Dubai is now home to two film festivals (*see p207*), encouraging an increase in homegrown, artistically credible film-making.

(see p207)

CENSORSHIP

Censorship is an issue for film-lovers in Dubai, who often have a hard time following a story after cuts made to meet cultural sensibilities leave the movie in tatters. Broadly speaking, the Dubai Department of Censorship will cut any nudity and overt sexual references, and any homosexual scenes. Political comments relating to Arab governments or anything deemed defamatory towards Islam are out, as is anything that comes even close to recognising Israel.

MULTIPLEXES

The following venues all tend to show similar programmes of English-language (mainly Hollywood) films, with a smattering of Arab and Hindi blockbusters. Hollywood and Bollywood films will carry Arabic subtitles.

CineStar

Deira City Centre mall, Garhoud (294 9000). **Tickets** Dhs30. **Screens** 11. **Credit** MC, V. **Map** p297 K2.

★ CineStar at Mall of the Emirates

Mall of the Emirates, Al Barsha (341 4222). **Tickets** Dhs 30. *Gold Class* Dhs110. **Screens** 14. **Credit** MC, V. **Map** p304 D2.

Grand Cinecity

Al Ghurair City, Rigga Road, Deira (228 9898). **Tickets** Dhs30-Dhs50. **Screens** 8. **Credit** MC, V. **Map** p299 K3.

Grand Cineplex

Next to Wafi City, Garhoud (324 2000). **Tickets** Dhs30-Dhs35. **Screens** 10. **Credit** MC, V. **Map** p297 J3. *Photo p206.*

INSIDE TRACK
NONSENSICAL SCHEDULES

Dubai's haphazard film schedules can make filmgoing in the emirate something of a lucky dip. Often, the cinemas serve up a puzzling combination of lame action B-movies that went straight to DVD everywhere else in the world two years ago, and really, really good Oscar-winning films... at least six months later than more or less everywhere else in the world. Then again, you can get lucky and, for no particularly good reason, see a blockbuster in Dubai before everyone else – *Transformers* was released over here before it reached the UK, and X-Men prequel *X-Men Origins: Wolverine* was shown before both its US and UK premières.

About the author – Film

Laura Chubb is Film editor for the weekly Time Out Dubai *magazine.*

Dubai is a city of decadence, so why shouldn't this extend to filmgoing? A Dhs100 Gold Class cinema ticket at Cinestar at Mall of the Emirates (*see p205*) or Grand Class cinema ticket at Grand Dubai Festival City (*see below*) allows you to stretch out in a luxury recliner, enjoy table service and view a film in more convivial surroundings than usual. It's advisable to call ahead and check availability, especially at weekends.

★ Grand Dubai Festival City
Dubai Festival City (232 8328). **Tickets** Dhs30-Dhs100. **Screens** 12. **Credit** MC, V. **Map** p297 L3.

★ Grand Megaplex
In the China Zone of the Ibn Battuta Mall (366 9898). **Tickets** Dhs30-Dhs50. **Screens** 21 (including IMAX screen). **Credit** MC, V. **Map** p304 A2.

Grand Mercato
Mercato Mall, Jumeirah Beach Road (349 9713). **Tickets** Dhs30-Dhs50. **Screens** 7. **Credit** MC, V. **Map** p302 C12.

Grand Metroplex
Dubai Metropolitan Hotel, Interchange 2, Sheikh Zayed Road (343 8383). **Tickets** Dhs30-Dhs55. **Screens** 8. **Credit** MC, V. **Map** p296 G5.

LOCAL CINEMAS

The following cinemas show a mix of Malayalam, Tamil and Hindi films, usually with Arabic (but not English) subtitles.

Galleria Cinema
Hyatt Regency Hotel, Al Khaleej Road, Deira (273 7676). **Tickets** Dhs30. **Screens** 2. **No credit cards. Map** p299 J1.
Screens new Malayalam and Tamil releases.

Lamcy Cinema
Next to Lamcy Plaza, Karama (336 8808). **Tickets** Dhs25. **Screens** 2. **No credit cards**. **Map** p297 J3.
Screens new Hindi releases.

Grand Cineplex. *See p205.*

Movies Under the Stars.

OUTDOOR CINEMAS

★ **FREE** **Movies Under the Stars**
Wafi Rooftop Gardens, Wafi City (324 4100).
Tickets Free. **Screens** 1. **Map** p297 J3.
Watching a film at this wonderful venue is an experience that a movie buff should not miss. There are Sunday screenings of double bills from 8pm to midnight, October to May. *See also below* **Inside track**.

INSIDE TRACK
MOVIES UNDER THE STARS

Wafi Rooftop Gardens at the impressive Wafi City mall is a great location for Dubai's only outdoor cinema – and, even more of an incentive for impecunious movie fans, there is no admission charge. Cinema-goers can lie back on bean bags while enjoying **Movies Under the Stars** (*see above*). The venue screens themed double bills every Sunday (for example, there was the recent Steve Carell mini-festival which showed *The 40-year-old Virgin* and *Anchorman* back-to-back). Unlike the normal practice in most of the world's outdoor cinemas, the complex closes in the summer months, thus protecting punters from the stifling 40 plus degrees temperatures.

FILM FESTIVALS

In 2004, Dubai launched the inaugural **Dubai International Film Festival** (www.dubai filmfest.com; *photo p208*). Attracting stars such as George Clooney, Morgan Freeman, Laurence Fishburne and Oliver Stone, the festival has succeeded in crossing cultural boundaries with exemplary line-ups of Arab, Indian, Far Eastern and Western films, alongside meet-and-greet forums, educational programmes and plenty of parties. But the festival is still in its infancy and, despite the hype, will have to work hard to convince the star names it craves to travel from Hollywood in the middle of December.

Dubai is also home to the **Gulf Film Festival** (www.gulffilmfest.com), which was launched in 2008. Predominantly screening films from the Gulf region, this festival provides more of an insight into the Arab world's burgeoning film industry.

Theatre

Dubai's theatre scene is very much in its early stages, but at least the venues themselves are impressive. The quality of the productions

About the author – Theatre
British-born writer **Ele Cooper** *is assistant editor of the monthly* Time Out Dubai Kids *magazine.*

Dubai International Film Festival. *See p207.*

varies considerably, depending on whether they're performed by a touring company (2009 has already seen visits from the English National Ballet and the West End's *The Lady in Black*) or produced locally (musicals starring children from Dubai schools). There will usually be something worth watching – although the country's strict censorship laws mean that you won't always see a full, uncut version of the original script.

Public performances of Emirati poetry, song and dance are mainly limited to ceremonial occasions and traditional displays at the Heritage & Diving Village (*see p70*).

THEATRES

Ductac
Mall of the Emirates (341 4777/www.ductac.org). **Map** p304 D2.
Short for Dubai Community & Arts Centre, Ductac comprises the Centrepoint Theatre, a beautiful two-tiered auditorium with a seating capacity of 543, the smaller Kilachand Studio, which stages more niche shows and holds 151 people, the Manu Chhabria Art Gallery, and several dance and art studios. As well as mainstream plays and concerts, the centre shows work by local photographers and artists.

First Group Theatre
Madinat Jumeirah (366 6546/www. madinattheatre.com). **Map** p304 D1.
A clean, modern, comfortable venue seating 450 people, the First Group Theatre has a busy programme ranging from African dance troupes to a recent production of *Annie*, the cast of which featured local schoolchildren. It's buried within the Madinat complex, so you can also have a mosey round the souk in the interval and take your pick from masses of restaurants afterwards.

INSIDE TRACK
NOISY NEIGHBOURS

Don't expect to enjoy your film in silence at any of Dubai's cinemas. For many filmgoers, especially teenagers, films serve merely as a backdrop to frenzied text messaging and mobile phone conversations, garrulous socialising, the noisy consumption of snacks and, in some cases, bouts of prolonged snoring. A few well-aimed tuts are usually about as far as anyone goes in combating the problem. Further occasional discomfort comes from over-enthusiastic air-conditioning, which can make auditoriums feel like wind tunnels – remember to take a light wrap or a pullover.

Health & Fitness

Work off or soothe away the excesses of your holiday.

Dubai has worked hard to market itself as a luxurious beach and shopping destination for Westerners, and part of that drive has found form in the many establishments that have sprung up dedicated to coddling you when on holiday. The beaches are pristine – often because they're brand new – and when you've finished tanning then the many hotel spas are on hand to pummel, smooth and moisturise skin that the fierce desert sun has dried. And should Dubai's round of shopping and eating show signs of working its way onto the waist, there are dozens of establishments on hand to get rid of the flab.

BEACH CLUBS

Providing you're in Dubai during the cooler months – September to the end of May – you'll be blown away by the private beaches, most of which are set in hotel grounds. There isn't mile upon mile of sand, but what there is, is perfect. Spending the day on a hotel beach can be costly if you're not a guest, but it's an experience that you shouldn't miss out on, even if it's just for one day. You'll be waited on hand and foot while you lie on your sun lounger. With the sun setting at around 6pm, it's worth waiting to see how quickly it disappears over the horizon.

There are some public beaches, but these aren't as impeccably looked after as those at hotels. For people on a budget, there are a couple of non-hotel beaches open to the public where you pay a nominal fee, Jumeirah Beach Park and Al Mamzar. Both beach parks tend to get busy, particularly on Fridays, when most shops don't open until at least 4pm, and on Saturdays; but they do have maintained public conveniences, kiosks and sun loungers.

Al Mamzar

Al Mamzar Creek, by the Sharjah border (296 6201). **Open** 9am-6pm daily. **Admission** Dhs5. **No credit cards. Map** p299 K1.
If you don't fancy the crowds at Jumeirah Beach Park, head for Al Mamzar. It doesn't have a café by the beach, but shower facilities and kiosks are dotted along the coast. There are sun loungers, but these tend to be in the main areas, so if you want a quieter spot, take a beach mat and camp down for the afternoon. Friday is busy, like most places in Dubai, but you should enjoy some peace and quiet during the week. The beach is a good size, unlike at some hotels.

Club Joumana

Jebel Ali Golf Resort & Spa, Sheikh Zayed Road, Exit 13, past Interchange 7 (883 6000/ www.jebelali-international.com). **Open** 9am-6pm daily. **Admission** *Sun-Thur* Dhs150; Dhs60 reductions. *Fri, Sat* Dhs250 incl lunch; Dhs125 reductions. **Credit** AmEx, MC, V. **Map** p304 A2.
Located about half an hour's drive from the centre of Dubai, Club Joumana is known for its friendly staff, and peace and quiet. Miles from the bustle of the city centre, here you might choose to stretch out and doze on the club's lush lawns or indulge in a variety of water sports available on the private

---

INSIDE TRACK
ALTERNATIVE THERAPIES

Those interested in holistic healing have the pick of the pack in Dubai. Psychics, past lives readers, crystal therapists and feng shui experts abound, which is odd, considering psychics are technically illegal here. Our favourite, though, is the comparatively sane colour therapy at **Spa Dunya** (Jumeirah Beach Residence, The Walk, 04 439 3669). The treatments are classic, and customised using your colour preferences.

---

beach. Activities include waterskiing, windsurfing, banana boating and sailing (catamaran and laser), and boat and fishing trips can also be organised. Back on dry land, Club Joumana boasts four flood-lit tennis courts, a glass-backed squash court and a badminton court. There are also two freshwater pools, a seawater pool and a children's pool. Nearby is a par-36 nine-hole golf course and practice facilities. Make sure you get there early at the weekend, as they often have to turn people away after 10am.

Club Mina

Le Meridien Mina Seyahi Hotel, Al Sufouh Road, Jumeirah (399 3333/www.lemeridien-minaseyahi.com). **Open** 9am-7pm daily. **Admission** *Sun-Thur* Dhs150 incl lunch; Dhs75 reductions. Members only Fri, Sat. **Credit** AmEx, MC, V. **Map** p304 B1.
One of the trendier clubs in town, Club Mina's private beach stretches for about a kilometre, and hosts many of the city's beautiful people whenever a powerboat race comes to town. If you can't beat 'em, join 'em: the relaxed beachside Barasti restaurant is a terrific place for a meal. Its facilities include three large swimming pools and two smaller pools for children.

Dubai Marine Beach Resort & Spa

Dubai Marine Beach Resort & Spa, Beach Road. (346 1111/www.dxbmarine.com). **Open** 7am-sunset daily. **Admission** *Sun-Thur* Dhs175; Sun-Thur Dhs90 children. *Fri, Sat* Dhs250; Fri, Sat Dhs130 children incl lunch. **Credit** AmEx, MC, V. **Map** p300 D8.
The resort, which is a favourite with the odd super-model, features two pools, a children's pool, a private beach and a tennis court; non-members can only book the court for tennis lessons.

Habtoor Grand Resort & Spa

Habtoor Grand Resort & Spa, Dubai Marina (399 5000/www.grandjumeirah.habtoor hotels.com). **Open** 8am-8pm daily. **Admission** *Sun-Thur* Dhs200; Dhs175 reductions. *Fri, Sat* Dhs225; Dhs150 reductions. **Credit** MC, V. **Map** p304 B1.
This is a busy beach club with three pools, one of which is a children's pool with a slide. If you're feeling energetic, there's beach volleyball, two floodlit tennis courts, two squash courts and water sports galore. You can have a break from the children by enrolling them in the junior Jungle Club. If you need a bite to eat, there are plenty of restaurants.

Hiltonia Beach & Pool

Hilton Dubai Jumeirah Hotel, Al Sufouh Road, Jumeirah (399 1111/www.hiltonworldresorts. com). **Open** *Beach* 7am-sunset daily. *Pool* 7am-8pm daily. **Admission** *Sun-Thur* Dhs180; *Fri, Sat* Dhs250. **Credit** AmEx, MC, V. **Map** 304 B1.

Armonia Spa at Sheraton Jumeirah.

There's no shortage of things to do here: water sports include parasailing, kayaking, jet-skiing, kneeboarding and fishing trips. Or you could just lie beside the pool and beach. As you'd expect from a Hilton hotel, the pools are surrounded by landscaped gardens, and there's a fairly pleasant beach.

Jumeirah Beach Park

Jumeirah Beach Park, Jumeirah Beach Road (050 858 9887/349 2555). **Open** 8am-11pm daily (ladies only Mon). **Admission** Dhs20/car or Dhs5/person. **No credit cards**. **Map** p302 A15.

There aren't that many facilities at the beach, but if you're after some relaxation, pack up your beach bag, grab a sun lounger and chill out for the day. This is one of the cheapest beaches in town, meaning that it's always busy. There's also a café selling junk food, a barbecue area, a children's playground and changing rooms.

Pavilion Marina & Sports Club

Jumeirah Beach Hotel (348 0000/www. jumeirahbeachhotel.com). **Open** 10am-7pm daily. **Admission** Dhs400; Dhs200 reductions. **Credit** AmEx, MC, V. **Map** p304 E1.

This upmarket beach club is popular with families as there are so many activities to choose from. If you're after water sports, windsurfing, water-skiing, kayaks, banana boat rides and yacht charters are all available, and if you simply feel like lounging by the water, there are four pools. People who like their sports to be land based can book themselves in for a few sets of tennis or practice their putting on the mini-driving range. If you're feeling like a break from the little ones, then simply pack them off to Sinbad's Kids' Club.

Ritz-Carlton Beach Club

Ritz-Carlton Dubai Hotel, Al Sufouh Road, Jumeirah (399 4000/www.ritzcarlton.com). **Open** 7am-7pm daily. **Admission** Dhs500 peak; Dhs300 off-peak; Dhs300 reductions peak; Dhs150 reductions off-peak. **Credit** AmEx, MC, V. **Map** p304 B1.

Despite the amount of construction work all around, the Ritz-Carlton Beach Club is still a spectacular place. For starters, there's a 350m (120ft) stretch of private beach as well as vast landscaped gardens. Facilities include four floodlit tennis courts, a grass soccer pitch, two squash courts, pitch and putt golf and a comprehensively equipped gym. Personal trainers are on hand to answer any fitness questions, and classes available include power yoga and women-only 'aerotennis', a cross between aerobics and the racket sport. The spa now features two women-only treatment rooms, taking the overall total to ten, with a range of seductive options stretching from Balinese-style massage to Scentao hot stone therapy. Water sports can be organised on request at additional cost.

1847. *See p216.*

Sheraton Jumeirah Health & Beach Club

Sheraton Jumeirah Beach Resort, Al Sufouh Road, Jumeirah (399 5533/www.starwood hotels.com). **Open** 7am-10pm daily (no pool lifeguards after 7pm). **Admission** Dhs100; Dhs50 children; free under-6s Sun-Thur; Dhs125 adults Fri, Sat. **Credit** AmEx, MC, V. **Map** p304 A1.

As well as two swimming pools, two floodlit tennis courts and two squash courts, the club has a gym packed with the usual array of bikes, steppers, rowing machines and treadmills. Add volleyball, a range of water sports, a sauna and steam room, and you won't run out of things to do in a hurry. Or you could just treat yourself to a hot stone massage (50 minutes, Dhs310) or a vitamin facial (60 minutes, Dhs425) at the Armonia spa.

INSIDE TRACK
CHEAP CUTS

Formul'a French Hairdressing Academy (Knowledge Village, Lot 11, Office G02, 04 438 0122) provides free haircuts and practically free dye jobs (you just pay for the cost of materials). Granted, students are doing the styling, but they do a pretty good job. Appointments at 9.30am and 1.30pm.

ARTS & ENTERTAINMENT

Akaru Spa. *See p216.*

HEALTH CLUBS

There are gyms and health clubs galore in Dubai, with a lot of hotel fitness centres vying for the local market as well as hotel guests. Many of these hotels sell day passes, which allow you to use their gym, pool and beach facilities. Although this adds up if you're living in the city, it's worthwhile if you're on holiday. Since most of Dubai has sprung up in the last decade, the gyms and spas are all pretty new, with modern equipment and trendy decor. The conservative local culture means that lots of gyms are for men or women only, or that there are separate gyms. You normally find, at the very least, that there are separate saunas and steam rooms. If there is one gym, there will often be women-only or men-only times, so it's worth ringing ahead before you go to check you can work out when you want to. If you're looking for professional instruction in a gym, you might not find it here. Staff tend to be unqualified, so ask about qualifications before you book a personal training session.

Aviation Club
Garhoud (282 4122/www.aviationclub.ae).
Open 6am-11pm daily. **Price** Dhs1,200/mth.
Credit AmEx, MC, V. **Map** p297 K3.

Home to Dubai's prestigious tennis tournament and one of the few clubs to establish itself on the Deira side of the Creek, the Aviation Club is an incredibly popular option. It boasts an impressive list of facilities, namely ten floodlit tennis courts, a swimming pool with 25m lap lanes, two squash courts, a dedicated spinning studio, a sauna, a steam room, plunge pools and a fully equipped gym. The club's aerobics studio continues to be the biggest and busiest in Dubai, hosting several fat-busting classes a day.

Big Apple
Jumeirah Emirates Towers, Boulevard Mall, Sheikh Zayed Road (319 8661/www.jumeirah emiratestowers.com). **Open** 6am-11pm daily. **Price** *Gym* Dhs50/day; Dhs530/mth. *Classes* Dhs35. **Credit** AmEx, MC, V. **Map** 296 H4.

Tucked away on the lower levels of the Jumeirah Emirates Towers, the Big Apple is a highly polished chrome and steel affair, the epitome of modern urban fitness centres. It lacks swimming, sauna or steam room facilities, but is armed to the teeth with state-of-the-art equipment, meaning you probably won't find yourself hanging around to use the treadmill or stepper. Aerobic classes cover everything from body pump to spinning, and in the winter there are a couple of outdoor sessions on offer. If you fancy a fitness overhaul, book yourself in for an assessment and personal training session or two. One session is enough to deliver your own training regime.

Club Olympus
Hyatt Regency Hotel, Deira Corniche (209 6802/ www.dubai.regency.hyatt.com). **Open** 6am-11pm daily. **Price** Dhs150/day. **Credit** AmEx, MC, V. **Map** p299 J1.

Friendly, professional staff attract a varied clientele to this city centre club. Classes range from aerobics to yoga; also provided are a gym and running track, which circles the two floodlit tennis courts. A pair of squash courts, an outdoor swimming pool, a sauna, a steam room, a jacuzzi and a splash pool complete the line-up of facilities; the outside deck is particularly popular in the cooler winter months.

Colosseum Muay Thai Health & Fitness Club
Montana Building, Zabeel Road (337 2755/ www.colosseumuae.com). **Open** 6am-midnight Sat-Thur; 9am-9pm Fri. **Price** Dhs40/session. **Credit** AmEx, MC, V. **Map** p299 J5.

Colosseum is a dedicated martial arts centre open to visitors as well as residents. The club has five boxing studios, an outdoor swimming pool, sauna and jacuzzi. There are regular karate, Thai boxing, aikido and kick boxing classes.

Fitness First
Ibn Battuta Mall (366 9933). **Open** 6am-11pm Sat-Thur; 7am-9pm Fri. **Price** Dhs100/day. **Credit** AmEx, MC, V. **Map** p304 A2.

The well-known health club chain Fitness First now has quite a few branches in Dubai. Members can choose from a host of classes, and can also take full advantage of the saunas and steam room.

Other locations Al Mussalla Tower, Bur Dubai (397 4117); BurJuman Centre (351 0044); Dubai Festival City (375 0177); Dubai International Financial City (363 7444); Satwa (398 9030); Uptown Mirdif (288 2311).

Griffin's Health Club

JW Marriott, Deira (607 7755/www.marriott. com). **Open** 6am-11pm daily. **Price** Dhs77 Sun-Thur; Dhs99 Fri, Sat. *Classes* Dhs30. **Credit** AmEx, MC, V. **Map** p297 K1.

There are two squash courts, an outdoor swimming pool, a spa and a jacuzzi as well as a gym with a separate cardio room at this reasonably priced health club. Classes include aerobics, spinning and step.

Health Club & Spa

Shangri-La Hotel Dubai (405 2441/www. shangri-la.com). **Open** 6am-midnight daily. **Price** Dhs180 Sun-Thur; Dhs220 Fri, Sat. *Classes* Dhs40. **Credit** AmEx, MC, V. **Map** p303 F12. Despite its upmarket location, this is a distinctly average hotel-based gym; however, the off-peak membership rates are reasonable. If you prefer classes to workouts, then go to the many hatha yoga, martial arts and salsa classes on offer.

Amara. *See p216.*

ARTS & ENTERTAINMENT

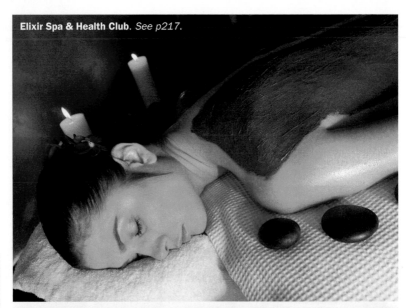

Elixir Spa & Health Club. *See p217.*

Lifestyle Health Club

Sofitel City Centre Hotel, Port Saeed (603 8825/www.accorhotels.com). **Open** 6.30am-11pm Sat-Thur; 8am-8pm Fri. **Price** *Gym* Dhs50/day. *Classes* Dhs30. **Credit** AmEx, MC, V. **Map** p297 K2.

This hotel-based club stretches over three floors: the reception, two squash courts, sauna and steam room are on one level; the gym and aerobics studio on the next; and an outdoor swimming pool and floodlit tennis court are on the roof. The gym is packed with resistance and cardiovascular machines; different aerobics classes are held each day in the studio.

Pharaohs Club

Wafi l, off Oud Metha Road (324 0000/www. waficity.com). **Open** 7am-10pm Sat-Thur; 9am-9pm Fri. **Price** Dhs1,200/mth; Dhs450/wk. *Classes* Dhs35. **Credit** AmEx, MC, V. **Map** p297 J3.

Still one of the most prestigious clubs in Dubai, Pharaohs provides members with luxurious surroundings and an impressive array of facilities. There are well-equipped gyms for men and women. Steam rooms, plunge pools and jacuzzis are also available, as well as a large swimming pool and separate pool in which, with a flick of a switch, you can attempt to swim against the tide. The club also boasts a climbing wall, three floodlit tennis courts, two squash courts and a comprehensive range of fitness classes.

Radisson Health Club

Radisson BLU Deira Dubai Creek (222 7171/ www.deiracreek.dubai.radissonBlu.com). **Open** 24hrs daily. **Price** Dhs55 Sun-Thur; Dhs85 Fri, Sat. **Credit** AmEx, MC, V. **Map** p299 J3.

What makes this gym stand out is that it is one of only two 24-hour gyms in town, so you have absolutely no excuse not to fit a session into your busy schedule. If, however, you like group exercise classes, this isn't the place as none is available. Facilities include an outdoor swimming pool, a tennis court, a squash court, a steam room and a sauna.

Shapes Wellness & Spa

Dubai Knowledge Village (367 2137/www. shapeshealthclub.com). **Open** 6am-9pm Sat-Thur. **Price** Dhs35/day. **Credit** MC, V. **Map** p304 C2.

A great gym for men and women who are trying hard to lose the lard. The owner, Sam, thinks treadmills are tedious, so instead there are lots of interesting classes available to help you achieve your weight loss goals, such as salsa and belly dancing. There's a separate women-only gym and a steam room to unwind in after class.

U Concept

Village Mall, Jumeirah (344 9060/www. uconcept6.com). **Open** 6am-9pm Sat-Thur. **Price** Dhs300/personal training session. **Credit** AmEx, MC, V. **Map** p300 D9.

An ultra-trendy, members-only gym, U Concept creates personal training and nutrition programmes with the busy professional in mind. If group exercise is your bag, give U Concept a wide berth, as group classes aren't part of its philosophy. Sports massage and therapy is also available, as well as private yoga and Pilates classes.

Willow Stream Spa & Health Club

Fairmont Dubai, Sheikh Zayed Road (311 8800/www.fairmont.com). **Open** 6am-midnight daily. **Price** Dhs200. **Credit** AmEx, MC, V. **Map** p301 G9.

This medium-sized gym offers one of the best views in town. There's nothing more awful than working out in a basement with no natural light, so here the windows have been fitted all the way round the gym, making it possible to watch the planes fly by outside. There are also plenty of TVs to keep you occupied and entertained during your workout. The day pass includes the use of a steam room and sauna, and there's a separate gym available for women.

SPAS

Holidays in Dubai revolve around five-star hotels, so it's no surprise that there's a spa culture here. Whether you've come to Dubai for some upmarket relaxation time or are travelling on a budget, you shouldn't miss out on a spa session. Not all spas are in hotels, and with the huge Indian population, some interesting Ayurvedic treatments are available. As well as the usual facials and massages, you can also find a plethora of alternative therapies.

Cleopatra's Spa. *See p217.*

ARTS & ENTERTAINMENT

Givenchy Spa. *See p218.*

1847

Boulevard at Jumeirah Emirates Towers, Sheikh Zayed Road (330 1847). **Open** 9am-10pm daily. **Price** Dhs220/hr massage. **Credit** AmEx, MC, V. **Map** p296 H4.

One for the gents, 1847 provides a range of high-end services, from shaves and facials, to manicures, pedicures and massages. *Photo p211.*

Other locations Grosvenor House, West Marina Beach Dubai (399 8989); Jumeirah Beach Residence (437 0252).

▶ *For more about what may be Dubai's best business hotel, see p106.*

Akaru Spa

Aviation Club, Garhoud (282 8578/www. akaruspa.com). **Open** 10am-10pm daily. **Price** Dhs265/hr massage. **Credit** AmEx, MC, V. **Map** p297 K3.

This pleasant, warmly decorated spa offers facials, massages and body wraps; but for pure, lulling, dream-like ambience, opt for one of their signature packages. We particularly like 'relax', which con-

sists of a body scrub, aromatic body massage and a facial. At Dhs475, it's an expensive offering, but as indulgences go, it's wonderful. *Photo p212.*

Alasalla Spa

Dubai Ladies Club (349 9922/www.dubai ladiesclub.com). **Open** 8am-10pm daily. **Price** Dhs280/hr massage. **Credit** AmEx, MC, V. **Map** p302 A15.

Treatments are Arabian-inspired and specifically for women. Choose one of their many hammam sessions; once you've tried one of those, you'll want to become a regular visitor.

Amara

Park Hyatt Dubai (602 1660/www.dubai.park. hyatt.com). **Open** 9am-10pm daily. **Price** Dhs420/hr massage. **Credit** AmEx, MC, V. **Map** p297 K3.

Amara is set in the Park Hyatt Dubai's Moroccan-style hotel, and is probably the trendiest spa in the city. If your environment matters to you as much as your treatment, book yourself in here and it's unlikely you'll be disappointed. Each of the treatment rooms comes with a private courtyard and outdoor rain shower. After your session, you'll be treated to herbal tea and dried fruits in the courtyard, and given some relaxation time. The spa exclusively stocks Anne Semonin's herbal products, and also uses local organic brand Shiffa and the exclusive Carita brand. Personal trainers can be booked for Dhs175 per hour. *Photo p213.*

Angsana Spa

Level 2, Marina Walk, Dubai Marina (368 4356/ www.angsanaspa.com). **Open** 10am-10pm daily. **Price** Dhs330/hr massage. **Credit** AmEx, MC, V. **Map** p304 B1.

Angsana's signature treatment is the Dhs500 Angsana massage, a two-hour pummelling with oils that mixes Asian and European techniques. Facials cost from Dhs320, and massages cost from Dhs350. **Other locations** Arabian Ranches (361 8251); Emirates Hills (368 3222); Montgomerie Golf Course (360 9322).

Assawan Spa & Health Club

Burj Al Arab Hotel, Beach Road, Jumeirah (301 7338/www.burj-al-arab.com/spa). **Open** 6.30am-10.30pm daily. **Price** Dhs600/hr massage. **Credit** AmEx, MC, V. **Map** p304 E1.

This lavishly decorated club is located on the 18th floor of Dubai's iconic landmark, enjoying spectacular views of the Gulf. There are separate men's and women's areas boasting a total of eight spa treatment rooms, a sauna, a steam bath, a plunge pool, a jacuzzi and a solarium. Espa and La Prairie facials are available, as well as wraps, massages and hot stone treatments. Don't expect all this to come cheap – a one hour basic massage will set you back Dhs600 – but if you're seeking a truly once-in-a-lifetime experience, this is the place. Non-guests can also book treatments here (minimum duration two hours), subject to availability.

Atlantis Spa

Atlantis, The Palm (426 1020). **Open** 10am-10pm daily. **Price** Dhs510/hr massage. **Credit** AmEx, MC, V. **Map** p294 A2.

Indulge yourself at one of the iconic hotel's 27 treatment rooms. If your feet need soothing after your workout, world-renowned foot specialist Bastien Gonzalez has a team of specialists at the spa ready to buff and polish your toes.

Cleopatra's Spa

Wafi, off Oud Metha Road, Bur Dubai (324 7700/www.waficity.com). **Open** 8am-8pm daily. **Price** Dhs325/hr massage. **Credit** AmEx, MC, V. **Map** p297 J3.

For the ultimate in spa treatments, you can't go far wrong with the luxurious Cleopatra's. As the name implies, the whole facility has an Egyptian theme; larger-than-life statues outside Wafi Pyramids give

way to a far more sophisticated and visually striking interior. The usual facials, massages and wraps complement some very different treatments. Among these is the gorgeous aroma stone massage, in which the body is massaged with hot, energy-filled 'batu' stones from Indonesia and exotic oils. Ayurvedic treatments are also provided, as is ionithermie, a detox and slimming treatment to tone muscles and smooth the skin. *Photo p215.*

Elche Natural Beauty Retreat

Villa 42, Street 10, behind Jumeirah Plaza (349 4942/www.elche.ae). **Open** 10am-8pm Sat-Thur. **Price** Dhs325/hr facial. **Credit** MC, V. **Map** p300 D9.

This idiosyncratic spa offers organic skincare treatments for women by trained Hungarian therapists, with facials starting at Dhs325. Herbalists hand-pick the ingredients, and the company's founder, Ilcsi Molnar, a beautician and herbalist, makes up the lotions and potions.

Elixir Spa & Health Club

Habtoor Grand Resort & Spa, Dubai Marina (399 5000/www.habtoorhotels.com). **Open** 9am-8.30pm daily. **Price** Dhs320/50min massage. **Credit** AmEx, MC, V. **Map** p304 B1.

The Habtoor's spa has five treatment rooms, a dry float room and tanning booth. The spa offers something for men and women, with massages starting from Dhs320 and facials from Dhs450. *Photo p214.*

Raffles Amrita. *See p218.*

Givenchy Spa

One&Only Royal Mirage, Al Sufouh Road, Jumeirah (399 9999/www.oneandonlyresorts. com). **Open** 9am-9pm daily. **Price** Dhs345/50min massage. **Credit** AmEx, MC, V. **Map** p304 C1.

The magnificent Health & Beauty Institute at the Royal Mirage Spa covers an area of 2,000sq m (21,500sq ft), divided into two levels. On the upper floor, the formal Givenchy Spa has separate areas and opening times for women; the rest of the time, it's mixed. It features 12 treatment rooms including an exclusive suite for private consultations, a resting area and a Givenchy boutique. The lower floor boasts an oriental hammam with a traditional heated marble massage table, two steam rooms and two private massage rooms. The institute marries contemporary decor with the hotel's Moroccan-fort theme; the result is arguably the most heavenly escape in Dubai. Two jacuzzis, a whirlpool and a plunge shower are also on hand. *Photo p216.*

Grand Spa

Grand Hyatt Dubai (317 1234/www.dubai. grand.hyatt.com). **Open** 9am-9pm daily. **Price** Dhs350/hr massage. **Credit** AmEx, MC, V. **Map** p297 K3.

This modern and tasteful candlelit spa stocks luxurious New York brands June Jacobs and Bella Lucce. Well-trained therapists perform skin-enhancing facials from Dhs350 and massages from Dhs300.

H2O Male Spa

Jumeirah Emirates Towers (319 8181/www. jumeirahemiratestowers.com). **Open** 9am-11pm daily. **Price** Dhs350/55min massage. **Credit** AmEx, MC, V. **Map** p296 H4.

H2O provides a range of therapies for men, including manicures, pedicures, tanning, waxing, facial therapy and massage. For something different, however, give the Flotation Pool (Dhs300) and Oxygen Lounge (Dhs75-Dhs300) a try. The first is a unique relaxation treatment involving an hour inside a salt water tank, floating in privacy while listening to soothing music – said to be as refreshing as eight hours of deep sleep. And in case you didn't feel refreshed enough after that, give the Oxygen Lounge a go. Muscles are eased on the active massage Cosmos chairs, while the user is treated to a dose of pure oxygen and 3D films.

Mandara Spa

Monarch Dubai, Trade Centre roundabout (501 8888/www.themonarchdubai.com). **Open** 9am-10pm daily. **Price** Dhs465/hr massage. **Credit** AmEx, MC, V. **Map** p301 G9.

One of the most Zen-like spas to hit Dubai, Mandara Spa is the perfect bolthole for the vexed and stressed. Try the signature Mandara Massage, Dhs950 for 95 minutes, which has two therapists working at the same time.

Raffles Amrita

Raffles Dubai (314 9869/www.dubai.raffles.com). **Open** 9am-9pm daily. **Price** Dhs399/hr massage. **Credit** AmEx, MC, V. **Map** p297 J3.

Try the 'Romantic Retreat' package: Dhs1,199 per couple buys 90 minutes of baths, massages and relaxation. *Photo p217.*

Ritz-Carlton Spa

Ritz-Carlton Dubai Hotel, Al Sufouh Road, Jumeirah (399 4000/www.ritzcarlton.com). **Open** 9am-10pm daily. **Price** Dhs450/50min massage. **Credit** AmEx, MC, V. **Map** p304 B1.

The heady Balinese theme at the Ritz-Carlton Spa is a well-executed concept, running throughout the decor and artwork and extending to the treatments, which include a Balinese Boreh massage and a

Spa InterContinental.

Talise.

Pumpkin and Cinnamon Body Glow. There are a total of ten treatment rooms and a salon dedicated to hair and beauty treatments, as well as a jacuzzi, sauna and steam room. European and Arabian-inspired treatments are also available, such as the Chocolate Indulgence.

Spa InterContinental

InterContinental Dubai Festival City (701 1257). **Open** 8am-10pm daily. **Price** Dhs400/hr massage. **Credit** AmEx, MC, V. **Map** p297 L3.
It's home to the only Natura Bisse treatments in the emirate (we recommend the Natura Bisse Diamond Facial, Dhs1,150) and treatment rooms have views over the Creek. Organic range Just Pure and the local brand Shiffa are also available.

Taj Spa

Taj Palace Hotel, Al Maktoum Street, Deira (211 3101/www.tajhotels.com). **Open** 7am-8pm daily. **Price** Dhs275/hr massage. **Credit** AmEx, MC, V. **Map** p299 L3.
Three different styles of massage are available at this atmospheric and relaxing spa. A one-hour basic Balinese, Ayurvedic or Swedish massage costs Dhs320. Friendly staff will happily recommend appropriate in-depth treatments according to the desired effect, and facials and various acts of delightful pampering are also available. As well as separate saunas and steam rooms, the spa also features a swimming pool and a jacuzzi.

Talise

Al Qasr, Madinat Jumeirah (366 6818/www. madinatjumeirah.com/spa). **Open** 9am-10pm daily. **Price** Dhs465/50min massage. **Credit** AmEx, MC, V. **Map** p304 E1.
Many different treatments are on offer to rejuvenate tired travellers, from massages with exotic oils to more scientific healing and wellness therapies. The Talise Pure Awakening is the signature treatment at this superior spa, and includes a massage, foot acupressure and eye therapy for Dhs475. Facials and massages start at Dhs465 for 50 minutes.

Willow Stream Spa

Fairmont Dubai, Sheikh Zayed Road (332 5555/www.fairmont.com). **Open** 6am-midnight daily. **Price** Dhs320/hr massage. **Credit** AmEx, MC, V. **Map** p301 G9.
High-quality treatments are available at the sublime Willow Stream Spa, which covers just under 4,000sq m (40,000 sq ft). As well as separate whirlpools, saunas and steam rooms for men and women, it also has two large outdoor swimming pools, positioned to catch the morning and afternoon sun respectively. There is a wading pool for children, and a lounge that is open to all. As for treatments, guests can enjoy a vast range of seductive options, including everything from the rose massage with mini facial to the sea salt body scrub, as well as facials, skin treatments and waxing.
► *The Fairmont Dubai is a fine hotel; see p106.*

Music & Clubs

Dubai's strict laws are tempered with signs of increasing diversity.

Long regarded as the 'party emirate', Dubai is home to countless nightclubs and bars of varying quality and salubriousness, and regularly attracts top DJs. Of late, the emirate's club scene has begun to diverge dramatically: where once house and R&B ruled the day, it's now not unusual to hear high-profile venues playing indie, electro, soul and even metal. Just be aware that Dubai's crowds come out to play late, so clubs may seem dead until midnight or even 1am, which leaves a couple of hours of partying before home time.

The live music scene is also growing: although the expensive and complicated licensing laws have traditionally restricted musicians to playing in house cover bands, local talent can be seen at dedicated amateur nights and also supporting the bigger international names that come to play in the city.

About the author

James Wilkinson *is the editor of the Music and Nightlife sections in the weekly* Time Out Dubai *magazine.*

BUR DUBAI

★ Chi

Al Nasr Leisureland, near the American Hospital/Lamcy Plaza, Oud Metha (337 9470/ www.lodgedubai.com). **Open** 8pm-3am daily (Chi Garden area closed summer). **Admission** varies. **Credit** AmEx, MC, V. **Map** p297 J3.

Pretty much the biggest club in Dubai, both in size and popularity, the 3,500-capacity Chi has become the default weekend jaunt for vast swathes of Dubai's population, thanks to its multi-room, multi-genre music policy. The three sub-rooms, including the swanky VIP area, usually play some form of R&B, indie and house, and the gargantuan Garden venue is given to a different act each week, from huge DJs like Tiësto to bands like the Charlatans and De La Soul. Keep your eyes peeled for celebrities too, particularly of the footballing variety.

Chill

Royal Ascot Hotel (355 8500). **Open** 3pm-3am daily (closed summer). **Admission** varies. **Credit** AmEx, MC, V. **Map** p298 H4.

Treading an uneasy path between classy and cheesy, this alfresco bar-cum-club hosts pool parties on weekend days and deep/Balearic house nights afterwards. The vibe is generally relaxed and friendly, and the series of fancy-dress parties early in Chill's life has attracted a mixed crowd of flamboyant types and businessmen. As well as the usual bevvies and food, punters can also get reflexology massages. However, Chill's decor remains its weak point: despite attempts at an upmarket vibe, it resembles an Ikea showroom – and we're really not sure about the Astroturf.

Elegante

Royal Ascot Hotel (355 8500). **Open** 10pm-3am Thur, Fri. **Admission** varies. **Credit** AmEx, MC, V. **Map** p298 H4.

Located just up the road from the notoriously grubby Waxy O'Conner's Irish pub, Elegante does its best to project an image of class in an area better known for its seedy clubs. Get past the velvet cords and no-nonsense doormen and you'll find yourself surrounded by a mixed crowd of dressed-up, arms-up clubbers, particularly on the popular R&B nights.

Submarine

Dhow Palace, Al Kuwait Street near Bur Juman (359 9992). **Open** 6pm-2.30am daily. **Admission** varies. **Credit** AmEx, MC, V. **Map** p301 G6.

Buried beneath the Dhow Palace Hotel, this dark 'n' dingy, nautically-themed club is a great venue in search of an identity. Go on any given night, and you could wind up listening to anything from minimal techno to reggae to death metal bands – all depending on which promoter is being courted by the manager at the time. Still, it does lend the place a certain charm, and the dark, cosy atmosphere is unlike any other club in Dubai. *Photo p223.*

FREE Wafi Rooftop
Pyramids, Wafi City, Oud Metha Road (324 7300/www.waficity.com). **Open** 8pm-midnight Fri & Sun (closed summer). **Admission** free. **Credit** AmEx, MC, V. **Map** p297 J3.
Wafi Rooftop is situated between two other venues (Seville's and Carter's, both perfectly fine drinking joints in their own right). Decorated with fake rocks and real grass, it plays host to two popular events throughout the winter. Fridays are taken up by Peanut Butter Jam, in which local bands play covers and original tracks to crowds lounging on bean-bags, and Sundays feature Movies Under the Stars, a double bill of mostly mainstream movies.

DEIRA

★ Alpha
Le Méridien Village (217 0000/www. platinumlistdubai.com). **Open** 7pm-3am Sun-Wed; 4pm-3am Fri, Sat. **Admission** varies. **Credit** MC, V. **Map** p297 L2.
Converted from an old Greek restaurant, this strange-looking club quickly became the go-to place for people looking for something a little different, thanks to its anything-goes Friday nights. It's not the biggest place in the city, but the cosy atmosphere and eclectic music selection – nights can include anything from drum 'n' bass to Motown to indie – have made it a favourite. The venue is also one of the only places in Dubai in which to see smaller, less-established non-UAE bands as well as local artists.

Festival Centre
Festival City (232 5444/www.dubaifestival city.com). **Open** times vary. **Admission** varies. **Credit** AmEx, MC, V. **Map** p297 L3.
Often regarded as a shopping mall with pretensions, Festival Centre nevertheless regularly plays host to

Wafi Rooftop.

the city's top imported talent by building stages onto the massive swathes of tarmac (affectionately referred to as the 'car parks'). Whether it's a solo show from the likes of Kylie Minogue and Maroon 5 or one of the annual festivals (*see p225* **Fest of Times**), the chances are high that Festival Centre will be involved. The Centre is also exploring smaller musical avenues, with local bands performing in the mall's rear dock area on occasion.

★ New Asia Bar & Club
Raffles Hotel, Wafi complex (04 314 9780). **Open** times vary. **Admission** varies. **Credit** MC, V. **Map** p297 J3.
After dabbling – as many bars do – with an unimaginative couples-only/dress-to-the-nines door policy, New Asia Bar & Club took a step back and became more inclusive. Which is good news for anyone who wants to dance in the shadow of a massive Indiana Jones-esque stone head in the top of a giant pyramid. Still a pricey joint, New Asia nevertheless does well at bringing in popular, big-name DJs, and is worth a visit for the spectacle alone. *Photo p224.*

Plan B
Wafi complex (04 324 0000). **Open** 7pm-2am Tue-Fri. **Admission** varies. **Credit** MC, V. **Map** p297 J3.
It's just a two-minute walk from New Asia, but Plan B couldn't be more different from its high-flying neighbour. The entertainingly goofy, multicoloured interior wouldn't look out of place on a kids' TV

> ### INSIDE TRACK
> ### TAKING LICENCE
>
> Any alcohol-serving venue wishing to host a band for the night must buy a music licence for each individual band member for each individual night (unless they are residents, in which case long-term licences can be purchased). This means that appearances by international live bands are few and far between, so expect such performances to be heavily in demand.

ARTS & ENTERTAINMENT

Possibly the best beach bar in the world.

BARASTI, DUBAI'S ORIGINAL BEACH BAR OPEN WEEK IN, WEEK OUT – "TIL LATE. JOIN US.

For more information call: Barasti at Le Meridien Mina Seyahi
04-399 3333, or visit www.minaeffect.com

barasti

Submarine. *See p220.*

series (if you took out the lairy, boozed-up Ted Baker-attired types) and a rotating series of (largely house music-based) nights have made it a popular and unpretentious place to party.

JUMEIRAH

★ FREE 360°

Jumeirah Beach Hotel (406 8744/www.jumeirah beachhotel.com). **Open** 4pm-2am Fri, Sat; 5pm-2am Sun-Thur (closed summer). **Admission** free. **Credit** AmEx, MC, V. **Map** p304 E1.

Situated at the end of its own pier, 360° provides panoramic views of Dubai's ever-expanding coast-line, including the adjacent Burj Al Arab. With sofas, shishas and sundowners every night, it's an immensely popular venue – particularly on the weekends, when international dance DJs are shipped in to entertain the crowds. Indeed, if you don't get down there early, you can expect a long queue – even if you're on the guest list (which can be accessed online via www.platinumlistdubai.com). It can get a bit shabby, however; just try to overlook the ciga-rette burns on the sofas.

Apartment

Jumeirah Beach Hotel (406 8000/www. jumeirahbeachhotel.com). **Open** 9pm-3am Tue, Thur, Fri. **Admission** varies. **Credit** AmEx, MC, V. **Map** p304 E1.

Located at the back of Jumeirah Beach Hotel, just a stone's throw from 360° (*see above*) and the Burj Al Arab, this two-roomed club has proved consistently popular with Dubai's clubbers, though its electro/R&B-themed nights are hardly treading new ground. Still, it's a fine place in which to party. The doormen can be a little strict, but have at least one girl in your group and you should be fine.

FREE Boudoir

Dubai Marine Beach Resort & Spa, Beach Road (345 5995/www.dxbmarine.com). **Open** 9pm-3am daily, couples only. **Admission** free. **Credit** AmEx, MC, V. **Map** p300 D9.

This swanky, wannabe Paris-style club prides itself on exclusivity, which should give you some idea of the attitude of the crowd inside – whether that's a good thing or not is down to you. The couples-only, dress-to-impress policy keeps the riff-raff out, while allowing the predominantly Lebanese audience to enjoy their R&B and commercial dance tunes. If you

---

INSIDE TRACK
WINTER SONGS

As the choking heat of summer lifts, Dubai's alfresco venues come alive – which means Wafi Pyramids (Pyramids, Wafi City, Oud Metha Road, 324 7300, www.waficity.com) rings to the sound of Peanut Butter Jam, the Friday night, live-band event featuring local talent playing covers and originals to a laid-back, beanbag-lounging crowd.

New Asia Bar & Club. *See p221*.

have money to burn and fancy a giggle, order a magnum of champagne and watch as the music cuts out while it's brought to you. Seriously.

First Group Theatre

Souk Madinat Jumeirah (366 6550/www. madinattheatre.com). **Open** times vary. **Admission** varies. **Credit** AmEx, MC, V. **Map** p304 D1.

Located in the labyrinthine Souk Madinat Jumeirah, the First Group Theatre – formerly Madinat Theatre – was, until the completion of the Palladium (*see p226*), the only place in Dubai for a little bit of culture. Sadly, culture and Dubai are essentially antithetical, so opera is limited to a couple of shows a year, and most of the content is adaptations or small-scale imports of Broadway and West End plays, such as *Annie* and *The Woman in Black*.

★ FREE JamBase

Souk Madinat Jumeirah (366 8888/www. madinatjumeirah.com). **Open** 7pm-12.30am Mon-Sat. **Admission** free. **Credit** AmEx, MC, V. **Map** p304 D1.

Once regarded as the best venue in the city for nightly live music, JamBase is now merely a very, very good live music bar with a varied covers band and a huge audience of diehard fans. Still, if you're up for a dance and don't mind aeons-long waits at the understaffed, overtaxed bars, then this should more than suffice.

★ Madinat Rooftop

Souk Madinat Jumeirah (366 8888). **Open** times vary (closed summer). **Admission** varies. **Credit** AmEx, MC, V. **Map** p304 D1.

Once upon a time, Trilogy was Dubai's undisputed king of the nightclub scene. Then, for reasons unknown (though much speculated upon), it was closed down. Now all that remains is the rooftop area (although rumours persist that Trilogy will open in full once more), but it's not such a great loss, since that was always the best part anyway. With spectacular views and a consistently good roster of left-field DJ talent (DJ Yoda and Gilles Peterson have played the venue), its Thursday night shows have become the place to be. *Photo p226.*

THE MARINA

DMC Amphitheatre

Dubai Media City, off Interchange 5, Sheikh Zayed Road (391 4555/www.dmc-communityguide.com). **Open** times vary. **Admission** varies. **Credit** MC, V. **Map** p304 B2.

An expansive outdoor area set in the middle of the city's media enclosure, the Amphitheatre comes

ARTS & ENTERTAINMENT

Fest of Times

The best of the region's music festivals.

Although it has nothing to compare with the likes of Glastonbury or Burning Man (for obvious reasons in the latter's case), Dubai hosts several music festivals a year, even though few manage to survive long enough to become regular fixtures. **Dubai International Jazz Festival** (www.dubai jazzfest.com), normally held in January or February, is a good example of one that has: though it's hardly Montreux, the festival is a huge crowd-puller. This is helped by decidedly un-jazzy headliners – James Blunt in 2009, for example – but these performers are usually accompanied by fairly credible international jazz acts.

For something a little harder, **Dubai Desert Rock Festival** (www.desertrock festival.com), normally in March, is a long-standing moshfest of extreme proportions, and the most important event on any respectable headbanger's calendar. Once a relatively inclusive event – past guests have included Muse and The Prodigy – it got an all-metal makeover in 2009 to capitalise on the Middle East's massive

metal fanbase, bringing in acts like Opeth, Arch Enemy and Motörhead.

At the opposite end of the scale is the **Chill Out Festival** (which also normally takes place in March), which usually gathers together a tasty selection of downtempo DJs, bands and solo musicians for a two-day unwindathon.

A little way out of town, November's **Coma** – which is pronounced 'comma' – (www.comafestival.com) is the UAE's first big dance music festival, and is held on Al Maya Island off Abu Dhabi. Starting in the morning and continuing for 24 hours non-stop, it's surely the most intensive festival on the books.

But for our money, the best bet by far is the Abu Dhabi edition of world music festival **Womad** (www.womadabudhabi. ae). This opened in May 2009 with acts including Robert Plant and Youssou N'Dour, and proved so popular (with around 80,000 people turning up) that the 2010 edition was announced on the second night. It's well worth the two-hour trip out of the city.

complete with real grass and its own lake. In recent years it has hosted a number of one-off international performances from the likes of Fergie from the Black Eyed Peas. However, its out-of-the-way location makes the more central Festival City a more popular option for touring bands.

Palladium

Dubai Media City, off Interchange 5, Sheikh Zayed Road (391 4994). **Open** times vary. **Admission** varies. **Credit** MC, V. **Map** p304 B2.
Opened in the spring of 2009, this $68 million venue is a one-stop culture shop with the capability to host full-scale operas, Broadway-level theatrical productions, live music acts, exhibitions and seminars. It certainly dwarfs its nearest competitor, the First Group Theatre (*see p225*), although it is a little more out of the way.

SHEIKH ZAYED ROAD

400 Club

Fairmont Dubai, Sheikh Zayed Road (332 5555/www.fairmont.com/dubai). **Open** times vary. **Admission** varies, couples only. **Credit** AmEx, MC, V. **Map** p301 G9/G10.
Cut from the same silken cloth as Boudoir, the 400 Club is built to hold exactly 400 occupants, many of whom, it often seems, have had appointments with plastic surgeons in the recent past. It's a playground for rich – or wannabe-rich – Lebanese couples, and

the music is typically an unadventurous mix of Arabic tunes and commercial house. Still, the actual venue is pretty and the dance floor usually vibrant.

Ductac

Mall of the Emirates (324 7300/www.ductac.org). **Open** times vary. **Admission** varies. **Credit** AmEx, MC, V. **Map** p304 D2.
Located in the Mall of the Emirates of all places, this cool, non-profit theatre plays host to all kinds of community-based events, from jazz quartets to art exhibitions to amateur stage productions of *High School Musical*. It's worth checking out the website to see what's on that week – the chances are that it will be something worth considering.
▶ *For more about the enormous Mall of the Emirates, see p159.*

Zinc

Crowne Plaza Dubai Hotel, Sheikh Zayed Road (331 1111/www.ichotelsgroup.com). **Open** 10pm-3am daily. **Admission** varies. **Credit** AmEx, MC, V. **Map** p301 G10.
A Sheikh Zayed Road venue that is popular with flight crews, Zinc has a large central bar and experienced resident DJs. The decor is metallic chic, but the general atmosphere is more down-to-earth than those in most other venues on the strip. Zinc's resident DJs, all unabashed crowdpleasers, supply a soundtrack of commercial house tunes and R&B. Unspectacular, but consistently entertaining.

Madinat Rooftop. *See p225.*

Sport

From extreme relaxation to extreme sport, this city has it all.

Whether it's cliffhanging from the Hajar mountains, putting a sail to the wind off Dubai Marina or reeling in a monster mahi-mahi on the East Coast, the UAE has it all, in characteristic abundance. But aside from the wacky sports and the legion of 4x4s that tear up its deserts every weekend, there's been a significant development of grassroots sports in recent years. So if you want to join a local football team, scream your lungs out for your national Sevens rugby squad or watch Goran Ivanisevic smash a tennis racket in the midday heat, Dubai has got it covered.

SPORTS VENUES

★ Aviation Club
Next to the Emirates Airline Training Centre, Garhoud (04 282 4122/www.aviationclub.ae). **Map** p296 K3.
The Aviation Club, by virtue of being the city's premier tennis venue, is a venue that is now firmly on sports fans' radar. It's hosted the Dubai Tennis Championships since its inception and also has excellent gym facilities, with courts for hire and several fitness classes running every day.

Dubai Sports City
Emirates Road, next to Dubai Autodrome (04 425 1111/www.dubaisportscity.ae).
Inaugurated with a successful series of Pakistan versus Australia cricket matches as part of the Chapal Cup in 2009, this huge development (loudly) boasts of its 60,000-seat outdoor stadium, 10,000-seat indoor stadium and 25,000-seat dedicated cricket stadium. Home to the International Cricket Council and the Manchester United Soccer School, Dubai Sports City is also the proposed site for many of the upcoming major sporting events. Keep an eye on the website, which has a calendar. *Photo p229.*

★ Insportz
Street 17a, Al Quoz (04 347 5888/ www.insportzclub.com). **Map** p294 C3.
A hub for sports in the depths of the industrial quarter, this is the place not only to see a myriad of minor

About the author
Chris Lord *is Sport & Outdoor listings editor in the weekly* Time Out Dubai *magazine.*

leagues meet and compete, but also to get in on it yourself. There are several small-scale cricket and five-a-side football leagues who meet regularly here.

The Sevens
Al Ain Road (04 321 0008/ www.dubairugby7s.com).
A 50,000-seat stadium, purpose-built for the sevens variant of rugby union, this venue is also home for local rugby clubs, including the Arabian Gulf Rugby Football Union team which competed in the Rugby World Cup Sevens in 2009. *Photo p231.*

PARTICIPATION SPORTS

Archery

Sharjah Golf & Shooting Club
Near Tasjeel Auto Village, Sharjah (06 548 7777/www.golfandshootingshj.com). **Open** noon-10pm daily. **Price** *Longbow* Dhs70 for 20 arrows. *Crossbow* Dhs90 for 10 bolts. **Credit** MC, V.
Shooting an arrow from a bow is a lot harder than it looks, and thus all the more rewarding when you eventually get it right. The club provides expert, safety-conscious tuition, and also caters to those with a penchant for crossbows.

Climbing

★ Pharaoh's Club
Wafi, near Creekside Park, Oud Metha (324 0000). **Open** 7am-11pm Sat-Thur; 9am-9pm Fri. **Price** Dhs55 for one hour with an instructor. Dhs45 for two hours free climbing. **Credit** AmEx, MC, V. **Map** p297 J3.

Experience the difference

Whether it's the excitement of learning to play camel polo, the thrill of desert off-road action or the challenge of Dubai's world class golf courses, Gulf Ventures will ensure your experience of Arabia is truly magical.

Dubai Sports City. *See p227*.

The UAE's first major climbing wall is 15m (50ft) tall, with a variety of climbing challenges set up to test everyone from the novice to the expert. It's also quite a friendly, sociable spot, and there's plenty of people coming and going to give you a leg-up.

Crab hunting

Lama Tours

(334 4330/www.lama.ae). Pick up from Dubai every day at 4.30pm. **Price** Dhs280 per person, minimum four people. **Credit** AmEx, MC, V.
Perhaps one of the most unique activities available in the UAE, crab hunting involves Lama Tours picking you up from anywhere in Dubai, ferrying you over to the Flamingo Beach Resort in Umm Al Quwain and setting you loose in the mangroves to spear as many crabs and squids as you can, under the moonlight. The resort will then cook your kill for you afterwards. It's a fun, albeit slightly raw, way to bag yourself some fresh-as-it-comes seafood.

Cycling

Dubai Roadsters

Wolfi's Bike Shop, between 2nd & 3rd Interchange on Sheikh Zayed Road (339 4453/www.wbs.ae). **Price** *Rides* free. *Bike hire* Dhs100 per day. **Credit** MC, V. **Map** p294 C3.
The Dubai Roadsters meet every Sunday and Tuesday evening at 7.30pm at Nad Al Sheba. There's also a two-hour meet for slightly more experienced riders every Friday at 5.30am (6am in winter) from the Lime Tree Café on Jumeirah Beach Road, for two to four hours cycling.

Desert trips

Although there are plenty of tour operators advertising to take visitors on organised trips into the sands, if you want to do more than just get jostled about in the back seat of a landrover, try a desert driving lesson. Or if you want to feel the sand flying in your face and can cling on to a wildly juddering steering wheel, have a bash at dune buggying. With only the odd bemused camel as spectator, you can roar through sand and scrubland at breakneck speeds, slalom round shrubs, and scream like a banshee all the while. Perfect for adrenaline junkies.

★ Desert Rangers

Dubai Garden Centre Building, Sheikh Zayed Road (340 2408/www.desertrangers.com). **Price** *Dune buggying* Dhs450 for 90 mins of dune buggying including pick up and drop off. *Dune bashing* Dhs295 per person. **Credit** AmEx, MC, V.
Tear up the desert. The price includes transport, drinks, headgear and insurance. *Photo p233*.

Fishing

It's early morning on the East Coast of the UAE. You've been waiting for a bite for half an hour, and have watched the mountains in the distance emerge from the fog. But just as your grip loosens slightly, there's a sudden tug on the line. You swing the rod high and the reel whirrs into life as a behemoth of a dorado,

glimmering yellow and bright green, leaps up and back into the water with a crash. You brace on the side of the boat as the rod bends double. He's well hooked, and it's going to take some fighting to bring him aboard. Sound like fishing as you imagined it? Forget measly catches and exhausted, overexploited waters, the big fish are out here.

Jebel Ali Golf Resort & Spa
Jebel Ali Resort (04 883 6000). **Price** Dhs1,750 for 4hrs. **Credit** AmEx, MC, V.
Although you set off from the rather unpromising and largely industrial environs of Jebel Ali, the departure point means that you can get out to deeper waters, and away from Dubai's encroaching development, more quickly. Experienced crew offer jigging, popping and a sociable journey. Maximum seven people per trip.

ME Charter
Various locations (050 653 8724/www. mecharter.com). **Price**s from Dhs500/hr. **Credit** AmEx, MC, V.
A British run company with a large range of boats from fishing to luxury yachts, and excellent offers to suit a variety of budgets.

Meridien Al Aqah
Dibba Road, Fujairah (09 244 9000). **Price** Dhs1,850/4hrs. **Credit** AmEx, MC, V.
Meridien provides trolling, spinning and fly fishing expeditions, all with instruction. There's a maximum of six people per trip.

★ Nautica 1992
Managed from the Habtoor Grand Beach Resort & Spa, Jumeirah (050 426 2415/www.nautica 1992.ae). **Price** Dhs3,500 for up to eight hours of deep sea fishing. Dhs2,500 for up to four hours trawling/bottom fishing. **No credit cards**.
One of Dubai's most established watersports companies, Nautica runs expertly manned fishing trips in search of kingfish, queenfish and trevally.

Golf

Bookings for tee times can be made through a central reservations office on 380 1234, or online at www.dubaigolf.com. The UAE Golf Association (380 1777, www.ugagolf.com) is the governing body for the sport in this country. Affiliate yearly membership costs Dhs200 and entitles players to reductions on green fees, lessons and merchandise at all UAE clubs.

Arabian Ranches Golf Club
Arabian Ranches, Emirates Road, off Interchange 4 by the Autodrome (366 3000/ www.arabianranchesgolfdubai.com). **Open** 24hrs for room reservations and golf. **Price** Dhs610 morning; Dhs 435 afternoon Sun-Wed. Dhs715 Thur-Sat. **Credit** AmEx, MC, V.
In association with Nicklaus Design, and formerly known as the Desert Course, this 18-hole par 72 grass course is the brainchild of Ian Baker-Finch. Part of a bigger residential complex, the course has a floodlit driving range, putting and chipping greens, and par three pitch-and-putt facilities.

The Sevens. *See p227.*

ARTS & ENTERTAINMENT

Desert Rangers. *See p229.*

Dubai Creek Golf & Yacht Club

Opposite Deira City Centre Mall, Garhoud (295 6000). **Open** *7am-2.40pm (last 18-hole tee-off) daily.* **Price** *18 holes Dhs695; 9 holes Dhs420 Sun-Wed. 18 holes Dhs795; 9 holes Dhs480 Thur-Sun.* Includes shared cart and bucket of range balls. **Credit** AmEx, MC, V. **Map** p297 K3.

The front nine of this luxury 18-hole, par 71 course was redesigned by local star Thomas Bjorn. The par five 18th crowns this stunning course in the centre of the city. Luxury villas line the avenue leading to the landmark Creekside clubhouse, a towering building constructed in the guise of a traditional sail. The meandering road also passes the 225-room Park Hyatt Dubai hotel.

Els Golf Club

Dubai Sports City, Emirates Road (425 1010). **Open** *7am-4.20pm daily. Driving range 7am-9.30pm daily.* **Price** *18 holes Dhs795.* **Credit** AmEx, MC, V.

The great Ernie Els designed this course to reflect the local landscape, attempting to create a 'desert links' in the process. Tee off from one of the four teeing areas that launch you on to the 7,538 yard course and see if he succeeded. *Photo p237.*

★ Emirates Golf Club

Sheikh Zayed Road, off Interchange 5 (380 2222/www.dubaigolf.com). **Open** *6am-3pm (last tee-off) daily.* **Price** *Faldo course Dhs795. Majlis course Dhs995.* **Credit** AmEx, MC, V. **Map** p304 B2.

Home to two fine courses and a Bedouin tent-inspired clubhouse, this is the most eye-catching golf venue in the region. The 7,101-yard Majlis course – the first grass facility in the Middle East – is home to the Dubai Desert Classic. The Majlis course is accompanied by the 7,127-yard Faldo course, redesigned by the golf star in 2005 from the original 'Wadi' course. The Majlis course is par 72, and the Faldo is par 73 courses and both make good use of the natural rolling desert terrain to ensure a serious test for players of all abilities. Many experts consider this to be the top club in Dubai. Non-members looking to play here should book 18-hole sessions at least three days in advance through the Central Reservation Line (380 1234).

Four Seasons Golf Club

Al Rebat Street, Al Badia (601 0101/www. fourseasons.com/dubaigolf). **Open** *6am-9.30pm daily.* **Price** *Dhs850.* **Credit** AmEx, MC, V. **Map** p297 L4.

Al Badia golf course is the focal point of this Dubai Festival City golf wonderland. Designed by Robert

INSIDE TRACK
KUSHTI LIFE

One of the most bizarre yet fascinating (and free) spectator sports takes place in a car park in Deira near Dubai Creek. Watch Pakistani expats get down in the sand in the traditional Kushti style of wrestling from 5.30pm every Friday. Head to Dubai Fish Market and follow the crowds around this time.

Fishing. *See p229.*

ARTS & ENTERTAINMENT

Trent Jones II, the 18-hole championship course has a desert oasis theme, and there is also a golf academy on site to help improve your game.

Montgomerie
Emirates Hills, Sheikh Zayed Road, off Interchange 5 (390 5600/www. themontgomerie.com). **Open** 6.30am-sunset (last tee-off); twilight game 2.30pm-nightfall. **Price** Dhs795 Thur-Sat; Dhs695 Sun-Wed. **Credit** AmEx, MC, V.

The Montgomerie, designed by Scottish Ryder Cup star Colin Montgomerie, covers more than 200 acres of undulating links-style fairways. With 14 lakes and 72 bunkers to avoid, drive placement is key here. Look out for the 13th hole and what is claimed to be the largest single green in the world, covering a staggering 5,394sq m (58,000sq ft). Less competitive golfers who simply want to practice will enjoy the Academy by Troon Golf, which boasts a state-of-the-art swing studio, a nine-hole, par three Academy course, short game area, putting greens and 'dummy' fairway – all floodlit.

Horse riding

Jebel Ali Horse Riding
Jebel Ali Golf Resort & Spa (883 6000). **Open** 7am-6pm daily. Closed July-Sept. **Price** Dhs150 for 1hr lessons for adults and over-5s. **Credit** AmEx, MC, V.

Learn to ride around the paddock here or, if you're a fully trained rider, head out to the desert around the hotel complex for a Dhs200 session.

Hot-air ballooning

Balloon Adventures Dubai
(285 4949/www.ballooning.ae). Early morning pickup from various locations around Dubai. **Price** Dhs950 per person, including refreshments. **Credit** MC, V.

Soar high over the Al Ain desert before taking a 'magic carpet' float low over the dunes, spotting running gazelle and camels on some unspoken, nomadic journey. The trip provides a peaceful perspective on the country. The minimum age is five.

Jetskiing

Kempinski Hotel Ajman

Ajman (06 714 5555/www.kempinski-ajman.com). **Open** *Beach* 6am-6pm daily; *watersports* until 10pm daily. **Price** Dhs150 for 20mins, additional beach entrance fee Dhs150 (Dhs200 on weekends and public holidays). **Credit** MC, V.

Although you can engage in most watersports off the coast of Dubai, jetskiing is the exception. To do that you have to make a short 30-minute drive to Ajman, where you can engage in all the action you could hope for. With a wide open, unblemished horizon, the sea really does feel your own.

Karting

Dubai Autodrome

Off Sheikh Zayed Road, at Interchange 4 (367 8700/www.dubaiautodrome.com). **Open** times vary. **Price** Dhs100 for a 15-minute session. **Credit** AmEx, MC, V.

This 5.4km (3.3-mile) circuit is sanctioned by the FIA (Federation Internationale de L'Automobile) and has six different configurations. It also has a race and driving school and a CIK-approved karting track. The Autodrome now also has an indoor, air-conditioned track available all year around and perfect for the summer heat. Children from seven to 12 can use the special karts provided.

XXL Expats

Where to work off the excesses of the Dubai lifestyle.

It's no secret that a lack of pavement, a continual searing sun and a penchant for *shawarmas* can leave Dubai's expats a little on the rotund side after a few months. Fear not, there are ways to beat the dreaded Dubai spread.

Run with...
Dubai Road Runners (340 3777), who meet every Saturday at Safa Park in Al Wasl. It costs Dhs5 to take part and they're a sociable bunch. Free for students.

Cycle with...
Dubai Roadsters (339 4453/050 644 3524). Based at Wolfi's Bike Shop (between Interchange 2 & 3 on Sheikh Zayed Road, www.wbs.ae), the Dubai Roadsters host very popular cycle rides, twice a week, up to the Nad Al Sheba area. There's also a two-hour meet every Friday at 5.30am from the Lime Tree Café on Jumeirah Beach Road. Contact Wolfi beforehand if it's your first time.

Swim with...
Hamilton Aquatics (050 250 5216). Hamilton hosts over 70 classes per week with eight different teaching levels for all ages. Venues at Wellington International, Gems World Academy in Al Barsha and Jumeirah College. Around Dhs50 a session.

Walk with...
Keenfit (050 559 7137/www.keenfit-me.com) as they wander the malls armed with poles. Yes it's odd, yes it's oh so Dubai, but it's also quite a natty, social way to burn off brunches. Twenty-minute

training with poles offered to newcomers. All walks are lead by a skilled instructor. Call or see website for details.

Train with...
Dubai Amateur Football League (050 396 5135/www.dxb.leaguerepublic.com). There are three competitive divisions in the men's league. Women should take a look at Dubai Women's Football Association (050 702 7841/www.dubaiwfa.com/www.dubaiwfa.com).

Bounce with...
Basketball Academy of Dubai (050 457 1706/www.badubai.com). There are open pick-up sessions indoors every Tuesday evening from 8pm at Dubai International Academy, costing Dhs20. A great place to get on a team.

Suffer with...
other heaving expats as they get put through army-style paces on a boot camp. Fitness 02 (050 955 6129/www.fitness02.com) advertises 'renegade' bootcamps and military sports cross-training for all fitness levels. Call for prices and the schedule.

Serve with....
Clark Francis Tennis (282 4540/050 624 0162/www.esportsdubai.com). The club has qualified teachers available for instructing groups and provides private lessons throughout the city, including at the Aviation Club and the Grand Hyatt hotel. See the website for details of its successful tennis league.

Bags packed, milk cancelled, house raised on stilts.

You've packed the suntan lotion, the snorkel set, the stay-pressed shirts. Just one more thing left to do – your bit for climate change. In some of the world's poorest countries, changing weather patterns are destroying lives.

You can help people to deal with the extreme effects of climate change. Raising houses in flood-prone regions is just one life-saving solution.

Climate change costs lives.
Give £5 and let's sort it *Here & Now*

www.oxfam.org.uk/climate-change

Be Humankind Oxfam

Kitesurfing

North Kites
*Al Bahar showroom, Jumeirah Beach Road
(394 1258).* **Price** Dhs250 per lesson, including
equipment. **Credit** AmEx, MC, V.
North Kites sells the boards and kites you need to
start the sport, provides lessons, and can also give
you details of other instructors.

Paintballing

Sharjah Paintball
*Sharjah Golf & Shooting Club (050 203 2288/
www.paintballuae.com).* **Open** 10am-midnight
daily. **Price** Dhs75 (weekdays) or Dhs 80
(weekends) for 2hrs. **Credit** MC, V.
Sharjah Paintball is open to groups of six to 20 people and, despite being a little way out of the centre
of Dubai, it is a first-rate paintball experience, with
several fields and options for plenty of scenarios.

Parasailing

Nautica 1992
*Based at the Habtoor Grand, Dubai Marina
(050 426 2415/www.nautica1992.ae).* **Open**
10am-5pm daily. **Price** Dhs250 15min solo
flight; Dhs400 tandem (with weight limit).
Credit AmEx, MC, V.
Nautica is one of Dubai's best known and longest
established watersports companies. It operates out
of the Habtoor Grand hotel complex.

Sailing

Bluesail
*Jebel Ali Golf Resort & Spa, Joumana Club
(888 0234/www.bluesailyachts.com).* **Open**
9am-5.30pm daily. **Rates** Dhs4,000-Dhs6,000/
half day charter; Dhs6,000-Dhs9,000/8hr charter.
No credit cards.
The highest-qualified RYA sailing school in the
Middle East offers power and sail training for all levels, from novice through to RYA Yachtmaster.
There are 42ft sail yachts available for charter and
corporate events, with charter prices including a
qualified skipper. Powerboat Level 1 and 2 training
is also available.

★ Dubai Offshore Sailing Club
*Jumeirah Beach Road, by Miraj Gallery, KFC &
Hardees (394 1669/www.dosc.ae).* **Open** 9am-
4pm daily. **Rates** *Group lessons* Dhs200/2hrs.
Admission Dhs10 (week); Dhs25 (weekend).
Credit AmEx, MC, V.
This club is typically abuzz with eager sailors.
Recognised by the Royal Yachting Association, the
DOSC provides courses all year round in optimists,
lasers and toppers (the Friday and Saturday Cadet
Club is popular with younger enthusiasts). There are
races every Friday, mooring facilities are provided
and the club runs a full social calendar. Note that
non-members must be invited by member.

Scuba diving

The massive constructions off the shore of
Dubai might have marred visibility, but the
country's East Coast (from Dibba to Fujairah)
still has some beautiful waters. Most of these
companies will take divers out to the east,
where you can train for a PADI. A number of
companies also offer snorkelling excursions.

Al Boom Diving
*Near Iranian Hospital, Al Wasl Road (342 2993/
www.alboomdiving.com).* **Open** 8am-10pm daily.
Credit MC, V.
Al Boom is a PADI-certified diving centre provid-
ing courses from beginner to instructor, as well as
daily diving trips to Fujairah and Musandam. The
PADI Discover Scuba course is Dhs550 and its Open
Water course costs Dhs2,350 including transport
and DAN insurance.

Emirates Diving Association
*Heritage & Diving Village, Al Shindaga (393
9390/www.emiratesdiving.com).* **Open** 8am-3pm
daily. **No credit cards**.

Els Golf Club. *See p233.*

Ski Dubai.

If you are already a trained diver, join EDA for Dhs100 a year to receive newsletters and information about diving in the UAE, as well as trips abroad.

Nomad Ocean Adventures
Dibba Harbour, Mussandam (050 885 3238/ www.discovernomad.com). **Open** by appointment daily. **No credit cards.**
A PADI resort and EDA dive centre with full diving facilities for trips and courses of all levels. Prices start from Dhs600 for full diving package including dinner, breakfast and accommodation. It's a 90-minute drive from Dubai; call for detailed instructions on how to get there.

Pavilion Dive Centre
Jumeirah Beach Hotel, Umm Suqeim (406 8827/ www.jumeirah.com). **Open** 9am-6pm daily. **Credit** MC, V. **Map** p304 E1.
The Pavilion, an accredited PADI dive centre, can have you exploring a real shipwreck in no time. The PADI Discover Scuba Boat Dive costs Dhs450, and the Open Water Diver course costs Dhs2,050.

Skiing and snowboarding

Ski Dubai
Mall of the Emirates (409 4000/www. skidxb.com). **Open** 10am-midnight daily.
Price Dhs180/2hrs; Dhs 150/2hrs children.
Lessons Dhs150-Dhs220. **Credit** AmEx, MC, V.
Map p304 D2.

Who wouldn't want to come to the desert and go skiing? One of Dubai's craziest ideas has become one of its biggest hits. Since it opened, Ski Dubai has developed into a firm favourite among tourists and expatriates, especially during the steamy summer months. For one incredibly low price you can hire all the necessary equipment (sans gloves and hats) and slide down the desert's biggest anomaly.

Surfing

Surf Dubai
Lessons held at Burj Al Arab open beach, Jumeirah (433 1783/www.surfingdubai.com).
Price Dhs200 for ABC Surfing session; Dhs475 for private lesson. **No credit cards. Map** p304 E1.
The surf might not rank with the best in the world, but Dubai does have a dedicated and passionate group of surfers who are equally eager to pass their knowledge on. Surfing season out here is November to April, beginners boards are provided by instructors and their website has predicted surf times.

Trekking

★ Absolute Adventure
(345 9900/www.adventure.ae). **Price** varies between treks. **Credit** MC, V.
Scramble up mountains, walk the wadis and wander through some of the most dramatic and atmospheric landscapes in the region. The treks that this Dibba-based company provide tend towards the East Coast and to the Musandam, an exclave of Oman at the tip of the peninsula. We recommend the coastal Aqaba to Lima trek, with dolphin spotting and spectacular views from the heights.

Wakeboarding & waterskiing

In case you're wondering, wakeboarding is a cross between snowboarding, waterskiing and surfing. It's currently one of Dubai's in vogue sports. But waterskiing remains very popular in the warm water off the coast.

Dubai Water Sport Academy
Dubai Marina, Marina Walk (050 303 9700).
Open 6am-7pm daily. **Price** Dhs150 for 15mins. **Credit** AmEx, MC, V. **Map** p304 B1.
The Academy has qualified instructors for monoski, barefoot, wake and kneeboarding.

Wakeboard School
Al Jazeera Hotel & Resort, Al Ghantoot (050 768 9504/www.thewakeboardschool.com).
Price Dhs100/20 mins. **Credit** AmEx, MC, V.
Set in an ideal saltwater channel on the UAE's largest private beach, the Wakeboard School is run by local champion Tom Ellis, and is just 20 minutes drive from Jebel Ali.

ARTS & ENTERTAINMENT

Escapes & Excursions

Musandam. *See p264.*

Abu Dhabi

A · B · C

1

ARABIAN

GULF

Ras Laffan

Khor Laffan

Port Zayed

Free Port Zone

Dhow Harbour

Carpet Souk

Iranian Souk

The Club

Jazirat Bu Ash Shu'um

AL MEENA

Le Meridien Abu Dhabi
4 9 1

Abu Dhabi Mall

Al Diar Capital Hotel

Cemetery

Sheraton Abu Dhabi Hotel & Resort

Cemetery

Mosque Gardens

Le Royal Meridien

Beach Rotana Hotel & Towers
1 3 6 7

SAADIYAT BRIDGE

QASR EL BAHR

Lulu Island

Millennium Hotel Abu Dhabi

Volcano Fountain

7 10 4 6

Al Ain Palace Hotel

Capital Gardens

Madinat Zayed Shopping Centre

Gold Souk

AS SALAM ST

SEA PALAI ROAD

EASTERN RIN

Al Noor Hospital

Crowne Plaza Hotel

MADINAT ZAYED

Police Station

Clock Tower

ITTIHAB SQUARE

AL HOSN

Fotouh Al Khair Centre

Cemetery

AL DHAFRAH

Cultural Foundation

Old Fort & Al Hosn Palace

Grand Mosque

Bus & Taxi Station

HAZAA BIN ZAYED ST

AL WAHDAH

NEW AIRPORT ROAD

i

AL MANHAL

Al Muhairy Centre

Central Hospital

SHEIKH RASHID BIN SAEED AL MAKTOUM

Al Mahnal Palace

AL TABBIYAH

AL KARAMAH

MUSSALA EL EID

National Theatre

Flagpole

Breakwater

AL KHALIBIYAH

Khalidiya Garden

AL ROWDAH

Khalifa Gardens

Municipality

KHALIDIYAH STREET

KHALIFA BIN ABDEL AZIZ ST

AN NAHYAN ST

Mushrif Palace

Marina Mall

Municipal Market

Khalidiya Children's Garden

Ministry of State

ZAYED THE FIRST STREET

KING KHALID BIN ABDEL AZIZ ST

Hilton Abu Dhabi
3 2 9

Ras Al Bateen

Emirates Palace
2 4 8

AL KHUBEIRAH

Police Station

Cemetery

AL BATEEN

Bateen Palace

SAEED BIN TAHNOON

AL KHALEEJ AL ARABI STREET

7

Al Dana Ladies' Beach

AR RAS AL AKHDAR

BAINUNAH STREET

SULTAN BIN ZAYED STREET

InterContinental Abu Dhabi

Abu Dhabi Golf & Equestrian Club

Khor Al Bateen

5

A · B · C

Hideriyyat

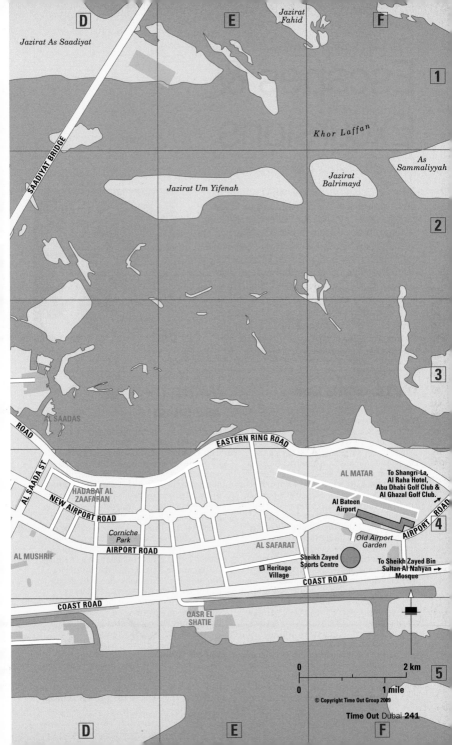

Escapes & Excursions

Explore the UAE's other attractions.

Although it was the British who brought the seven emirates of Abu Dhabi, Ajman, Dubai, Fujairah, Ras Al Khaimah, Sharjah and Umm Al Quwain together as the Trucial States, it was the late Sheikh Zayed Al Nahyan – the much-mourned former leader of Abu Dhabi, whose death in 2004 brought dignitaries here from all over the world – who cemented the place of the United Arab Emirates in the world. The country was formed in 1971 and, buoyed by the collective strength of this union and the foresight and fortunes of Abu Dhabi in particular, each emirate has since grown in status.

THE LIE OF THE LAND

The UAE is situated on the eastern spur of the Arabian peninsula. To the north-west is Qatar; Saudi Arabia is to the west and south, and Oman to the south-east and north-east (for map, *see p290*). It goes without saying that Dubai leads the way in accommodating and entertaining tourists, but away from the glitz lies the wider UAE's tapestry of sun-drenched beaches, cool mountain escapes and bustling cities rich with cultural experiences. Just short of two hours drive south from Dubai is the capital of the UAE, **Abu Dhabi** (*see below*) and, closer still, to the north, there are unexpected pockets of quiet reflection amid the chaos of **Sharjah** (*see p259*). Adventure abounds further north in the wild reaches of **Ras Al Khaimah** (*see p260*) and superb snorkelling and diving is on offer at **Fujairah** (*see p258*) and along the East Coast.

Be warned, however, that public transport remains primitive. Buses are as cramped as they are economical, and rarely will you see a tourist aboard one. Nonetheless, the government's determination to build smooth, efficient highways is paying off. Our advice, if you're heading out of Dubai, is take the wheel of a 4x4 on short-term hire and explore the UAE's delights at your own pace.

Within the UAE

ABU DHABI

Spurred on by a heady dose of sibling rivalry, the nation's capital is plotting to become the Gulf's cultural hub. Less than 50 years ago, the entire emirate of Abu Dhabi was a near-empty desert populated by Bedouin tribes and small villages. Its initial elevation to economic prominence was the result of pearl cultivation until global recession, coupled with a thriving pearl industry in Japan, put paid to that and relegated Abu Dhabi to the position of poorest emirate. But the discovery of huge offshore oil reserves in 1958, and the subsequent rule of Sheikh Zayed, totally transformed its fortunes. As recently as 30 years ago, the capital city was still short of a reliable electricity supply and roads. Now its expanse of highways are heavy with traffic, and the whole city is embarking on a process of development that (along with neighbouring Dubai) is almost unprecedented in modern times.

BLACK GOLD

Having noted that the island stood as a natural stronghold – and also offered fine fishing – the Bani Yas Bedouin tribe settled in Abu Dhabi in the 1760s. They dubbed the region Abu Dhabi

Wild About Dhabi

Meet the UAE's original inhabitants.

Despite Abu Dhabi's rocket ride into the 21st century, there are still plenty of reminders of its wilder past. First is a close encounter of the natural kind with Don Revis' **Kayak Abu Dhabi** (050 542 0820, www.kayakabudhabi.com). Don runs eco tours of one of the city's most precious and declining natural resources: its mangroves. Along the way, there are excellent opportunities for some bird-spotting as well as opportunities to learn something about the intricacies of this extraordinary ecosystem.

Another day out with conservation in mind is a visit to the **Abu Dhabi Falcon Centre** (02 575 5155). To all intents and purposes, it's a working veterinary clinic; it takes in 4,500 falcons a year from clients across the Gulf. As such, tours must be booked in advance (Sat-Thur), but once there, you will learn a lot more about this symbol of the UAE than you ever thought possible. From showing how a broken wing is mended to holding one of the birds, Dr Magit Muller is an amiable guide and this is a trip not to miss.

Another establishment to recently open its doors to the public is the **Abu Dhabi Wildlife Centre** (www.abudhabiwildlife centre.com). Run by the indomitable Ronel Smuts and her family, it was originally a centre for stray and rehabilitated animals from across the UAE (its cheetahs were rescued from the back seat of a car in Dubai), but evolved into a fabulous wildlife and breeding facility. It's an amazing opportunity to get up close and personal with everything from lions and crocodiles to caracals, monkeys and tortoises. What better opportunity to get to meet some of the planet's rarest and most beautiful creatures?

Emirates Palace. *See p247.*

('Father of the Gazelle') and would thereafter lead a largely unchanged existence for nearly 200 years. Legend has it that the city owes its unorthodox name to gazelle tracks found by a wandering party of Bedouin hunters. The nomads followed the tracks into a shallow inlet of the sea, only to discover that they emerged again on the shore of the facing island, and ended at a spring of fresh water. They quickly returned to their base in the Liwa oasis and reported the discovery to their leader, Sheikh Dhiyab bin Isa, who decreed that the island should thereafter be known as Abu Dhabi in honour of their guides.

The discovery of a freshwater well encouraged the ruling Al Nahyan family to relocate from its home in Liwa to Abu Dhabi, securing the city's first steps on its rise to prominence. The good times continued through the 1800s, as residents grew prosperous from the seemingly endless supply of pearls that were found off Abu Dhabi's lengthy coastline. Then came the aforementioned worldwide pearl recession and Abu Dhabi's subsequent decline, which forced potentate Sheikh Shakhbut bin Sultan to investigate other potential sources of revenue. Somewhat fortuitously, he granted drilling rights to the British – who had been present in the region since 1892 in the role of overseers of a protectorate – and the search for oil began.

In 1958, huge offshore oil reserves were found. Abu Dhabi became the first of the Gulf States to export oil in 1962, earning an estimated US$70 million per year throughout the 1960s. Today, roughly two million barrels of oil are exported from the United Arab Emirates every 24 hours. Current estimates suggest this will continue for the foreseeable future.

The British left the Gulf region in 1971, and the seven factional emirates united to form the UAE, declaring Abu Dhabi the provisional capital. Sheikh Zayed Al Nahyan was welcomed as the new state's first president, and duly returned to power every five years before his death, when his son, Sheikh Khalifa bin Zayed bin Sultan Al Nahyan, assumed control. In 1996, the word 'provisional' was dropped from Abu Dhabi's title, making it the official capital city.

THE TOURISM CARD

When the government declared it wanted to turn Abu Dhabi into a tourist destination, some people scoffed. After all, why go to Abu Dhabi when the ultimate tourist city is just down the road? Yet more than US$100 billion of developments are being built over the next three years, including a reported 50 top-end hotels and a new airport that will process up to 20 million passengers a year.

Top Gear

Formula 1 comes to the UAE.

The roar of F1 engines is something the capital can expect to get used to over the coming seven years. Abu Dhabi is at the forefront of a sporting calendar set to turn the capital into a major attraction, and having pipped their Dubai rivals to hosting the UAE's first **Grand Prix**, the city duly set about turning its Yas Island into the sort of racing showpiece that would show its upstart neighbour who was really the boss.

Costing an estimated $40 billion and set to be completed before the first race is run on 1 November 2009, the track is a calling card for the city, quite literally in fact. For the glistening 50,000-seat stadium will be one of the first things that visitors see as they land at Abu Dhabi airport. But the plan is to bring people in not only for the Grand Prix, but all year round. Yas Marina Hotel is the only hotel with not just a harbour large enough to accomodate the super yachts of visiting billionaires but a Grand Prix circuit running through its very heart. The circuit itself can be split into two separate tracks and will provide facilities for kart and drag racing, as well as allowing mere mortals to test their motoring skills at the new Ferrari Theme Park.

It's a grand plan, and just part of an ongoing bid to turn the emirate into a sporting haven. The **Abu Dhabi Golf Championship** (Jan) is now well established at its home at the National Course, but two new Championship courses on Saadiyat Island, including Gary Player's Ocean Course, are set to test the competition's loyalties. Elsewhere, the **Capitala World Tennis Championship** (Jan) will bring the game's top players to Zayed Sports City in the New Year, while the **Red Bull Air Race** (Apr) remains a popular attraction in the skies above the Corniche beach. But surely one of the biggest new sporting attractions is the upcoming **World Club Cup Football Championship**, which Abu Dhabi is hosting in December 2010 and 2011. A chance to see the world's top clubs compete for a genuine trophy on UAE soil is an unmissable opportunity and a sure sign that there is more to come in the future.

Religion Calling

'What does Islam mean?' and other questions.

'Do the different colours of the scarves mean anything?' a rather thin, nasal Australian voice enquires. The guide gives a genial smile and removes his headscarf to better demonstrate his answer. Emboldened by this, another voice pipes up: its owner is male and, although dressed in traditional Arabic dress, he betrays a gruff, American accent. 'How many times a day do you have to pray?' it enquires. Again the guide smiles and gestures towards a honeycomb-shaped clock on the wall depicting five separate times arranged around two dates (the Gregorian and Islamic calendars).

In the minutes that follow, he goes on to describe what happens during prayer time, why women pray in separate areas and how a Muslim man can marry more than one wife. All the while, eager hands shoot up from an audience sat cross-legged on the world's largest carpet underneath the

world's biggest chandelier. Welcome to the **Sheikh Zayed Mosque**.

Guided tours of the mosque began back in early 2008. Teams of wandering visitors from all over the world are taken daily (except at weekends) around the grounds, shown the prayer halls, the wash areas and introduced to some of the finer aspects of Islam. It is a humbling experience and one well worth the time. But perhaps the best part of the mosque tour is that it ends in a giant question and answer session, with visitors' hands shooting up to ask various questions about Islam, Arabic culture and the history of the UAE. It's not just a day trip and a chance to see the world's third biggest mosque up close, but a better opportunity to understand the Arabic world.

Sheikh Zayed Mosque is on Airport Road. For enquiries call 800 555. Entrance and tours are free, with tours taking place from Sunday to Thursday at 10am.

And if the emirate's ambitious schemes work out, there's no reason that the new airport shouldn't be tested. Plans have been unveiled for entire communities to be created on Al Reem Island, Lulu Island and Al Raha Beach, as well as reconstruction work and new facilities all over the city's main island. Five-star hotels, golf courses, restaurants, spas and parks are going to be appearing all over the emirate.

The most intriguing project is Saadiyat Island, and in a noisy statement of intent, the four main buildings in the island's cultural sector have been designed by four of the world's leading architects: Frank Gehry has designed the world's largest Guggenheim gallery, Japanese designer Tadao Ando has created a Zen-concrete Maritime Museum, and Frenchman Jean Nouvel's Classical Museum, and Zaha Hadid's Performing Arts Centre are two entirely contrasting yet incredibly inventive buildings in their own right.

At its heart though, Abu Dhabi remains a traditional Middle Eastern city, which means it's advisable to watch your behaviour even when just passing through. Overt drunkenness and lasciviousness should be confined to private places, and revealing outfits are best avoided, especially during Ramadan. Gone are the days when such offences would result in jail time, but too much skin on show will still attract slack-mouthed stares from pretty much everyone you meet.

Sightseeing

Residents will tell you that Abu Dhabi is the cultural heart of the UAE, and the **Cultural Foundation** takes pride of place. In recent years, it has hosted art exhibitions and local and international performing artists such as the Royal Philharmonic Orchestra. However, from May 2009 it moved its cultural and arts programme to the National Theatre in Al Manhal.

To realise just how far the city has come in such a short space of time, visit the **Heritage Village**, a faithful representation of a small nomadic camp. Follow this with a visit to **Emirates Palace** (*photo p244*) which, like Dubai's Burj Al Arab, is often referred to as a seven-star hotel as it offers a lot more than the average five star. As well as being a popular music venue for the likes of Coldplay, George Michael and Andrea Bocelli, Emirates Palace has become a worthy host for temporary art exhibitions. The Picasso exhibition in 2008 drew 50,000 visitors to the hotel, and elsewhere in the city a number of independent galleries such as the Ghaf Gallery, Salwa Zeidan Gallery and the Al Qibab Gallery have transformed Abu Dhabi's art scene.

Arabia is famous worldwide for its thoroughbred horses, and the Emirati people follow horse racing with a passion. The breeding of winning horses is a serious business, and the Golf & Equestrian Club (02 445 5500, www.adec-web.com; map p240 C4) holds races every Sunday from November to April. In a surprisingly efficient use of space, there is a par-72 golf course located within the racetrack, which closes two hours before the racing begins. Non-member green fees for 18 holes are Dhs230 (Saturday to Wednesday) or Dhs240 (Thursday and Friday). More fun, but less prestigious, is a round at Al Ghazal Golf Club (02 575 8040, www.alghazalgolf.ae), an 18-hole sand course chiselled into land alongside the airport. The city's golf pedigree was raised by the National course at the Abu Dhabi Golf Club (02 558 8990, www.adgolfclub.com), which has played host to the Abu Dhabi Golf Championship since it began, and it will be raised further still when Gary Player's signature ocean course opens on Saadiyat Island in late 2009.

The city is also home to a pleasant network of parks. In the centre is **Capital Gardens** (map p240 B3), an assortment of manicured lawns gathered around a central pond which is known to erupt into aquatic action whenever the mood takes it. Refreshments come courtesy of vending machines and a small cafeteria. The picnic tables are popular on warm winter evenings, and it's always well lit and clean. **Khalidiya Garden** (map p240 B4) is noisy, but great for children and full of colourful inflatables, although for a quiet stretch, the **Old Airport Garden** (map p241 F4), next to the ice-skating rink, has swings for the children, is beautifully ornamental and manages to remain tranquil even with the little ones haring around. Trainspotter types might even fancy a gander at one of the largest flagpoles in the world (map p240 A4), which stands at the end of Abu Dhabi's breakwater.

Cultural Foundation

Opposite Etisalat building, Airport Road (02 619 5223). **Open** 8am-2pm, 5-9.30pm Sat-Thur; 5-8pm Fri. **Admission** varies. **Map** p254 B3.

This vast centre for the arts is proof of a very real desire to stimulate artistry in a land where so much energy is put into making cold hard cash. As you might expect from a building with such a noble purpose, there's a hushed atmosphere throughout the network of corridors and arched courtyards. The summer months excluded, the Foundation fills its lecture halls with residents drawn by international acts – primarily musicians, but speakers and actors too. The Foundation publishes a wealth of Islamic texts and is home to the National Archives.

Lulu Island.

FREE Heritage Village

Breakwater, across from Marina Mall (02 681 4455). **Open** 9am-1pm, 5-9pm Sat, Mon-Thur; 5-9pm Fri. **Admission** free. **Map** p240 A4.
Get a whiff of what life was like for Abu Dhabi's Bedouin by viewing a reconstruction of their traditional desert encampment, including a goat's hair tent and a campfire with coffee pots. There are also plenty of old-fashioned craft shops to enjoy, but we love it for the fresh, traditional doughnuts, which are cooked on the spot.

Beaches & islands

Some of the city's five-star hotels have their own stretch of sand, varying in size, which non-guests can use for a charge of somewhere between Dhs80 and Dhs100 for a day pass. Sadly, the best bit of beach in the city is attached to the Emirates Palace and is strictly for hotel residents only.

As an alternative, Abu Dhabi has several public beaches, and there are scenic (albeit rugged) stretches around the peninsula (up past the InterContinental Abu Dhabi), but without facilities like changing rooms and shops. For a little more privacy, women can avoid the male of the species altogether at Al Dana Ladies' Beach. But by far the most popular and convenient remains the corniche beach, a vast, man-made stretch of sand skirting Abu Dhabi's seafront. A small fee of Dhs15 is payable upon entering, although the beach is divided into family and bachelor areas.

There is no need for the more adventurous tourist to stop at the shore, however. Abu Dhabi is unique among the emirates in its wealth of islands. Over 200 of them, varying in size and level of habitation, lie just off the coast. Small wonder that hopping from island to island is one of the emirate's more popular pastimes. If you don't own a boat, you can hire one – with captain – from a hotel beach club or one of the marinas. This is the safer option in any case, as the water is dangerously shallow in places, and would-be captains must be able to navigate the treacherous dredged channels.

The large island opposite the corniche is **Lulu Island** (map p240 A4), a man-made landmass that's famous for having been built with no real purpose in mind. Now it appears that it will be filled with housing, and is due to be linked to Abu Dhabi by a number of bridges and tunnels; but if you can make your way out there, the beach is still currently open to the public, daily, until 8pm.

Motor about three miles (five kilometres) south of Abu Dhabi and you'll come to **Futaisi Island**, an inhabited isle some 15 miles (40 kilometres) square, that is privately owned by Sheikh Hamad bin Hamdan Al Nahyan. Home to old quarries from which stone for Abu Dhabi's forts was once dug, the island is now a tourist retreat and nature reserve. Boats run to and from their office (02 666 6601) in Al Bateen Marina at 10am and 5pm. Once there, you can rent a chalet and ride horses. Some 240 kilometres west of Abu Dhabi, near Jebel Dhanna, is **Sir Bani Yas Island**, a hotel and nature reserve where various conservation programmes are run (*see p249* **This is the Wildlife**).

This is the Wildlife

Have an adventure in the wild without sacrificing life's luxuries.

AL MAHA DESERT RESORT & SPA

If you think Dubai has sold its soul to overdevelopment, **Al Maha Desert Resort & Spa** will be a pleasant surprise. The resort sits in the middle of the desert around 45 minutes from Dubai – an oasis of Bedouin-style luxury bungalows overlooking an infinite sea of undulating dunes and *ghaf* trees. The property is nestled smack bang in the middle of the **Dubai Desert Conservation Reserve** (www.ddcr.org), which became an official member of the International Union for Conservation of Nature thanks to the successful reintroduction of the Arabian oryx, a spiky-horned beast that was extinct in the wild until a few years ago.

To date, there are around 200 oryx roaming the resort, along with gazelles and a variety of other native creatures like the rare sand cat (though they are near impossible to spot), the Arabian red fox, gerbils and even Ethiopian hedgehogs. Most of the 225 square kilometres (87 square miles) of protected desert is off limits to the public unless accompanied by a few select Dubai-based tour operators, which makes staying at Al Maha all the more exclusive.

Although the eye-watering prices may be out of reach to most, it will be worth every dirham when you witness wildlife meandering around the dunes from the comfort of your own private infinity pool. Oryx and skipping gazelles graze so close you can practically hear them chewing. Each of the 42 suites comes equipped with every luxurious whim under the sun – from a decanter of fine sherry to an art easel and oversized bathtubs. There's ample opportunity to explore the rest of the desert reserve – game park style – with 4x4 drives, wildlife walks, desert camel treks and falconry displays.

Al Maha Desert Resort & Spa

www.al-maha.com/04 3034222.
Getting there Al Maha Desort Resort & Spa is in the Dubai Desert Conservation Reserve on the Dubai-Al Ain highway (E66). When coming from Dubai, the turn-off (careful, it's easily missed) is after exit 50 to Murquab. From Abu Dhabi, take Emirates Road and follow it to exit 44. Follow the signs to the Al Ain highway (E66).

SIR BANI YAS ISLAND

It may have the swanky five-star **Anantara Desert Islands Resort & Spa**, but the real attraction of this island off the coast of Abu Dhabi is the unbelievable amount of wildlife it is home to.

Sir Bani Yas Island has been transformed into a veritable Galapagos of the Middle East, with so many animals frolicking freely, it's as though Noah's Ark was shipwrecked nearby. The island was originally the private retreat and royal nature reserve of Sheikh Zayed bin Sultan Al Nahyan, the former ruler of Abu Dhabi and president of the UAE, and today it has been redeveloped into one of the UAE's most pristine wildlife reserves.

Guests staying at the 64-room Anantara resort have exclusive access to all 87 square kilometres (34 square miles) of the island, which is home to rare creatures like a herd of around 400 free-roaming oryx (the largest herd in the world), gazelles and a truly wondrous array of exotic species that include giraffe, flamingoes, hyenas and cheetahs. There are even plans to remove the fences dividing the species, so predators can perform their normal function of weeding out the weaker specimens among the herds of herbivores and thus create a natural ecosystem.

The island has become a haven to marine and avian life, in large part due to the more than 2.5 million plants and trees that have been planted by the developers who have worked on the island.

Guests can explore the thriving mangroves in a guided kayak tour, take in the natural habitat of marine species like flying fish, or go snorkelling in the surrounding sea (there are plans to open a dive centre), home to turtles and dugongs.

Desert Islands Resort & Spa

Sir Bani Yas Island (02 801 5400/ www.desertislands.anantara.com).
Getting there Jebel Dhanna is about 210 kilometres (130 miles) to the west of Abu Dhabi, along the continuation of Sheikh Zayed Road. Boats to Sir Bani Yas run from the Jebel Dhanna pier, but officially are only open to guests of the Desert Islands Resort and staff of the island. The Desert Islands Resort runs seaplane flights from Abu Dhabi airport.

Sardinia.

There are many other small, uninhabited islands of green dotted around out to sea, but still within easy reach of the city. Popular outcrops include **Bahraini**, **Cut** and **Horseshoe**, but all are good for a day's exploring and secluded sun-soaking. You'll often find a cluster of windsurfers taking brief respite on **Surf Reef**, gathering themselves amid the swirling offshore breezes. However, rubbish is a major problem on many of the islands as there is no service yet to have it removed, so make sure to always remove what you take with you.

Al Dana Ladies' Beach

Near the Hilton Abu Dhabi, Corniche Road (02 665 0129). **Open** noon-6pm Sat-Wed; 10am-6pm Thur, Fri. **Admission** Dhs10. *Parking* Dhs5. **No credit cards**. **Map** p240 A5.
Al Dana beach is a totally man-free environment, and has a cafeteria and swimming pool. It is typically open until dusk (around 6pm).

Corniche Beach

Corniche. **Admission** Dhs15. **No credit cards**. **Map** p240 A4.
Opened in 2008, this man-made two-kilometre stretch of golden sand on the east coast has become a major attraction for the city. Skirted by the corniche walkway, a popular spot of joggers and walker, the beach is divided into bachelor and family areas, and has a number of cafés to provide some much-needed refreshment.

Restaurants & cafés

Abu Dhabi is currently on an upward spiral in terms of dining opportunities. Although the superior (and licensed) restaurants are almost all within five-star hotels, there are familiar fast-food outlets and some charming independent restaurants down many of the side streets.

Al Fanar

Le Royal Méridien Abu Dhabi, Khalifa Bin Zayed Street (02 674 2020). **Open** 12.30-3pm, 7-11pm daily. **Main courses** Dhs40-Dhs60. **Credit** AmEx, MC, V. **Map** p240 B3 ❶
Say what you like about revolving restaurants, but the views from up here are excellent. The food is also first-rate, and Al Fanar's popular Friday brunch affords diners the opportunity to drink an unlimited amount of champagne, thus ensuring that the room really does spin.

Bice

Hilton Abu Dhabi, Corniche Road (02 681 1900). **Open** noon-3pm, 7-11pm daily. **Main courses** Dhs40-Dhs60. **Credit** AmEx, MC, V. **Map** p240 A4 ❷

There's a fine line between paying too much for simple Italian food and seeing wonderfully simple Italian food ruined by fussiness. It's a line that's walked pretty well at Bice. Polished oak floors, beautifully crafted chairs and a splendid in-house pianist define a setting that is rich in atmosphere; the food is of the highest quality and the menu has some great vegetarian options. Bice also has one of the best wine cellars in the city.

Bord Eau

Shangri-La Hotel, Qaryat Al Beri (02 509 8888). **Open** 7pm-midnight daily. **Main courses** Dhs100-Dhs150. **Credit** AmEx, MC, V.

The French do two things extremely well – art and food – and both have made like Napoleon and invaded foreign shores. Bord Eau presents a gallery of fine food, with all but two dishes on the menu flown in from France. The menu changes every three months on a seasonal basis, and can appear confusing at first, with starters and mains separated into four categories, including signature and Escoffier. To sum up: it's as good as you'd get in France.

Finz

Beach Rotana Hotel & Towers, next to Abu Dhabi Mall, north end of Ninth Street (02 644 3000). **Open** 12.30-3.30pm, 7-11.30pm daily. **Main courses** Dhs60-Dhs80. **Credit** AmEx, MC, V. **Map** p240 C2 ❸

If you have a hankering for seafood, there are few places better in the entire country than this excellent restaurant. From a comfy vantage point in the spacious and beautifully designed dining room you can peer into the large open kitchen and see the staff preparing your meal, and in the other direction you are able to enjoy sea views.

Mezzaluna

Emirates Palace, Corniche Road (02 690 8888). **Open** 12.30-3.30pm, 6.30-11.30pm. **Main courses** Dhs150-Dhs200. **Credit** AmEx, MC, V. **Map** p240 A4 ❹

Most of the restaurants at the Emirates Palace are underwhelming, but this Italian is excellent. From the complimentary appetisers to the sabayon dessert prepared at your table amid flames, the meals here are usually difficult to fault. If you're determined to eat at the Emirates Palace, this is your best bet.

One Café

Khalidiya, next to the BMW showroom (02 681 6500). **Open** 9am-10pm Sat-Thur; 2-10pm Fri. **Main courses** Dhs60-Dhs80. **Credit** AmEx, MC, V. **Map** p240 B4 ❺

Entering the One Café (located on the first floor of the popular home accessories store) is the equivalent of walking into a UAE episode of *Friends*: everyone looks relaxed and happy to be there, enjoying the food and good conversation. An excellent spot for some lunchtime refuelling.

Rodeo Grill

Beach Rotana Hotel & Towers, next to Abu Dhabi Mall, north end of Ninth Street (02 644 3000). **Open** 12.30-3.30pm, 7-11.30pm daily. **Main courses** Dhs60-Dhs80. **Credit** AmEx, MC, V. **Map** p240 C4 ❻

With its dark wooden furniture and grand green leather chairs, you could easily mistake Rodeo Grill for an elegant English gentlemen's club, rather than Abu Dhabi's best steakhouse. The cuts are the finest you'll find in town, the wine list is impressive and the chocolate soufflé is a mountain of cocoa-fuelled decadence. Recommended.

Sardinia

Abu Dhabi Health & Fitness Club (02 446 5455). **Open** noon-3pm, 7-11pm daily. **Main courses** Dhs150-Dhs200. **Credit** AmEx, MC, V. **Map** p240 C4 ❼

Although the location may not be that promising (it's tucked away round the back of a fitness club), Sardinia comes as a genuine and delightful surprise. Its food earned it the 'Best Restaurant' prize at the Abu Dhabi Eating Out Awards.

Sayad

Emirates Palace, Corniche Road (02 690 8888). **Open** 12.30-3pm, 6.30-11.30pm daily. **Main courses** Dhs150-Dhs200. **Credit** AmEx, MC, V. **Map** p240 A4 ❽

There was a point when Sayad was becoming the Middle East's equivalent of the Ivy, as celebrities such as Will Smith and Jamie Foxx dined here in town. Accordingly, the prices are A-list, but despite the grand setting it's not horribly overblown and the seafood is excellent. From the rich foie gras to the delicate Canadian lobster salad with mango and watermelon, the menu is classy throughout and when the bill arrives, it's on a big wave of white chocolate dotted with truffles – a gesture almost as grand as the price.

Talay

Le Méridien Abu Dhabi, north end of Sheikh Zayed Second Street (02 644 7800). **Open** 12.30-3.30pm, 7-11.30pm daily. **Main courses** Dhs50-Dhs60. **Credit** AmEx, MC, V. **Map** p240 C2 ❾

Talay is the pick of the restaurants located in Le Méridien's picturesque Culinary Village, and its traditional take on Thai food is best enjoyed at one of its beachside tables – even though you'll have to arrive early to be sure of securing one. Try the signature tom yam seafood soup, with its squid, shrimp and serious chunks of oyster mushroom deftly seasoned with coconut milk and lemongrass.

Pubs & bars

By 2015, it seems likely that Abu Dhabi will be a great after-dark city, but for the time being you'll have to get on the road to Dubai for a place to party. Many of the city's bars are currently little more than depressing dives, but as more hotels open over the coming years, nightlife options will increase rapidly. That said, there are a still a few places worth visiting if you're looking for somewhere to go out in the capital.

Captain's Arms
Le Méridien Abu Dhabi, north end of Sheikh Zayed Second Street (02 644 7800). **Open** noon-1am daily. **Admission** free. **Credit** AmEx, MC, V. **Map** p240 C2 ❶
The Captain's Arms generally meets with the approval of expats, although this may have less to do with the nautical theme and more to do with the cheap pints available during happy hours – hours that stretch well beyond 60 minutes. During the cooler months, its pretty, albeit diminutive, terrace is the busiest place in town.

Heroes
Crowne Plaza Abu Dhabi, Hamdan Street (02 621 0000). **Open** noon-2am Sat-Wed; noon-3am Thur, Fri. **Admission** free. **Credit** AmEx, MC, V. **Map** p240 B3 ❷
An expat favourite, this American-style diner/sports bar is busy most nights and is a fair bet if you're after drinks and huge portions of comfort food – the giant spare ribs are the biggest served to man since the bronto-ribs that tipped over Fred's car in the opening credits of *The Flintstones*. Regular drink deals and a monthly comedy club, the Laughter Factory, ensure Heroes usually has a convivial atmosphere with barstools occupied by people happy to talk the night away. A DJ plays all the oldies on Thursday nights and the band does passable renditions of Nirvana, Aerosmith, the Beatles and the Red Hot Chili Peppers.

Jazz Bar
Hilton Abu Dhabi, Corniche Road (02 681 1900). **Open** 7pm-1.45am Sun-Fri. **Admission** free. **Credit** AmEx, MC, V. **Map** p240 A4 ❸
Home to one of the better bands in town, the Jazz Bar is understandably popular with the city's more sophisticated drinkers. The candlelit tables cannot be pre-booked, and often fill up early, and it's rare that the place doesn't get busy later in the evening. It's not cheap by any means, but if you're after a classier place for a drink than the average pub and want live music, then the Jazz Bar hits the spot.

Oceans
Le Royal Méridien Abu Dhabi, Khalifa Bin Zayed Street (02 674 2020). **Open** noon-3pm, 7-11pm daily. **Admission** free. **Credit** AmEx, MC, V. **Map** p240 B3 ❹
Technically, it's a restaurant, but they put on the odd good night here in the small bar area, and monthly Ministry of Sound nights. There's a wood-decked

Sax Restaurant Club.

outdoor terrace and, if the right DJ is playing, it attracts a decent crowd. It's also next door to Sax (*see below*), so you can flit between the two.

Rock Bottom Café
Al Diar Capital Hotel, Meena Street (02 678 7700). **Open** noon-2.30am daily. **Admission** free. **Credit** AmEx, MC, V. **Map** p240 B2 ❺
A quick perusal of this bar's clientele and you'll be in little doubt as to why it's so named: the live entertainment oscillates between an ear-splittingly loud band and a DJ playing run-of-the-mill tracks to a dancefloor full of unsuspecting tourists, touchy-feely ladies and denim-clad bikers. It's the kind of place that springs to mind at 1am when you're trying to think of somewhere that serves alcohol and is open.

Sax Restaurant Club
Le Royal Méridien Abu Dhabi, Khalifa Bin Zayed Street (02 674 2020). **Open** 9pm-2am Sat-Thur; 9pm-3am Fri. **Admission** free. **Credit** AmEx, MC, V. **Map** p240 B3 ❻
Low-lit and relatively snug, Sax is a good bet if you're after a meal with live entertainment. After 10pm, it's usually packed with the well-dressed set.

Trader Vic's
Beach Rotana Hotel & Towers, next to Abu Dhabi Mall, north end of Ninth Street (02 644 3000). **Open** 12.30-3.30pm, 5pm-12.30am daily. **Admission** free. **Credit** AmEx, MC, V. **Map** p240 C2 ❼

The food is more miss than hit, but the cocktails at this Polynesian-themed grog house are out of this world. The Tiki Puka Puka, for example, is a notoriously potent rum-based headspinner. A grass skirt-wearing band plays most nights and keeps the crowds happy. Thursday nights are packed.

Shopping

You won't want to be traipsing around the streets of the city if it's hot, and there's little you'll be missing anyway; many of the shops sell little more than cheap junk and badly counterfeited goods. For serious shopping you're better off heading to the two modern malls: **Abu Dhabi Mall** and the **Marina Mall**. These similarly sized, American-style shopping centres have quick and easy food courts, cinemas, and wares ranging from domestic goods to designer labels.

But by far the most interesting (and hectic) shopping experience in the capital is at the **Iranian souk** in Port Zayed and the **carpet souk** off Mina Road (map p240 B2). The Iranian souk sells goods fresh off the boats that arrive from Iran every three or four days. On sale are all manner of carpets, ornaments, terracotta trinkets and the like. It is also one of the finest spots in the city to procure some quality horticulture, not to mention venus flytraps the size of your fist. Haggling is regarded as a kind of sport in these parts, so you should indulge in a round or two as much to pass the time as to procure bargains.

Traditionally, the souks are the prime source of traditional knick-knacks as well as the predictable range of Celvin Kline shirts and Hogo Boos aftershave. The same cannot be said of the recently opened **Qaryat Al Beri Souk**, however. More along the lines of Dubai's Madinat Jumeriah, it contains a smattering of carpet, jewellery and clothes shops alongside a branch of the Abela deli and the excellent chocolaterie Choco-La. But most people come here for the food, and a steady supply of good bars and restaurants, including the likes of Left Bank, Ushna, Sho Cho and the Meat Company, provides more than just a place to rest weary feet and recharge your batteries.

Abu Dhabi Mall

North end of Ninth Street (02 645 4858/www.abudhabi-mall.com). **Open** 10am-10pm Sat-Wed; 10am-11pm Thur; 3.30-11pm Fri. **Map** p240 C2.
Connected to the Beach Rotana Hotel & Towers, this large shopping centre keeps on attracting bigger and better brand names to complement what is an already solid range of outlets. It has mainstream names including Tommy Hilfiger and Guess, as well as gems like Pull and Bear and Kenneth Cole, a cinema and a noisy food court.

Marina Mall

The Breakwater (02 681 2310). **Open** 10am-10pm Sat-Wed; 10am-11pm Thur, Fri. **Map** p240 A4.
Thanks to a recent expansion, the Marina Mall has vastly improved in quality, with an increasing number of designer brands having outlets here. The prices are the same as those in other major cities around the world.

Where to stay: beach resorts

Al Raha Beach Hotel

Al Raha Beach, Shahama city (02 508 0555/www.ncth.com). **Rates** Dhs1,000-Dhs1,600 double. **Credit** AmEx, MC, V.
Set apart from the cluster of hotels in the city centre by a 15-minute drive, the Al Raha Beach Hotel is a five-star property that is unique in Abu Dhabi for the fact that it has a number of two-, three- and four-bedroom beach villas. These can be rented for a short holiday or a longer stay, and are wonderfully decorated. There's also a lovely infinity pool with views of the Gulf, as well as the UAE's largest nightclub, Enigma, which isn't particularly good.

Beach Rotana Hotel & Towers

Next to Abu Dhabi Mall, north end of Ninth Street (02 644 3000/www.rotana.com). **Rates** Dhs950-Dhs1,260 double (excl 16% tax). **Credit** AmEx, MC, V. **Map** p240 C2 ❶
Probably the most family-oriented of the top hotels in the city, the Beach Rotana is connected to Abu Dhabi Mall, meaning shopaholics don't have far to walk. It's wonderfully elegant inside, with a welcoming lobby and rooms that are spacious and stylish. The premium rooms have luxury bathrooms with jacuzzis and rain showers. The beach is small, but there's a children's pool as well as an adult one and

---

INSIDE TRACK
TAXIS

There are a number of taxi companies in Abu Dhabi, but there are two fundamentally different kinds of cab: silver taxis, and yellow and gold ones. The new silver cabs are strictly monitored, and run on a set meter rate in line with Dubai. The older (and often more run-down) yellow cabs are far cheaper. On the meter, you can travel the length of the city for less than Dhs15, but drivers aren't monitored, and often turn their meters off and quote extortionate fees, particularly at peak hours or when they see the whites of a tourist's eyes. By all means barter, but you generally shouldn't pay more than Dhs20-Dhs25 to travel anywhere on the island.

ESCAPES & EXCURSIONS

the obligatory swim-up bar. A first-rate gym is on site for visitors who want to keep up their fitness regime while away from home.

Emirates Palace
Corniche Road (02 690 9000/www.emirates palace.com). **Rates** Dhs1,450-Dhs1,870 double (excl 16% tax). **Credit** AmEx, MC, V. **Map** p240 A4 ❷
If you've ever wondered what sort of hotel you could build for US$3billion, the Emirates Palace is the answer. Despite the hyperbole, it does feel like an actual palace, and has regularly accommodated royalty. Rooms have plasma screens as standard, and the top-of-the-range accommodation comes with a room for your bodyguard and a private butler to take care of your every need. The beach and pool areas are outstanding, but room service can be slow and not all the in-house restaurants are worth the price. Still, even if you can't afford to stay here, it's worth a visit for afternoon tea.

Hilton Abu Dhabi
Corniche Road (02 681 1900/www.hilton.com). **Rates** Dhs650-Dhs2,600 double (excl 16% tax). **Credit** AmEx, MC, V. **Map** p240 A4 ❸
Set in a fine location overlooking the Gulf, the majority of the Hilton's rooms have been renovated over the last couple of years. Guests enjoy unlimited access to the beach club, which sports a private stretch of sand and pleasant spa. The hotel is also home to some of the better food and drink outlets in Abu Dhabi.

Le Méridien Abu Dhabi
Tourist Club area, Sheikh Zayed Second Street (02 644 6666/www.lemeridien.com). **Rates** Dhs1,200-Dhs2,800 double (excl 16% tax). **Credit** AmEx, MC, V. **Map** p240 C2 ❹
This pleasant hotel is situated by the beach and centred around the tranquil Méridien Village, a stretch of greenery with a variety of excellent alfresco food and drink outlets. There's an on-site spa centre that provides traditional Turkish hammam treatments, but the nightclub, Gauloises, can be a depressingly sleazy experience.

Sheraton Abu Dhabi Hotel & Resort
Corniche Road (02 677 3333/www.starwood. com/sheraton). **Rates** Dhs700-Dhs1,300 double (excl 16% tax). **Credit** AmEx, MC, V. **Map** p240 B2 ❺
Although best as a business hotel, the Sheraton does have a pleasant outdoor area set among palm trees, with pools for children and adults, a private lagoon and a small beach. The rooms are modern in decor and are fully equipped, but they tend to be on the small side. Nevertheless, it's a functional five-star with some good bars and restaurants on site, including a popular Italian restaurant and sophisticated but quiet cocktail bar.

Where to stay: city hotels

Crowne Plaza Abu Dhabi
Hamdan Street (Fifth Street) (02 621 0000/ www.crowneplaza.com). **Rates** Dhs650-Dhs1,150 double. **Credit** AmEx, MC, V. **Map** p240 B3 ❻
Centrally located, the Crowne Plaza is in a prime position for people who want to take full advantage of Abu Dhabi's shopping activities, although it's a little dated by today's standards. The Roman-style rooftop pool is a major plus for visitors, and the popular basement bar Heroes provides entertainment for the evenings.

Le Royal Méridien Abu Dhabi
Khalifa Bin Zayed Street (02 674 2020/ www.lemeridien.com). **Rates** from Dhs900 double (excl 16% tax). **Credit** AmEx, MC, V. **Map** p240 B3 ❼
Arguably the top business hotel in the city, this plush, 31-storey building resembles an ordinary city skyscraper in all respects bar the revolving Al Fanar restaurant that slowly slides around the roof of the building. Suites in the Royal Tower are excellent, and the rest of the hotel's rooms are more than adequate. The Méridien also has an impressive number of restaurants and bars on site, although the Illusions nightclub is best avoided.

Millennium Hotel Abu Dhabi
Khalifa Bin Zayed Street (02 626 2700/ www.millenniumhotels.com). **Rates** Dhs750-Dhs1,150 double (excl 16% tax). **Credit** AmEx, MC, V. **Map** p240 B3 ❽
The Millennium is a central hotel with large rooms overlooking both the capital gardens and the corniche, providing great views whichever side of the building you are in. The decor is a nice mix of dark woods and marble, and competent staff conduct their business with unobtrusive efficiency. The hotel is popular with business travellers as well as B-list stars. It has a boutique feel, and a modern gym and pool to while away a day in before you hit the town. Then again, you could stay put and enjoy a leisurely meal at the hotel.

Resources

Hospital
Al Noor *Khalifa Bin Zayed Street (02 626 5265).* **Map** p240 B3.

Internet
Street Net Café *Abu Dhabi Mall, north end of Ninth Street (02 645 4141).* **Open** 10am-11.30pm daily. **Price** Dhs15/hr. **No credit cards.** **Map** p240 C2.

Police station
Police HQ *Sheikh Zayed First Street (02 446 1461).* **Map** p240 A4.

Jahili Fort. *See p256.*

Post office
Central post office *East Road (02 621 1611).* **Open** 8am-8pm Sat-Wed; 8am-6pm Thur. **Map** p240 B2.

Tourist information
Ministry of Information & Culture *near police station, Airport Road (02 444 0444).* **Open** 7.30am-2pm Sat-Wed. **Map** p240 C3.
There are plans to move the tourist office to the city centre; contact the Ministry for up-to-date details.

Getting there

By bus
The buses and minibuses that leave from Bur Dubai bus station cost about Dhs20. Despite the set timetable drivers usually wait for the bus to fill up before they set off. Buses and minibuses will drop you off at the bus station in the centre of Abu Dhabi, from where cheap local taxis are available.

By car
From Dubai, Abu Dhabi is a straight drive of 150km (95 miles) down the Sheikh Zayed Road. The road turns into Airport Road as you enter Abu Dhabi, and the city (where the roads are on a grid system) is fairly easy to navigate.

By taxi
The journey from Dubai to Abu Dhabi will cost you Dhs220 to Dhs250 if you flag a taxi down in the street, but make sure the seatbelts are working, as the journey down Sheikh Zayed Road to the capital is not always the best advert for road safety. You're probably better off with Al Ghazal Express – an Abu Dhabi-based taxi operator – who will come to collect you in Dubai and take you to the capital for a flat fee of Dhs150 (the return journey, oddly, is Dhs225). It's a cheaper set fee and the cars are far superior, in terms of both comfort and safety, than standard Abu Dhabi cabs. Bookings can be made by calling 02 444 5885 directly, which is cheaper than going through a hotel. If you're travelling alone, you could take a shared taxi from Bur Dubai bus station at a cost of Dhs50. The taxi waits until there are four passengers before departing, so you could be waiting for anything from ten minutes to an hour.

AL AIN

The UAE's third city is a sleepy place where very little happens, which is the appeal for many. About 160 kilometres (100 miles) east of Abu Dhabi and the same distance south-east of Dubai, Al Ain is a 90-minute drive from either, but there are also domestic and international flights to Al Ain International Airport (03 785

5555). Despite being sparsely populated, it's a large, sprawling city that appears to be home to around half the world's roundabouts.

The UAE's **Natural History Museum** (Al Khubaisi, 03 761 2277) and **Al Ain Museum** (Zayed Bin Sultan Street, 03 764 1595) together house the country's largest collection of historic artefacts, and although they're hardly presented in the most engaging manner, it's a good place to investigate if you're interested in what conditions were like in the UAE before they struck black gold. The nearby **Al Ain Zoo & Aquarium** (Zoo roundabout, by the traffic police HQ, 03 782 8188) is the biggest zoo in the country.

Don't be tempted by the **Hili Fun City** theme park – it's a wasteland of decay and decrepit rides, the vast majority of which are, according to the signs, 'permanently closed due to safty (sic) reasons'. But the recently reopened **Jahili Fort** (*photo p255*) is well worth your attention, not only to see how a traditional fort would look, but to visit the excellent Wilfred Thesiger exhibition, a fantastic photographic portrait of the great British explorer and travel writer, who documented these lands in his classic travel book *Arabian Sands.*

The best time to visit Al Ain is during the winter, when time can be spent exploring ancient archaeological sites and the hot springs in the Jebel Hafeet mountains. Jebel Hafeet is also the site of archaeological finds that date back to the end of the fourth millennium BC. The hills around here are pockmarked with caves, which can be explored by adventure groups. A point to bear in mind is that the

---

INSIDE TRACK
BUSES

Taxis to Dubai or Al Ain from Abu Dhabi usually cost between Dhs200-Dhs250, so it makes sense to head out by bus. The central bus station on Muroor Road has three kinds of coach: the new silver and maroon Emirates Express, the old multicoloured ones, and the smaller white minibuses. These buses don't work to schedules, but leave when full, so the smaller minibuses leave more frequently and thus cost a bit more (Dhs25) than the large coaches – although you will be crammed in what feels like a tin can, travelling at breakneck speed, with 14 sweaty gents and no air-conditioning. The Emirates Express buses, particularly the new ones, are luxurious by comparison; and at just Dhs15, they are cheaper too. We think it pays to be patient.

Liwa.

elevation of the land makes Jebel Hafeet a good few degrees cooler than both Dubai and Abu Dhabi, which means it's bearable here even in the height of summer.

Al Ain Rotana Hotel

Zayed Bin Sultan Street (03 754 5111/ www.rotana.com). **Rates** Dhs550-Dhs750 double (excl 16% tax). **Credit** AmEx, MC, V.
The low-rise Rotana boasts a striking swimming pool and modish, nicely turned-out rooms. Tennis courts, a well-stocked gym and superb massage facilities are further draws. This is the classiest hotel to be found in the city.

Hilton Al Ain

Follow signs from city centre to Sarroj (03 768 6666/www1.hilton.com). **Rates** Dhs450-Dhs900 double (excl 16% tax). **Credit** AmEx, MC, V.
This good-value branch of the Hilton empire has large, comfortable rooms that are equipped with balconies on which you can take your time to grapple with the generous breakfasts. Sink-in armchairs, bouncy beds, more satellite channels than you could possibly want and speedy room service make this a good option if you're after a lazy weekend.

InterContinental Al Ain Resort

Near Al Ain Mall, Ernyadat Road (03 768 6686/www.ichotelsgroup.com). **Rates** Dhs400-Dhs700 double (excl 16% tax). **Credit** AmEx, MC, V.
A sprawling complex that's the focal point of the Garden City's social life in the evenings, the InterContinental hosts a series of good outlets and clean, functional rooms. Popular with families for its network of swimming pools and the laid-back attitude of the staff, this is a fine hotel to stay in.

LIWA

Liwa – the famous fertile crescent of the nation and the gateway to the Empty Quarter – should be on everyone's list of places to experience during a visit to the UAE. Only three hours by car from Abu Dhabi, Liwa's desert scenery and rugged terrain is a world away from urban living. The oasis features plenty of freshwater pools and date plantations, and is home to the Bani Yas tribe – the Bedouin ancestors of Abu Dhabi's ruling family.

Sightseeing

Don't look to visit Liwa if you're in the mood to let your hair down – this is no place to come looking for a party. What it does offer is a welcome respite from busy bustle of Dubai's 21st-century city life; visitors head here for the grand silence that echoes in the expanses of the Empty Quarter and the beauty of the vast dunes that roll into the distance. When you visit, it's worth taking a drive around the series of villages, stopping off at points of interest such as the remarkably well preserved fort and the oasis of Qatuf which – for people who have read *Arabian Sands* – is where Sir Wilfred Thesiger camped during his visit to Liwa back in 1947. The wells that Thesiger mentions in his book are still here, over 60 years later, right by the mosque.

You mustn't leave Liwa without experiencing the magisterial beauty of the desert. The star attraction here is **Moreeb Hill**; at 358 feet, it's the country's biggest sand dune, and plays host to the annual Moreeb Dune Championship for cars and motorbikes. The intrepid or foolhardy (delete as appropriate) can attempt to scale the shifting sand mound in a 4x4. If that sounds a tad too intimidating, more sedate camel and horse treks can be organised by the Liwa Hotel (02 882 2000) at dawn and dusk, as well as belly dancing shows out in the sands and desert camping. For desert safaris, try Off Road Adventures (www.arabiantours.com).

Where to stay

The four-star **Liwa Hotel** (02 882 2000, www.ncth.com) is your only option and, thankfully if rather unexpectedly given the lack of competition, it's not a bad one. The 66-room resort overlooks the Rub al Khali desert and is surrounded by some of the highest sand dunes in the world. Spacious, well-equipped rooms are arranged around a sun-drenched pool and provide stunning views of the dunes rolling out to the horizon. Facilities include four floodlit tennis courts, a volleyball court, a swimming pool, saunas, a jacuzzi and a steam room. There's also a children's pool and playground area to keep the hotel's younger residents entertained. A selection of decent restaurants and bars – including an evening terrace for shisha – complete the food and drink choices. During the sizzling summer months, the hotel has some excellent offers.

A luxury five-star retreat – Qasr Al Sarab – is due to open in the Empty Quarter in 2009, thereby increasing accommodation options deep in the desert. When completed, the hotel will have 150 rooms, 60 villas, a spa and an observatory from which guests can watch the sun rise and set over the desert.

Getting there

From Dubai, head 135 kilometres (84 miles) west along the Dubai–Abu Dhabi highway until you reach the Mafraq turning. Go straight towards Tarif and turn left 23 kilometres (14 miles) later when you see a sign for Dhafrah and Shah fields. Drive south following signs for Hmeem on the edge of Liwa. Turn right and head for the villages and oases. For more detailed directions and a map, visit www.ncth.com.

THE EAST COAST

Fujairah might seem like the quieter, less flashy cousin to the other emirates, but it merits a little more exploring. One unique and unmissable spectacle is **bull butting**, a sight so odd and rare that it's worth tagging a whole trip around. The origins of this unusual sport, known as *mnattah* (which means 'head butting' in Arabic), are shrouded in mystery, but it's thought to have originated when the Portuguese came to the Gulf in the 16th century, seizing hold of the Arabian spice trade and leaving behind a fervent passion for bovine warfare. If you happen to be in town on

Bull butting in **Fujairah**.

Masafi Friday Market.

a Friday afternoon, head to the bull fighting arena along Corniche Road, just after the coffee pot roundabout, next to Café Maria. Don't worry about blood and spears though; this is a fight between two beasts, rather than bull versus toreador and no blood is spilled, though much beastly sweat flows. The spectacle draws carloads of people from across the emirate every week. The action kicks off when two bulls are led into the dirt arena and, with a flurry of guttural grunting and dust, the animals butt each other, locking horns, and push until one becomes submissive. Although the bulls run loose, a handler skirts around them brandishing a cane in case they become too wayward. There are inevitably some hairy moments as the bulls lurch too close, but its otherwise harmless fun to watch.

On your way to Fujairah, stop at the **Masafi Friday Market** on the main road (E88) from Dubai and the west. Oddly, it's open every day of the week apart from the promised Friday. It's a peculiar sight; with big, tented carpet stalls lined up along the road outside the town. You'll also find fruit and veg vendors, locally made pottery and unlikely inflatable toys. Even if you're not specifically looking for a chunky rug, or a blow-up whale, it's still worth a quick nose about.

Worth a little more time for history buffs is Fujairah's old town. The **Fujairah Museum** at Al Gurfa Street and Al Nakheel Road (09 222 9085) houses a fairly decent collection of archaeological artefacts in a rather grungy-looking museum, including ancient Islamic bronze coins excavated from a farm in Mirbah,

rock art from Wadi Al Hail, old tools and Bedouin jewellery. For a sense of the town itself, head for the **souks** selling meat, fish and vegetables off Al Gurfa Road, where locals haggle over the price of dates, melons and mangoes, and Pakistani butchers proudly show off their produce.

Another local curiosity is **Bidiya Mosque**, which is further north along the coastal road between Dibba and Khor Fakkan. This tiny structure is the oldest and smallest mosque in the UAE, dating from 1446, predating the Portuguese invasion of the area by more than 50 years.

For nature lovers, there's a tiny enclave of the emirate of Sharjah around a ten minute drive south from Fujairah along the coast, which is home to **Khor Kalba**, one of the world's oldest mangrove forests and one of the few places where you might see the rare white-collared kingfisher. When the tide is high, the mangroves can be explored in a canoeing trip with Dubai based tour company Desert Rangers, the only firm approved to take tourists through this delicate ecosystem (04 340 2408, www.desertrangers.com).

Where to eat

If you think the faux stone façade at **Al Meshwar Restaurant** (Hamad Bin Abdullah Road, Fujairah, 09 2231113) is wacky, wait until you see the interior, with its grotto-like surrounds, complete with flowing waterfall and hanging ferns. The downstairs café (which has Wi-Fi) serves snacks such as falafel, and upstairs serves a better range of traditional Lebanese fare, from basic *shawarmas* to seafood dishes. If you go to **Sadaf** on Al Corniche Road, Fujairah (near the Hilton Hotel, 09 223 3400) you'll need a hardy appetite, because the portions at this Iranian chain are huge. Serving traditional Persian food like grilled meat platters and kebabs, the restaurant also does western dishes like chicken schnitzel. For classier and pricier fare, head to the **Hilton Fujairah** next to the coffee pot roundabout on Al Gurfa Street (09 222 2411, www.hiltonworld resorts.com) which has a range of culinary options certain to sate any cravings for club sandwiches, pasta, seafood and the like.

Getting There

By bus
Buses to Fujairah cost Dhs25 and they depart every half hour from the Deira taxi stand near Al Nasr Square in Dubai. You will have to make alternative travel arrangements on your way back, as there is no bus service from Fujairah to Dubai. Contact the RTA for more information (800 9090, www.rta.ae).

By car
Fujairah is around 130 kilometres (80 miles) from Dubai via Al Dhaid and the journey should take around an hour and a half. Take the

Khatt Springs.

E11 towards Sharjah airport and the E88 to Dhaid and Masafi. If you are heading to Dibba, turn left at the Masafi roundabout and, if you are going to Fujairah town, turn right.

By taxi
You can take a metered cab from Dubai to Fujairah or Dibba and the trip should cost around Dhs250. To return to Dubai, you'll need to take a Fujairah taxi, which should be cheaper at around Dhs150.

RAS AL KHAIMAH

Ras Al Khaimah has been labelled 'the Wild West of the UAE'. It's a slightly giddy claim: there are no cowboys, the gold is found in the souks rather than the hills and as far as we can tell, no one has ever been scalped. But one look at the desolate mountains offers an explanation: the craggy barreness is like something from a Sergio Leone film. Full of small villages and archaeological sites, this stretch of the **Hajar Mountains** has provided the UAE's hiking fanatics with years of exhausting and exhilarating entertainment. The well-known 'Stairway to Heaven' for example, an 11-hour hike that involves sheer drops of thousands of feet, should not be tried without an experienced guide. Try Dubai-based Absolute Adventure (050 625 9165, www.adventure.ae), which runs various trips in the mountains of Ras Al Khaimah.

For wadis, try **Wadi Galeela**, which is on the way to Khasab from Ras Al Khaimah. Explorer Tours (042861991, www.explorer tours.ae) organises trips on a fantastic trail towards the start of 'Stairway to Heaven' (the best time is between November-March). The trek can take up to 12 hours though shorter routes are available too. And what will you see? Abandoned settlements, stone houses and even graveyards.

For less strenuous mountain-going experiences, head for **Khatt Springs** on Al Jazeera Road. These naturally occurring warm waters have become a big tourist attraction for Ras Al Khaimah, and have been adapted into a mini-spa, with pools of warm water that lower blood pressure and aid relaxation. For the paltry sum of Dhs25 (or for free, if you're staying at the hotel), take the plunge. For a bit more pampering, the **Khatt Springs Hotel & Spa** (07 244 8777) provides everything from traditional mudpacks to the latest technological trickery, though sceptics might raise their eyebrows at some of the more 'mystical' treatments.

For a bit of culture and history, the **National Museum of Ras Al Khaimah** in the Old Town (07 233 3411) is a good bet. Make your

Sultan Qaboos Grand Mosque.

way past the rather sullen guards, and you'll find a lovely, tree-lined courtyard and the most detailed information in Arabic and English of any of the northern Emirati forts. If you want any more information on the area, try the **Ministry of Information & Culture** (off King Faisal Road, 06 765 6663, www.uaeinteract.com).

Where to eat

There's not much available, but you could try **Churchill's** (Al Muntasir Street, opposite Dubai Islamic Bank, Al Nakheel, 07 228 2822) though the drinks selection is limited, and its food is terrible. As well as a nightly karaoke session, it features a dart board, free bar snacks, a pool table and a palpable air of numb regret. The **Grand** on Al Muntasir Street, four buildings down from Al Nakheel Hotel, Al Nakheel (07 228 7685, 07 228 4250) has quality food and good-sized portions, and the **Phoenicien** outside Hilton Ras Al Khaimah (07 228 8793) serves up Lebanese food and is populated by helpful (if reserved) staff.

Getting there

From Dubai, take Emirates road – the route is well signposted.

Beyond the Borders
MUSCAT

Muscat has managed to modernise without turning the city into a strip of gargantuan shopping malls and even today, with thousands of expats, it's managed to retain an enchanting Omani culture. You only have to look at the buildings, with their arches and white-washed walls, to feel a true sense of Arabia, and stroll through the city's streets, particularly the carefully maintained old town, to see true Arabian authenticity.

Culture vultures should try to visit the Sultanate during January, when the annual **Muscat Festival** (www.muscat-festival.com) transforms parks and beaches into a cultural explosion of traditional dance, crafts and farming techniques. To get a better idea of the colourful history of the city, head to the museum **Bait al Baranda** in Muttrah (+968 24 714 262), which would't be out of place in a European capital. Its imaginative, interactive displays are a great way to get to grips with Muscat's past. Another must-do on any itinerary is the **Sultan Qaboos Grand Mosque** in Khuwair, which is open to tourists Saturday to Wednesday from 8am to 11am (women must be fully covered). This awe-

Muttrah Souk.

inspiring structure once contained the world's largest Persian carpet measuring around 20,000 square metres (215,000 square feet) – until Abu Dhabi stole the title with another gargantuan rug – but don't worry, the glittering Swarovski chandeliers and intricately carved rosewood doors still make it one of the world's most impressive mosques.

But the biggest draw to this peaceful country is the natural environment. Visit **Qurum Beach** and watch the sand teeming with footballers as the sun sets or, for a more peaceful vibe, the Oman Dive Centre's (+968 24 824 240) white sand beach is a good bet. And if you love fishing, Muscat will fulfill your desires. Jump on a deep sea fishing expedition with Gulf Leisure Tours (+968 99819 006) and haul in a massive tuna, or take it easy with a snorkelling trip where dolphin spotting is guaranteed. For shopping, any local will point you in the direction of the **Muttrah Souk**, and

its labyrinth-like laneways could keep you contented for days. It is full of jumbled trinkets, tat, and genuine antiques.

But above all, do everything you can to stay outdoors. Try the palm-fringed wadis like **Wadi Tiwi** or **Wadi Shab**, both with unbelievably clear, deep, naturally formed pools; or the **Hajar Mountains**, where you can trek or canyon in beautiful natural surrounds. Most of these spots and Oman's best coastline (like **White Beach**) are only a couple of hours drive away from the centre of Muscat. And only 150 kilometres (90 miles) south along the coast is **Ras Al-Jinz**, a protected area where green turtles lay and hatch their eggs all year round. Visitors to the **Ras al-Jinz Scientific & Research Centre** (+968 96 550606, www.rasaljinz.org) learn all about the fascinating, ancient creatures. For tours, contact Oman World Tourism (+968 24 313 333, www.omanworldtourism.com)

Where to eat and stay

Take a seat in the picturesque garden of **Kargeen Café** in Madinat al Qaboos (+968 24 692 269), where you can sit on comfortable cushions and drink a refreshing mint juice while puffing a shisha. For breakfast, do as the locals do and go to **D'Arcy's Kitchen** (+968 24600 234), a perennially popular café in Shatti Al Qurum with bumper breakfasts served all day long. For dinner, don't miss out on a curry at the always excellent Indian restaurant, **Mumtaz Mahal** in Qurum (+968 24605 907). Afterwards, you can nip next door to the lively **Left Bank** bar (+968 24693 699), which serves up a mean mojito.

Muscat wouldn't be Muscat without its fabulous range of flashy hotels like the **Chedi** (+968 24 542 400, www.ghmhotels.com), the **Shangri-La** (+968 24 776 666, www.shangri-la.com) and the **Al Bustan Palace** (+968 24 799 666, www.ichotelsgroup.com) – all equipped with restaurants and bars worthy of a sundowner to further soak up the beautiful coastline. Even if you're not staying at the Al Bustan Palace, you would be foolish not to visit to gawp at the incredible lobby, which towers some 40 metres (130 feet) high. The hotel is an iconic building in Muscat's history, and it's been redeveloped with a number of top-notch restaurants to enhance its appeal for visitors. For a culinary extravaganza to remember, the molecular gastronomy displays at the hotel's signature restaurant Vue by Shannon Bennett (+968 24 799 666) will have you talking for weeks.

Tourist information

There is no tourist office in Muscat. For tourist information, contact the Ministry of Tourism (+968 2458 8700, www.omantourism.gov.om).

Visa requirements

Citizens from most GCC, EU countries and the US can get a two-week tourist visa at the border or airport on arrival, but you might want to check with the Omani embassy to ensure your country hasn't been removed from the list.

Getting there

By air
Oman Air, Emirates Airlines, Gulf Air, Saudi Arabian Airlines and Etihad all fly to Muscat.

By car
From the UAE, reaching Muscat is fairly straightforward, with a highway leading straight to Oman's border, so you're unlikely to get lost. But it's worth buying a map, since once you cross the UAE border, you'll realise that their Omani neighbours never took to signposting. Before you head off, check if your insurance is also valid in Oman, otherwise you may not be allowed into the Sultanate. And don't forget to have your passport stamped at the borders.

By coach
Comfort Line runs returns from Dubai to Muscat (24 702 191).

Wadi Shab.

ESCAPES & EXCURSIONS

ESCAPES & EXCURSIONS

MUSANDAM

Musandam has earned itself the unusual nickname of the Norway of Arabia thanks to its dramatic, cavernous fjords and rocky mountain backdrop. There's precious little to do here except admire the scenery, though despite its diminutive size, there's a winningly varied feel to the main town of **Khasab**, which creates a surprisingly buzzing atmosphere. Smugglers have been shuttling back and forth from Iran to Khasab since time immemorial. Their booty ranges from goats (a princely sum of OMR85 a pop, apparently) and garments, to cigarettes and more ungodly and intoxicating substances.

Surrounded by a beautiful plateau of grey mountains that wash pink as the sun rises, the Musandam's claim to natural fame is the striking blue channels of water which are teeming with marine life, including frolicking dolphins. These fjords are also home to **Telegraph Island** a desolate lump of rock which was once part of the British Empire's attempt to run a cable from Bombay to Basra. It's thought to be the very spot where 'going round the bend' became a euphemism for going mad. Posted on the island for long periods with only the surrounding grey mountains for company and the task of laying cable, quite a few Brits lost it.

Located three hours or so from Dubai (depending on the border crossing), Musandam makes the perfect spot for an overnighter or a day excursion. Camping is possible on the public beach, though if you're just visiting for the day, the best way to appreciate the mind-boggling stillness and beauty of the northernmost tip of Oman is undoubtedly on a dhow trip (try Khasab Travel & Tours, +968 2673 0464, www.khasabtours.com). These wooden vessels are made even more alluring courtesy of thick Arabic carpets and gigantic cushions, and as you kick back to observe the passing mountains emerge from the placid waters, the only interruption you are likely to hear is the sound of the boatmen whistling to indicate the presence of dolphins swimming alongside. On a full-day cruise, it's possible to travel the entire length of the khor (around 17 kilometres or 11 miles); on a half day, the furthest you will get is Telegraph Island, where the boat will moor, the fluorescent fish will gather in the crystal-clear water and you can swim and snorkel to your heart's content. If you don't mind a bit of haggling, then you can always arrange a price with a fisherman from **Khasab Harbour** or even **Dibba Harbour**, which is another fishing harbour only a 90-minute drive from Dubai (try Al Marsa tours, at Al Marsa, +968 2683 6995, www.musandamdiving.com)

Another rather unique site in this region is the isolated town of **Kumzar**. Occupied by around 3,000 people, sporting dilapidated cannons on the beach, a run-down mosque and hundreds of munching goats; Kumzar is quite eerie when deserted in summer, but unique in that locals speak an entirely distinctive language, a mixture of Persian, Portuguese, Arabic and, some claim, English. Isolated from the land, it's only really accessible from the water, and takes around an hour by speedboat. If you want to check out what's happening beneath the water, head for the **Golden Tulip Resort**, which has a dive centre on site (+968 26 73 05 01, www.musandam-diving.com) providing daily dive excursions on speed boats as well as the full range of dive courses.

Aside from immersing yourself in Musandam's unique scenery, a bit of culture can be found at **Khasab Castle**, on the waterfront near to the harbour. Built by the Portuguese in the 16th century, when they controlled the trade coming through the Strait of Hormuz, this impressive fort makes a worthwhile distraction from all the natural attractions in the area. There's not all that much to see inside, but the views out across the water can be spectacular, especially around sunset. There's also **Bukha Fort**, which is just off the main road between the UAE border at Tibat and Khasab. As with Khasab Castle, the fort at Bukha was built by the Portuguese, though it was renovated in the early 1990s.

Where to eat

Dibba restaurant at the **Golden Tulip Khasab Resort** near the public beach (+968 26 73 07 77, www.goldentulipkhasab.com) has lunch and dinner buffets – highlights include a smoky *shish taouk* and a nicely piquant dish of meatballs with pine nuts and tomatoes. There's an à la carte menu available too at the English Pub which takes care of nightlife, unless you fancy a jaunt to the hotel's Arabic nightclub, replete with fleshy Moroccan dancers, who wobble salaciously and may not be to everyone's taste.

Getting there

From Dubai, follow the Emirates Road all the way north to Ras Al Khaimah City.

At the clock roundabout turn right. Drive on with the golf course on either side and pass through two sets of traffic lights before turning left. From here there are no more turn offs before you reach the UAE/Oman border at Al Darah – so don't forget your passport. After the border a spectacular road hugs the shoreline for 38 kilometres (24 miles) before you reach Khasab.

Directory

Getting Around

ARRIVING BY AIR

Dubai International Airport
switchboard 224 5555/
flight information 216 6666/
www.dubaiairport.com.
One of the most acclaimed airports in the world, DIA recently underwent an elaborate and extravagant expansion programme, with a new third terminal opened at the end of 2008 exclusively for Emirates airline flights.

Almost all major airlines arrive at Terminal 1. Here the Dubai Duty Free (224 5004) is the last port of call for the purchase of alcohol before entering Dubai's 'hotel-only' licensing restrictions (*see p271* **Customs**). Airport facilities include internet and banking services, shops, restaurants, business services, bars, pubs, a hotel and a regular raffle that gives you the chance to win a luxury car. Tickets cost Dhs500, but the odds are favourable as there is a draw every time 1,000 are sold.

The smaller Terminal 2 caters largely for charter flights, cargo and commercial airlines from Iran, and the CIS countries (former Soviet Republics such as Belarus, Moldova, Armenia, Ukraine and Georgia). There is also a VIP terminal known as Al Majlis.

A card-operated E-Gate enables travellers who carry the relevant 'smart card' to check in and travel unhindered, using nothing more than their fingerprints for identification.

To and from the airport

DIA is in Garhoud, about 5km south-east of the city centre.

If you're staying at one of the big hotels, you'll get a complimentary shuttle bus or limousine transfer to and from the airport. Otherwise, taxis are the most convenient and practical form of transport. There is a Dhs20 surcharge on pick-up from the terminal (instead of the usual Dhs3). This means that the journey from the airport to Bur Dubai costs around Dhs40, and the return journey is Dhs20 or so. It takes about ten minutes to get to Bur Dubai; Jumeirah, Dubai Marina

and the hotel beach resorts are about half an hour away.

There are bus links to and from both terminals every 20 or 30 minutes for around Dhs3, although times are somewhat erratic and routes can be lengthy. Route **401** goes from the airport to Al Sabkha bus station and the **402** goes to Al Ghubaiba, running through the centre of the city. From Deira station, located opposite the Al Ghurair Centre on Al Rigga Road, the numbers **4, 11** and **48** will take you straight to Terminal 1, as will the **33** and **44** from Bur Dubai. All buses are air-conditioned.

It's now also possible to take the **Dubai Metro** line to and from the airport, with stops for terminals located on the city's Red Line. Single journeys cost between Dhs1.8 and Dhs6.5, or Dhs14 for a day pass offering unlimited travel. Call 227 3840 or 800 9090 for more details, or visit www.rta.ae.

Airport parking

There are short- and long-term parking facilities available at the airport. Tariffs range from Dhs10 per hour in the short-stay car park to Dhs120 per day for up to ten days in the long stay.

Airlines

All airlines operating regular flights into DIA are listed on the airport website; some of the most popular are listed below. Note that some airlines ask you to confirm your flight 72 hours before departure, and that cheaper tickets will often incur a penalty fee for alteration or cancellation.

Air France *602 5400/*
www.airfrance.ae.
British Airways *reservations & ticket sales 307 5777/8000 441 3322/www.britishairways.com.*
Emirates *214 4444/*
www.emirates.com.
Etihad Airways *02 250 58000/*
www.etihadairways.com.
Gulf Air *271 3111/3222/*
www.gulfairco.com.
KLM *319 3777/www.klm.com.*
Lufthansa *343 2121/*
www.lufthansa.com.

Qatar Airways *229 2229/221 4210/www.qatarairways.com.*
Royal Brunei *information 351 4111/ticket sales 316 6562/ www.bruneiair.com. (No alcohol served on board.)*

ARRIVING BY ROAD

The UAE is bordered to the north and east by Oman, and to the south and west by Saudi Arabia. Road access to Dubai is via the Abu Dhabi emirate to the south, Sharjah to the north, and Oman to the east.

There is no charge for driving between emirates, but travel to or from Oman or Saudi Arabia requires you to show your passport, driving licence, insurance and visa. Crossing the Oman border costs Dhs30 per person for those with UAE residency and Dhs60 for those on a visit visa. Before you travel, it's always worth checking www.omanaccess.com/ explore_oman/visa1.asp for all the latest visa requirements.

On the journey, your car is likely to be searched; carrying alcohol is prohibited. All the highways linking Dubai to the other emirates and Oman are in good condition. Ensure your vehicle and the air-conditioning are in good working order, as it is inevitably hot at most times of the year, and the drive through the Hajar Mountains to Muscat, the capital of Oman, takes approximately five hours. Check with Immigration (398 0000) before you leave for any important changes in travel policy. For traffic enquiries, contact RTA (800 9090, www.dubaipolice.gov.ae). *See also p267* **Navigation**.

ARRIVING BY SEA

There are boats to Dubai from Iraq and Iran; journey time is more than two days, and costs around Dhs580 return. For schedules and details you should contact the **Dubai Ports Authority** (881 5555, www. dpa.co.ae). Alternatively, if you're travelling north, you can call **Rashid Port** (345 1545), which operates sea routes to Port Bandar Abbas and Port Bandar Lankah in Iran, and Port Umm Qasr in Iraq.

NAVIGATION

Thanks to its modern highway system, it's fairly easy to get around most of Dubai. However, in some places the existing infrastructure has struggled to cope with the growth of the city, most notably the Garhoud and Maktoum bridges spanning the Creek and the Shindagha tunnel underneath it. During rush hours (7-9am, 1-2pm, 5-8pm Sun-Thur), serious tailbacks can develop, although these do not appear as bad as they once were. A third bridge, Business Bay, opened in March 2007, with a Floating Bridge and a wider Garhoud both added in 2008. A suspension bridge across the Creek – the world's largest, naturally – is due to open in 2012.

Despite the relatively good road system, Dubai can be a dangerous place to drive in. There are high numbers of road accidents and deaths, caused largely by speeding and poor lane discipline. Many drivers tailgate, chat away on their mobiles and do not use their indicators or mirrors.

The easiest way to get around by road is in a taxi (*see below*). Water taxis or *abras* (*see below*) are also available on the Creek, but won't help you get around the whole city. The red line, Dubai Metro's first route, opens in September 2009, with its trains running from Jebel Ali Free Zone to Rashidiya. The green line, which will go from Jaddaf to Al Qusais, is scheduled to open in March 2010, with further lines following in the next few years. Dubai's public buses are not tourist friendly, and are primarily used by people unable to afford cars or taxis. The biggest problem with getting around Dubai, though, is the lack of an accurate system of street names. Some of the larger roads and streets are known by their name, but most are just numbered. This means your destination is usually identified by a nearby landmark, typically a hotel or building. *See also p269* **Addresses**.

PUBLIC TRANSPORT

Buses

The public bus system is rarely used by tourists, due to the convenience of taxis and the Metro. The service is cheap but routes can be convoluted and times erratic.

Timetables, prices and route maps are available from the main bus stations of Al Ghubaiba in Bur Dubai (342 11130) and by the gold souk in Deira (227 3840). You can also call the main information line (24 hours, seven days a week; 800 9090) or visit www.rta.ae.

Should you brave a bus trip, try to have the correct money since change for larger notes is rarely available. All bus stops are request stops. Eating, drinking and smoking are not allowed on board; the front three rows of seats are reserved for women. Note that passengers without tickets are liable for prosecution.

Monthly bus passes can be purchased for Dhs95 (only valid on certain city routes) or you can purchase a rechargeable pre-pay card. These are available from the depots at Al Ramoul and Al Qusais.

Metro

The driverless, fully automated Dubai Metro is due to open on 9 September 2009, starting with the 52km (32-mile) **Red Line** which will run from Jebel Ali Free Zone to Rashidiya, passing through Mall of the Emirates, Burj Dubai, Bur Dubai and the airport along the way. The **Green Line**, its second route, is scheduled to start running from March 2010, going from Jaddaf to Al Qusais. Plans are afoot for further lines but no details were available at time of going to press. The trains, which will run every three minutes and 43 seconds on average, will provide free Wi-Fi. All trains and stations will be air conditioned, as will the walkways that access them. Waves were made with the news of just how cheap the Metro will be – between Dhs1.8 and Dhs6.5 for single journeys and Dhs14 for a day pass offering unlimited travel. However, this is Dubai, so naturally there will also be a 'gold car' at the front of each train boasting a more luxurious interior and wider leather seats, an 'exclusive lighting design' and a panoramic view through the train's front window – at an increased price, which hadn't been disclosed at time of going to press. Call 227 3840 or 800 9090, or visit www.rta.ae for more details.

Monorail (Palm Jumeirah)

Opened in April 2009, the **monorail** runs the 5.5km length of the Palm Jumeirah. More of a tourist attraction than a useful mode of transport, it glides between just two stations: Gateway Towers and Atlantis, the vast pink hotel at the Palm's tip. The trains are automatic and driverless, although an attendant is on board at all times. Four trains (set to increase to nine with the opening of Dubai Metro) operate between 8am and 10pm daily, with singles costing Dhs15 and returns a wallet-offending Dhs25. Once the Metro is open in September 2009, the monorail is also planned to stop at the Tecom station, where passengers can connect onto the main rail network. Call 04 390 3333 for more information.

TAXIS

Official taxis are well maintained, air-conditioned and metered. Fares are Dhs1.6 per kilometre with a Dhs3-Dhs3.50 cover charge depending on the time of day (between 10pm and 6am, it's more expensive). The two biggest companies are the **Dubai Transport Company** (208 0808) and **National Taxis** (339 0002), and the metres of taxis booked on the phone will start at Dhs6-Dhs7, again depending on time of day. There is a Dhs10 minimum fare on all journeys. Unofficial taxis are best avoided, as they tend to be older cars with poor air-con and they may rip you off. If it's the only option available, be sure to agree on a price before entering the car. Taxi drivers usually have a reasonable grasp of English, so you shouldn't find it too difficult to explain where you want to go.

If you're in an outlying area of the city you should consider booking a taxi by calling 208 0808. Fares for longer journeys outside Dubai should be agreed in advance (there is also a 12-hour service available, with petrol and driver included).

Drivers have a reputation for being honest, so if you leave something in a taxi, your driver might find a way to return it to you. Failing this, call the company you used and give the time, destinations (to and from) and taxi number, and they will do their best to help.

WATER TAXIS

Abras are water taxis that ferry both Dubai workers and tourists across the creek for Dhs1. The boats run between 5am and midnight, carry about 20 people and take just a few minutes to make the crossing from Bur Dubai on the south bank of the Creek to Deira on the north, or vice versa.

DIRECTORY

DIRECTORY

DRIVING

People drive on the right in Dubai. A vehicle licence may be secured at Dhs320 for the first registration, which is thereafter subject to annual renewal – following a road-worthiness test – at a charge of Dhs370. Driving licences issued by some overseas governments may be used to obtain a Dubai licence. Seatbelts are compulsory in the front seats and recommended in the back. In residential areas, the speed limit is normally between 40kph (25mph) and 80kph (50mph). On the highways within the city, it's 100kph (60mph); outside the city limits, it's 120kph (75mph).

Although there are, in theory, fines and bans for a whole series of offences, in practice enforcement of these is pretty erratic. While you may have to pay up to Dhs1,500 if you're caught going through an amber or red light, don't expect much in the way of road rules or driving etiquette if you venture out by car. *See also p267* **Navigation**.

Traffic fines & offences

A comprehensive official traffic police website (www.dubaipolice. gov.ae) lists details of licence requirements, contact numbers and fines for offences. All offences are listed under Kiosk Locations and Violations.

There is a zero-tolerance policy on drinking and driving. If you are caught driving or parking illegally by the police, you'll be issued with a *mukhalifaa* (fine). If caught by a speed camera you'll normally be fined Dhs500, although if you're speeding at excessive levels this may be higher. When hiring a car, it's routine to sign an agreement of responsibility for any fines you may incur. You can check whether you've racked up any traffic offences on www.dubaipolice. gov.ae or call 800 7777. Fines can be paid online, or at the Muroor (Traffic Police Headquarters), near Galadari Roundabout on the Dubai-Sharjah road.

Traffic accidents

If you are involved in a serious traffic accident, call 999; if it's a minor collision, call the police on 398 1111. If you do not report scratches or bumps to the traffic police, insurers will almost certainly reject your claim. Third-party vehicle insurance is compulsory.

If the accident was a minor one and no one was hurt, move the car to the side of the road and wait for the police to arrive. If there is any doubt as to who is at fault, or if there is any injury (however slight), do not move the car, even if you are blocking traffic. If you help or move anyone injured in an accident, the police may hold you responsible if anything happens to that person.

Breakdown services

There are two 24-hour breakdown services, the **AAA** (Arabian Automobile Association) (800 4900, www.aaauae.com) and **IATC Recovery** (International Automobile Touring Club) (800 5200, www.iatcuae.com).

If you are driving when the car breaks down, try to pull over on to the hard shoulder. The police are likely to stop and will give assistance. If you're in the middle of high-speed traffic, it will be unsafe to get out of the car. Instead, use a mobile to call the police from the relative safety of your vehicle. Other breakdown services (not 24-hour) include the following:

Ahmed Mohammed Garage *050 650 4739.*
Dubai Auto Towing Service *359 4424.*

Vehicle hire

Most major car-hire companies have offices at Dubai airport (15 companies have 24-hour outlets there) and five-star hotels. Before renting a car, check the small print, and especially clauses relating to insurance cover in the event of an accident, as this can vary from company to company.

Drivers must be aged over 21 to hire a small car, or 25 for a medium (two-litre) or larger 4x4 vehicle. You'll need your national driving licence (an International Driving Permit is best, although it isn't legally required). You'll also need your passport and one of the major credit cards. Prices range from Dhs77 per day for a small manual car, to Dhs1,000 for something like a Lexus LS430. Motorbikes are not available for hire in Dubai.

Autolease *224 4900.*
Avis *224 5219.*
Budget *224 5192.*
Cars *224 5524.*
Diamond Lease *220 0325.*
Europe *224 5240.*
Fast Rent A Car *224 5040.*

Hertz *224 5222.*
Patriot *224 4244.*
Thrifty *224 5404.*
United Car Rentals *224 4666.*

Fuel stations

There are 24-hour petrol stations on all major highways. Most petrol stations also have convenience stores selling snacks and drinks.

Parking

Many areas in the city centre have introduced paid parking in a bid to reduce congestion. Prices are reasonable (Dhs1 or Dhs2 for a one-hour stay, depending on location), but this hasn't made it easier to secure a parking space. Paid parking areas are operational at peak times (generally from 8am to noon and 4pm to 9pm), and it's free to park there outside these hours and on Fridays or public holidays. If you park illegally or go over your time limit, the penalty charge is Dhs100-Dhs150. Generally your car hire company will pay the fines for you and charge them to you at the end of your lease.

Particular black spots include the warren of streets in 'old' Bur Dubai, the stretch of Sheikh Zayed Road between the Crowne Plaza and Shangri-La hotels and most of Deira. Parking in shopping malls is free in most places although BurJuman is an exception, charging Dhs10 per hour and only granting free parking to people spending Dhs100 or more or visiting between the hours of 12.30pm and 2.30pm or after 6pm. There tend to be huge queues at all the malls on Thursday and Friday evenings.

Most hotels have extensive parking facilities for visitors.

Road signs

Road signs are in English and Arabic, but the sheer scale of the American-style highway system means you have to stay alert.

WALKING

The city was not designed for pedestrians. Certain areas lack pavements and the sheer size of some highways can mean waiting up to 20 minutes just to cross. It is not uncommon for pedestrians to take a taxi just to get to the other side of the road. Due to the heat and humidity, an outdoor stroll is out of the question between June and September.

Resources A-Z

ADDRESSES

Since it's not divided into separate postcodes, Dubai can be difficult to navigate. Although street addresses are slowly being introduced to the city, at present all official locations are simply given postbox numbers. The majority of roads are numbered, but not identifiable by anything other than nearby landmarks. Any resident here will happily point you in the direction of the Ritz-Carlton or the Jumeirah Beach Hotel, but few will know an actual address. Taxi drivers know most of the significant landmarks, but it's always worth carrying a map with you just in case. The most common reference points are hotels, shopping malls, restaurants and some of the bigger supermarkets such as Spinneys and Choithrams.

It's not a bad idea to invest Dhs45 in a copy of the *Dubai Explorer Street Map*, which is available from all bookshops, or any Emarat petrol station.

We've included a number of useful city maps at the end of this guide; *see pp326-336.*

AGE RESTRICTIONS

You must be aged 18 to drive in Dubai (21 to rent a small car, 25 to rent a large one) and to buy cigarettes, although the latter rule does not generally appear to be vigorously enforced.

In restaurants and bars, you must be 21 to drink. It is illegal to buy alcohol from an off-licence without a licence. Issued by the Police Department to non-Muslims holding a residence visa, these are valid for one year only, but are easily renewable. Alcohol can only be bought from two legal suppliers, a+e and MMI.

ATTITUDE & ETIQUETTE

A cosmopolitan city with hundreds of different nationalities, Dubai has a well-deserved reputation for being tolerant and relaxed. It is, however, a Muslim state and must be respected as such. Most 'rules' concerning cultural dos and don'ts are basic common sense and courtesy, with particular respect needing to be shown for Islam and the Royal Family.

General guidelines

In formal situations, it is polite to stand when someone enters the room and to offer a handshake to all then men in the room on entering. Only offer your hand to an Arab woman if she does so first. It is courteous to ask Muslim men about their family, but not about their wives. You may find yourself addressed by a title followed by your first name by expat workers – for instance, Mr Tom – and it's not unusual for a woman to be referred to by her husband's name – Mrs Tom, say – so don't take offence.

Although the last ten years have seen attitudes relax, avoid offending locals with public displays of affection and flesh. This is particularly true during Ramadan (when everyone is expected to dress more conservatively) and at the Heritage Village, but in nightclubs you won't find dress codes any different from those in the West. Topless bathing is not allowed, even on the private beaches, and sometimes women are asked not to wear thongs. Be respectful about taking photographs and always ask for consent. Communication can at times be frustrating, but patience is crucial in a nation where time holds a different significance and civility is paramount.

For further information contact the **Ministry of Information & Culture** on 261 5500 or the **Sheikh Mohammed Centre for Cultural Understanding** on 353 6666 or at www.cultures.ae.

In terms of getting by on a day-to-day basis, 'information', 'expansion' and 'efficiency' are buzzwords in Dubai. Although the range of personal services can sometimes astound, the all-too-common collapse in communication can also astonish. There is a tendency to be keener to help than actually having the capability of carrying it through, with telephone conversations often leaving you more confused than when you started.

Far less harrowing is using the internet (*see p273*) – there are countless websites that offer straightforward facts and advice for tourists. In this guide, contact websites have been given in addition to the telephone number wherever possible.

BUSINESS

Dubai has been incredibly proactive in its bid to establish itself as the business hub of the UAE. Every effort has been made to welcome new business and its corporate care is the envy of the rest of the world. Dubai's economy is aided by low labour costs, minimal taxes, free zones, a secure convertible currency and a liberal community.

This safe environment has attracted international interest on a scale unrivalled elsewhere. The city's main economic activities are non-oil trade, oil production and export, and, more recently, tourism.

Airport business centres

All passengers using Dubai International Airport can use these 24-hour facilities:

Airport International Hotel Business Centre *216 4278/ www.dubaiairport.com.* **Map** p297 L2.
24-hour facilities comprising five meeting rooms (capacity six to 18 people), one conference room (capacty 60 people), eight workstations, state-of-the-art communication systems, and full secretarial and support services.
Global Link *Departures level, near Gate 16, Terminal 1, Dubai International Airport (216 4014/ 216 4015/www.dubaiairport.com).* **Map** p297 L2.
This business centre at the airport provides passengers with six ISD booths, workstations, internet connection, fax and secretarial services.

Conference & exhibition organisers/office hire

With large halls and spacious showrooms readily available in all the major hotels, Dubai is able to handle any seminar, conference or trade exhibition. The city's comprehensive facilities can cater for everything from small meetings through to major international conventions.

Several public institutes have also been developed especially to host significant events, such as the **Dubai International Convention Centre** (332 1000, www.dwtc.com), which annually hosts GITEX, one of the top IT exhibitions in the world. Most of the city's hotels provide business facilities/venues with all the necessary support services. Otherwise, the **Dubai World Trade Centre** or DWTC (info@dwtc.com; www.dwtc. com) and **Dubai Chamber of Commerce & Industry** (DCCI) are two excellent points of contact if you're looking for services and recommendations.

Dubai Chamber of Commerce & Industry *Baniyas Road, on the Creek, Rigga, Deira (228 0000/*

www.dcci.gov.ae). **Open** 8am-4pm Sun-Thur. **Map** p299 K4.
The DCCI exhibition halls and auditoriums are large, flexible spaces developed to accommodate exhibitions, trade and social fairs, and new product launches.
Dubai International Financial Centre *Emirates Towers (362 2222/www.difc.ae).* **Open** 8am-6pm Sun-Thur. **Map** p298 H4.
The DIFC is an onshore capital market designated as a financial free zone. It's designed to offer financial services and to support new initiatives, with the focus on banking services, capital markets, asset management & fund registration, reinsurance, Islamic finance and back office operations.
Dubai World Trade Centre *Sheikh Zayed Road, near Za'abeel roundabout, Satwa (332 1000/ www.dwtc.com).* **Open** 8am-5pm Sun-Thur. **Map** p296 H4.
The DWTC incorporates the Dubai International Convention Centre. It comprises nine interconnected, air-conditioned exhibition halls covering 37,000sq m (14,285sq ft), which are available for lease either on an individual basis or in any combination of multiples.

Courier companies

The companies listed below provide freight-forwarding, domestic, logistical, catalogue packing and moving services. They also offer source and delivery services (meaning they will find what you want and deliver it). Open 24 hours a day, they can be contacted by telephone and internet. They all accept major credit cards. The UAE postal service, EMPOST, offers an express delivery service known as Mumtaz Express (*see p275*).

DHL *800 4004/www.dhl.com.*
FedEx *331 4216/www.fedex.com.*
TNT *800 4333/www.tnt.com.*

Hours

In 2006, the government working week changed from a Thursday/ Friday weekend to a Friday/ Saturday weekend. This was done to make the working week closer to that of the West. Although some people still have a Thursday/Friday weekend, most residents in the UAE either have a Friday/Saturday weekend or work a six-day week with only Friday off. Working hours

during the day can also vary, with a few firms still operating a split-shift system (normally 8am-noon and 4-8pm), although this is becoming increasingly rare.

Licences

The basic requirement for all business activity in Dubai is a licence (commercial/professional/ industrial) issued by the Dubai Department of Economic Development. To apply, contact the **Ministry of Economy and Commerce** on 295 4000, www.uae.gov.ae.

Sponsors

The regulation of branches and representatives of foreign companies in the UAE is covered in the Commercial Companies Law. This stipulates that companies may be 100 per cent foreign-owned providing a local agent (UAE national) is appointed. These agents will assist in obtaining visas in exchange for a lump sum or a profit-related percentage. The exceptions to this rule are the free zones, where no local sponsor is required.

Translation services

There are dozens of different communities in Dubai, covering many languages and dialects, but English is widely spoken, particularly in a business context. If you need something translated into Arabic you can try one of the following. (Note: none accepts credit cards.)

Eman Legal Translation Services *Room 104, 1st Floor, above Golden Fork Restaurant, Nasr Square, Deira (224 7066/ ets@emirates.net.ae).* **Open** 9am-6pm Sat-Wed; 9am-2pm Thur. **Map** p299 L3.
Ideal Legal Translation & Secretarial *Room 17, 4th Floor, above Al Ajami Restaurant, Al Ghurair Centre, Al Riwqa Street, Deira (222 3699/ideal@emirates. net.ae).* **Open** 8am-1pm, 3-7pm Sat-Wed; 8am-5pm Thur. **Map** p299 K3.
Lotus Translation Services *Room 411, 4th Floor, Oud Metha Office Building, Oud Metha Street, near Wafi Centre, Bur Dubai (324 4492/lotrnsrv@ emirates.net.ae).* **Open** 8.30am-1.30pm, 2-6pm Sun-Thur. **Map** p297 J3.

Useful organisations

American Business Council
*16th floor, Dubai World Trade
Centre, Sheikh Zayed Road (340
7566/www.abcdubai.com)*. **Open**
8am-5pm Sat-Thur. **Map** p301 G10.
British Business Group *BBG
Office, Conference Centre, British
Embassy, Al Seef Road (397 0303/
www.britbiz-uae.com)*. **Open**
8.30am-5.30pm Sun-Thur. **Map**
p299 J4.
**Department of Economic
Development** *DCCI Building,
Baniyas Road, Deira (222 9922/
www.dubaided.gov.ae)*. **Open**
7.30am-2.30pm Sun-Thur.
Map p299 K4.
**Dubai Chamber of Commerce
& Industry** *DCCI Building, next
to Sheraton Hotel, Baniyas Road,
Deira (228 0000/www.dcci.gov.ae)*.
Open 8am-4pm Sun-Thur.
Map p299 K4.

CONSUMER

Although people flock to Dubai to
shop, there are no statutory rights
to protect consumers, except the
right to recover the paid price on
faulty goods. However, unless you
are prepared to take it to court,
exchange is as far as many stores
will go. Tourists with consumer-
related problems and enquiries
can contact the **Department
of Tourism and Commerce
Marketing** (223 0000, www.
dubaitourism.ae). For complaints
about purchased items, the
**Emirates Society for
Consumer Protection** in
Sharjah (06 556 3888) may also
be able to assist, and the **Dubai
Economic Development
Office** (222 9922) will try to help
people who have problems with
expiry dates and warranties.

CUSTOMS

There is a duty-free shop in the
airport arrivals hall. Each person
is permitted to bring into the
UAE four litres of alcohol (be
they spirits or wine), two cartons
of beer, 400 cigarettes, 50 cigars
and 500g of tobacco. No customs
duty is levied on personal effects
entering Dubai. For more extensive
explanations on any duty levied
on particular products, see the
Dubai Airport website, which
has links to the Municipality site:
www.dubaiairport.com, or call
224 5555.
    The following are prohibited
in the UAE, and import of these
goods will carry a heavy penalty:
controlled substances (drugs),
firearms and ammunition,
pornography (including sex toys),
unstrung pearls, pork, raw seafood
and fruit and vegetables from
cholera-infected areas.
    For further information on
what you can and can't bring
into the country, call the Dubai
Customs hotline on 800 4410 or
check out www.dxbcustoms.gov.ae.

DISABLED

Generally speaking, Dubai is not
disabled-friendly. Although things
are improving, many places are
still not equipped for wheelchair
access. Most hotels have made
token efforts, but functionality
still plays second fiddle to design,
meaning that wheelchair facilities
have largely been swept under the
carpet. Those that do have some
specially adapted rooms include
the Burj Al Arab, Sofitel City Centre
Hotel, Crowne Plaza, Emirates
Towers, Hilton Dubai Creek, Hilton
Dubai Jumeirah, Hyatt Regency,
Jumeirah Beach Hotel, JW Marriott,
Oasis Beach Hotel, Madinat
Jumeirah, Ritz-Carlton Dubai,
Renaissance, One&Only Royal
Mirage and Sheraton Jumeirah.
    The airport and major shopping
malls have good access and
facilities, and some of the Dubai
Transport taxis (208 0808) are
fitted to accommodate wheelchairs.
There are designated disabled
parking spaces in nearly all of
the city's car parks; to use them
you'll need disabled window
badges, though many able-bodied
drivers fail to respect this.

DRUGS

Dubai adheres to a strict policy
of zero tolerance for drugs.
There are lengthy sentences and
harsh penalties for possession
of a non-legal substance, and there
have been several high-profile
cases of expatriates serving time
for such offences. Drug importation
carries the death penalty, although
no executions have been carried
out in the last few years. But
even association with users and
importers carries a stiff penalty.
For more information see the
Dubai Police website, online at
www.dubaipolice.gov.ae.

ELECTRICITY

Domestic supply is 220/240 volts
AC, 50Hz. Sockets are suitable for
three-pin 13 amp plugs of British
standard design; however, it is a
good idea to bring an adaptor with
you just in case. Adaptors can also
be bought very cheaply in local
supermarkets such as Carrefour or
Spinneys. Appliances purchased in
the UAE will generally have two-
pin plugs attached. For queries get
in touch with the Ministry of
Electricity on 262 6262.

EMBASSIES &
CONSULATES

For enquiries about visa, passport,
commercial and consular services
as well as press and public affairs,
contact your country's embassy or
consulate. In Dubai, they are
usually open 8.45am to 1.30pm from
Sunday to Thursday. If you need to
contact an official urgently, don't
despair; there is usually a number
on the embassy's answer service
for help outside working hours.
    Your embassy provides
emergency legal services (the stress
being on 'emergency', since it has
no authority over the UAE legal
system if you are caught breaking
the law), consular and visa services,
and educational information and
advice. For a list of all embassies in
Dubai log on to www.dwtc.com/
directory/governme.htm.
For embassies abroad visit
www.embassyworld.com.

Australia *1st floor, Emirates
Atrium Building, Sheikh Zayed
Road, between Interchange 1 & 2
(508 7100/www.austrade.gov.au)*.
Open 8am-3.30pm Sun-Wed;
8am-2.45pm Thur. **Map** p296 G5.
Canada *7th floor, Juma Al Bhaji
Building, Bank Street, Bur Dubai
(314 5555/www.canada.org.ae)*.
Open 8am-4pm Sun-Thur.
Map p299 J5.
France *18th floor, API World
Tower, Sheikh Zayed Road (332
9040/www.consulfrance-dubai.
org.ae)*. **Open** 8.30am-1pm, Sun-
Thur. *Visas* 8.30-11am Sat, Fri.
Map p301 G9.
India *Al Hamaria Diplomatic
Enclave, Consulate area, near
BurJuman Centre (397 1333/www.
cgidubai.com)*. **Open** 8am-1pm,
2-4.30pm Sun-Thur. **Map** p299 J5.
New Zealand *15th floor, API
Tower, Sheikh Zayed Road (331
7500/www.nzte.govt.nz)*. **Open**
8.30am-5pm Sun-Thur. **Map**
p301 G9.
Pakistan *Khalid bin Waleed Road,
near BurJuman Centre (397 3600)*.
Open 7.30am-noon Sun-Thur.
Map p299 J5.

DIRECTORY

Russia *Al Maktoum Street (223 1272).* **Open** 11am-1pm Sun-Wed; 10am-noon Thur. **Map** p299 J3.

South Africa *3rd floor, Dubai Islamic Bank Building, Bank Street, Bur Dubai (397 5222/www.south africa.ae).* **Open** 8am-4pm Sun-Thur. *Consular* 8.30am-12.30pm Sun-Thur. **Map** p299 J5.

United Kingdom *British Embassy Building, Al Seef Road, Bur Dubai (309 4444/www.britain-uae.org).* **Open** *Passports* 8am-1pm Sun-Thur (collection noon-1pm). *Visas* 7.30-11am Sun-Thur (collection 1-2pm). *General* 7.30am-2.30pm Sun-Thur. Hrs change during summer; call for details. **Map** p299 J4.

USA *21st floor, Dubai World Trade Centre, Sheikh Zayed Road (311 6000/www.dubai.usconsulate.gov).* **Open** (to public) 12.30-3pm Sun-Thur. **Map** p301 G9.

EMERGENCIES

For **police**, call 999; for **ambulance**, call 998 or 999; and for the **fire brigade**, call 997. The **coastguard** can be contacted on 345 0260; there is also a helicopter service. If you dial 999 or 282 1111, in an emergency Dubai Police will send a police helicopter, which they guarantee will be with you within eight minutes.

See also p275 **Police**; *below* **Health** for a list of hospitals.

GAY & LESBIAN

Homosexuality is, in effect, prohibited in the UAE and there are no gay cafés, bars or pubs. Although there is a small gay community in Dubai, it is not centralised around a specific region and there is no official gay presence in the city.

HEALTH

Dubai has well-equipped public and private hospitals. Emergency care for all UAE nationals, visitors and expatriates is free from the Al Wasl, New Dubai and Rashid hospitals. All other treatments are charged to tourists, so it's definitely advisable to have medical insurance as well as travel insurance.

The **General Medical Centre** (349 5959) on Jumeirah Beach Road is open 8am to 7pm Saturday to Wednesday and 8am to 1pm on Thursday. Should you require

further information call the **Ministry of Health** (MOH) on 306 6200 or the **Department of Health & Medical Services** (DOHMS) on 337 1160. Both are open during normal government hours, from Sunday to Thursday.

For people whose countries have a reciprocal medical agreement with the UAE, further treatments are available. Dubai hospitals are clean and safe.

Accident & emergency

All the hospitals below have 24-hour A&E departments, but only emergency cases at the A&E of public hospitals are seen free of charge.

Contraception & abortion

Most pharmacies prescribe contraception over the counter, with relatively few contraceptives requiring prescriptions. It is widely known (although officially illegal) that this includes the morning-after pill. The American Hospital has a Family Planning clinic (309 6877), and the Canadian Hospital (336 4444) offers consultation.

Abortion is illegal in the UAE unless recommended by a doctor who is concerned about the mother's survival. Written permission is needed from either the husband or guardian.

Dentists

Good dentists are readily available in Dubai, including orthodontists and cosmetic dentists, though prices can be hefty. For a 24-hour emergency dental service, phone 332 1444. **Dr Michael's Dental Clinic** (349 5900, www.drmichaels. com) and the **Scandinavian Dental Clinic** (349 3202) both come highly recommended.

Doctors

Most of the big hotels have in-house doctors, as do the majority of the hospitals. Alternatively, there is the **General Medical Centre** (349 5959), or you can ring your local embassy for its recommendations (*see p271* **Embassies & consulates**).

Hospitals

The three main Department of Health hospitals in Dubai are listed below. For more information, visit www.dohms.gov.ae.

Al Wasl Hospital *Oud Metha Road, south of Al Qataiyat Road, Za'abeel (324 1111/www.dohms. gov.ae).* **Map** p297 J3.

New Dubai Hospital *Opposite Hamria Vegetable Market, after Hyatt Regency Hotel, Deira (271 4444/www.dohms.gov.ae).* **Map** p298 H2.

Rashid Hospital *Oud Metha Road, near Al Maktoum Bridge, Bur Dubai (337 4000/A&E 219 1000/www.dohms.gov.ae).* **Map** p297 J2.

The following are five private hospitals in Dubai that have Accident & Emergency departments. Note that all private health care must be paid for, including emergency care. Hospitals are required to display price lists for all treatments at reception.

American Hospital Dubai *Off Oud Metha Road, between Lamcy Plaza & Wafi Centre, Al Nasr, Bur Dubai (336 7777/ www.ahdubai.com).* **Map** p297 J3.

Canadian Hospital *Ground Floor, Gulf Towers (336 4444).* **Map** p297 J3.

Emirates Hospital *Opposite Jumeirah Beach Park, next to Chili's restaurant, Jumeirah Beach Road, Jumeirah (349 6666/ www.emirateshospital.ae).* **Map** p302 A15. As well as an A&E facility, the Emirates Hospital has a 24-hr walk-in clinic (though you're required to pay Dhs200 for the first consultation).

Iranian Hospital *Corner of Al Hudeiba Road & Al Wasl Road, Satwa (344 0250/www.irhosp.ae).* **Map** p300 E9.

Welcare Hospital *Next to Lifco supermarket in Garhoud, Deira (282 7788/www.welcare hospital.com).* **Map** p297 K3.

Insurance

Public hospitals in Dubai will deal with emergencies free of charge. They have good facilities and their procedures (including the use of sterilised needles and the provision of blood transfusions) are reliable and hygienic.

Medical insurance is often included in travel insurance packages, and it is important to have it unless your country has a reciprocal medical treatment arrangement with the UAE. Although travel insurance typically covers health, it is wise to make sure you have a package that covers all eventualities, especially as for serious but non-emergency care you would need to attend a private hospital or clinic, where treatment can be expensive.

Opticians

See p181.

Pharmacies

There is no shortage of extremely well stocked and serviceable pharmacies in Dubai and no formal policy of prescription: all you need to know is the name of the drug you need. Normal opening hours are 8.30am to 1.30pm, 4.30pm to 10.30pm Saturday to Thursday and 4.30pm to 10.30pm Friday, but some open on Friday mornings as well. A system of rotation exists for 24-hour opening, with four chemists holding the fort at any one time for a week each. For a list of the 24-hour pharmacies on duty, check the back of the local newspapers or head online to www.dm.gov.ae.

Alternatively, you can call the DM Emergency Offices on 223 2323: they will be able to point you in the direction of the nearest pharmacy.

Prescriptions

Most drugs are available at the pharmacies without prescription. In rare instances when this isn't the case, pharmacists dispense medicines on receipt of a prescription from a GP.

STDs, HIV & AIDS

To secure residency in Dubai, you have to undergo a blood test and anyone identified as HIV positive is not allowed to stay in the country. Tourists do not have to be tested, but should you become ill and have to be hospitalised, expect to find yourself on the next plane out if tested positive for HIV. Despite there being no official figures, it's widely accepted that there is a genuine problem with sexually transmitted diseases, due in part to the large numbers of prostitutes working in the city.

Sunburn/dehydration

The fierce UAE sun means that heatstroke and heat exhaustion are always a risk, especially in summer. Sunglasses, hats and high-factor sun creams are essential, particularly for children, and the importance of drinking large quantities of water to stave off dehydration cannot be overemphasised.

Vaccinations

No specific immunisations are required for entry to Dubai, but it would be wise to check beforehand – a certificate is sometimes required to prove you are clear of cholera and yellow fever if you are arriving from a high-risk area. Tetanus inoculations are recommended if you are considering going on a long trip.

There are very few mosquitoes in the towns and cities, and since it's not considered to be a real risk, malaria tablets are rarely prescribed for travel in the UAE. If you are planning to camp near the mountains or explore wadis in the evening, cover up and use a suitable insect repellent. If in any doubt, consult your doctor before you travel to Dubai. Polio has been virtually eradicated in the UAE and hepatitis is very rare.

ID

ID is necessary for car hire as well as entry into bars and clubs if the bouncers don't think you look over 21. Passports are the most requested type, so have copies made in advance. Plans are well underway to issue all UAE residents with 'smart cards', which are set to replace all other forms of identification (including driving licences, and labour and health cards). Primarily introduced to increase the speed and efficiency of services and provide a population census, it will link to all government departments and carry personal information like the individual's blood group, fingerprints and other biological characteristics.

INSURANCE

Although the crime rate in Dubai is exceptionally low, it is still worth insuring yourself before you travel. Travel insurance policies usually cover loss or theft of belongings and medical treatment, but be careful to check what is included before you leave, and any clause that might be disputed, especially if you're intending to take part in activities like desert off-roading and scuba diving.

Car insurance will be covered by any creditable, authorised car hire company and anyone holding a valid licence should be able to get insurance. However, do check whether you are covered for insurance for the Sultanate of Oman. Since many parts of the UAE have a 'porous' border, you may find yourself driving within Oman without warning (the road to Hatta, for example, will take you through Oman in several places).

Medical insurance is often included in travel insurance packages and it is vital to have it, since health care in private hospitals can be extremely expensive. Emergency care is available free of charge at the government hospitals (*see p272* Health). Be careful to keep all your documents and receipts of any medical payments you make, as you will have to claim them back later. For a list of insurance companies, check out www.yellowpages.ae.

INTERNET

Dubai is leading the way in the global movement towards an electronic government. Not only is the internet often the most efficient way of finding useful information here, but you can now seemingly do everything online, from paying a traffic fine to reporting a lost licence.

The government organisation, Etisalat, controls the server and is the regulator of content. Consequently there is an element of censorship, with pornography, dating and gambling sites blocked, along with a few photography and social networking sites. If the network fails there can be no service at all for hours at a time, although thankfully this is uncommon. In the past, internet users in free zones have been able to bypass censorship, although this situation is expected to change in the near future so that nobody can bypass the proxy. VoIP (Voice over Internet Protocol) programmes, such as Skype, which allow you to make cheap or free calls over the internet, are illegal and cannot be accessed. You can contact Etisalat by dialling 101, or visit www.etisalat.com.

The EIM (Emirates Internet & Multimedia) kiosks provide public access to email, news and business information, enabling users to access the net from anywhere, irrespective of their

DIRECTORY

email provider. Kiosks can be found in airport waiting areas, shopping centres and hotel lobbies, and take various methods of payment. Costs range from Dhs5 to Dhs15 an hour. Most hotels have some form of internet access and there are net cafés dotted around the city. For a list of internet cafés, check out www.yellowpages.ae.

Al Jalssa Internet Café *Bur Dubai (351 4617).* **Cost** Dhs10/hr. **Map** p299 H5.
Coffee Bean Café *Aviation Club, Garhoud (282 4122).* **Cost** Dhs15/hr. **Map** p297 L3.
Dubai Cafe.net *Sheikh Zayed Road, near Emirates Towers (396 9111).* **Cost** Dhs10/hr. **Map** p296 H4.
Giga Planet Network Café *Garhoud, near International School (283 0303).* **Cost** Dhs5/hr. **Map** p297 K2.

LANGUAGE

Although Arabic is the UAE's official language, English is widely spoken and understood by nearly everybody. For some basic vocabulary, *see p280*.

LEFT LUGGAGE

There is a left-luggage storage facility at the airport. Costs are Dhs10 per bag per half day (12 hours) for a normal sized bag or Dhs15 per half day for an oversized bag.

LEGAL HELP

Dubai has strict laws, severe sentencing, no free legal aid and no equivalent of the Citizens Advice Bureau. Should you require legal help or advice, contact your country's embassy (*see p271* **Embassies & consulates**). Foreign embassies cannot override any law in the UAE and will not sympathise if you claim ignorance of those laws, but they can offer advice and support and give details of your legal status and options. Otherwise, contact the **Ministry of Justice** for advice on 295 0004.

The government has also set up a **Department for Tourist Security** (800 4438), whose purpose is to guide visitors through the labyrinth of the law and to liaise between tourists and the Dubai police. For a full list of law firms, see www.yellowpages.ae.

LIBRARIES

You must be a resident to borrow from Dubai's libraries, but most will be happy for you to browse or use the reading room, where there is usually a broad selection of English-language books. The **Dubai Municipality Central Library** allows the public to view its collections online, offering title searches, browsing and capability to reserve books from home. Dubai Municipality has launched its new **eLibrary**, which allows registered members to read hundreds of books, magazines and foreign newspapers online. The library can be contacted on 226 2788, or at www.libraries.ae.

DM Library *Al Ras Street, opposite St George Hotel, near Gold Souk, Al Ras (226 2788/www.libraries. ae).* **Open** 8am-9pm Sun-Thur. **Map** p298 G3.
Dubai Lending Library *International Arts Centre, opposite the mosque, Jumeirah Beach Road (337 6480).* **Open** 10am-noon, 4-6pm Sat-Thur. **Map** p300 D9.

LOST PROPERTY

A few years ago, theft in Dubai was extremely rare, but instances of bag snatching are becoming more common. If you are a victim of crime, contact the nearest police station or report it to the special **Tourist Police** unit (800 4438), necessary for the validation of your travel insurance claims.

If you lose something, most unclaimed items are taken to a general holding unit known as **Police Lost & Found**, which can be contacted on 216 2542.

If you have lost something on a bus or *abra*, call the public transport information line on 800 4848 and ask for Lost & Found. If you leave something in a taxi, get in touch with the relevant company (*see p267*). The **airport** has a contact number for lost baggage (224 5383 for all airlines). To minimise the aggravation of losing important documents, always make a copy. Should you lose your passport, report it immediately to the police and contact your embassy (*see p271* Embassies & consulates).

MEDIA

Despite the creation of Dubai Media City (complete with the slogan 'freedom to create'), the media in the UAE is still subject to government censorship, although direct clashes are rare as most organisations operate a policy of self-censorship. This means you'll never see anything that criticises the UAE royal families or the government, and there are no scenes of nudity in any films or TV programmes. Although censorship is becoming more relaxed in some areas (many references to alcohol and images of bikini-clad babes are now allowed), it is unrealistic to expect objective political coverage in local newspapers.

Most international publications are available here, although the black marker pen of the censors ensures that overtly sexual images are covered up.

Newspapers & magazines

There are four English language daily newspapers in Dubai: *Gulf News*, *Khaleej Times*, *Gulf Today* (Dhs2-Dhs3) and a free paper *7 Days* (Dubai's equivalent to London's *Metro*). All publish local and international news. *Gulf News* also publishes a free tabloid, *Xpress*, which comes out on Thursday. *The Times* and *The Sunday Times* are also available, although the Middle East editions are different to the UK version of the newspaper and they avoid subjects that might be considered to be sensitive in the region.

The city's magazine sector has become increasingly competitive in recent years and there is now a wealth of magazines published in Dubai. Monthly and weekly entertainment and listings magazines include *Time Out Dubai*, *What's On* and *Connector*. Lifestyle magazines include *Emirates Home*, *Viva* and *Identity* (interior decoration), *Ahlan!*, *OK Middle East* and *Grazia*.

There are free tourist magazines available in some hotels around Dubai, although most of them are of dubious quality.

Radio

Dubai has five English-language radio stations, featuring a mixture of British, Canadian and Australian DJs. Unfortunately, the quality of programming on them is generally pretty low, with an over-reliance on chart music, too many advertisements and plenty of opportunities for unsubtle product placement.

Channel 4 FM, 104.8 FM
Modern chart, dance and R&B.
City 101.6 FM
Part Hindi, part English.
Dubai Eye 103.8 FM
Bridges the gap between
conventional music and talk radio.
Dubai FM, 92.0 FM
Government-run station that
plays a mixture of older hits
and contemporary chart music.
Radio 1 FM, 100.5 FM
Modern chart, dance and R&B .
Radio 2 FM, 99.3 FM
Easy listening.

Television

The Dubai government runs the
English-language channel **Dubai
One**, which shows a mixture of
sitcoms, popular series and movies.
Most residents and hotels have a
satellite package of some form, with
Showtime and **Orbit** among the
most popular, thanks to offerings
like ShowMovies, BBC Prime and
the Discovery Channel. Over the
past couple of years, MBC has been
making big waves as a free service
with MBC's Channel 2 screening
films 24 hours a day and MBC4
showing the latest TV series from
the US. English Premiership
football is screened on Showtime's
ShowSports channel.

MONEY

The national currency is the
dirham. At the time of going to
press, UK£1 was equal to Dhs6.05.
The US$ has been pegged to the
dirham at a fixed rate of Dhs3.6725
since 1980. Bank notes come in
denominations of Dhs1,000 (silver),
Dhs500 (red), Dhs200 (blue), Dhs100
(red), Dhs50 (purple), Dhs20 (blue),
Dhs10 (green) and Dhs5 (brown).
There are Dhs1 coins and then 50,
25 and 10 fils, though you'll rarely
use these lower denominations.

ATMs

Visitors will have no problems
finding ATMs in Dubai. These are
in every major hotel and mall, and
on most of the busier streets. Most
credit cards and Cirrus- and Plus-
enabled cash cards are accepted.
Check with your personal bank
for charges for withdrawing
cash overseas.

Banks

There are a number of international
banks in the city such as HSBC,
Citibank, Standard Chartered and

Lloyds TSB, as well as locally
based operations such as the
National Bank of Dubai and
Dubai Islamic Bank. They offer
comprehensive commercial and
personal services and transfers,
and exchanges are simple.
    Bank opening hours are normally
8am to 1pm Sunday to Thursday
and 8am-noon Saturday. All banks
are shut on Fridays.

Bureaux de change

Rates vary and it's worth noting
that the airport is the first place
you can, but the last place you
should, change your money. There
are several money changers in the
city centre (Bur Dubai and Deira)
who tend to deal only in cash but
whose rates (sometimes without
commission) can challenge the
banks', particularly with larger
sums of money. Travellers' cheques
are accepted with ID in banks
and hotels and other licensed
exchange offices affiliated with the
issuing bank. There is no separate
commission structure but exchange
houses make their money on the
difference between the rates at
which they buy and sell.
    Below are some reliable bureaux
de change in the city:

Al Fardan *Al Fardan
Headquarters, Nasr Square,
Maktoum Street, next to Citibank,
Deira (228 0004/www.alfardan
exchange.com).* **Open** 8.30am-
8.30pm daily. **Map** p299 L3.
Al Ghurair *BurJuman Centre, Halid
Bin Walid Road, Bur Dubai (351
8895).* **Open** 10am-10pm Sat-Thur;
2-10pm Fri. **Map** p299 J5.
Thomas Cook Al Rostamani
*Next to Al Khajeel Hotel, Road 14,
Al Nasr Square, behind HSBC
bank, Deira (222 3564/www.
alrostamaniexchange.com).* **Open**
9am-9.30pm Sat-Thur; 4.30-9.30pm
Fri. **Map** p299 L4.
Phone this branch for details of the
company's other locations.
UAE Exchange Centre *Ground
floor, Mall of the Emirates (341
3132).* **Open** 10am-10pm Sun-Wed;
10am-midnight Thur-Sat. **Map**
p304 D2.
Wall St Exchange Centre *Near
Naif Police Station, Naif Road,
Deira (800 4871).* **Open** 8am-
10.30pm Sat-Thur; 8-11.30am,
2-10.30pm Fri. **Map** p299 J2.

Credit cards/cheques

All major credit cards are accepted
in the larger hotels, restaurants,

supermarkets and shops.
Acceptance of cheques is less
widespread. Bouncing cheques
is a criminal offence and can result
in heavy fines – even, in some
cases, a jail sentence.
    The UAE was slow to jump on
the debit card bandwagon and
no chip card service is available.
A handful of the bigger chain
stores accept Visa Electron and
Switch cards; always check with
individual retailers.

Tax

Famous for its absence of direct
taxation – meaning thousands
of expat workers enjoy tax-free
salaries – Dubai does have some
'hidden' taxes, such as the ten per
cent municipality tax included in
food and hospitality costs, and,
for those with a licence, a sales tax
on alcohol from off-licences (often
a steep 30 per cent). There is
no corporate tax except for
oil-producing companies and
foreign banks.

OPENING HOURS

The concept of the Saturday/
Sunday weekend doesn't apply
in the Middle East, since Friday
is the holy day for Muslims.
The weekends used to vary
enormously with people either
having a Thursday/Friday weekend
or a Friday/Saturday weekend.
In 2006, though, the government
working week changed to a Friday/
Saturday weekend, making a
more unified working week across
the UAE.
    Unfortunately, there are no
clear-cut rules when it comes to
retail outlets. The most common
shopping hours are 10am to 1pm
and 4pm to 9pm for stand-alone
stores, but shops in malls are open
10am to 10pm and often until
midnight on the weekends. The
main exception is Friday, when
some business don't open until
2pm or 4pm.

POLICE

In an emergency, call 999. If you
just want information, www.dubai
police.gov.ae is a good place to
start. If you want to report
something confidentially or think
you have witnessed something
illegal, there is a hotline (Al
Ameen Service) on 800 4888
or go to www.alameen.ae.
    For more on emergencies,
see p272.

DIRECTORY

DIRECTORY

POSTAL SERVICES

The Emirates post is run solely by Empost and works on a PO box system, although a postal delivery service is planned for the future. All mail in the UAE is delivered to centrally located post boxes via the Central Post Office. With Dhs220 per year and an email address you can apply for a personal PO box and will be notified by email when you receive registered mail or parcels. There is also a service that delivers parcels to your door for Dhs9.

Hotels will handle mail for guests and you can buy stamps at post offices, Emarat petrol stations, many supermarkets and greeting card shops. Shopping malls such as Deira City Centre, Lamcy Plaza and Mall of the Emirates have postal facilities. Delivery takes between two and three days within the UAE and from three to seven days for deliveries to Europe and the USA. The service can be irritatingly erratic, so don't be surprised if sending something to your home country takes a little longer than expected.

All postal enquiries can be directed to the Empost call centre on 600 599999, 8am to 8pm Saturday to Thursday. Alternatively, phone the Emirates Post Head Office on 262 2222, 7.30am to 2.30pm, Saturday to Wednesday.

Central Post Office *Za'abeel Road, Karama (337 1500/www. empostuae.com)*. **Open** 8am-11.30pm Sat-Wed; 8am-10pm Thur; 8am-noon Fri. **Map** p297 J3.

PROHIBITIONS

The law is very strict with regards to the consumption of alcohol (other than in a licensed venue or a private residence), illegal drugs, gambling and pornography. Israeli nationals are not allowed into the UAE; however, following a recent change in policy, other nationalities can now enter the UAE with an Israeli stamp in their passport.

RELIGION

Islam is the official religion of the United Arab Emirates. Around 16 per cent of the local population is Shi'a Muslim and the remainder Sunni Muslim. Dubai is the most multicultural and therefore most tolerant of the emirates and other

religions (except Judaism) are respected, but it is still a Muslim state. The faithful congregate five times a day to pray and you will hear the call to prayer being sung from local mosques all over Dubai.

Tourists need to be extra sensitive if they are visiting during Ramadan, the ninth month of the Muslim calendar, lasting approximately one month, when Muslims fast during daylight hours to fulfil the fourth pillar of Islam. Determined by the lunar calendar, the dates vary annually, moving forward by roughly 11 days each year. During this period, bars will not serve alcohol before 7pm and clubs are shut as no loud music or dancing is allowed. Eating, drinking or smoking in a public place during daylight hours is forbidden, though some restaurants erect screens to allow people to eat and drink in private. In 2010, Ramadan is expected to commence from around 11 August (depending on the sighting of the moon) for 30 days.

For details of how to behave, *see p269* **Attitude & etiquette** and *p278* **When to go**.

Owing to its relative tolerance, Dubai has a variety of Christian churches and Hindu temples. For details of places of worship, see www.yellowpages.ae. The list below is a guide to non-Muslim places of worship:

Church of Jesus Christ of Latter-day Saints *395 3883.*
Emirates Baptist Church International *349 1596.*
Holy Trinity Church *337 0247.*
International Christian Fellowship (ICF) *396 1284.*
New Covenant Church *335 1597.*
Saint Mary's Church *337 0087.*
United Christian Church of Dubai *344 2509.*

SAFETY & SECURITY

Although at odds with some perceptions of the Middle East, Dubai is actually one of the safest places in the world to visit. However, bag-snatching and pickpocketing do seem to be on the increase, so, as with other countries, be vigilant and don't leave your belongings unattended. The other problem issues tend to be restricted to areas such as money laundering that don't tend to impact directly on the tourist or resident.

Security is high, and most accommodation blocks and malls are well-manned by private guards.

Nevertheless, it is always a good idea for visitors to take out travel insurance, and to follow the normal precautions to safeguard themselves and their valuables during their visit.

STUDY

Dubai has developed an extensive and respected education system in only 30 years. UAE nationals enjoy very high standards of free education, whereas expats tend to send their offspring to private schools and colleges. There are more than 100 of these, catering for all nationalities.

If you wish to learn Arabic, there are a number of language centres in the city, by far the most popular of which is the Arabic Language Centre.

Arabic Language Centre
Dubai World Trade Centre, Sheikh Zayed Road (308 6036/info@dwtc. com). **Open** 8am-6pm Sun-Thur. **Map** p301 G10.
Arabic courses for all levels are held on a termly basis throughout the year.

TELEPHONES

The international dialling code for Dubai is 971, followed by the individual emirate's code: 04 for Dubai. Other area codes are Abu Dhabi 02, Ajman 06, Al Ain 03, Fujairah 09, Ras Al Khaimah 07 and Sharjah 06. For mobile phones the code is 050 or 055. Drop the initial '0' of these codes if dialling from abroad.

Operator services can be contacted on 100; directory enquiries are on 181 or 151 for international. Alternatively, consult the *Yellow Pages* online at www.yellowpages.ae, which in many cases can be quicker and less frustrating. To report a fault call 170.

Making a call

Local calls are very inexpensive and direct-dialling is available to 150 countries.

Cheap rates for international direct calls apply from 9pm to 7am and all day on Fridays and public holidays. Pay phones, both card- and coin-operated, are located throughout the UAE. To make a call within Dubai, dial the seven-digit phone number; for calls to other areas within the UAE, simply dial the area code followed by the

seven-digit phone number.
To make an international phone
call, dial 00, then the country code
(44 for UK; Australia 61; Canada 1;
the Republic of Ireland 353; New
Zealand 64; South Africa 27; USA 1;
France 33; India 91; Pakistan 92;
Russia 7), then the area code,
omitting the initial 0, followed
by the phone number.

Public telephones

There are plenty of public
telephones, which accept either
cash or phone cards. Phone cards
for local and international use are
available in two denominations
(Dhs25 or Dhs40) from most
Etisalat offices, supermarkets,
garages and pharmacies.
 Coin-operated phones take
Dhs1 and 50 fils coins.

Mobile telephones

Dubai has one of the world's
highest rates of mobile phone
usage and practically everyone
has at least one cellular phone. A
reciprocal agreement exists with
over 60 countries allowing GSM
international roaming service for
other networks in the UAE. There
is also a service (Wasel) that
enables temporary Etisalat SIM
cards (and numbers) lasting 60
days (or until your Dhs300 credit
runs out) for use during your trip
if your network is not covered, or
if you do not have a GSM phone.
Calls are charged at local rates
with good network coverage.
See p273 Internet.

TIME

The UAE is GMT+4 hours, and
has no seasonal change of time.
So, for instance, if it is noon in
London (winter time), it is 4pm
in Dubai; after British clocks move
forwards for BST, noon is 3pm
in Dubai.

TIPPING

Hotels and restaurants usually
include a ten to 15 per cent
service charge in their bills;
if not, adding ten per cent is normal
if not obligatory. Unfortunately,
this inclusive charge usually goes
straight to the restaurant and
rarely reaches the pockets of
the people who served you, so
if you're particularly impressed
by the standards of service you've
encountered, you will need to tip in
addition to the inclusive total.

It is common to pay taxi drivers
a small tip, just rounding up the
fare to the nearest Dhs5 being
the norm. For other services
(supermarket baggers, bag carriers,
petrol pump attendants, hotel
valets) it is usual to give at least
a couple of dirhams.

TOILETS

There are well-kept free public
toilets in malls and parks, and
most hotels will let you use their
facilities free of charge. Petrol
stations have conveniences but
their condition varies. Toilets in
souks and bus stations are usually
for men only, and are often
unfamiliar to Western visitors –
a simple squat toilet set in the
floor, with no seat or toilet rolls.

TOURIST INFORMATION

The Department of Tourism &
Commerce Marketing (DTCM)
is the government's sole regulating,
planning and licensing body for
the tourism industry in Dubai.
It has information centres around
the city, the most immediately
useful being in the airport arrivals
lounge (224 5252). Its one-stop
information centres aim to answer
any visitor queries, provide maps,
tour guides and hotel information,
as well as business and conference
advice. Most of the larger shopping
malls have their own centres
providing visitor information.

**Department of Tourism &
Commerce Marketing** *10th-12th
Floors, National Bank of Dubai
Building, Baniyas Road, Deira
(223 0000/www.dubaitourism.ae).*
Open 7.30am-2.30pm Sat-Wed.
Map p299 K4.

VISAS & IMMIGRATION

Visa regulations are liable to
change, so it is always worth
checking with your travel agent
or with the UAE embassy in your
home country before leaving.
Overstaying on your visa can
result in detention and fines
(a penalty charge of Dhs100 per
day that you're over). Nationals
of Israel are not permitted to enter
the UAE. Your passport must have
at least two months (in some cases,
six) before expiry for you to be
granted admission into the UAE,
so check before booking your flight.
Nationals of the following countries
will not need to obtain a visa
before travelling to Dubai or the

UAE; they will receive it upon
arrival at the airport.

Americas Canada, USA.
Asia Brunei, Hong Kong, Japan,
Malaysia, Singapore, South Korea.
**GCC (Gulf Cooperation Council)
countries** Bahrain, Kuwait, Oman,
Qatar, Saudi Arabia, UAE.
Oceania Australia, New Zealand.
UK Citizens of the UK will be
granted a free visit visa on arrival
in the UAE: passports will be
stamped with the visa as you pass
through immigration at any airport
in the UAE. Although the visa is
usually stamped for 30 days, it
entitles the holder to stay in the
country for 60 days and may be
renewed once for an additional
period of 30 days for a fee of
Dhs500.
Western Europe Andorra,
Austria, Belgium, Denmark,
Finland, France, Germany, Greece,
Iceland, Ireland, Italy,
Liechtenstein, Luxembourg,
Monaco, the Netherlands, Norway,
Portugal, San Marino, Spain,
Sweden, Switzerland, Vatican City.

To establish or confirm the
permitted duration of your stay,
you should contact the UAE
embassy or consulate in your
country at the addresses below.
Failing that, the contacts given
in Travel advice (*see p269*)
will keep you up to date with
the latest visa requirements –
which seem prone to regular,
unannounced changes.

UAE embassies abroad

Australia *12 Bulwarra Close,
O'Malley ACT 2606, Canberra,
Australia (2-6286 8802).* **Open**
9am-3.30pm Mon-Fri.
Canada *45 O'Connor Street,
Suite 1800, World Exchange
Plaza, Ottawa, Ontario, K1P 1A4
(613 565 7272/safara@uae-
embassy.com/www.uae-embassy.
com).* **Open** 9am-4pm Mon-Fri.
France *3, Rue de Lota, 75116
Paris (4553 9404).* **Open** 9am-4pm
Mon-Fri.
India *EP 12 Chandra Gupta
Marg, Chanakyapuri, New Delhi
110021 (687 2822).* **Open** 9am-
3pm Sun-Thur.
Pakistan *Plot No.122, University
Road, Diplomatic Enclave, PO
Box 1111, Islamabad, Pakistan
(227 9052).* **Open** 9am-3pm
Sun-Thur.
Russia *Ulofa Palme Street,
4 Moscow – CIS (2374060).*
Open 9am-4pm Mon-Fri.

DIRECTORY

South Africa *980 Park Street, Arcadia 0083, Pretoria, South Africa (342 7736/9).* **Open** 9am-5pm Mon-Fri.
UK & Republic of Ireland *30 Prince's Gate, London SW7 1PT (020 7581 1281/embcommer@cocoon.co.uk).* **Open** 9am-3pm Mon-Fri. *Visa section* 9am-noon Mon-Fri.
USA *3522 International Court, NW Washington DC, 20008 (202 243 2400/New York office 212 371 0480).* **Open** 9am-4pm Mon-Fri.

Multiple-entry visas

Multiple-entry visas are available to business visitors who have a relationship with a multinational company or other reputable local business, and who are frequent visitors to the UAE. This type of visa is valid for six months from date of issue and the duration of each stay is 30 days. Validity is non-renewable. The cost of such a visa is Dhs1,000. The visitor must enter the UAE on a visit visa and obtain the multiple entry visa while in the country. The visa is stamped in the passport.

96-hour visa for transit passengers

As a way of promoting Dubai's city tours, passengers who stop at Dubai International Airport for a minimum of five hours are eligible for a 96-hour transit visa which enables them to go into the city for that period of time. Passengers wanting to find out about this are advised to go to the Emirates Airport Services Desk in the airport arrivals hall prior to immigration to make a booking for one of the several tours on offer. You need a copy of your hotel booking (fax or email printout). The visa is US$50. This visa is available only to people travelling onwards from Dubai and not returning to their original country of departure.

WATER & HYGIENE

The tap water in Dubai comes from desalination plants, and although technically drinkable, it doesn't taste great. Most people choose to buy their drinking water, which costs only Dhs1-Dhs2 for a litre bottle; but do be wary of the ridiculous mark-ups at certain bars and restaurants. Outside Dubai, avoid drinking water from the tap – you might even want to use bottled water for brushing your teeth.
Standards of food hygiene are

extremely high in Dubai, though caution should be shown if trying some of the smaller roadside diners. If in doubt, avoid raw salads and *shawarmas* (meat cooked on a spit and wrapped in flatbread). Outside the city limits, milk is often unpasteurised and should be boiled. Powdered or tinned milk is available, but make sure it is reconstituted with pure water. You may also want to avoid dairy products, which are likely to have been made from unboiled milk.

WEIGHTS & MEASURES

The UAE uses the metric system, but UK- and US-standard weights and measures are understood.

WHAT TO TAKE

Lightweight summer clothing is ideal in Dubai, with just a wrap, sweater or jacket for cooler winter nights and venues that have fierce air-conditioning. The dress code in the UAE is generally casual, though guests in the more prestigious hotels such as the Ritz-Carlton and the Royal Mirage do tend to dress more formally in the evening. Since you are visiting a Muslim country, bikinis, swimming costumes, shorts and revealing tops should be confined to hotel beach resorts. Bars and clubs are really no different from those in the West, with tans shown off to the max. That said, visitors should dress conservatively when travelling to and from these venues. With such a wealth of shopping facilities, including some of the world's largest malls, there is precious little you can't get hold of in Dubai. Visitors can't buy alcohol from off-licences – so be sure to stock up at Dubai Duty Free when you arrive at the airport.

WHEN TO GO

Climate

Straddling the Tropic of Cancer, the UAE is warm and sunny in winter and hot and humid during the summer months. Winter daytime temperatures average a very pleasant 24°C, though nights can be relatively cool: perhaps 12-15°C on the coast and less than 5°C in the heart of the desert or high in the mountains. Local north-westerly winds (*shamals*) frequently develop during the winter, bringing cooler windy conditions as well as occasional sandstorms.

Summer temperatures reach the mid-40s, but can be higher inland. Humidity in coastal areas averages between 50 and 60 per cent, reaching over 90 per cent in summer – even the sea offers no relief as the water temperature can reach 37°C. Rainfall in Dubai is sparse and intermittent. In most years it rains during the winter months, usually in February or March. Winter rains take the form of short, sharp bursts and the very occasional thunderstorm. Generally appearing over the mountains of the south and east of the country, these rumbling cloudbursts can give rise to flash floods, but on average rain falls only about five days in a year.

In terms of when to go, you really can't go wrong if you visit any time between November and March, as you're virtually guaranteed beautiful weather every day. June to September can be unbearably hot and humid during the day, although hotel bargain deals can still make it an attractive proposition. Also bear in mind when Ramadan is taking place.

Public holidays

There are two kinds of public holidays: those that are fixed in the calendar, and those religious days that are determined by the lunar calendar and therefore vary from year to year. The precise dates are not announced until a day or so before they occur, based on local sightings of phases of the moon.
The fixed dates areas follows:

New Year's Day 1 Jan
Mount Arafat Day 11 Jan
Accession of HH Sheikh Zayed as Ruler of the UAE 6 Aug
UAE National Day 2 Dec

The variable dates are as follows:

Eid Al Adha a three-day feast to mark the end of the haj pilgrimage to Mecca
Ras al-Sana the start of Islamic New Year
Mawlid al-Nabi the prophet Mohammed's birthday
Lailat al Mi'raj the accession day of the Prophet Mohammed
Eid Al Fitr three days marking the end of Ramadan.

WOMEN

The cultural differences between locals and expats in Dubai are obvious, and the traditional advice for women in any big city – catch taxis if you're unsure about the area, don't walk alone at night and so on – should still be heeded, but all women here tend to enjoy a high standard of personal safety. Wearing revealing clothing in a public place will attract stares, some of simple condemnation and others of a more lascivious nature. That said, physical harassment is rare, as the local police are swift to act against offenders.

The traditional *abaya* (long black robe) and *sheyla* (head scarves) worn by Emirati women are less and less seen on younger women, who tend to wear Western-style clothes in the city. The metal face masks (*burkha*) are now largely reserved for the more conservative women in rural areas. This development in itself goes some way to illustrate the changing roles of women in the UAE. With the advent of an education system available to women (female students now outnumber male) and the government's active encouragement of women in the workplace, attitudes have clearly changed.

Dubai International Women's Club (DIWC) *Opposite Mercato Mall, Beach Road, Jumeirah (344 2389).* **Open** 8am-5pm Sat-Thur. **Map** p302 C12.
This is a social club with around 150 members, which meets four times a month. The club organises charity events, not only in Dubai but also overseas.
International Business Women's Group *345 2282/ www.ibwgdubai.com.*

The IBWG is an organisation for women in the business world, and meets on a monthly basis to exchange ideas and offer advice. Call or check the website for details of forthcoming meetings. Alternatively, you can log onto www.expatwoman.com for advice and information on meeting other female expats.

WORKING IN DUBAI

Dubai holds many attractions for prospective newcomers, especially the enticing tax-free salaries. If you are considering working in Dubai, it is worth visiting first to get a feel for the lie of the land. Dubai is a relatively small business community, so even a week's worth of well-planned networking can be fruitful in terms of making contacts – there is a real 'who you know' attitude here, so come armed with your best first impressions and plenty of friendly pushiness.

There are also several employment agencies and recruitment consultants online to help you; try www.yellowpages. ae for a full list of Dubai-based work agencies. Although UK-based recruitment organisations can be hit and miss, companies like the South African-based www. ananzi.co.za and local giant www.bayt.com have earned themselves sound reputations.

To be able to work in Dubai, either an employer must sponsor you or your spouse must do so. If you managed to secure employment from home, the process of becoming a fully-fledged

Dubaian is a little smoother, but it can still take some time. New recruits generally arrive on a 60-day visit visa. This entitles you to work for the stipulated period, while your employer gets the residency ball rolling with the Immigration Department. It's advisable to have several copies of your passport as well as plenty of passport photos for the numerous forms. Your employer should provide a comprehensive list of the paperwork required – check before you fly out in case you need to bring original education certificates or other proofs of qualification.

In order to gain residency in Dubai you'll also need to pass tests for HIV/AIDS, hepatitis and other infectious diseases. It is fairly standard to be offered extra medical insurance as part of your package, but once you have received your health card you are entitled to use any of the public hospitals in Dubai. Health Cards need to be renewed every year, residency visas and labour cards only every three years. For further general information and advice about setting up in business in Dubai, visit www.ameinfo.com. *See p269* **Business**.

Dubai Naturalisation & Residency Administration (DNRA) *Trade Centre Road, near Bur Dubai Police Station, Bur Dubai (398 0000/www.dnrd. gov.ae).* **Open** 7.30am-7.30pm Sun-Thur. **Map** p301 H8.
The DNRA presides over procedures and laws related to expatriate entry and residence in the United Arab Emirates (including tourist visas).

THE LOCAL CLIMATE

Average temperatures, humidity and rainfall in Dubai.

	High (°C/°F)	Low (°C/°F)	Max Humidity (%)	Rainfall (mm/in)
January	23 / 73	14 / 58	90	12 / 0.5
February	23 / 74	15 / 59	89	19 / 0.7
March	27 / 80	17 / 63	85	12 / 0.5
April	31 / 88	21 / 69	83	4 / 0.1
May	36 / 97	24 / 76	80	0 / 0
June	38 / 100	27 / 80	85	0 / 0
July	39 / 103	29 / 85	80	1 / 0
August	39 / 103	30 / 86	82	0 / 0
September	38 / 100	27 / 81	85	0 / 0
October	34 / 93	23 / 74	87	1 / 0
November	30 / 86	19 / 67	86	2 / 0
December	25 / 77	16 / 61	88	18 / 0.7

For links to see the latest satellite images of the weather conditions in the Middle East and Europe, go to http://www.uaeinteract.com/uaeint_misc/weather/index.asp.

Further Reference

DIRECTORY

LANGUAGE

Arabic is the official language of
Dubai, and Urdu and Hindi are also
widely spoken and understood,
but English is the predominant
spoken language.

Some basic words and phrases
are given below in phonetics.
Capitals are not used in Arabic,
but are used below to indicate hard
sounds. With Arabic possessing so
many different dialects and sounds
from English, transliterating is
never easy. We've opted to go for
a mainly classical option.

Basic vocabulary

hello *marhaba*
how are you? *kaif il haal?*
good morning *sabaah il khayr*
good evening *masaa' il khayr*
greetings *'as-salamu 'alaykum*
welcome *'ahlan wa sahlan*
goodbye *ma' 'is-salaama*
excuse me *afwan*
sorry *'aasif*
yes *na'am*
no *laa*
God willing *insha'allah*
please (to a man) *min fadlak*
 (to a woman) *min fadlik*
thank you (very much)
 shukran (jazeelan)
I don't know *lasto adree* or
 laa 'a-arif
who? *man?*
what? *matha?*
where? *ayina?*
why? *lematha?*
how much? (cost) *bekam?*
how many? *kam?*

Numbers

zero *sifr*
one *waahid*
two *itnain*
three *talata*
four *arba'a*
five *khamsa*
six *sitta*
seven *sab'a*
eight *tamanya*
nine *tis'a*
ten *'ashra*

Days & times

Sunday *al-ahad*
Monday *al-itnayn*
Tuesday *al-talata*
Wednesday *al-arba'a*
Thursday *al-khamees*
Friday *al-jum'a*
Saturday *al-Sabt*
hour *sa'aa*
day *yom*
month *shahr*
year *sanah*
today *al yom*
yesterday *ams/imbarah*
tomorrow *bukra*

Getting around

airport *matar*
post office *maktab al barid*
bank *bank*
passport *jawaz safar*
luggage *'aghraad*
ticket *tath karah*
taxi *taxi*
car *say-yarra*
city *madina*
street *share'h*
road *tareeq*

BOOKS

For a more detailed list of Arabic
authors and bookshops, visit
www.uaeinteract.com.

Frauke Heard-Bay *From Trucial
States to United Arab Emirates*
In 1971, the seven sheikdoms at
the southern end of the Gulf, the
Trucial States, formed the state
of the United Arab Emirates; it
was soon a member of the UN,
OPEC and the Arab League. This
academic volume examines
the historical and social movements
that have shaped the present-
day UAE.
Denys Johnson-Davies (transl),
Roger MA Allen (ed)
Arabic Short Stories
A charming and insightful set
of tales from the Middle East.
Alan Keohane
Bedouin: Nomads of the Desert
This photographic portrait pays
tribute to the tribal customs that
survive among those who continue
their annual journey across the
desert. It's a very timely reminder
of the importance of preserving
the UAE's ancient traditions.
TE Lawrence *Seven Pillars
of Wisdom: A Triumph*
The extraordinary account, by
Lawrence of Arabia himself, of the
war of the tribes against the Turks.

Edward Said *Reflections on
Exile & Other Essays*
Powerfully blending political and
aesthetic concerns, Said's writings
have revolutionised the field of
literary studies.
Freya Stark *A Winter in Arabia:
A Journey through Yemen*
There were a number of great
travellers and adventurers in
the 1930s, but Freya Stark was
unusual in being a woman. This
is here account of the peoples
and tribes of the Yemen.
Wilfred Thesiger *Arabian Sands*
One of the classic travel books.
Thesiger recounts the time he spent
with the Bedouin, and their travels
across the Empty Quarter of Saudi
Arabia in the days before 4x4s
and air-conditioning.

MAGAZINES

For the top events, meal deals
and local listings, pick up a copy
of *Time Out Dubai*. Free listings
magazines are also distributed at
various malls.

TRAVEL

Dubai Explorer publishes useful
maps, including *Off Road Explorer*
and *Underwater Explorer*.

UAE Yellow Pages

www.uae-ypages.com
Full of local listings.

WEBSITES

www.timeoutdubai.com
www.timeoutabudhabi.com
Insider's glimpses of what's
happening when and where.
www.uaeinteract.com
Website of the Ministry of
Information & Culture, with
information on the UAE.
www.dubaitourism.co.ae
General tourist information.

Transport

www.dubaiairport.com
News from Dubai International
Airport.
www.dpa.co.ae
Messages about water transport
from the Dubai Ports Authority.
www.rta.ae
Bus timetables and schedules.

Index A-Z

Note: page numbers given in **bold** indicate section(s) giving key information on a topic: those in *italics* indicate images.

INDEX

INDEX

INDEX

Advertisers' Index

Please refer to the relevant pages for contact details.

Make the most of London life

Maps

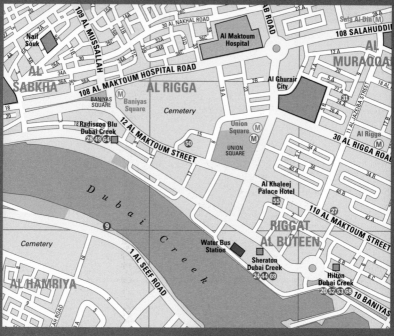

Major sight or landmark		
Railway stations		
Parks		
Hospitals		
Metro stations	Ⓜ Ⓜ	
Area name	**AL RAS**	

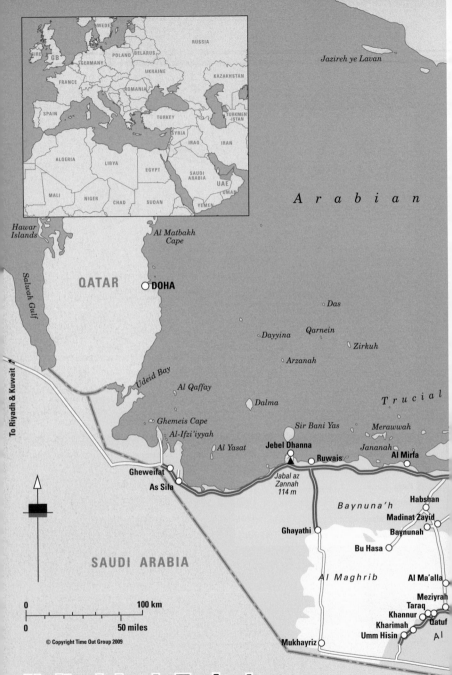

Jazireh ye Lavan

A r a b i a n

Al Matbakh
Cape

Hawar
Islands

Salwah Gulf

QATAR ○ **DOHA**

Das ○

Dayyina ○   Qarnein ○

Zirkuh ○

Arzanah ○

T r u c i a l

Udeid Bay

Al Qaffay ○

To Riyadh & Kuwait

Dalma ○

Ghemeis Cape ○

Merawwah

Sir Bani Yas

Al-Ifzi'iyyah ○

Al Yasat ○   **Jebel Dhanna**   Jananah

Ruwais ○   **Al Mirfa** ○

Gheweifat ○

As Sila ○   Jabal az
Zannah
114 m   **Habshan** ○

B a y n u n a ' h

Madinat Zayid ○

Ghayathi ○   **Baynunah** ○

Bu Hasa ○

SAUDI ARABIA   A l   M a g h r i b   **Al Ma'alla** ○

Meziyrah ○

Taraq

Khannur ○   **Qatuf** ○

Kharimah ○   Al

0   100 km   **Umm Hisin** ○

0   50 miles

© Copyright Time Out Group 2009   **Mukhayriz** ○

United Arab Emirates

Whatever your carbon footprint, we can reduce it

For over a decade we've been leading the way in carbon offsetting and carbon management.

In that time we've purchased carbon credits from over 200 projects spread across 6 continents. We work with over 300 major commercial clients and thousands of small and medium sized businesses, which rely upon our market-leading quality assurance programme, our experience and absolute commitment to deliver the right solution for each client.

Why not give us a call?

T: London (020) 7833 6000

Street Index

STREET INDEX

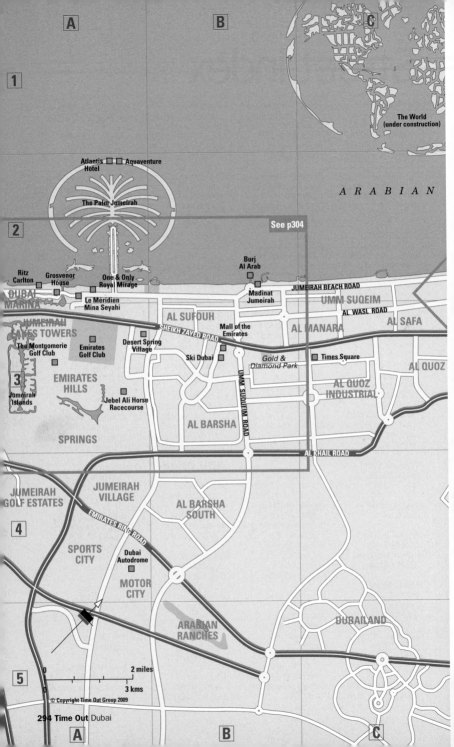

A B C

1

The World
(under construction)

ARABIAN

Atlantis □ □ Aquaventure
Hotel

The Palm Jumeirah

2

See p304

Burj
Al Arab □

Ritz
Carlton □
Grosvenor
House □
One & Only
Royal Mirage

Madinat
Jumeirah

JUMEIRAH BEACH ROAD

DUBAI
MARINA

Le Méridien
Mina Seyahi

AL SUFOUH

UMM SUQEIM

AL WASL ROAD

AL SAFA

JUMEIRAH
LAKES TOWERS

SHEIKH ZAYED ROAD

Mall of the
Emirates

AL MANARA

The Montgomerie
Golf Club □

Emirates
Golf Club □

Desert Spring
Village

Ski Dubai □

Gold &
Diamond Park

□ Times Square

AL QUOZ

3

EMIRATES
HILLS

AL QUOZ
INDUSTRIAL

Jumeirah
Islands

Jebel Ali Horse
Racecourse

AL BARSHA

UMM SUQEIM ROAD

SPRINGS

AL KHAIL ROAD

JUMEIRAH
GOLF ESTATES

JUMEIRAH
VILLAGE

AL BARSHA
SOUTH

4

EMIRATES RING ROAD

SPORTS
CITY

Dubai
Autodrome □

MOTOR
CITY

DUBAILAND

ARABIAN
RANCHES

5

0   2 miles
0   3 kms
© Copyright Time Out Group 2009

A B C

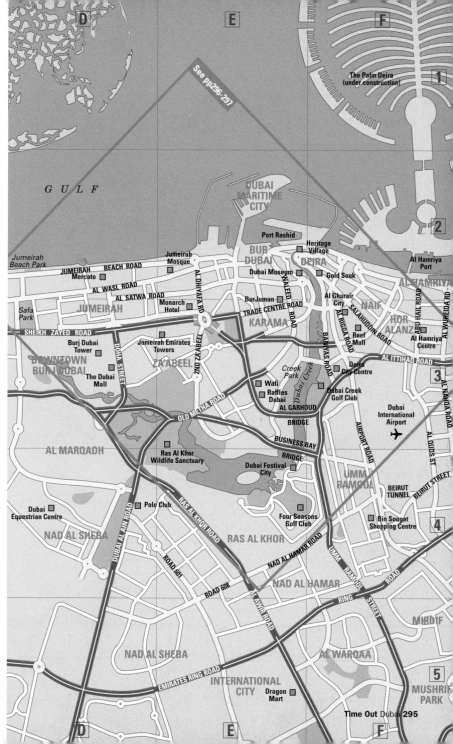

F

0   2 km

0   1 mile

© Copyright Time Out Group 2009

❶ Hotels pp86-109
❶ Restaurants & Cafés pp110-142
❶ Pubs & Bars pp143-152

ARABIAN

GULF

G

Port
Rashid

Dubai
Maritime
City

AL DAGHAYA

AL SHINDAGHA

AL MINA

*Dubai
Dry Docks*

See pp300-301

AL HUDAIBA

Dubai Marine Beach
Resort & Spa

AL BADA'A

Dubai Zoo

See pp302-303

JUMEIRAH

AL SATWA

Towers Rotane
Hotel

Jumeirah
Beach
Park

AL WASL

JUMEIRAH

BEACH ROAD

Safa Park

AL SAFA ROAD

AL WASL ROAD

Al Safa Complex
(Park'n'Shop)

Metropolitan
Hotel

296 Time Out Dubai

F

G

H

See pp298-299

AL KHALEEJ ROAD

AL SOUQ
AL KABEER

AL
RAS

AL RAFFA

AL MANKHOOL ROAD

MANKHOOL

AL ADHID ROAD

AL MINA ROAD

AL DHIYAFHA

ROAD

AL
KIFAF

2ND ZA'ABEEL RD

Trade
Centre

Fairmont
Dubai

Dubai International
Convention Centre

Jumeirah Emirates
Towers
60 114 129
131 29 34 36
43

Dubai International
Financial Centre

Dusit Dubai

Al Murooj
Rotana

RAS AL KHOR ROAD (E 44)

SHEIKH ZAYED ROAD (E 11)

Burj Dubai

Souk al Bahar
The Palace

The Dubai Mall
28 39 62 82 30
The Address
57 19 33

Al Manzil
68 122

Qamardeen

AL MARQADH

H

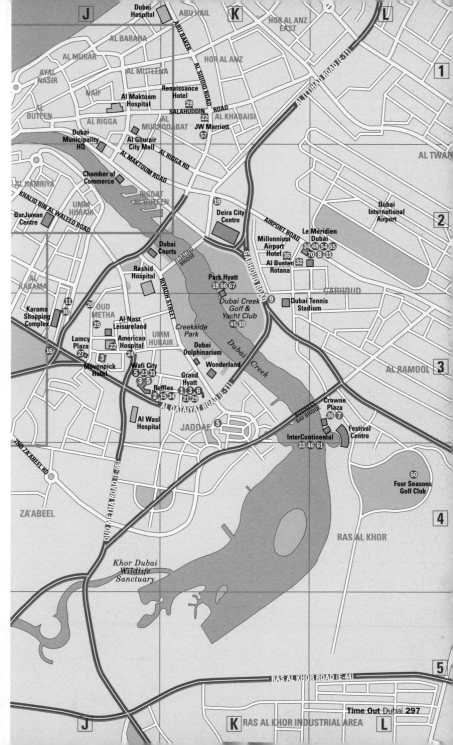

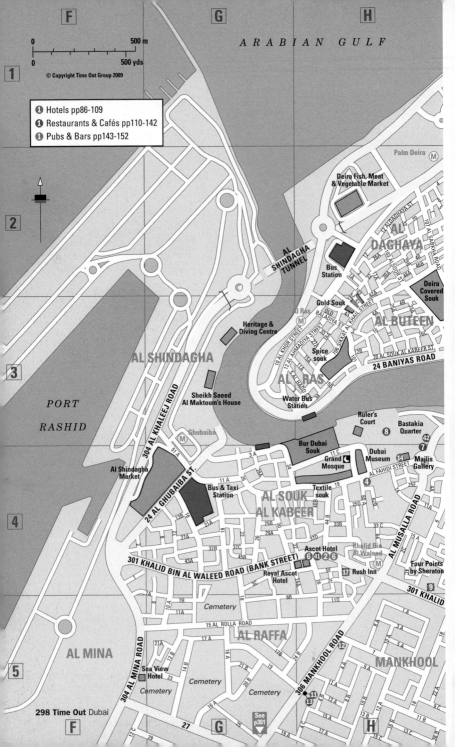

F **G** **H**

ARABIAN   GULF

1

0 _____ 500 m
0 _____ 500 yds
© Copyright Time Out Group 2009

❶ Hotels pp86-109
❶ Restaurants & Cafés pp110-142
❶ Pubs & Bars pp143-152

Palm Deira Ⓜ

Deira Fish, Meat
& Vegetable Market

AL
DAGHAYA

2

AL
SHINDAGHA
TUNNEL

Bus
Station

Deira
Covered
Souk

AL BUTEEN

Heritage &
Diving Centre

Al Ras Ⓜ

Gold Souk

AL SHINDAGHA

Spice
souk

AL RAS

24 BANIYAS ROAD

3

Sheikh Saeed
Al Maktoum's House

Water Bus
Station

Ruler's
Court

Bastakia
Quarter

Ghubaiba Ⓜ

PORT

RASHID

Bur Dubai
Souk

⑧

42
7

Al Shindagha
Market

Grand
Mosque

Dubai
Museum

14

Majlis
Gallery

AL FAHIDI STREET

④

Bus & Taxi
Station

AL SOUK
AL KABEER

Textile
souk

24 AL GHUBAIBA ST.

4

301 KHALID BIN AL WALEED ROAD (BANK STREET)

Ascot Hotel

⑥④①②⑥

Khalid Bin
Al Waleed Ⓜ

Four Points
by Sheraton

Royal Ascot
Hotel

⑰ Rush Inn

9

301 KHALID

AL MUSALLA ROAD

Cemetery

15 AL ROLLA ROAD

AL RAFFA

⑫

MANKHOOL

5

AL MINA

Sea View
Hotel

Cemetery

Cemetery

306 MANKHOOL ROAD

⑪
⑬

See
p301

304 AL MINA ROAD

298 Time Out Dubai

F **G** **H**

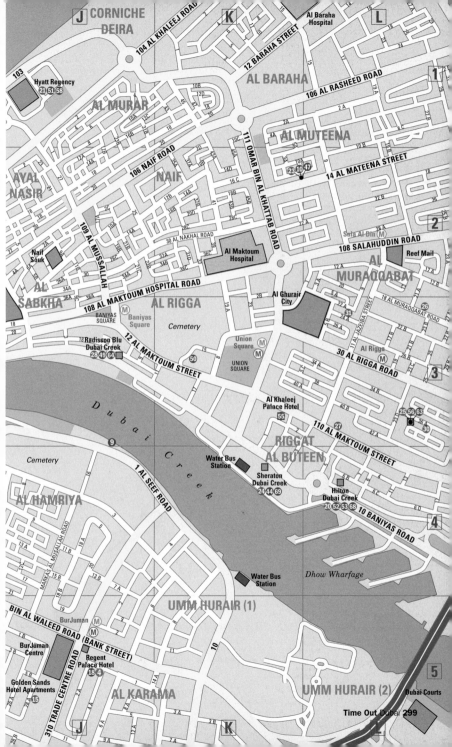

6

*Dubai
Dry Dock*

AL MINA

0   500 m

0   500 yds

© Copyright Time Out Group 2009

❶ Hotels pp86-109
❶ Restaurants & Cafés pp110-142
❶ Pubs & Bars pp143-152

7

304 AL MINA ROAD

Capitol Hotel **7**

305 AL DHIYAFHA RD

A R A B I A N

G U L F

8

10
❶
Jumeirah
Rotana Dubai

5 A

10 A

15 A

3 A

JUMEIRAH (1)

AL BADA'A

7 A

5 B

30 B

13 A

Dubai Marine Beach
Resort & Spa

39 74
16 17

Palm Strip

Jumeirah
Mosque

13 B

15

17 B

21 A

*Dubai Open
Beach*

77

21 B AL HUDAIBA ROAD

23 C

Iranian
Mosque

23

9

Magrudy Centre

12 B

23

84

Iranian
Hospital

25

306 AL SATWA ROAD

The Village

Jumeirah
Centre

302 JUMEIRAH BEACH ROAD

Jumeirah
Plaza

304 AL WASL ROAD

29 A

8 B

29

27 B

31

31 B

33 B

6 B

35 A

37 A

35 B

Beach
Centre Mall

39 B

37

35 B

39

41

45 A

10

Sheikh Mohammed Centre
for Cultural Understanding

47

49

51

53

See
p303
▼

Dubai Zoo

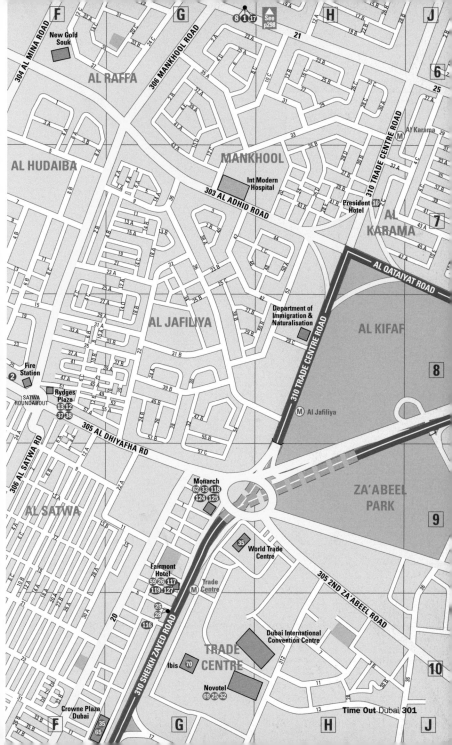

0 — 500 m
0 — 500 yds
© Copyright Time Out Group 2009

11

① Hotels pp86-109
① Restaurants & Cafés pp110-142
① Pubs & Bars pp143-152

302 JUMEIRAH ROAD

Mercato Mall

Town Centre

12

A R A B I A N

G U L F

311 AL UROUBA STREET

13

14

JUMEIRAH (2)

302 JUMEIRAH ROAD

304 AL WASL ROAD

Jumeirah Beach Park

15

JUMEIRAH (3)

302 Time Out Dubai

Majlis Ghorfat Um Al Sheef **A** **313 ALATHAR ST**

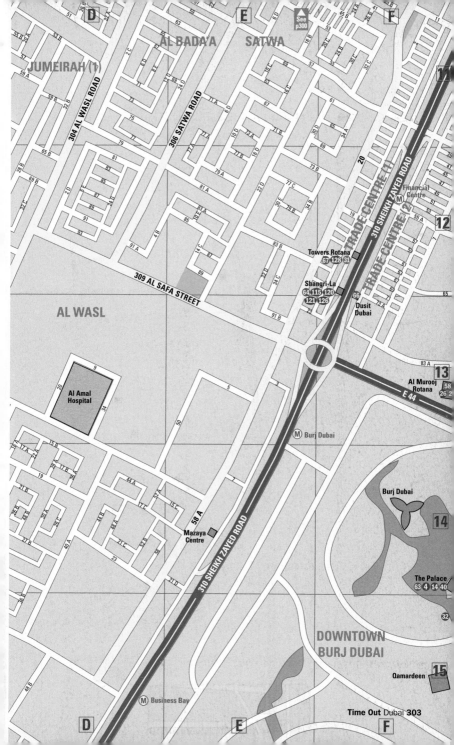

BIBLIO RPL Ltée
G – MARS 2010

1 Hotels pp86-109
1 Restaurants & Cafés pp110-142
1 Pubs & Bars pp143-152

A   B   C   D   E

1   2   3

© Copyright Time Out Group 2008

2 kms
1 mile